Tommy Douglas

Tommy Douglas

with all good wishes,
Doris Shackleton

Doris French Shackleton

Best wishes.
T. C. Douglas

McClelland and Stewart Limited

McClelland and Stewart Limited,
The Canadian Publishers,
25 Hollinger Road,
Toronto, Ontario.
M4B 3G2

ISBN 0-7710-8116-2

Printed and bound in Canada
by T. H. Best Company Limited
Don Mills, Ontario

Contents

To Carellin and Alexis,
citizens of a later time.

Acknowledgements

The writing of this book owes a great deal to the cooperation of a number of people who over a period of months during 1973 and 1974 agreed to recorded interviews. Many have been quoted at length in these pages. Tommy Douglas submitted cheerfully to hours of questioning. Others were: F. R. Scott, A. M. Nicholson, J. H. Brockelbank, F. C. Williams, Mrs. J. E. Powers, Mrs. J. Clarke, Grant MacNeil, Bill Davies, Joan Tulchinsky, Joyce Nash, H. S. Lee, Allan Blakeney, Howard Green, Hans Brown, Shirley Sutherland, T. H. McLeod, Clifford Scotton, Grace MacInnis, Stanley Knowles, M. J. Coldwell, David Lewis, Eleanor McKinnon, J. F. Parkinson, Graham Spry, Clarence Fines, Margaret Stewart, and Irma Douglas. To all of these people, my thanks for their time and interest. I am also grateful for conversations and correspondence with Beatrice Trew, Paul Helstrom, Joe Phelps, Isobel Bergstrom, Douglas Fisher, A. W. Johnson and numerous other associates and acquaintances of the subject of this book.

To Tommy Douglas himself I can only express my gratitude. He was generous not only with his time but with the written records of a long and fascinating political career. The present book, as many readers will soon remind me, is not the whole story. It is my hope that Tommy will presently make time to write his memoirs, to fill the many gaps. If this book does no more than create a public appetite for his own account of things, it will have served some purpose.

I am also indebted to Allan R. Turner, Provincial Archivist, Trevor Powell and Ed Morgan of the Saskatchewan Archives, to Clifford Scotton for making available the CCF papers lodged in the Public Archives, and to Richard McLennan for assistance in combing recent Douglas papers. I am particularly grateful to Clifford Scotton for reading the manuscript and giving helpful advice.

My sincere thanks to the Canada Council for assistance through its "Explorations" program and to my publishers for this further evidence of their interest in publishing the books of many hues which make up the political history of Canada.

As for Roberta Atchison, who typed presentable copy from my personal hieroglyphics, the credit must be hers for getting to the finish wire on time.

7

Introduction

How, in 1974, year of complete disenchantment, to write the story of a Baptist minister in politics? Richard Nixon, they say, is a Quaker, which underlines – what? That a man may keep his name on a church register and have the morals of an alley cat? This is no new discovery. But it casts a dark shadow on all men who profess religion and walk a political path.

The tenuous connection between public and private virtue is a theme worth unending examination. The drawback in discussing the subject now is that some generations are more credulous than others. Our own is not credulous at all. We believe currently that true private morality is to be without standards of morality, and that true public morality does not exist. The whole structure of government, we have begun to say, is so inevitably corrupt, and so incapable of intervening on the moral side of things, that the only safe way to vote is for a government that will do least for us. Vote for a handsome devil and trust he will be lazy in office.

There were some editorial writers who saw in the Watergate trials a triumph for American democracy, an example to all the world. In that wretched recital of deception. Others remarked that political corruption goes on everywhere, and people are used to it. The sham continues for the purpose of fooling some naive souls, and also because there is no other way to govern. The one editorial is maddeningly blind, the other depressingly resigned.

If, then, we have become almost immune to the persuasive habits of politicians, believing governments by definition incompetent and corrupt, it is hardly the time to produce a biography of Tommy Douglas. It risks being read only by way of novelty, as a repository of quaint, old-fashioned ideas. (Despite the fact that the subject is alive and well, and was recently returned to parliament in the election of July, 1974, with a respectable plurality while half his NDP colleagues were beaten by Liberals or Conservatives.) The crunch is whether you are prepared to believe Douglas when he talks of a "better way of life" made possible by government. Whether you are prepared to believe that *he* believes it, or ever did.

I have known Douglas – as well as most CCF-NDP'ers know him – over a period of perhaps thirty years. I have interviewed scores of people, most of whom searched their vocabularies for words to express admiration. I have interviewed some who questioned his motives, seeing them as more "human" than angelic, and some who found his authority galling, and for the life of me I could not refrain from questioning the motives or the competence of those who disparaged him. I shall include these comments, though, for "balance". I sense the dilemma of Judith Robinson, one-time columnist for the Toronto *Telegram*, who was much taken with Douglas and in a 1953 piece, having described his success as a spellbinder, added, "The Premier of Saskatchewan is that sort of political campaigner. Try to discover how he does it and a difficulty develops. Since he had you coming right along most of the way the detachment essential to scientific inquiry is hard to regain."

Because there is nothing a journalist loathes so much as the suspicion that he has been gullible, few journalists have written about Douglas, and, for that matter, few books have been written about his regime in Saskatchewan. Writers felt they were on safer ground, somehow, in describing William Aberhart or John Diefenbaker, whose quirks and idiosyncrasies are commonly conceded.

Perhaps for much the same reason, authors like Peter Newman are capable of writing in 469 pages a "breathtakingly frank recreation of the stumbling march of events and the personalities that danced darkly across the Canadian political stage between 1963 and 1968" – according to the dust jacket of *The Distemper of Our Times*, (Toronto: McClelland and Stewart, Limited 1968) – giving scarcely more than three lines throughout to either the newly formed New Democratic Party or to its national leader, T. C. Douglas. To Newman, both were irrelevant to the "real" political world, exactly as many people shut away religion from "real" affairs, referring to it only when sad things such as death occur in a family.

The skepticism of contemporary writers puts me on the defensive. I can retaliate with Blais Pascal, who said, "Men hate and despise religion but they fear it may be true," or I can draw their attention to Viscount Morley, who in an 1876 book on Rousseau, wrote, "Those who would treat politics and morality apart will never understand the one or the other." But the skepticism doesn't go away; one can't expect it to.

Neither can I disregard our times, and write for a future day when people may be ready once more to organize a party to legislate a New Jerusalem. I don't believe history repeats itself that way or that the marvellous naivete which maintained a CCF government in office for twenty years in Saskatchewan will come again. What "times" are ahead are beyond conjecture, except that the chances of them being parlous are quite safe.

I am tempted to say, "to hell with it", and simply write the book. Believe it or not, believe Douglas or not, as you like.

But it would be wrong to leave this introduction in such a state of gloom. It would be a disservice to my subject. Tommy Douglas is so light-hearted, so buoyant in manner, that the most solemn of biographers must take his disposition into account. During his earliest years in parliament another Scot, Angus MacInnis, sat on the CCF benches in dour contrast to Tommy. MacInnis was a craggy man of unrelenting integrity. When someone in the group once happened to ask when Angus was born, Tommy quipped, "Born? I thought he was quarried."

He is full of wisecracks. He has the "sunny ways" once ascribed to Sir Wilfrid Laurier, and if there is any political figure in Canada's past whom he resembles, it is that eloquent and much loved early Prime Minister, whose small features under a broad forehead indeed have a certain similarity to Douglas', though Douglas so far lacks the white, silky halo.

Douglas is cheerful in manner, vastly energetic and practical, and he has absorbed within himself, without malice, all the accidental let-downs and devastatingly deliberate put-downs of normal political life. He nurses no grudges. It appears there is always a job at hand to do.

It is much easier to write of Douglas as part and parcel of the events, than to segregate and attempt to dissect him. He is of very little help to a biographer intent on that kind of analysis. He will say "I" once in a paragraph, and slip at once, comfortably, into "the party" or "the government" and "we". It seems not to be shyness or modesty, for he can brag without shame of what "we" achieved, but a fastidious nature that shows itself in his responses. He will not have you come too near.

If he indulges in self examination it is never a public act, and I venture to say he does very little of it in private. Once, in an aside at some social affair, he said in regard to this book, "You won't find me very interesting. I never do anything but work." It was the nearest he ever came to discussing his own personality, temperament, sins, or virtues.

So the book must be written as the events took place. Through it all Tommy Douglas will be there, and you will perhaps be able to understand what kind of person he is. The events, in summary, were these: he was born in Falkirk, Scotland, in 1904, and came to Canada as a boy. He was educated in Winnipeg and Brandon, and he was ordained as a Baptist minister in 1930. He was a candidate for the Farmer-Labour Party in the Saskatchewan election of 1934, and defeated; and a candidate for the CCF in the federal election of 1935, and elected. He resigned from federal politics in 1944 to enter the Saskatchewan election as a candidate and as the leader of the provincial CCF party. The party was elected, he became Premier, and the CCF under his leadership won the elections of 1948, 1952, 1956, and 1960. In 1961 he resigned to become the first national leader of the New Democratic Party. In 1971 he resigned from leadership, but he retains his seat in the House of Commons as a private member.

He gave Canada public health insurance, and lost his own seat in the backlash. He demonstrated in one province the democratic socialist concept of a "mixed economy" (part public, part private) strongly directed toward supplementing and supporting low private income, and toward egalitarian principles in education, health, housing, and the arts. He involved the people in government with extraordinary success. He created a public service of unmatched calibre and imaginative enterprise.

Across Canada he is known as a great orator. In parliament he spoke in defence of the west against the more powerful east, the workers against corporate power, all of Canada against a more powerful neighbouring state. He held his party on the side of civil liberty against the popular panic of the FLQ crisis in 1970.

As to tributes and testimonials, these will appear throughout the book. His party regards him variously. Parties are never satisfied. Keeping a provincial government in office for twenty years was all very well, but why did he lead the New Democratic Party for ten years without taking power in Ottawa? Still, they admire him.

Frank R. Scott, eminent constitutional lawyer and Montreal poet, a leader of the early democratic socialist movement in Canada, said in an interview:

"The three most prominent in the early days – Woodsworth, Coldwell and Douglas –' were quite different in their characters and their capabilities. Woodsworth was the philosophical and spiritual leader of the movement, an inspiring figure, but remote really from the ordinary people, a person to be enormously respected, absolutely trusted, but not the mover of masses. Coldwell also was a somewhat retiring person on the public platform – not retiring but not terribly effective – fundamentally a parliamentarian, happiest in the House of Commons, where he did a superbly good piece of work.

But Tommy was It. Tommy related the whole thing to people, to every type of person. He knew how to speak to them, to get their interest, and use his enormous gift of wit and humour to the greatest advantage. He was never very terrifying in his ideas even when putting forth bold CCF policy and he was able to put it into words that made it seem perfectly sensible and reasonable to ordinary people. And he was therefore the best."

Chapter One
Falkirk and the Clydeside

The oldest son of the oldest son was named Thomas. The family lived in Falkirk, in Stirlingshire, Scotland, and their men all worked as iron moulders in the celebrated Carron Iron Works. "Celebrated" even in very early days, for the word is used in Blackie's *Imperial Gazeteer* of 1855. Falkirk has a long history. Even at that date the town and its iron industry were prospering. The Carron Iron Works had been founded to make cannon for Wellington in the Peninsular Wars. (It was also a name well known to the households of the early maritimes and central provinces of Canada. Carron made stout box stoves, well suited to Canadian winters.)

Thomas Douglas, grandfather of the "Tommy" who reached political heights in Canada, had eight sons and a daughter. The men were all iron moulders by trade, Presbyterian by faith, and Liberal in politics. As Tommy remembers it, their politics had become somewhat more fervent than their religious observance. The senior Thomas had presided at a great meeting in the Falkirk Town Hall when Gladstone opened his Midlothian campaign, an occasion he recalled with pride. Political argument was the meat to his meal. He was a man who liked to talk and to laugh, who recited Burns with gusto and fine feeling. He had a "natural eloquence" according to his grandson, who recalls the long narrative, "Tam O'Shanter", recited in its entirety for his benefit, and the chilling excitement of the verse:

"Ah Tam! Ah Tam! Thou'll get thy fairin'!
In hell they'll roast thee like a herrin'!"

It was Burns rather than nursery rhymes that Tommy listened to in his parents' and grandparents' houses. And Burns made a lasting impression. Tommy will still quote you Burns at the drop of a hat. He is still, in 1974, so much in demand on Burns Night in Canada that bookings are made with his secretary two years in advance and he is guest at two or sometimes three Burns banquets in a row.

Poetry and stories were part of his childhood. The Douglas men and women, like most Scots in their position, had only elementary schooling. Later one resorted to the public library in pursuit of self education. The Douglases made full use of the library. Grandfather Thomas liked to paint in oils. It was a workingman's family, but without the harshness of narrow poverty, whether of diet or spirit.

The Presbyterian observance had softened. Tom, the eldest of the eight sons, could recall stricter sabbaths – when shoes were cleaned, fires laid, and all other possible tasks performed on Saturday, to leave the Lord's Day as free from work as it was from pleasure. But by the time the sons were grown these customs had changed. There were social evenings of singing and dancing, and whiskey would be passed around in the grandfather Douglas home as young Tommy remembered it.

And the town itself was not an ugly or brutal place: Falkirk had been there long before the foundries grew up close by, and its ancient streets were little changed. The *Gazeteer* of 1855 describes it as

> situated on a gentle eminence in a beautiful and fertile country . . . it has a Free, and three U. Presbyterian churches, and several other Dissenting chapels; a number of well-conducted and well-attended schools; several public libraries, and religious and benevolent societies. . . .
>
> Falkirk is of great antiquity . . . In July, 1298, a battle was fought a little north of the town between the forces of Edward 1 and those of William Wallace, in which the latter was defeated . . . About one mile south of the town, a battle was fought on January 17, 1746, between the Highlanders under Prince Charles, and the royal forces under General Hawley, in which the former was victorious.

And this was still Falkirk as Tommy Douglas knew it, in the early years of his childhood. Bannockburn and a half dozen other ancient battlegrounds lie near grey Stirling Castle, home of the Argyle and Sutherland Highlanders, his own father's regiment. From the castle's ramparts the far Highlands were visible: the Grampians, Ben Lomond, and the other magic names. They have become as familiar to generations of Canadian schoolchildren as Carron stoves were to Canadian grandparents. Ballads and iron stoves were both exported from this region to the oldest British colony. But with the immigrant settlers came much more. With them came a new political radicalism.

Tom Douglas joined the Argyle and Sutherland Highlanders to serve in the Boer War, and later in India. He returned "sickened", his son says, by the butchery of battle and the thankless lot of a foot soldier. An iron moulder again, he joined the Labour Party.

Thomas Senior evicted him from his house.

The grandfather owned two small stone houses, thatched first, later roofed with slate, and he lived in one and rented the other to Tom when he married. There Tommy was born, the first grandson, on October 20, 1904, and duly christened Thomas Clement.

Politics separated the family only briefly. Tom, with his wife and child, had not been long in their new terrace house in Falkirk's Sunnyside district – the home Tommy remembers best – when grandfather Thomas appeared at their door announcing that he had "come to see the boy". The breach was healed.

One by one the seven uncles went Labour. Eventually, at the time of the First World War, grandfather Thomas took an occasion when Tom was home on leave in Falkirk to take him aside and say, "Well, you'll be glad to know I've joined that damned Labour Party of yours." The Douglases were one again.

Their district had sent Keir Hardie, the first Labour member, to parliament. The conversion of the Douglases was part of a massive swing from the Liberals to Labour. It has never changed. When Premier Tommy Douglas went back to visit Falkirk (It was an anniversary occasion for the Carron Iron Works. Douglas was accompanied by Senator Arthur Roebuck, whose great-grandfather was the founder of Carron.) he discovered that the town was in the middle of a by-election. At a banquet given by the mayor, a Labour man, Douglas politely enquired about the election, and the mayor pointed out to him the Union candidate, present at the table. "In Scotland," Douglas explains, "the Liberals and Conservatives got together long ago, and gave up the farce of playing in's and out's." The Union choice was the local squire, an Army regular, an Oxonian. Douglas expressed some alarm to the mayor because he had seen the Union candidate's posters everywhere, but no sign of those of the Labour candidate.

The mayor reassured him. "Ah yes, they have the posters, and the pamphlets, and the speeches on the wireless. But we have the votes." Douglas was back in London when he read the by-election results in a newspaper. Labour had won again, three-to-one.

Tom Douglas, Tommy's father, was a big, rugged man who like Thomas senior had his gentler side. He spent time in his small garden, where he grew roses. He broke with family tradition not only in politics. He was against his son learning the iron moulder's trade, or any other. He wanted education for Tommy, and a rise to better things.

Tommy was small and sickly, and during his first years much under the influence of his mother. Annie Clement was the daughter of Highland parents who had come down to Glasgow speaking only Gaelic. Andrew Clement, her father, worked in the huge cooperative wholesale near the Glasgow waterfront. The family was Conservative, and Baptist. Andrew had been a Baptist lay preacher, and before that a member of the Plymouth Brethren.

At sixteen, Annie had gone to work in the cotton mills in Paisley. She was a small woman of considerable spirit, fond of poetry and the long romantic novels she and other members of the family brought home regularly from the library. Sometimes she gave little recitations at home entertainments, and she took pride in drilling her children in their school "memory work". On Sundays she read to them a chapter or two from Stevenson or Scott, after which the book was put away till another weekend. Frequently when Tommy was sick she read to him.

When he was nearly six, Tommy had a bout of pneumonia. Shortly after recovering from this, he fell and cut his right knee on a stone. It seemed a small injury, but it failed to heal. Osteomyelitis affected the lower femur, close to the knee cap.

The first of many operations on the knee was performed at home by the local doctor who arrived in his black top hat with his small bag in his hand. The kitchen table was pressed into service; mother and grandmother administered chloroform. No sooner had the doctor left than a suture came loose; there was considerable bleeding, and the doctor had to be found and brought back to repair the damage. The leg was still in poor shape when the family made its first migration to Canada.

Uncle William had been the first to migrate, and sent back favourable reports, though later he returned to Falkirk. Tom was the second to go, in 1910. Annie and their three children, Tommy and two younger sisters, Isobel and Nan, soon followed to join him in Winnipeg.

One of the more fanciful accounts of this exodus appeared as a *Reynolds News* "Profile", on March 4, 1962, and is cherished in Tommy's scrapbook. Headed "Frontiersman" it relates: "When he was six, young Tommy Douglas left Scotland with his parents to resettle in the bleak frontier country of Saskatchewan. There he learned to fight for the virgin land, fight the long harsh winters when the thermometer dipped to forty degrees below zero; broiling summers when it soared above the century; to fight pests, droughts and marauding Indians."

Winnipeg's North Side was not quite the environment pictured by *Reynolds News*, but it had its challenges.

The family rented a house on Gladstone Street, about eight blocks from the Vulcan Iron Works where Tom had found a job. It was a neighbourhood of frame houses, with outdoor toilets. Immigrants from every country in Europe crowded there; only the Douglas family and one other on their street were of British descent. Not far from them was J. S. Woodsworth's All People's Mission. Tommy went there for the boys' sports program. It was the only recreation centre in the district. Woodsworth was a slight man with a brown beard, recognized as the head of the Mission but not readily approachable.

Here in Winnipeg Tommy started elementary school, but progress was hindered by repeated flare-ups of osteomyelitis. He was frequently on crutches; repeatedly in the Sick Children's Hospital. One winter he attended school chiefly through the generous help of two neighbourhood boys who decided to haul him there on a sled. They were east European boys, one Polish, and one Galician. They spoke little English and wore clothes that looked odd to Tommy. He knew their mothers wore *babushkas* and their fathers wore heavy peasant coats. In his helplessness, he wondered at their readiness to help him. Unquestion-

ably the surprised recipient of good works learns more racial tolerance than the doer. Tommy never forgot what he owed those other
immigrant boys.

Later, in hospital for a major operation, he experienced one of the
most significant events of his life. As a ward patient he received only the
routine attention of the physicians on duty. He learned that his leg would
probably have to be amputated. By accident, an orthopaedic surgeon
going through the ward observed him and discussed his case with the
students in tow behind him. The surgeon, Dr. R. H. Smith, (he later
became commander of the Eleventh Field Ambulance, and was killed in
France) decided that the case would provide a valuable teaching project.
He obtained permission from Tommy's parents to operate, believing he
could save the leg, although the knee might be permanently stiffened.

The operation was performed with unexpected success. Tommy
recalls Dr. Smith and the retinue of students grouped around to view the
results, and the doctor saying "It is too bad he cannot bend his knee."
Tommy said, "Doctor, I *can* bend it," and did so. Dr. Smith was elated,
the students were filled with admiration, and Tommy had a right leg that
allowed him to hike, to pedal a bicycle, to play soccer, to win amateur
boxing tournaments, and to campaign through strenuous elections. It
was not until 1945 that a further injury brought a return of the old
infection.

Tommy also had a lasting insight into what it meant, in those days, to
be poor. He said:

> My father had no coverage for accidents or medical needs. There
> was no workman's compensation, and there was nothing for the
> families of the poor. To go to an orthopaedic surgeon was, for us,
> simply out of the question. And if my father had been seriously
> disabled in his work by the molten metal which did, several times,
> burn him severely, there would have been no money to take care of
> my mother, my sisters or myself.
>
> When I thought about it, I realized that the same kind of service
> I got by a stroke of luck should have been available to every child in
> that ward, and not just to a case that looked like a good specimen for
> exhibition to medical students.

The Medicare program of Saskatchewan when Tommy was Premier
came directly from the fear of a poor boy that he would lose his leg, and
a sense of the unfair caprice that saved it for him.

War broke out in 1914. Tom Douglas felt compelled to return to
Scotland and enlist again. The family decided that, rather than continue
alone so far from him, they would go back also and live in Glasgow with
the Clement grandparents. They sailed on the "Pretoria", which travelled
without lights through the dangerous Atlantic waters. In the Irish Sea
they waited for a destroyer to escort them into the harbour. The ten-

year-old boy found the occasion immensely thrilling, as he watched the sailors at their guns while the destroyer circled round them.

Back in Scotland, Tommy completed elementary school and then, largely financing his own education, was enrolled at a high school Academy. The family was not financially secure. As a soldier, Tom Douglas received $1.10 a day: $1.00 was assigned to his wife and there were no additional allowances for her or the children. Annie Douglas sold sewing machines to augment the family income. Tommy took part-time jobs which were readily available in a Glasgow short of manpower and humming with war activity.

But first he had to establish his status with his peers. When asked if, at that age, he had any sense of a special calling that might raise him above other lads, he replied, "Not much! I was too busy, being rather small, just keeping my head above water." And that seems to have been the case. He was a pugnacious youngster when he felt threatened. He had an early encounter with a tough gang on what was then Clarence Street, down near the wharves, and parallel to Paisley Road where the Academy was located. Tommy had to pass Clarence Street to get to school. The gang shouted, "Canuck", knocked off the little pork-pie hat he wore the first day, and looked with some derision at the knickers, gartered below the knee, that all schoolboys in Canada then wore. Tommy decided that if he had to be knocked around he might as well settle things with the top boy. The top boy was rather large, and named Geordie Sinclair. When Geordie issued an order to Tommy, the "Canuck" refused to obey. "Do it or I'll belt you," Geordie said, and proceeded to belt him. Tommy threw a punch back. He arrived home much later with a bloody nose and cut ear. Mother and grandmother urged him to avoid further trouble by hurrying straight home next day by another street, but an uncle advised the women to leave him alone to work it out in his own way. So the following day after school Tommy went straight for Clarence Street and accosted Geordie: "If you haven't had enough I'll give you some more. Are you ready?" Whereupon Geordie gazed down on Tommy and pronounced benignly, "You've had enough, Canuck." The initiation was over, and Tommy had won his right to return to Scotland.

Tommy later found it odd that Canadian schoolboys don't fight to anything like the extent of the numerous pitched battles of his own youth.

Far from experiencing any early intimations of a high calling, Tommy at that time would have chosen to be a sailor. Paisley Road paralleled the metal-tongued shipyards and great wharves of Glasgow, where ships of every registry plied their quickened wartime industry. The famous Clydeside was Tommy's second home.

He distinguished himself well enough at school, though he did not labour unduly at his lessons. He had a facile memory and a natural ease of expression. History and literature were what he liked most. He took part in dramatics and in sports, particularly football. The Academy also provided him with a teacher of elocution, a circumstance of some importance. The teacher recited Burns in a way that made Tommy, who had soaked up Burns since babyhood, now feel that he was hearing him for the first time.

The place of Robert Burns, poet, lies, as everyone knows, close to the core of Scotland. The popular writer of travel books, H. V. Morton, described his pervasive presence:

> Everyone in Scotland has grown up with Burns; many quote him who have never read a line of him, because his songs are in the air, his verses are something heard round the fireside; and it is never possible to tell when a man of humble birth and education quotes the poet whether he is quoting from the printed page or merely remembering something which he has known all his life. . . .
>
> Centuries of repression spoke in him. . . . In his voice, clear and unhesitant, one heard all the joys and sorrows which lay unspoken for generations in the heart of men who work with their hands. This great silence he broke magnificently. He sang in thirty-six years all the things that men like him in every other particular but that of expression had failed to sing for centuries. No wonder he died young. It was a great strain on the throat.[1]

The social message of the poet was coming through to Tommy now. But it was something more than this. Something in the potential power of the human voice reached the young pupil. He learned to project his rather light voice; he copied the sonorous phrasing of his elocution teacher.

Annie Douglas had steered her own family to the Baptist faith; they now went to chapel. On Sundays Tommy would go not only in the company of his mother and grandparents but frequently also in the evenings, on his own. He went less from piety than for the pleasure of hearing the discourse of the preachers, how they developed a sermon from a text, how they struck dramatic chords from their written pages, how they read Holy Scripture. Theatre or other public entertainment was not easily available. But the gift of words which many of the dissenting preachers possessed fed the mind with powerful exhortation and rich imagery.

Douglas also recalls that once he went alone to hear Lloyd George at St. Andrew's Hall. "It set me up for a week," he said. Lloyd George and Aneurin Bevan were two of the greatest orators in his recollection.

There was a close affinity between the religious and the political oratory of Douglas' time. Many of the British Labour members had been preachers in the non-conformist sects – the Baptists, the Methodists, the Congregationalists. "The Labour Party," Clement Attlee once said, "owes more to Methodism than to Marx." During the Great Strike of 1926, the dissenting churches were turned into soup kitchens for the strikers. And the heroic verse which Douglas later made his own, a resounding call to Canadians who may have been puzzled by the allusion but were in no doubt about its impact and intent, was from Blake's poem, "The New Jerusalem", adopted as a hymn by the British Labour Party.

"I shall not cease from mortal strife,
Nor shall my sword rest in my hand,
Till we have built Jerusalem
In this green and pleasant land."

Tommy Douglas spent four important years of his early youth in the political ferment of the Clydeside.

"Glasgow is as factious as it is rich," wrote the seventeenth century preacher, Thomas Moorer. According to Robert Middlemas in an excellent description of much later date, "In the late nineteenth century the tough argumentative faculty, hitherto almost exclusively engaged in the pursuit of theology, spilled over into politics."[2]

Here the Independent Labour Party (ILP), successfully breaking political allegiance loose from the Liberals, was founded in 1893 by Keir Hardie, and had developed a remarkably able workingclass leadership by 1908. In 1906 James Keir Hardie had published his "Declaration of Socialism". Johnston published "Our Noble Families" in 1908 and 1909: "the most caustic arraignment of the Scottish aristocracy ever committed to print."[3] And other pamphleteers exposed the dismal state of public health and housing in Glasgow.

Always a radical thorn in the side of the British Labour Party, the ILP was rich in altruism and had nothing but scorn for the compromisers. Says David Lowe in *Souvenirs of Scottish Labour*: "The Scottish Labour Movement was not founded on materialism . . . The instinct for freedom and justice which animated the Covenanters and Chartists also inspired the nineteenth century pioneers. Their heroes were Jesus, Shelley, Mazzini, Whitman, Ruskin, Carlyle and Morris. The economists took a second place. The crusade was to dethrone Mammon and to restore spirit, and to insist that the welfare of the community should take precedence of the enrichment of a handful."

Middlemas, in a somewhat sedate introduction to his account of this turbulent epoch, states: "The Clydesiders . . . had certain obvious characteristics – being devoted to their ideals, high-minded in their politics and well-loved in their constituencies – but these qualities are present in many politicans and as it may be taken for granted that few men enter public life without at least the illusion of public service, they need not be unduly emphasized."[4]

There is something very striking about that grudging paragraph, written ten years ago by a man who was Senior Clerk of the House of

Commons at Westminster, as it reveals an attitude not only toward Labour and the ILP but toward political democracy itself at the time of writing. The motivation of politicians was expected to be admirable. Political perfidy might occur, but was not the norm. Public confidence in public morality existed, strongly reinforced by groups such as the Fabians and the ILP, renewing over generations a persistent belief in the efficacy of government to serve the common good. The alienation of so many voters in Britain as well as America in the subsequent decade is in striking contrast.

By the time of the First World War the ILP was close to its peak. A fierce opposition to the war, on grounds of socialism and international brotherhood, brought the ILP into conflict with the senior British Labour Party. Some of its members were arrested and jailed for publishing articles against conscription. But the radical party was in full strength, marching toward a resounding political success in the general election of 1922.

The fiery oratory of ILP leaders blistered the ears of listeners in Glasgow Green, that city's Hyde Park. There Tommy Douglas heard Jimmy Maxton, the wildest rebel of them all, urging the workers to down tools and stop the making of munitions. Maxton was "well known as a platform orator with a thin hatchet face and mane of long black hair which fell across his face giving it a saturnine and piratical appearance."[5]

Douglas recounts a favourite story about these times. He and his chum, Tom Campbell, had two preferred out-of-school haunts. One was Glasgow Green, where they listened to Jimmy Maxton, Willy Gallacher, and other socialists, along with a variety of soapbox evangelists who denounced the King, praised Kaiser William, and otherwise behaved as outrageously as fancy led them. The boys' second choice for Sunday entertainment was the Kelvin Grove Museum, a penny fare on the tram from Paisley Road, but a dream world away in the historic splendours it contained.

In 1953 Premier Douglas visited Glasgow following the coronation of Queen Elizabeth, and was guest speaker at a dinner on George Square, arranged in his honour by Glasgow's (Labour) Lord Mayor, Sir Hector MacNeil. Asked if there was any guest he would particularly wish to meet, Tommy named Alan Morton, who played centre for the Glasgow Rangers. And asked if there was a spot he would particularly like to revisit, he chose the Kelvin Grove Museum. The mayor's car picked him up the following morning for a visit to the museum, and he was astonished to see a bronze bust of Jimmy Maxton. Said he to Sir Hector, "It confirmed my impression that there is nothing the upper classes are so fond of as a dead radical."

To help pay his school fees in those years, Tommy began work as a soap boy. He worked from 4:00 to 8:00 p.m. daily, and all day Saturdays, at a barber shop where he rubbed soap into tough whiskers, down a long line of high chairs. Since the barber shop was next door to a munitions factory, the whiskers were full of grime and black sand, and a boy's fingers could be rubbed raw at the job. When the barber had proceeded down the row with his razor, it was again Tommy's turn to finish off with a towel and a dust of powder.

He made six shillings a week, and twice that much in tips. To miss none of the harvest of tips, he prevailed on a clever uncle, a joiner by trade, to design a little box which was placed in a prime position at the cashier's desk. All beautifully engraved it read "For the Boy". At Christmas, to inspire the proper spirit, he decorated it with a sprig of holly. "I sometimes made two pounds at Christmas," Tommy said.

Tommy was in fact prospering in wartime Glasgow. During the summer holiday when he was thirteen he got a chance to work in a cork factory for thirty shillings a week. The cork factory belonged to a Mr. Hunter, and was located right beside the main suspension bridge over the Clyde. Mr. Hunter considered Tommy an adaptable lad and promoted him to office work, answering the phone and taking orders, for the magnificent weekly wage of two pounds ten. It was more than his father had ever made as a moulder. And Hunter had other ambitions for Tommy. He had no sons of his own, and he proposed to pay Tommy's way to night school to learn Portuguese and Spanish, and then send him off on voyages as a buyer. Tommy was, in fact, doing so well that he neglected to return to the Academy that fall.

Tom Douglas came home on leave in November, 1918. He was not at all pleased that Tommy had dropped out of school. Perhaps hoping to set his son back on the proper course, he seriously considered not returning to his regiment when his leave was up. It was obvious that the war was nearly over in any case. Annie Douglas prevailed on him not to break his good record, and they all trooped down to see him off on November 10. Next day came the Armistice, but Tom could not be with his family for the lengthy period of demobilization.

There had been serious family discussions about staying on in Scotland, or returning again to Winnipeg. They made the decision to return. The soldier's family would have their passage at government expense, and so on very short notice, on New Year's Day 1919, Annie Douglas and the three children sailed out of Liverpool. Tom Douglas would join them a few months later.

The 1919 voyage was memorable. Inspired by the New Years occasion and the end of the war, the crew had drunk so heartily that the cargo was not securely fastened and it shifted; the boat took a dangerous list. Several hundred Canadian troops on board moved the cargo and brought the ship to an even keel, relieving the minds of those on board. Later in the voyage a flu epidemic raged, and there were funeral services on deck and burials at sea.

Tommy Douglas was glad to return to Canada. Whatever the prospects in the cork business, the Old Country did not seem to compare with the New. His father had become deeply intolerant of the old class ways in Scotland, and so had he. From the boy's point of view, it was a question of foolish restrictions, of having to live up to the uniform of the Academy and not associating with lesser boys, and on the other hand of finding one's movements severely curtailed by feudal privilege. He said,

> When I wanted to go on a hike with a pal, we would take a streetcar as far as possible, till we were out of the city. But everywhere we went, signs said, 'Trespassers Will Be Prosecuted.' We couldn't go through fields, or through woods. I had been used to roaming the banks of the Assiniboine and the Red, taking a couple of ground sheets to make a little tent so we could sleep overnight, but that was impossible in Scotland. Six thousand acres were fenced off for the Duke of Sutherland, to hunt deer twice a year. It didn't appeal to a boy who had spent a few years in Canada. Mother was glad to go back too, and Father after he got there.

Immigrants to Canada and the United States in those years shared a resolute intention to better themselves. Tommy Douglas, throughout his career, saw *opportunity* as essential. "I don't care if a man has to work hard," he said, "but there should be some possibility of improving his life." Some basic security, and a great deal of opportunity, were the requirements. "Not to *have* more," he said, "but to have the opportunity to reach ahead to something better."

Such is not the philosophy of the recent (1970) best seller by Charles Reich, *The Greening of America,* nor of the new-leisure school. It is not the philosophy of the sensual man. It defines "quality of life" in different terms. It is not, primarily, acquisitive.

"I haven't kept a lot of old photographs or mementos," Douglas said. "I have no squirrel instinct. I don't hoard much of anything." His possessions at the end of his career are modest. The philosophy is mobile, active, striving, impatient of waste and disorder. Driving through the logging woods of Vancouver Island in the spring of 1974, other occupants of the same car deplored the ugly devastation of the crudely slashed timberland. But Douglas stirred restlessly as he saw the wasted wood left on the forest floor, and talked of new techniques perfected in Scandinavia to salvage it.

That evening at a meeting in his west coast riding, he told a questioner, "I may get the dickens from some members of my party for saying this, but I don't really favour a Guaranteed Annual Income. Except in certain cases. What I favour more is a constant *shelf* of projects for young people to do. There is lots of work to be done in Canada, if we are to achieve the kind of society people have a right to expect."

Chapter Two
Preparatory Years, Winnipeg and Brandon

When the Douglas family moved to Winnipeg for the second time, the Scottish ILP had preceded them. In the late spring of 1919, Winnipeg was in the throes of a general strike. The most virulent of its leaders was R. B. Russell, a machinist from the Clydeside, while William Cooper, a cabinet-maker from Aberdeen, had propagated the cause of worker solidarity in the labour press. The strike may have been – and was – widely denounced as an uprising on the pattern of the year-old Russian Revolution. But it was in fact led by a score or so of British immigrant workers. Only one of them was associated at a later date with the Communist Party.[1]

When Annie Douglas and her three children arrived in Winnipeg again, they rented a house on Gordon Street, near their former neighbourhood. Tommy, now fourteen, found a job at once as a messenger boy for the Ultra Drug Company, earning six dollars a week. Then an advertisement for an apprentice in the printing trade led him to the Richardson Press, which produced the *Grain Trade News* and did printing for Dawson Richardson Publications. He was taken on, and he worked as an apprentice printer for five years, until he acquired his journeyman's papers.

His personal association with the Winnipeg Strike was of course little more than a period of high excitement in his teens. Only in later years did he draw some conclusions from the strike about the nature of organized labour in Canada. But he was, by accident, present during one of its street battles. He was delivering the *News* around the Grain Exchange offices on the Saturday afternoon of June 21, 1919, when he heard the hubbub of the crowd in the street. There had been parades and counter-parades for weeks, and there had been a minor riot on the same spot on June 10. This was the major disturbance. Douglas and a young friend climbed up a pole and reached the roof of a two-storey building on Main Street near the corner of Williams Street, and from this grandstand watched the melee. They saw the Mounties charge with clubs and guns, saw a streetcar overturned and set on fire, saw a man shot. The crowds milled back and forth. It was a wild afternoon in Winnipeg, with two casualties and many men injured, and it marked the culmination of the General Strike.

Douglas identifies himself and his companion in a newspaper photograph of the scene, showing the galloping Mounties, the packed crowds, and the two figures on a rooftop. It was reproduced in a commemorative account of the affair by Earle Beattie.[2] "We were too stupid to be scared up there," Douglas said. "We were just excited by it all."

His father had returned from the war that spring. Although he appears not to have participated in marches or riots, he was one of the returned men who had found few jobs available while the cost of living was soaring. Many veterans attached themselves to the explosive strike situation. The strike had started with a walkout of building and metal trade employees, and had spread until the key services of the city completely collapsed. The strikers had quit work in an impressive display of strength on May 15 but had maintained the peace. Strike leaders instructed their members against demonstrations and violence and advised them in the *Daily Strike Bulletin* to "just eat, sleep, play, love, laugh and look at the sun." It was the veterans, having joined the strikers, who first took to the streets. Soon there were marches of anti-strike groups with detachments of "special police", civilians recruited to uphold the Citizens Committee of One Thousand which had been organized by the professionals and businessmen of the city. Part of the wrath of the veterans was directed against "aliens" who had taken jobs in Winnipeg while they fought the war, a predictable reaction in the chaotic uncertainty of that demobilization period.

The Strike Committee asked for a settling of grievances: higher wages, the right to collective bargaining, reinstatement of jobs to all strikers without recrimination. But the rhetoric of some strike leaders, especially those influenced by the One Big Union (OBU) organized that March in Calgary, suggested a basic upheaval of society. The OBU roots were British, though it owed something to the Industrial Workers of the World (I. W. W.) of the United States. The OBU saw society in simplistic terms of producers and non-producers; their objective was to get power into the hands of the producers. Dedicated to its own universal solution it ignored traditional politics, including Labour Parties. It was a short-lived phenomenom.

But the utterances of strike leaders terrified the authorities. The panic reaction of the government was remarkably similar to the reaction of Trudeau and Bourassa to the FLQ "crisis" of 1970. The Meighen Government of 1919, convinced that an armed revolution in the Bolshevik style was upon them, passed amendments to the Immigration Act and the Criminal Code to permit them to deport the British-born leaders of the strike, moved the Mounted Police and heavy arms to Winnipeg, quelled the street marches with unnecessary force, and packed the leaders off to jail. Eastern papers screamed of Reds. Meighen declared that the "so-called strike was a cloak for an effort to overturn proper authority". Yet his argument "seems to be weakened by the fact that in police raids across Canada there was found no evidence of an attempt to arm any branch of the workers movement."[3] Within a year the jailed men were released, and many were promptly elected to city government, the provincial legislature, and the House of Commons. Sympathy swung to the strikers. The fancy rhetoric of the One Big Union faded into inconsequence: class was not implacably pitched against class.

Douglas' personal recollections of the period include standing at outdoor meetings to listen to such impassioned speakers as J. S. Woodsworth and Fred Dixon. Dixon was editor of the *Western Labour News*, possessing an "animal magnetism" that projected from the platform, and an intellect that got him acquitted in the trials following the strike, when he conducted his own defence. Dixon died soon after the Winnipeg events; if he had lived he would have assumed a leading role in Canada's left-wing politics.

As for Woodsworth, Douglas found that the mild-mannered minister from the All People's Mission became a different man on the platform. His voice became loud and almost harsh in tone, and he made so strong an impression on Douglas that it was Woodsworth to whom he turned for advice fifteen years later when the determination to organize the farmers and workers of Weyburn was changing the direction of his life.

Dixon had put Woodsworth in charge of the *Western Labour News* after his own arrest. Two days later Woodsworth was arrested as well, and part of the evidence against him at the trial was that he published "seditious libel", such as the passage from Isaiah which reads:

"And they shall build houses, and inhabit them; and they shall plant vineyards, and eat the fruit of them. They shall not build, and another inhabit; they shall not plant and another eat; for as the days of a tree are the days of my people, and mine elect shall long enjoy the work of their hands."

Douglas recalls that his father did not endorse the OBU. His union sympathies were along more traditional lines. And he also recalls the shock his parents felt when they heard that J. S. Woodsworth was arrested with others for his part (editing the strike newspaper) in that stormy month in 1919. "It's an awful disgrace when your minister goes to jail!" Douglas said.

But in retrospect, the impact of the strike on his later thinking had special significance in two ways. The frustration of World War One veterans in the demobilization period contributed heavily to fear of what might happen at the end of the next great war in 1945. It became imperative to plan for that new peace, and Douglas was one of his party's chief exponents on that theme. It was an important factor in the 1944 election of the CCF in Saskatchewan. And he rejected, as did his father, high-flown and simplistic solutions based on labour – as a class – taking political power. It did not fit the Canadian experience. Douglas is dubious about the existence of genuine "solidarity" among Canadian working people. If anyone in Canada, he says, is class-conscious it is the big "middle class" with which people in many occupations identify, and which is tinged with disdain for greasy plumbers and mere manual workers. But those blue-collar workers are not proud of their class, nor loyal to it; they are individually either anxious to get out of it, or at pains to deny any distinction between their occupation and any other. They are part of the "upward mobility" syndrome of North America. Political calculations in Canada have to be careful of "class".

However, back in 1919, Tommy Douglas had more immediate problems to think about. He was earning money that was very much needed to help his family get established in Canada. But Tom Douglas, when he arrived to join his family, was not at all pleased to find his son working in a print shop. He felt his son should be getting on with his education.

Tommy promised that he would go back to school as soon as possible, but he felt his father was "living in a dream world" if he thought the family could afford the luxury of a son in high school.

A sense of insecurity led the family to buy a house at the earliest opportunity – Tom's discharge gratuity was used as a down payment – and to pay off the mortgage in the shortest possible time. When Nan and Isobel finished elementary school they found work in Winnipeg department stores, to help out also.

Every morning Tommy's father got up in time to reach the Vulcan Iron Works to begin work at seven, and his custom was to arrive early, to allow time to change his clothes, lay out his tools and have a cigarette before the whistle blew. But he could not be certain. There were intermittent layoffs, and he might arrive at the plant to be told there was no work for him that day.

There was no unemployment insurance, no health insurance, no pension. And it was a dangerous job. Twice Tom had serious accidents, once when the molten metal hit his foot, and on another occasion close to his eye. If he had become disabled there would have been no protection for him or for his family.

The debt incurred to buy a house was the only one the family ever assumed. They put off buying a car until years later. In the twenties, like most Canadian families, they were just getting by.

"Christmas," Douglas said, "was not a time for electric trains." One Christmas his mother commissioned him to take two dollars downtown and buy gifts for the three children. The "big" present was a games board with Snakes and Ladders and Parcheesi on one side, Checkers on the other.

Tom Douglas was a tall, well built man, and his son, even when they argued, felt great respect and affection for him. He was a man of independent spirit, quick to anger, but also quick to regret harsh words. He was generously disposed to others, and would walk to the plant with newly-arrived immigrant workers and coach them in English, so they could cope with the foreman's orders. Occasionally after work he enjoyed a social time with his fellows at the Legion clubrooms, and he was keen on soccer.

His father had a scrupulous sense of honesty which would not let him dissemble for convention's sake. The family had again turned to the Baptist church. Tommy was baptized and joined the church at fourteen. Thus Annie Douglas and the children were anxious to make a good impression when the minister came one day to visit. Tom returned from work. He saw no reason to forego his usual custom. He announced to the minister, "I'm going to have a bottle of beer. Would you like one?" His wife and children were mortified, and only later was Tommy able to admire that forthrightness.

Annie Douglas was the religious influence in the home and it was she who took most pride in Tommy's growing interest in the church. His father had become cynical of the Christian offices performed by chaplains at the fighting front. He donated money to the Salvation Army, and stayed away from church.

The earliest occasion Douglas speaks of, when his platform skill evoked a profound audience response, involved a sympathetic moment shared by the father and son. Tom Douglas had shown an interest in the Masonic Order, but it was Tommy who involved himself deeply in the junior Order of De Molay. This youth organization had spread widely through the United States after the First World War. A chapter was formed in Winnipeg. One of its high moments was a dramatic production before a convention of Masons held in the old Board of Trade building at the corner of Portage and Main. The play concerned the life and death of the patron of the junior order, Jacques De Molay, the fourteenth century knight-at-arms who led expeditions against the Saracens, and was put to death as a heretic by Philip the Fair of France. Tommy took the title role and he threw himself heroically into the part. He spoke of that evening:

"My father was there and he was sparing of praise as in most things. When we came out he said, 'Let's walk.' which we did, for a distance of about four miles. I knew he had been deeply moved. There was never a word. We walked in silence. Going up the front steps he tapped me on the shoulder and said, 'You did no bad'."

There were other debating and theatrical opportunities, for Dr. Howden, one of the Masonic "dads" of De Molay, was also manager of the Winnipeg Theatre and found parts for Tommy in several plays. He thought Tommy should follow a theatrical career. Tommy was continuing the elocution lessons begun in Scotland, studying with Jean Campbell, a local teacher of some note.

He had other opportunities to practise stage craft with church and

28

the Boy Scouts. It was the era of "live" entertainment, and Tommy's talent was much in demand.

He was only slightly abashed one evening when he had to improvise a public prayer. He had been chosen as Chaplain of the De Molay chapter and had been given a manual with suitable prayers for all occasions. But as they were closing one evening, a boy got up in his place to say that there had been a very bad fire in Winnipeg, two or three children had been burned, and he thought a prayer ought to be said for the victims. Tommy had to get along without the manual, but he did manage a prayer. And he suspects that his effort that night led to the advice of a senior "dad", W. J. Major, later Attorney-General of Manitoba in John Bracken's government, who urged him to consider entering the ministry.

Tommy became a Scoutmaster when he was seventeen, and was fond of taking boys on camping trips, usually on bicycles. Camping out was a favourite summer pastime. In winter he went down to the OBU gym and learned to box. He was placed in the lightweight class; "I wasn't a great boxer but I was fast on my feet and could hit fairly hard." One evening in 1922 a friend, Harvey Stewart, called to ask him to go to the gym and spar with him. Harvey was entering the bouts for the provincial championship and suggested that Tommy try too. When he returned that evening Tom Douglas asked if he had put his name down for the bouts, and Tommy admitted that he had. His father was much annoyed. He thought it was very foolish of his son, a terrible waste of time. He refused to go near the bouts, and when Tommy turned up with injuries he received no sympathy at home.

But Tommy fought his way through the bouts to the lightweight championship of Manitoba that year, and successfully defended his title the following year.

"I was a bit of an oddity in the print shop," Douglas said. "I didn't join them in the evening at drinking parties or playing poker. At noon hour when there was a poker game going I was memorizing a recitation for the evening or getting a little talk ready. They didn't kid me, because I was provincial lightweight champion and you're not inclined to kid one of those."

An intriguing letter to Douglas was written in 1944 by a supporter anticipating his arrival in Edmonton to campaign in the Alberta election that year:

We are sure looking forward to hearing you again and I am sure you will have a good attendance. A good number from our plant will be there too. They are anxious to see the great little guy who could take a big fellow, let him train for two weeks and fight him bare knuckles and win. I'll never forget that episode just north of the Elmwood Park, Tommy, and of course I can't say that I have been a bit reticent about it and the many other things I am privileged to know of you.[4]

Tommy became a linotype operator when he was sixteen, and began to receive a full journeyman's pay of $44 a week before his five years' apprenticeship was up. He would get his union card (he still holds it) but a serious decision had to be made. If he continued in his trade he could look forward to promotion to foreman, and pay of $55 to $60 a week, a very good sum for those years. If he went back to school, as he had solemnly declared he would do "as soon as we're established" it would mean a precarious financial existence – and an uncertain future. For by now he knew that if he returned to study it would lead to the ministry.

Douglas is reluctant to talk about experiencing a "call". He is more apt to joke about impromptu prayers at De Molay meetings, or an early preaching assignment which he took at the town of Stonewall when he was eighteen. He went down by train. When he got off he looked about, and asked a boy the way to the Baptist Church. The boy shouted down the entire length of the platform "Hey, this kid says he's the new preacher!"

It was W. J. Major who persuaded Tommy to go back to his neglected education and enter the ministry. His mother was pleased with his decision. She had hoped to see him a minister, though there had been no urging.

He chose Brandon College, where he was permitted to take a combined course, completing matriculation and proceeding into theology, over six years. He enrolled at Brandon at the age of nineteen.

He supported himself by taking "weekend supplies". Many small churches in the west had to rely on student ministers to take their pulpits on Sundays. Usually a first-year student was not sent into the field, but Tommy was lucky. Dr. W. C. Smalley, Superintendent of Western Missions, who had despatched Tommy to Stonewall the previous summer, called on him again to take a service at the small town of Austin, not far from Brandon. They were closing down the church. The congregation was drifting away; they had decided they could no longer manage to support a church. Tommy was assigned to take the last few services and wind things up. With all the brash conviction of youth he confronted the congregation with questions. Why close the church when there were many young people in town who might be persuaded to attend? They agreed to keep the church going if he would stay on, and when he accepted they sent in a request for his services. He preached there every Sunday and during two summers. "The first summer I got around to all the farms on a bicycle. The next year they got me an old Ford car: it took me halfway and I pushed it the rest."

He was paid about $15 a Sunday. During his second and third years he took the church at Carberry – a Presbyterian church which was unable to find a minister and appealed to Brandon College for a student to help them out. In the following two years he preached at Baptist churches at Shoal Lake and Strathclair. He picked up extra money as well by reciting at local entertainments. It was still the "Chatauqua era". Monologues and recitations were much admired. He had a ready store of popular material, including Alfred Noyes' "The Highwayman", Pauline Johnson's "Legend of Qu'Appelle Valley", and Kipling's "If'. He considers that he made out rather well financially; he even managed loans to students who were harder up than he was. Brandon at that time specialized in two departments, the training of ministerial students, and geology. In the scramble to support themselves, some theologs could be found working during the summer on geological surveys – which paid more – while geology students sometimes were sent out to preach.

At Carberry, Tommy met a pretty, bright-eyed young girl who was a Methodist but had transferred to the Presbyterian church to hear him preach. Irma Dempsey was the daughter of a local farmer. The Dempseys were Ottawa Valley Irish. Irma's grandfather had left Ireland at the time of the great famine and settled near North Gower, close to Ottawa. They had moved to Manitoba to homestead before the turn of the century. When Irma finished high school at Carberry she enrolled at Brandon College to study music, and wound up her course, whether by accident or good timing, the same year that Tommy graduated with distinction and moved on to his first charge. Tommy says, "Of course they used to warn the girls at college to stay away from the theologs, or they'd end up in a drafty manse somewhere, getting their clothes out of a missionary box." But Irma, like Tommy was a cheerful optimist, and the prospect seemed to hold no terrors for her. Tommy was ordained in June, 1930, and they were married later that summer.

Brandon College at that period was an affiliate of McMaster University. It was not considered to be in any sense a radical outpost, but the deep agitation in religious thinking which permeated the western churches in those years reached into its classrooms. In fact, practising members of Baptist churches would have been disturbed to hear what the students were learning in the college they had founded.

The Baptist Church was so far from "left" in its thinking that it had just emerged from the *science vs. religion* controversy. Most young Baptists were fundamentalist when they entered Brandon. There, their ideas were challenged. Was Christianity concerned with individual salvation or with social behaviour? The ideas of the "social gospel" were in full flood.

One of Brandon's finest professors, Harris L. MacNeill, served as Acting Dean for many years during that period but was considered too modernist to receive the appointment. MacNeill taught Greek, which was for him and for his students an avenue to philosophy and far-reaching discussions. Economics was presented by Professor Burtenhard, who scrupulously presented various theories, including socialism. A course in socialism had been offered, and Tommy and several friends had signed up for it. However, in the fall they discovered the course had been withdrawn. The group went to Professor Burtenhard and argued for the course, which he reinstated. The students had been mildly socialist; taught by a reluctant teacher they emerged at the end of the year convinced that the Marxist theory was the right one.

When Tommy was asked, "What did you preach about in those years, at your 'supply' churches? Did you begin properly, with a text?" his answer was,

> Oh you always start with a text. But the bible is like a bull fiddle, you can play almost any tune you want on it. My background, being interested in social and economic questions, naturally inclined me to preaching the idea that religion in essence was entering into a new relationship with God and into a new relationship with the universe. And into a new relationship with your fellow man. And that if Christianity meant anything at all, it meant building the brotherhood of man. If you really believed in the fatherhood of God, if you believed what Jesus said, that we live in a friendly universe, then the brotherhood of man was a corollary to it. And that meant a helpful relationship between man and man, building a society and building institutions that would uplift mankind, and particularly those who were the least fortunate, and this was pretty well the sort of message I was trying to get across.

In Tommy's third year his head-of-the-class position was challenged by a newcomer, Stanley Knowles, who had previously attended college in Los Angeles, and had spent a year as a printer earning enough to go back to university. The two proceeded to divide the academic spoils between them in the next three years, though Knowles wound up at graduation with most of the gold medals. Tommy usually explained: "I tried to take the gold medals but they made me put them back." Knowles says, "Tommy was smarter, but I was better at writing exams."

Tommy in fact received gold medals in debating and oratory, and in his final year he was Senior Stick, head of the student body. His debating prowess won the college considerable honour when they fielded the only Canadian team to beat the touring Imperial Team from Great Britain. He was very active as well in student politics, and he found time to enter the college boxing bouts.

Recalling their shared student years, Knowles says, "Brandon was the time when we sorted out our religious and our social thinking. We went in as *conventional* young men accepting society. We came out convinced that something had to be done to make society more Christian."

Both men have retained an association with Brandon University. Douglas received an honorary Ll.D. in 1965, Knowles in 1967. In 1970 Knowles was invited to become Chancellor of the University.

In their final year, with thoughts on graduation and a first charge, both Douglas and Knowles accepted invitations to "supply" at the little city of Weyburn, Saskatchewan. The Calvary Baptist Church at

Weyburn was a friendly place, and became much attached to both young ministers, who preached on alternate Sundays through the winter of 1929-1930. Eventually a choice had to be made. A meeting of the congregation put the difficult matter to a vote. The ballots have never been opened to public view, but the official comment was that it was "close". Douglas received the invitation. He was ordained there in June, 1930, when he was twenty-five years old.

Stanley Knowles went instead to First Baptist Church in Winnipeg, and thence transferred to the United Church, which had been his earlier affiliation. His political career in Winnipeg has been uninterrupted since those days, and he has no regret that he lost the vote of the Weyburn congregation.

The real point is, he said, that Tommy went to Saskatchewan. And that was a fateful combination, as the next thirty years would prove.

Chapter Three
Saskatchewan

"I certainly wouldn't have chosen Saskatchewan as the locale for Canada's first democratic socialist experiment," Tommy Douglas said. "There wasn't a province west of New Brunswick that was less fertile ground."

Douglas was talking about economic resources. It would have been rather gratifying to have had some material abundance when one set about redistributing it. Saskatchewan had almost none.

In 1944 when the CCF took power it appeared as dry and empty as a cracked clay river bed between the last metropolis in Manitoba and the promise of foothills in Alberta.

Now that grain and oil have become internationally magnified Saskatchewan may begin to seem important to Canada. But certainly in the years before 1944, and for much of the time since, it has been possible for most other Canadians to regard Saskatchewan as so much extra mileage on the car getting to the west coast, or down east.

But a number of people have written about Saskatchewan, and some of us have spent years of our lives there. From these writings and this experience a different view of a unique piece of Canada emerges. It was the worst, but also the best place in the country for Tommy Douglas to set on its way to the New Jerusalem.

Lush grass grows out of deep soil, for hundreds of miles. The stark two facts of soil and sky are all there are. Neither is passive. The sky blazes with light, the earth freezes solid, thaws, is deeply fecund, dries, scorches, blows away. It is a mistake to see Saskatchewan in pale water colour drawings of limpid air and thin etched lines of wire and fence. More accurate artists like George Swinton of Winnipeg have painted sound and fury in heavy oils and that is in fact what the prairies, and most of all Saskatchewan, are like. It is hot and freezing and charged with the most furious and most simple of emotions.

It is as grand as a sea coast, but different. Here the soil is alive, its life is the preoccupation of the people. The rush of life in the spring, between the deaths of winter, sets the pattern of extreme contrasts.

Ralph Allen once wrote of:

> the union of a very old land and a very young people. . . . The prairies
> are older than the Nile, older than the hills of Jerusalem, older than

Galilee and the valley of the Jordan ... It took many millions of years to hew out its rocks and mountains, to bury its twenty-ton lizards and flying dragons, to sift and grind its soil, to hide its lakes of inflammable ooze and its underground hills of coal and metal ... Beginning a million years ago, mile-high glaciers crept through Canada, then melted, in four glacial periods. Like bulldozers, they pushed mountains of sand, humus and rock onto the prairies from the Canadian shield. The glaciers dug up clay and limes created in ancient seas. When they finally melted they left vast lakes. These silt-covered bottoms of melt-water lakes are today the richest wheat-lands of the prairie provinces.[1]

Plains Indians survived fairly well on the wild game of the grasslands. They were cruelly shunted aside by the Canadian government which opened up the land to immigrant farm development. The white settlers raised cereal crops, particularly wheat, for export. They tore up the soil without knowing that dry years would come and the winds would bring devastation. They raised some prodigious crops. They were also plagued by rust, grasshoppers, hail, and early frost, and only painfully and partially learned to cope with these adversities – there were years when they could only wait and endure.

What they faced is shown in the fact that of the first four people to die in Saskatchewan, two froze to death in blizzards, one drowned in the Saskatchewan River, and the other died of exhaustion fighting a prairie fire.

But a new population, having risked its own uprooting to arrive here, was not inclined to submit or retreat. The tests to their endurance provoked an heroic response.

In the exhilaration of the time Nicholos Flood Davin, who established the Regina *Leader* in 1883, wrote: "All the charms that belong to youth, hope, energy are found in the North-West; and the bracing influence of the new free land on mind and character is remarkable. The climate is akin to that which nurtured the warrior hordes, the Goths and the Vandals, who became the terror and ultimately the destroyers of the Roman Empire.[2]

A writer somewhat more staid, Hugh MacLennan wrote of Saskatchewan as an itinerant maritimer in 1961:

This is one of the sternest terrains I know inhabited by people living normal lives. . . .

I remember the feeling of fear it gave me as a boy when my mother told me of a relative who had gone to Saskatchewan from Nova Scotia, and how she had watched her son walking alone across the prairie to school until he became a tiny dot on the horizon.

MacLennan finds it remarkable that civilization so quickly came into being in this primitive violence:

Montreal had been settled for two centuries before it had a university, but the University of Saskatchewan was established five years after the land on which it stands had been incorporated within the province. A professor I met in Saskatoon only last year, originally a Nova Scotian and a man of vigour still, told me of the morning when he and one or two colleagues saw their first students appear, and that the first subjects they taught them were Latin and Greek. Fifty years later the University of Saskatchewan was one of the best in the country. . . .

These days when I visit Saskatchewan I remember how students from the farms starved during the depression years in order to get an education. I think how people cooperated, and thereby upheld the dignity of their species. I feel that here I have made at least a brief acquaintance with the kind of unconscious force which Tolstoy believed is decisive in history.[3]

The way in which the land was peopled was an invitation to political rebellion in due course. Immigration had been pressed in Europe with the blatancy of a medicine show. And the immigrants were being conned. They were not being invited to create a viable community, like the first colonies of New England and New France. They were brought in to serve the interests of the already established sections of the country, the industrial east. They would become a domestic market to help build the new industries of Ontario. This original subordination of the prairie region to the two-generations-older industrial east is detailed more specifically by W. L. Morton than by any other writer.

Louis Riel's adventures in Manitoba, according to Morton, began "the tradition of Western grievance". He pursues this idea:

The struggle of the Prairie West had begun, and it was to merge with the struggle against economic subordination to the capital and corporations of the East. The result of this struggle, both of its failures and its partial successes, was a release of that utopianism which has been endemic in western society since the French Revolution, and indeed in religious form since the Reformation, and which has always found a refuge and a stimulus on the frontiers of settlement.[4]

This view of prairie political behaviour is perhaps an exaggerated one. But it has much validity. The dramatic tension of prairie geography and climate was not suited to turn an immigrant people into docile consumers for eastern goods and eastern politics.

The Saskatchewan people came by the hundreds of thousands from the social and economic repressions of Europe. They were British, Germans, Ukrainians, Swedes, Norwegians, Poles, and a variety of other nationalities. The Scandinavians and British, in particular, brought with them some knowledge of cooperatives. It was this style of economic development that would blunt the worst of the poverty in a lean landscape.

But one should be cautioned. It was not quite as simple and inevitable a process as this suggests. Everything tends to become polarized in Saskatchewan. Not one but two streams of social behaviour have flourished in the province from the beginning. MacLennan wrote with admiration of the people who cooperated in order to survive; that was one stream and, as it turned out, the main one. The other was as virulent and rowdy a troop of free enterprisers as ever assailed the marketplace. And even today, one river of literature describes in awed tones the altruism of the men who organized the Wheat Pool, while another smaller but livelier flow of books tells of the traders who cheated the Indians, the land dealers, the liquor smugglers who crossed the United States border during the prohibition years, the gamblers, bootleggers, and prostitutes of early Moose Jaw. For people such as these, and for the respectable free enterpriser, tough, sentimental and ambitious, the Wheat Pool crowd was anathema. And this polarized division into free enterprisers and cooperators would find its natural expression in politics. Political leaders in the province have included not only those of the farthest left but those of the farthest right in the Canadian spectrum.

Both kinds of Saskatchewanites opposed the east, perpetuating Morton's theory of rebellion against subordinate status. But, in politics, the "free enterprisers" have found accommodation with the dominant parties of the east, even while they have protested the independence of their stance, or organized conspicuously around a local leader – a Gardiner or a Diefenbaker – and played down the party connection in eastern Canada.

The "cooperators" had to forge tenuous political links with new and uncertain eastern counterparts. The founding strength of their political faith was western.

The cooperators began with economic objectives. In the beginning, in 1902, the homesteaders formed a Territorial Grain Growers Association in opposition to the National Policy of John A. Macdonald, and particularly in opposition to the protective tariff structure which favoured eastern industry and at the same time placed a heavy burden on farmers in the extra costs added to machinery and farm equipment. The Association published the *Grain Growers Guide* which sparkled with utopian ideas, but the Association was non-partisan politically and lobbied successfully with the Liberal government in power at Regina. They persuaded the government, for example, to establish publicly-owned telephones and compulsory hail insurance in the twenties. In 1905 they had changed their name to the Saskatchewan Grain Growers Association. They were consulted openly and often by the provincial government, and one of their founders, W. R. Motherwell, was Saskatchewan's Minister of Agriculture from 1905 to 1918.

Premier Martin in a speech in Preeceville on May 2, 1920, wooed farm support by disassociating himself from federal Liberal policy on the issue of continuing the government's wartime Wheat Board. Martin brought J. A. Maharg, the Grain Growers president, into his cabinet. Maharg resigned a year later when Ottawa disbanded the Wheat Board, and the chummy relations between the Grain Growers and the Liberals began to melt away.

With wheat prices dropping dramatically from wartime levels, a new farm organization, much more militant, came into existence. It was the Farmers Union of Canada, founded at Ituna, Saskatchewan, and it was the farmers' parallel to the One Big Union of western labour. L. B. McNamee, a big Irish homesteader from Kelvington, was its president, and the secretary was a Swiss named Norbert Henri Schwarz, who persuaded the Union to adopt as its slogan: "Farmers of the world unite".

The Union set out to create a farmer-controlled system of grain marketing, and brought in Aaron Sapiro, "the Great Persuader", a passionate messianic lawyer from the United States, who sold the idea of a Wheat Pool like a new religion. The Pool came into being in 1924, and soon was to dominate the handling of Saskatchewan wheat, a powerful competitor to the private elevator companies.

The Farmers Union cultivated a sense of solidarity among its members, using the Marxist phraseology of the "class struggle" and opposing a "capitalist" class made up of private grain buyers, speculators on the Exchange, bankers, and middlemen. To tighten its bonds, it maintained a conspiratorial air, with closed meetings, passwords, "Brother" as a form of address, and the expulsion of any member who was not an "actual dirt farmer".

The *Regina Leader* in an editorial on July 4, 1925 said it had "long suspected that the mentality behind the Farmers Union of Canada was Communistic and promised nothing but evil."

The increasing radicalism of successive organizations of farmers reflected their frustration. Canada's economic and financial power was entrenched in the east; federal government policies seemed to favour it at every turn. The accepted historical description of the period focuses on the needs and the progress of industry:

> The agrarian pioneer phase had all but ended by 1920. The future expansion of the Dominion was now linked to the development of industrial capitalism, not merely in manufacturing but in the exploitation of such natural resources as timber and minerals and water power . . . Transportation facilities and an expanding home market guarded by a protective tariff had brought into being a substantial manufacturing industry.[5]

While western farmers called for more government action, to support and protect them from the wild fluctuation of grain prices on the world market and the cruel vagaries of the weather, eastern manufacturers wanted tariffs, but little action beyond tariffs, from the hands of government. McInnis says, " . . . the dominating emotion of Canadian industrialists was less the hope of favours yet to come than the fear of interference and impositions in the form of social legislation or tax burdens, and demands for economy and nonintervention were particularly directed against the federal government."[6]

In 1926, the farmers' movement was solidified by the union of the old Grain Growers Association and the Farmers Union. The new organization was called the United Farmers of Canada (Saskatchewan Section) (UFC (SS)), having its counterparts in the United Farmers of Alberta and the United Farmers of Ontario. They subscribed to political action in varying degrees, and their programs were radical for the times.

In Saskatchewan, an even more virulent wing developed in the Farmers' Educational League, with George Hara Williams of Semans as secretary. Williams had the distinction of being one of the first of the prairie-born generation to become a farm leader. The League backed him as president of the UFC (SS) in 1929, and he was elected.

The League set about educating its members with a will. At the same time the Wheat Pool Library, lending books by mail, did a tremendous volume of business among its isolated farm members. So did an Open Shelf Library run by the provincial government. Books on subjects like economics and sociology were borrowed over and over again by the avid readers of the prairies. Radicalism, utopianism, interest in the Russian experiment, sprouted and flourished.

In 1930 George H. Williams was not convinced that the people were ready for utopia. He wrote in a memo to the United Farmers executive in August 1930: "We have no guarantee of the time that will elapse before the people will discard this outworn system of private ownership and profit. I feel that at the present time an honest observer must admit that no more than twenty per cent of the agrarian population are willing to discard the system; that ten per cent do not know what to think and seventy per cent still cling to it."[7]

But that was 1930. The next few years were "bad times" of such magnitude that the psychology of the province shifted radically. The livelihood of the farmers in their pioneer homes, depending as it did on the vagaries of climate and on the fluctuations of prices for wheat in world markets, was unstable. The world-wide depression of the thirties brought catastrophe. Loss of markets for grain and livestock sent prices crashing. Added to that were unprecedented years of drought, when Saskatchewan's wheat crop yielded less than three bushels per acre, compared to an average sixteen bushels in good years. The prairie winds whistled, the dust blew thick, and nothing grew. In many districts of Saskatchewan, 90 per cent of the people were without any income and were forced to accept "relief". The destitution of that time, for a new, strong, spirited population, jolted Williams' cautious estimates of those farmers willing to change the economic system. Saskatchewan became ready for change.

Douglas said: "It (the depression) swept away most preconceived notions. People have to have a sense of the need for change before it comes. I've never believed that social change is brought about by rational thinking on the part of people. They take the next step forward because they have to in order to survive. Man likes to tread the beaten path. Only a great social upheaval can force him to move into some great new uplands of human behaviour."

If Saskatchewan's natural environment, manner of settlement, economy, and the crisis of the great depression, all seemed to lead toward receptive conditions for the democratic socialist experiment of the CCF, the political establishment of the province might have seemed rather to militate against it. The Liberal party, in power almost continuously since the province began, was entrenched so securely that it seemed beyond the most optimistic hopes of a populist party to unseat it. But by the Second World War, the Liberals had reached that pinnacle of arrogance from which governments are most readily toppled – a target for all the forces of wrath and discontent. In this respect too, Saskatchewan was ready for democratic socialism at the propitious moment.

Why Saskatchewan, and not Manitoba or Alberta? Although "the prairies" are lumped together in the minds of Canadians, wide political differences had developed in these provinces. What Douglas could do in Saskatchewan he might well not have been able to do in Alberta or Manitoba.

J. S. Woodsworth and other early Labour men had been elected to the House of Commons from Winnipeg. But there was a sharp dividing line between Winnipeg and the rural areas of Manitoba, and the socialists did not break that barrier until 1969 when Ed Schreyer, with a farm background, took them to unexpected victory. There was also a history of compromise. When Bracken accepted leadership of the successful farm group in 1921, he formed a government with a non-partisan flavour, known as the Liberal Progressives. During the Second World War his coalition government had included one CCF member, S. J. Farmer, as Minister of Labour. Bracken was so non-partisan, in fact, that he was eligible for a call from the federal Conservatives in quest of a new national leader in 1942. Says Stanley Knowles, now NDP member for Winnipeg North Centre: "This muddled political scene didn't give us much chance – not until the particular parties resumed their separate identities." Polarization appears to be one prerequisite to socialist success.

Alberta's politics were just as different from events in Saskatchewan. Alberta has been settled heavily by immigration from the United States, first by men in search of ranchlands, then by men in search of oil. Its first government, like Saskatchewan's, was Liberal, but the early farmer political movement took firmer root and the United Farmers of Alberta (UFA) elected a government in 1921. They remained in power for fourteen years of rather uninspired administration of no particular ideology, until they shocked the province with a scandal involving the premier, J. E. Brownlee, in 1934. Unable to cope with the economic trauma of the depression, the United Farmers' government was replaced by Social Credit, the monetary-evangelist party, in 1935. The new-born CCF struggled along with a few members and one or two seats in the legislature, but the thrust of the farmers' movement had been spent in the UFA. The swing had brought in Social Credit, which moved sharply to the right on taking office. The CCF (and later the NDP) experienced an almost total shut-out in political terms in Alberta.

Thus, in different ways, both Manitoba and Alberta tried out reformist administrations which either delayed the advent of the socialists or cut them off completely.

In contrast, the Liberals had an almost unbroken record of power in Saskatchewan until the CCF unseated them in 1944. And the Liberals had by that time become as corrupt in power as any Canadian administration since Confederation. They managed to keep the Conservatives, despite noisy and valiant election attempts, on the Opposition side. Even the Progressive party, a short-lived agrarian effort in the 1920s,[8] failed to elect more than six provincial members at Regina.

The Conservatives managed to break the Liberal hold only once, in 1929. It was a peak time for the Conservatives, with Bennett winning federal power a year later. In Saskatchewan there were two hell-bent elections, not unrelated to the sudden appearance in the province of the Ku Klux Klan. In 1929 the Conservatives were swept in, and in 1934 the Liberals emphatically threw them back out.

The organizers of the Ku Klux Klan arrived from Indiana late in 1926, and quickly established locals in Regina, Moose Jaw, and smaller centres. The game appeared to be largely pecuniary. The selling of memberships was an important feature, and leaders absconded with funds and were brought to trial.

Their paraphernalia, including the tracts and burning cross (electrically lit in Saskatchewan, to conform with fire regulations), and their titles of Imperial Wizard, Imperial Kligrapp (secretary), Great Titan, King Kleagle, were bizarre in the extreme, yet many sober citizens, including ordained ministers of the Anglican and some other Protestant churches, openly espoused their cause.[9]

Their appeal was to preserve Saskatchewan as Anglo-Saxon and Protestant, against the continuing large influx of European immigrants, many of whom were Roman Catholic. The rhetoric of the imported organizers, especially Dr. J. H. Hawkins, was particularly vicious: attacking the government's immigration policy he said, "You have said we are a great melting pot, but let us see that the slag and the scum that refuse to assimilate and become one hundred per cent Canadians is skimmed off and thrown away."[10] A self-proclaimed "ex-priest", J. J. Maloney, authored anti-Catholic pamphlets. The Liberal provincial government was assailed for permitting Catholic nuns to wear their religious garb when teaching in public schools.

Calderwood cites a considerable list of known Conservatives who were supporters or local leaders of the Ku Klux Klan.[11] James G. Gardiner, the Liberal premier, denounced the Klan in the Speech from the Throne in January, 1928, and in June that year he had the federal government deport Hawkins. He ripped into the Conservatives for their alleged connections with the Klan.

M. J. Coldwell, who had joined the Progressive party, later admitted to a good deal of sympathy with Gardiner's position at that period. But he was not to be spared from Gardiner's wide-swinging attack at the time, even though he and others were denouncing the KKK as vigorously as the Liberals were. Gardiner was a rough fighter, and he chose to include the Progressives with the Conservatives in having links with the infamous Klan.

Gardiner was rapped on the knuckles by the *Western Producer* (June 21, 1927) which said he "rather unwisely, and somewhat cheaply, linked the Progressives with the Klan by reference to such similar organizing techniques as utilizing paid organizers from the U.S., a reference to the Non-Partisan League of the Progressive past." And T. A. Crerar, the Progressive party leader who himself returned to the Liberal fold, commented after the 1929 election, "It is probably a fact that 75 per cent of the Progressive vote in 1921 was of Liberal antecedent. Gardiner's tactics in his efforts to annihilate them lost thousands of these people who are nominally Liberals and are sore and angry."

James Gardiner had once told a reporter, "You can't win elections with rosemary water and grain statistics". He had been Minister of Highways in the Dunning administration of 1922, and succeeded Dunning in 1926 as leader despite Dunning's preference for Agriculture Minister Hamilton. Gardiner's highway inspectors had become known as "The Highwaymen". He had discovered in the road system a ready-made structure to reach into all localities of the province to exert political pressure, and his use of this department was unashamed. That the highways of Saskatchewan were in deplorable shape throughout the Liberal regime was beside the point. The highway inspectors went into every community; organized Liberal workers in every poll to keep track of every vote; approved or disapproved, by way of reward or punishment, the contracts for public buildings; influenced the appointment of teaching staff and even of church ministers. All key party people had civil service jobs and were paid from the public treasury. They included the sanitary inspectors and liquor store managers. "Finally, the party organization was assisted throughout the province by newspapers, which gave their support in return for government printing contracts . . . The formal organization constituted a democratic facade which hid from the common gaze the naked autocracy of effective party management . . . Appointments were from the top down . . . The social cost of this corruption lay in the increased expenses of government due to an inefficient and padded civil service, to the costly and poorly planned roads and public works, and to uneconomical government purchasing."[12]

The Gardiner machine, overturned in 1929, rolled back into power in the next election. In the September 1934 issue of *Canadian Forum*, Burton J. Richardson wrote, "High Politics in Saskatchewan", analyzing the June election which had disposed of J. T. M. Anderson's short-lived Conservative regime. "Smooth as a streamlined motor car, steady as a steam-roller, slick as a new-ground piston, the Saskatchewan Liberal Party is the super-machine of Canadian politics," Richardson wrote. He pointed out that the machine had "nipped what even itself thought might be a CCF uprising".

Nipped also was Tommy Douglas' first attempt to get himself elected to the legislature of his province. The new CCF had offered slight opposition, except in a few ridings, to the triumphant Gardiner machine. One constituency that had looked promising for the CCF was Last Mountain. Three days before the election the Liberal organizer had the votes figured this way: Liberals: 2,760; Farmer-Labour (CCF): 2,753; Conservative: 1,031. The actual count was: Liberals: 2,719; Farmer-Labour (CCF): 2,705; Conservative: 1,341.

The Liberals were in power for another ten years. What made them seem doubly invincible was the support of the federal party, in power at Ottawa during much of their tenure of office. In fact when the federal Liberals ousted R. B. Bennett and the Conservatives the following year, in 1935, Canada had Liberal governments in Ottawa and in all the provinces except Alberta.

With the depression a second ready-made power structure was available to the Liberals at Regina – relief administration. The relief officers filled in any gaps left by "The Highwaymen". Who could vote against the man who decided the size of one's food allotment for the coming month?

Politics in Saskatchewan is violently alive and relentlessly partisan at every level, from the average voter to the members of the legislature. And "dirty politics" has been at least as bad, if not measurably worse, than in other sections of the country.

When Douglas recorded an extensive interview in 1958 he was questioned about the "personal vindictiveness" of the 1948 session of the Legislature, when Walter Tucker was Leader of the Opposition. Douglas replied:

> That is not so foreign to Saskatchewan. It is part of the tradition of the Gardiner machine. I remember coming to Weyburn in the fall of

1929 and Liberals, members of my congregation and good Christian people, would tell me the most awful things about Conservative leader J. T. M. Anderson and other Conservative cabinet ministers. They had illegitimate children around, they were scamps and scalawags, they were crooks. And I used to say, 'Surely you don't believe that. It's not substantiated. I understand you differing with them politically but this is streetcorner gossip that decent people shouldn't listen to.' But that was the atmosphere. That was the Gardiner tradition. If someone's against you politically, you break them. You get them fired from their jobs or boycott their stores, make life so miserable they get out. . . .

You should be able to differ on fiscal or economic policy without building up a personal hatred. One of the first years I was in parliament, I shared an office with M. J. (Coldwell), and a well-known Liberal came in and began to run down M. A. Macpherson who was a Conservative and had run against M. J. in 1934. M. J. turned on him like a lion. He said, 'Mr. Macpherson is a political opponent but he's one of the finest Christian gentlemen I've ever known. If that's all you have to say will you please leave.'

There is no need to stoop to personal vilification – this is part of the British tradition. And this the Liberal party has never understood.

To those who found rough-and-tumble politics normal and stimulating, just as to those who enjoyed the "free enterprise" economic scramble (and they were frequently the same people), the new wave of politics that came with the CCF was preachy and unconvincing. Some of them were won over, by the Douglas style and the Douglas conviction. But there remained the unrepentant ones, and it would be a serious mistake not to acknowledge their presence in Saskatchewan.

One of the liveliest chroniclers of this period of prairie history is James H. Gray, whose series of books is a brilliant account of those "bad times" as seen by a young man who did not join the CCF. In one of his books he says: "Between 1900 and 1915, the combined efforts of the government, railways and free-lance agents lured more than one million immigrants to the three prairie provinces. Their coming ushered in the bawdiest, brawlingest, and back-breakingest era in prairie history. It was also the most puritanical, law-abiding, Sabbatarian, and pietistic."[13] To a writer who draws his stories from the other tradition, the polarization of this unique society is equally clear.

In the *Canadian Forum* of April, 1935, the same, though younger, James H. Gray wrote "To Hell with Utopias" out of bravado and in response to the surfeit of talk of prairie reform. The *Forum* editor published Gray's piece in a spirit of tolerance, explaining that no one had written in defence of capitalism for some time. "How rich and beautiful

and intelligent will life be in Canadopia; and how insufferably *dull*! . . .
To Hell with Utopias! I wouldn't swap my front seat for this show for
one on the right hand of God, nor for one in Jim Woodsworth's lap
either," wrote young Mr. Gray.

The duality of Saskatchewan is a matter of sky against earth, of west
against east, of plenty and starvation, of black/white politicians, of the
cooperator and the unbeliever. It is a contest of magnificent proportions.
Only a province capable of such extremes could have the audacity to
create a small pocket of socialism deep in the centre of North America.

But one could be sure of this: it would never slip in gently. It would
require a fighter as redoubtable as any populist commander, to bring in
the victory.

This was the province Douglas came to as a young Baptist minister in
1930.

Chapter Four
Church to Politics

Tommy Douglas was ordained as a minister of the Baptist church in June, 1930, and married Irma Dempsey at her parents' home in Carberry, Manitoba, on August 30. The wedding was unspectacular. Neither the Douglases nor the Dempseys are a showy lot. The Reverend Mark Talney, who had married Tommy's sister Nan, officiated, and Stanley Knowles was present. Knowles and Douglas traded churches for two ' weeks, to give the couple a honeymoon in Winnipeg.

Irma was only nineteen and Tommy, at twenty-five, looked scarcely older. They took a small apartment on Second Avenue in Weyburn, furnished it for forty dollars and took up their new life with shared zeal and good spirit. The minister's salary was $1800 a year. Irma thought Weyburn was "just great". She found scope for her talent in preparing pupils for the annual music festival. They attended Weyburn symphony concerts. They, particularly Irma, liked to curl; they even played hockey with a small group of friends out at the Powers' farm on the Souris River. "Community things – ! You could never stop!" Irma said.

At home, Tommy played the clarinet sometimes while Irma played piano. She thought he performed quite well on the instrument but that diversion had to give way to more important things – "like everything else." Tommy soon had the church congregation extolling his praises, but Irma also made a good impression. She was small and composed, resourceful, and good humoured, an inestimable partner in Douglas' career. "She fell in with anything that was needed," the people of the church said. "She was a little shy. She never pushed herself forward. Reserved, but friendly."

Church members whom they liked and saw much of were John E. Powers and Ted Stinson and their wives; Powers and Stinson later opened a grocery store in Weyburn. Both attended the first political meeting of the Farmer-Labour Party in Weyburn with Douglas. Ted Stinson became his campaign manager.

When, in 1973, Mrs. Powers looked back to those happy occasions at her farm home with the Reverend Mr. Douglas and his wife and the Stinsons, she called him "Mr. Douglas" still. She would not say the Stinsons and the Powers had been his closest friends; she said, on reflection, "People dislike a minister having special friends."

But formality was not always in evidence. There are stories of Tommy's antic adventures. One was the visit of a former girl friend to Weyburn. He told Irma, "I think you'll like her. But it's a little difficult. She's very hard of hearing." Off he went to meet the girl at the station, and on the way home he cautioned, "Irma's a marvellous person, but there's just one thing. You'll have to raise your voice; she's quite deaf." While the two shouted their greetings Tommy slipped away, grinning, to let them resolve their mutual problem.

The mental hospital at Weyburn was to become the setting for some of Tommy's famous jokes. Like most of the jokes he treasured, they were usually on him. He was gathering material for his M. A. thesis on the subnormal family at the hospital one afternoon and stayed beyond his usual hour. A new attendant came on the ward. Tommy approached him and said he was ready to leave. The attendant said to sit down and wait for supper. Tommy said he was writing case histories for his M.A. The attendant said that was nice, so sit down and keep writing. "It took me an hour," Tommy said, "to get out of Ward B."

Douglas had wasted no time in bringing the young boys of the church and community together in a Tuxis Group and in Trail Rangers. One day he had a call from James Graham, the police magistrate. "I've got a number of boys appearing in court tomorrow morning. Will you come down?" Douglas listened the next morning while Magistrate Graham read the charges of breaking and entering and theft. There were a dozen boys of various sizes, all neglected, all unkempt in trailing suits belonging to adult males of the family. The school nurse, Anne Morton was there, and she put in a word for them. To send them off to the Industrial School in Regina was to provide them with a post-graduate course in crime, she pointed out. Their parents had been scolded and appealed to without success. Douglas discovered why he had been invited: there was nothing to be done, the magistrate said, but to put them all in his custody.

So Douglas arrived home with twelve of the least prepossessing junior criminals he had ever seen. Irma, a bride of six months, met the first problem by feeding them. Next they were taken to a barber who trimmed their hair without charge, and after that, members of the church with boys in the same age bracket were propositioned for clothes. The boys became something of a church project. The young people in church organizations were given the task of providing them with after-school and weekend social activities. By keeping in close touch, Douglas managed to steer his wards away from trouble and eventually into honest lives, but there was one close call. One Sunday when Douglas was out of town his gang broke into a store and made off with chocolates and cigarettes. The storekeeper called up Douglas, who tracked them down. Douglas ordered the boys to return what was left of the stolen goods, and report to church the next Sunday and to his study afterwards. He was finished with them, he said. They would have to go back to the magistrate and off to the Industrial School. The boys turned up at church, then sidled into his office. Douglas laid it on hard. They had let down all the people in the church who had believed in them and were so sure they would never steal again. The boys cried. There was a big reconciliation. They would try very hard, and this time there would be no more trouble. They started to leave. But Reggie, the toughest and smartest of the lot, turned at the door and came back. On Douglas' desk he emptied the contents of his pockets – Douglas' penknife and fountain pen lifted from the desk in the course of the lecture.

"Reggie," said Douglas, "turned out very well. In the latter part of the war I went overseas at the invitation of General A. G. L. McNaughton. When I was visiting one advance post the brigadier was extending me every courtesy, explaining my schedule, and he said he had a Provost group of four on motorcycles to escort me around. He presented them; the sergeant was Reggie. 'He's one of our best men,' the brigadier said, 'That sergeant seems to know every trick a man could pull before he does it. Splendid fellow.' "

The Baptist church became the scene of theatrical productions, including an ambitious Christmas pageant and a sunrise Easter service. Even on average Sundays outsiders attended to hear Douglas speak. Older members of the Baptist faith compared him to "the prince of preachers", Charles Haddon Spurgeon, who arrived from the rural countryside of England to take London by storm in the late nineteenth century. Bound copies of Spurgeon's sermons graced many Baptist homes in that period; it was high praise to find a likeness in Tommy Douglas.

A conversation, some impressions over a forty years' acquaintance, was taped in Mrs. Powers' living room in Weyburn. With her is Mrs. Jack Clark. Both women are widowed, and both their husbands worked in Tommy's first political campaigns. An abbreviated transcript:

Mrs. P.: Our church had the two young men coming from the university. We liked both Mr. Knowles and Mr. Douglas so much we couldn't decide, so we took a vote. Mr. Knowles was a little deeper in his sermons. But Mr. Douglas always gave us a good sermon. And he was fine with the young people.

Those were the depression times. There was no pasture for the stock; no feed. Every day you'd see people going north, just leaving the place, some to the Peace River.

Mrs. C.: We put damp towels around the windows and doors to keep out the dust in those days. You never saw green grass. We were in the worst of it, in Weyburn.

Mrs. P.: The East thought we were just poor managers, until the depression hit them too. Mr. Douglas helped organize the relief. . .

Mr. Douglas directed the church pageant at Christmas. Nearly everyone was involved in it. He had an elocution group. I wish you could have heard him on Bobbie Burns' night! He recited them one after the other. Once in the United Church, to a big crowd. . .

Of course Mr. Douglas was never political in church. But he was always for the underdog. That was always clear wherever he spoke.

His speeches always ended on a good note, something to live by.

Mrs. C.: In Regina in 1962, the Liberals and Conservatives ganged up on him. They were determined to get him.

Mrs. P.: We thought it was terrible. Mr. Douglas had done so much for Saskatchewan.

He wanted to do so many things for the people. He had them all planned in his mind.

Mrs. C.: The electricity on the farm. It seemed to me everybody should have turned CCF!

Mrs. P.: That was Mr. Douglas' idea too.

Mrs. C.: You drive up back roads and see all the farms lit up. The farmers' wives have everything we have in the city.

Mrs. P.: They didn't give him credit. Used to say he was just a little *upstart*. Hundreds never realized who gave it to them.

Mrs. C.: One lady said to me, 'You CCF all think he's a little tin god.' That type of person always had everything.

Mrs. P.: Mr. Douglas took that trip to Chicago, when he was taking that course, and saw all those people out of work. He used to say if he ever had a chance to hit that, he would hit it hard.

Douglas' ministry, in southern Saskatchewan, was in one of the areas that suffered most from the combined drought and depression. To the manse door came transient young men. Irma said: "They must have known they could get food because there was a steady stream of people. We never turned anybody down. I – still almost weep. Some poor soul always turned up – oh gosh, they never stopped coming. I'll never forget that period."

In an article written at that time Douglas said: "The religion of tomorrow will be less concerned with dogmas of theology and more concerned with the social welfare of humanity. When one sees the church spending its energies on the assertion of antiquated dogmas but dumb as an oyster to the poverty and misery all around, we can't help but recognize the need for a new interpretation of Christianity."

Douglas said his views met no conflict at his local church.

They were progressively minded people. But there was conflict at church conventions. At one convention I moved a resolution on social concern and I remember an older man strongly disagreed. He said the two classes are pre-ordained, the rich to learn benevolence and charity and the poor to learn gratitude. We should preach the gospel, that man should repent of his sins, come to God, be reconciled to Him and get ready for the next world.

Once, later in the '30s, I was asked to address some Baptist young people at a big convention in the east. There we were in a terrible economic depression, fascism sweeping over a large part of the world. The Jewish people were being persecuted, arrested in Germany and thrown into concentration camps. And here in the presence of these tremendous evil forces in the world, the best we could get at this group of young people was a resolution condemning dancing, condemning slot machines and wanting beer parlors closed an hour earlier.

His experience in Chicago disturbed him deeply. He was in the midst of M.A. studies from McMaster; he would take a summer course in economics at the University of Manitoba to complete his Masters degree. But the entire summer of 1931 was spent in Chicago in preparation for his Ph.D. At the university he worked with sociologist Arthur Erastus Holt. And he was sent with student teams to study the "jungles" along the Chicago tracks, where tens of thousands of transients lived in lean-to's, going out to beg or steal by day, and herded back to their confines by the police at night. Douglas had never seen poverty to match this.

They were not just bums and hobos. There were decent boys who had come from the same kind of home I had. The only difference was that I had a job and they didn't. That shook me. We found fellows who had worked on the railroads, bank clerks, some who had graduated in law and even medicine, and they couldn't find anything to do. There were little soup kitchens run by the Salvation Army and the churches. In the first half hour they'd be cleaned out. After that there was nothing.

They were not militant. Just despondent. Pushed around. It was impossible to describe the hopelessness.

In Saskatchewan the malevolent forces of weather could be blamed for misfortune. Only in the great city did Douglas fully acknowledge the man-made catastrophe. Nor was it any longer possible to believe that if a young man had the right stuff in him he would get ahead. In this class-ridden world it was traumatic to discover one's own kind reduced to despair and want. Until this happens, the easy habits of class conceit make it possible to rationalize poverty. The foreign immigrants in Winnipeg were foreigners; the dirt farmers around Weyburn were dirt farmers. But there in the Chicago jungles were professional men reduced to beggary.

Cliches are persistent. When one by one they are proved false, the basic disagreement with society itself, which every person hides in him somewhere, surfaces.

50

Douglas met Norman Thomas, veteran leader of the United States Socialist Party, in Chicago. They established a friendship that continued until Thomas' death. Douglas also attended some Socialist Party meetings which, he said,

> were pretty disillusioning affairs. At the first one, they sat around debating whether after the revolution people would eat in their own homes or would come to dining kitchens for communal meals. I made the great mistake of getting up and shooting off my mouth: 'What are you going to do *now*? Aren't you going to run some people for City Council? You have one of the worst councils in North America.' Mayor 'Big Bill' Thompson was in office then. Remember he got elected by promising to punch George V on the nose. He had taken every reference to England out of the textbooks in the schools. . . .
>
> But the Socialist Party people just swept you aside, quoted Marx and Lenin. The revolution would happen of its own accord and power would drop into your lap. These were not young people. They were old Marxian socialists. They knew the texts, but they wouldn't go to work. They had never adapted to the milieu of America. They always thought in terms of Germany and Russia before the revolution.
>
> That experience soured me with absolutists. I learned to be wary of people who say, 'If we can't have society completely socialist we don't want anything to do with it. We don't want to patch up the old system.' I've listened to that until I'm sick and tired of it.
>
> You don't press a button and an old society disappears and a new one is born next morning at seven o'clock. Society is changed organically; you slough off the old and the new takes its place. You do what you can for people and work for change. And I don't mind how hard people want to push. But I've no patience with people who want to sit back and talk about a blueprint for society and do nothing about it. I got that in Chicago.

Douglas read current socialist writings, including those of J. S. Woodsworth, M.P. for Winnipeg North. He was impressed by Britain's Fred Henderson's *The Case for Socialism*. A letter some years later to a supporter in Assiniboia, Saskatchewan refers to the book and the author:

> Dear Mr. Stuart: I am delighted to know that you have fallen under the spell of my friend Fred Henderson's *The Case for Socialism*. Interestingly enough, it was this book that finally helped me make up my mind as to what my social and political philosophy would be. I have distributed hundreds of copies of his little book and I would like to take the liberty of sending you a copy under separate cover. . . .
>
> You will be interested to know that Fred Henderson is still alive

and active. Mr. Coldwell and I had breakfast with him in London last fall. He drove all the way into London to see us. He is Mayor of Nottingham, although he is some eighty-six years of age. He sprouts new ideas as though he were twenty-one and seems to have unbounded energy. He and I have carried on a correspondence over the years, but it was certainly a great pleasure to meet him in the flesh and find that 'his eye was not dimmed nor his natural strength abated.'

Later Douglas explained, "At that time I thought, 'well, something's got to be done.' I didn't think in terms of politics (for myself). I thought in terms of the church making some pronouncements on social and economic conditions. Setting forth some sort of goals for a better type of society. That was as far as my mind went. I could do practical things."

He began to organize the unemployed. He set up an odd-job agency, a phone-in service that took calls for snow-clearing, odd repairs and household tasks, and the unemployed provided labour at twenty-five cents an hour.

The Douglases moved out of the apartment into a bungalow, where they would live until the move to Ottawa. Here young people used to gather, to sit and talk and read plays. They put on one or two plays a year in a local hall, charging a quarter for admission. In the church basement Douglas organized study groups for young people who had finished high school and reached the end of their education. He persuaded a retired English professor and other educated men of the community to help the young people take university courses extramurally.

He said, "I had two young fellows who finished high school, one with an average of 98 per cent and one of 96 per cent. They couldn't go on to University. There was just no way. Both of them later became commissioned officers in the RCAF. They took university on their veterans' credits and just kept on going. But at that time – . It was the sense of futility."

Through the Weyburn Ministerial Association, Douglas worked to collect money to pay freight charges on fruit and vegetables from British Columbia which were scheduled for dumping. The young men sorted the produce into bags at the Weyburn station, and people came with baskets or wheelbarrows to take it home.

The Baptist congregations in eastern Canada sent bales of goods, often the out-of-date stock from clothing stores. Everything was heaped in the church basement and people took what they needed. "Sometimes they wouldn't ask for anything. I remember a woman – they were respectable farmers near town. The women would come to church with just thin cotton dresses under their coats in winter. I asked her to wait, after church, and I said, 'How are you fixed for bedding at your place? Some has just come in.' Her eyes filled with tears and she said, 'We

52

haven't a sheet left in the house.' We loaded stuff up in the back of their old Ford car."

Douglas appeared before city officials to press for increases in relief rates. Businessmen were alarmed at the tax load.

I had a lawyer in my congregation. One morning I dropped in at his office and he took issue with me about having any part in this unemployment association. I said he saw only affluent clients, people concerned with the purchase and sale of real estate and so on. Had he ever seen the poorer part of the city? He said he'd lived in Weyburn twenty-five years. But I took him out to homes that had hardly any coal, the children had no clothes to go to school and hadn't had milk for a week. I took him to talk to the school nurse. He said he wouldn't have believed it. Weyburn had the highest relief schedules in the province but it didn't meet the need.

I learned a very hard lesson. You have to take a stand. Either with the sheep or with the fellow who's shearing them. The moment you take a stand with the unemployed you're in trouble with the taxpayers who say, 'If they get more I get less.' So the logical thing for preachers is to get back to nice generalities. 'We must all love each other. If there was more love, and everybody was honest and decent, we wouldn't have any of these troubles.'

I was becoming labelled as a dangerous radical in the community, stirring up the unemployed to ask for more money and sticking my nose in places that were none of my business. I had several bad set-to's with provincial relief officers who would come down to tell the city council they were spending too much money, they had to make cuts. And I would go before them with these cases of children needing milk and clothing and the school nurse's report. I was a nuisance.

Estevan, just south of Weyburn, was the scene of a bitter labour dispute and riot in September, 1931. Douglas had returned from Chicago. The Mine Workers Union (MWU), newly organized in the face of opposition from the coal mine owners, called a strike on September 8 to protest wage cuts and poor working and living conditions and to demand union recognition. The press and the general public were unsympathetic. Douglas and his wife visited Estevan and the coal mines at Bienfait, to see conditions for themselves. Irma, in particular, was appalled by the wretched shacks the men and their families rented from the mine owners, and their bondage to the company store from which they were obliged to buy their supplies at higher prices than in the town stores. When Douglas preached from his pulpit on the unfair conditions behind the miners' protest, his board received a strong complaint from the mine operators. But farm members of his congregation collected a truckload of food for Estevan.

The strike was a classic example of Communist Party intervention in a bad situation[2], giving the company an acceptable excuse (in the public view) for failing to alleviate real distress.

The precarious existence of the miners, who were trying to survive on part-time work, was put in jeopardy by wage cuts. They had supplemented their mine jobs with summer work on the farms – this was now gone. Now wages were cut from 37½ cents an hour to 32½ cents. Some miners were paid by the weight of the coal they brought to the surface, and they complained that they were continually short-weighted, and were docked for slack in the load, even though the slack was sold in the market. They complained of the extra time – up to an hour every morning – they were obliged to spend pumping water seepage before they began work. They were not paid for that time, nor for clearing out clay falls or helping to lay track.[3]

The grievances made a formidable list, but the local union committee was inexperienced. Then Sam Scarlett and James Sloan arrived from the MWUC headquarters in Saskatoon. Their militant language and their claim to support by the Red International of Soviet Russia, fell short of producing a conciliatory mood. Sloan turned down any suggestion of review by a board appointed under the Industrial Disputes Act, on the grounds that such boards had been anti-labour in the past.

The RCMP, at the request of the companies, brought in a detachment of extra men, while the Coal Operators Association engaged a private force of special constables to protect mine property.

Things came to a head three weeks after the strike was called. Anne Buller, labour organizer from Winnipeg, was scheduled to address a strikers' rally in Estevan. The town council passed a bylaw prohibiting parades or demonstrations, and the police were authorized to enforce the prohibition. But the miners were not informed of what was in store for them, and arrived in a cavalcade from Bienfait, passing down Estevan's main street, on September 29. A scuffle broke out, the police fired, and three strikers were killed.

A stone was erected in Bienfait cemetery by the Ukrainian Labour Temple to honour the men: it was inscribed with the three names, and "murdered in Estevan Sept. 29, 1931 by RCMP". Village authorities had "RCMP" obliterated, but the stone remains.

On October 3, Premier J. T. M. Anderson told the press that the trouble could have been averted except for "outside agitators", and spoke to the local branch of the Legion in Bienfait on October 13, urging the veterans to guard the community against revolutionary elements.

Influenced by scare stories in the Estevan *Mercury* and the Regina *Leader Post*, public opinion generally condemned the "Reds" for stirring up trouble. The *Mercury* said of the Communist-dominated MWUC: "Unless it is hit, and hit hard right now, there will be troublous times for good citizens."[4]

Canadian "good citizens" at that time, so soon after the Russian Revolution, were horrified at the thought of a "Bolshevik" conspiracy. It was a period when a number of prominent communists including Tim Buck were tried for seditious conspiracy under Section 98 of the Criminal Code, and eight including Buck served jail sentences for a political belief that was abhorrent, and frightening, to most Canadians.

Douglas condemned the crude intervention of Scarlett, Sloan, and Anne Buller. He saw the communists exploiting the misery of the workers with callous disregard for human safety and welfare, provoking the police to create confrontation as part of their assiduous effort to prepare the ground for revolution. He said that the local people suffered by this cruel game, while the communists skipped out of the situation.

This was not entirely true. Scarlett and Buller were in fact tried and served jail terms for their part in the riot. Any conciliation between the workers and the mine owners, even before the intervention of the communist "agitators" seemed doubtful indeed, while no direct responsibility was established on the part of the communists in the parade itself before the fatal shootings. But the communist tactics were certainly unfruitful, at best.

Douglas was labelled a "Red" for his support of the miners and the whole experience sharpened his dislike for communism as it operated in the thirties. While he would consider it a mistake to "give up on a good cause because there are a few communists in it", he subscribed wholeheartedly to the democratic socialist, anti-communist view. He despised communism because it disregarded humanist values and the right of an individual to a free choice.

Kenneth McNaught, Woodsworth's biographer, describes the political position:

> In those years also, there were men single-mindedly devoting their lives to the struggle to find a middle ground – a practical line of progress between the extremes of triumphant capitalism on the one hand, and the dogmatic violence of bolshevism on the other. There were men prepared to incur the odium usually directed at the suspected Red that they might explore the avenues leading to constitutional reform of a political and economic system which seemed to them to threaten a chronic debasement of all human values.[5]

During Woodsworth's years on the Vancouver waterfront, after his break with the Methodist church, he encountered a labour atmosphere "seething with revolutionary speculation, tremendous enthusiasm for the Russian experiment",[6] but he stayed with the so-called "revisionist" or British Fabian line. For this he earned some scathing criticism from his more doctrinaire comrades, as in a telegram he received after his arrest for his part in the Winnipeg Strike: "Congratulations on your martyrdom. Hope you deserved it."

Woodsworth maintained, "In Britain, revolution may appear to come more slowly than in Russia, but there will be no counter revolution . . . It may take a few years to work out, but when it's done it's done for good."[7]

But Douglas was unlike Woodsworth in that he was able to remain within his church affiliation while his political activities grew. He said, "I felt no enmity toward the church for having 'failed'. The church was doing its best."

Both ministers were part of the "social gospel" movement which galvanized leadership within the Protestant churches before the 1930s. Methodists, Presbyterians, and Congregationalists led the movement, along with smaller numbers of Baptists, who encountered more division within their church. M. J. Coldwell was an untypical Anglican, for the Anglican Church was not in general a part of the social gospel movement.

Some cynics saw the trend as an escape from theological complexities. Ministers pursued such matters as tariffs, the grain trade, and railway rates, certainly more immediate and probably more comprehensible.

> By 1917 all wings of the social gospel seem to have found a place of such prominence in the farmers' organizations that it might well be termed the religion of the agrarian revolt . . . E. A. Partridge, who pioneered more ideas and institutions of the western farmer than any other man, was motivated by a practical, ethical Christianity mixed with elements of Ruskinian socialism . . . One of the (social gospel's) most important functions was to forge links between proposed reforms and the religious heritage of the nation, in the process endowing reform with an authority it could not otherwise command . . . At one time or another most (of the reformers) could be found describing their enterprises in religious terms, and the social passion which marked their lives clearly entered that realm of ultimate commitments usually considered the province of religion.[8]

But Woodsworth, some years before Douglas faced the religion-and-politics dilemma, became convinced that the two were incompatible. He broke with the Methodist church not only because of its position in the First World War, when he accused it of turning into "a very effective recruiting agency", but because it appeared to him to be in the process of becoming the creature of wealthy men, so that successful ministers became financial agents rather than spiritual leaders.

Douglas, in the Baptist Church of the 1930s, was not forced to make the hard decision to renounce his religious affiliation. He continued to find his church, if not united, at least able to accommodate the social reformers in its midst. And in the little prairie city of Weyburn his intense preoccupation with the social needs of the times found very few objectors among his church membership. In fact, as in the examples of John Powers and Ted Stinson, the staunchest officials followed him into political battle, seeing that battle, as he did, as a continuation of the same great moral struggle.

Chapter Five
Farmer-Labour and the CCF

Douglas said he can fix no day or hour when the decision to enter politics was made. But the letter he wrote to J. S. Woodsworth in 1932 was as fateful a step as any, and no young preacher determined to stay *out* of politics should have sent it.

Douglas had organized the unemployed of Weyburn, with the sympathetic support of the railway and other union men of the town, into the Weyburn Labour Association. On the other hand, he was making extensive rounds of the farm districts, taking church appointments, including Stoughton, which were entirely rural, so the farmers' struggle had become equally familiar. He spoke to local meetings of the United Farmers of Canada (Saskatchewan Section), which was the cumbersome and ambitious title of the organization established in 1926 to unite earlier groups. The UFC (SS) was becoming increasingly politicized. The idea of bringing together these labour and farm groups pursued Douglas.

He wrote to J. S. Woodsworth, the Labour M.P. for Winnipeg, for advice. Perhaps the unified organization would be a massive lobby pressuring governments. Perhaps it would field candidates of its own. The urgent need was to organize all the depression's victims, to begin to fight. How should he proceed toward this end?

"There were so many events pressing on us," Douglas said. "There were the cooperatives and the Wheat Pool, and we all knew the Ginger Group of M.P.s at Ottawa with Woodsworth as chairman. During the Estevan strike I had helped get assistance from both the United Farmers and from the branches of the Independent Labour Party in Regina. I hadn't joined anything, but I saw the need to pull these groups together. I suppose the only thing they all had in common was a conviction that the so-called market economy wasn't functioning, and capitalism was not only incompetent but also very unjust."

Mr. Woodsworth answered promptly. By coincidence, he said, he had just received a letter on the same subject from Alderman Coldwell who was on the Relief Committee in Regina. He suggested that Douglas contact Coldwell, and he was sending a letter also to the alderman.

When Coldwell got his letter it was a Saturday; he had no school that day, and he proposed to his fifteen-year-old son Jack that they take the car, go down to Weyburn, and look up Douglas. In Weyburn they were directed to the Douglas house, and there they met a very young woman whom Coldwell embarrassed by asking whether her father was at home. Irma directed him to the church study, where Douglas was at work on his Sunday sermon.

Major James Coldwell, federal leader of the CCF after Woodsworth and until it dissolved into the NDP in 1961, was later regarded as an able parliamentarian of impeccable behaviour, whose highest word of praise would always be that the person in question was "one of the finest Christian gentlemen I have ever known." But this much-respected statesman was in 1932, according to Douglas, a "flaming radical".

"He was the most dynamic fellow I ever met. You see people were losing their homes, being put off their farms, going *hungry* – I went into a home north of Cedoux once where they had stewed gophers and coffee made of barley and nothing else. M. J. was outraged by these conditions. He and George Williams roused the prairies, became the centre of protest against these *unnecessary* hardships of the people."

Coldwell, born in Devon, imbued with British Labour Party philosophy, was principal of Thompson School in Regina. He was active in the Canadian Teachers' Federation, but that was a secondary interest. In 1925 he had run unsuccessfully as a Progressive candidate. With Clarence Fines, his assistant principal, he planned and set in motion the Regina branch of an organization they called the Independent Labour Party. It included an assortment of people who were not "labour" – the derivation was directly from the British Labour Party. Primarily it was set up to elect civic officials, and Coldwell and Fines, though subjected to the harassment of the Regina School Board, became aldermen with sweeping, unarguable majorities. Independent Labour Party branches were organized in Moose Jaw, Saskatoon, and Melville.

Coldwell gave weekly radio broadcasts, listened to by thousands. "Thoughtful little talks, on economic planning and the money system," Douglas recalls. Listeners sent in donations to keep him on the air.

Douglas described how the people turned to political action.

At that time Bennett was talking about 'sound money'. He said we couldn't have a publicly-owned central bank – it would ruin the market and cause grass to grow in the streets of every city in Canada. He was doing all the wrong things about the depression, just as Hoover had done.

People had little to read – they read everything we sent them. They got books from the Wheat Pool Library and the Regina Open Shelf Library. They read Hansard! The politicians would go crazy: at some of those meetings, with all the farmers in their overalls, they thought they could tell them anything they liked. Then some old farmer would get up and pull Hansard out of his pocket and say, 'On page so-and-so, this is what you said in parliament. It's not what you're saying now!'

The Swedes, the Finns, and the Norwegians were particularly responsive. The British settlers of Labour Party background were quick to become involved. Some United States immigrants were receptive, having brought with them the influence of the "Patrons of Industry", or that of Henry George and his "single tax" solution to economic ills, or the writings of Clarence Darrow.

Almost all occupational groups included some ready adherents. For the small town entrepreneurs the question was whether they could make a better buck under a system of each man for himself, or whether they should fall in with the farmers, standing together to work for "a change in the system" – government control of money, the railways, and the marketing of grain, for a start. Some chose the latter. School teachers and Protestant ministers found the policies of Coldwell and Woodsworth logical and convincing. Many such individuals made common cause with the farm population.

It was a fundamental kind of socialism that was growing in Saskatchewan. It was a vigorous, home-grown variety, in contrast to the bitter dogma of the ineffective and outcast United States Socialist Party. It viewed the other socialists of the world through a long telescope, and formed its own impressions.

Opinions might differ concerning the communist regime in Russia. Most had by now condemned it as totalitarian and oppressive. Others were lenient, arguing that socialism had to begin that way in backward Russia, but would inevitably develop into the ideal classless society. The inference was that countries with superior education could achieve the same aims by proper parliamentary procedure. They liked to say that a communist believes "the end justifies the means" and they grieved for the shortsightedness of this approach.

In 1924 Labour had had its first chance to govern Britain, and Saskatchewan socialists were unanimous in condemning Ramsay Mac-Donald for betraying socialist principles. With Britain's Independent Labour Party, they would have preferred to see MacDonald put forward a program that would invite defeat – since his was a minority government – and in so doing educate the masses, rather than achieve what limited reforms he could in alliance with the Liberals.

In 1932 Sweden had elected a democratic socialist government (which was to stay in power for the next forty-odd years, to the present time) and its conciliatory stance pleased the Saskatchewanites. Sweden became their favourite example of socialism in action. It was their proof that democracy was enhanced, not terminated, by socialism.

They drew something from each of these far-off radical developments. But Saskatchewan socialists were themselves probably as vigorous proponents of the philosophy of democratic socialism as might be found anywhere at that period.

Socialism no doubt came more easily in Saskatchewan because most of the capitalists were down east. There were no examples around, in the flesh, to temper condemnation of the insensitive, greedy plunderers who appeared in cartoons with top hats and cigars.

But, more important, the capitalist concept of a free market in which brains and enterprise could compete on a basis of individual merit has seldom looked less credible. The farmers had to sell their crops in the fall for whatever they could get; grain passed into the hands of the Grain Exchange where fortunes (in good times) could be made in speculation; the grain was sold in the spring at the prevailing price, without reference to the farmer who was starting his next round of production. He had no control over things like his machinery costs, which the tariffs and freight rates of the east made onerous; he had no control over the selling price of his product. Forced to borrow to survive in business, he was powerless before loan, interest, and mortgage rates imposed by banks and investment companies, all based in Ontario.

"Free enterprise" was a sour joke. Douglas put it succinctly for them: "It's every man for himself, as the elephant said when he danced among the chickens."

By its very nature, capitalism was chaotic. But orderly planning was an essential feature of the socialism of Saskatchewan. It spelled stability, security and progress.

" . . . the capitalist economy, by its own proud admission, had no conscious directing principle. Rather it put its trust in the invisible hand of the market, which was supposed to vector all private greeds into a common good.

"Capitalist intellectual life, then, was particularly schizophrenic. The system was increasingly scientific as to details, but irrational as a totality, and each triumphant period of production was crowned by an inexplicable crisis."[1]

Saskatchewan socialists affirmed a moral obligation to curb man's acquisitive impulses at a reasonable level, in order to spread the benefits of the economy more fairly. It was part of their creed that people should have personal freedom to the point where it begins to impinge on the rights of others. In all this, they were confident that the world could supply everyone with all that a man or woman could reasonably desire. They talked of "the age of abundance" into which mankind had entered. A favorite axiom was that "we have solved the problem of production; now we must solve the problem of distribution."

The yeast of their philosophy was democratic power. In this they were in the true socialist tradition as expounded in Michael Harrington's recent exhaustive study.[2] Harrington does not separate the socialists of the world into Marxists and Fabians on the basis of their democratic principles, as many in Canada do. Rather he dedicates himself to salvaging and reconstituting Marx as a democrat, except for one *slip of the tongue*. Harrington insists that when Marx invented the phrase, "the dictatorship of the proletariat", he "proposed . . . to help man become, for the first time, truly conscious and therefore the masters of their own destiny . . . As a political tactician, a philosopher and an economist, he regarded democracy as the essence of socialism." For himself and for North Americans, Harrington states the belief that socialism "is a possibility based upon the unprecedented development of technology and it can become an eventuality only when there is a *conscious majority* that masters that productivity and puts it to the service of human need." (italics added)

It is also worth noting that Marx, the father of socialism, based his hope on the *workers* of the world – not on the underprivileged or the poor or the disadvantaged as a class. Marx is scorned by some New Left writers because he rejected the drifters and the "dregs of humanity" whom he defined as the *lumpenproletariat*. Whether or not he had compassion for this bottom layer of society, he put little trust in it as an instrument of revolutionary change. He felt, rather, that this group could all too easily be subverted to fascist causes.

True to this tradition, the socialists of Saskatchewan were the "workers" in that society. They were not the village incompetents or the dull hired men who never acquired farms of their own. They were none of them rich or elitist; they were "dirt farmers" but they were the leaders of the farm communities; they were the coop organizers, and the Wheat Pool organizers, and the church workers. They practised self help and democratic association as a way of life: they were ready to become that "conscious majority". It was their passion to do the thing, to be part of the change, to make it happen.

It was this yeasty population that was responding to the call to organize as a political force. And while Douglas was "doing practical things" and in the process being drawn irresistibly into the current of political action, initiatives in organization had been taken by M. J. Coldwell and Clarence Fines in Regina, and by George Williams, and others in the rural areas.

Clarence Fines, vice-principal at Coldwell's school, was a uniquely pragmatic, shrewd young man who had grown up in a Conservative family and at high school in Stonewall, Manitoba, had won a public speaking prize for a speech on Arthur Meighen. He usually stepped into a treasurer's or secretary's position in an organization and skilfully helped guide it past dangerous shoals. In the fall of 1929 he and Coldwell, with J. S. Woodsworth, brought together a meeting they called the Western Conference of Labour Political Parties. They met again in Medicine Hat in 1930, and in Winnipeg in 1931, when Fines became president. He spent his year's term of office planning a union with the farmers' organization. Invitations were sent to any likely prospect who might be interested in "a new social order".

The United Farmers of Canada (Saskatchewan Section) had by a narrow margin at their 1929 convention defeated a proposal for direct political action. That only led to a spin-off group, the Saskatchewan Farmers' Political Organization, which inherited what was left of the Progressive Party and sponsored 13 candidates in the 1930 federal election (electing only 2). A number of able women were prominent in the organization, including Mrs. Louise Lucas of Mazenod. With the election out of the way they concentrated on bringing the farmers into the projected union with the Western Conference of Labour Political Parties. At the February 1931 convention of the United Farmers, the burning issue was again the resolution to go into politics. The resolution passed. Andrew J. Macauley, another socialist, succeeded George Williams as president. The Liberals in the organization resigned.

The convention was described in an article in a 1957 *25th Anniversary Booklet* by Carlyle King, now Academic Vice-President of the University of Saskatchewan: "The convention voted to go into politics amid wild cheering, only six dissenting in a throng of 600. They also passed a 'Charter of Liberty' which was 'equally red hot'. It called for nationalization of the CPR, socialization of currency and credit . . . and nationalization of all land and resources as rapidly as possible."

Fines invited the UFC (SS) to meet with the Labour Party conference in Calgary in 1932. The snowball was gathering momentum.

These were the developments Douglas and Coldwell discussed in the Baptist Church study at their first meeting in 1932. Coldwell was delighted that the young minister appeared so keen, so interested, so ready to "pitch in". For his part, Douglas felt an instant liking and deep respect for the older man, who became for some years his political mentor. They decided the first step would be to bring Douglas' Labour Association into the Independent Labour Party. A rally was planned at the Weyburn Exhibition Grounds. So well known was Coldwell through his radio talks that he drew a crowd of one thousand. Douglas was elected president of the branch. He sold memberships in the new political group, and he also appeared as guest speaker at a district meeting of the UFC (SS) in Estevan. He congratulated the farmers on their recent decision to enter politics. Labour, he said, had been politically active for several years but wasn't making much headway. Was it time to join forces?

There was some talk in Weyburn, of course, about these activities. He was called a "Red", or accused of being duped by the "Reds". Yet most of his church congregation supported his move. The economic conditions of 1932 were so serious that people feared collapse – any effort to find a way out was not to be dismissed with scorn. Not only the farmers but also the townspeople who depended on their trade were desperately hard up. Lawyers who had once prospered took to typing their own letters because they could not pay a secretary $25 a month. No one could take satisfaction in prevailing economic conditions.

On July 25, 1932, the Saskatchewan Independent Labour Party held its second convention in Regina. Coldwell, re-elected as president, pointed the way they must travel: "The Labour Party cannot adopt the suicidal policies of those who want to see conditions get so bad that people will be goaded to revolt. Nor must we join those who wish to patch up a thoroughly worn out economic system. Neither brute force nor blind optimism are acceptable . . . In the face of all the things that beset us we must plan or perish."

Two days later on July 27, in an unused building on the Exhibition Grounds while the annual Saskatchewan Exhibition was underway, the hoped-for political union with the farmers took place. The UFC(SS) – and fortunately we can now discard this title – met with the ILP. Their joint conference created the Saskatchewan Farmer-Labour Party. George Williams, representing the much larger farm group, withdrew his name in nomination for president in favor of M. J. Coldwell. Williams knew how popular Coldwell had become throughout the province, and he was also concerned that his recent Russian adventure would prejudice people against the party. An executive was formed with seven farmers and seven labour representatives – among the latter was Douglas, at the age of twenty-seven the youngest of the group.

One of the solemn moments of the convention was a pledge by Coldwell not to betray their trust. The memory of the Progressives who had broken ranks and drifted into the Liberal party was still a sore point with most of the people present. This time it would be different, Coldwell vowed.

"The task before us is difficult. We have to appeal not to the passions of people but to their intellect. It can be done," said Coldwell.

A month later the inter-provincial conference for which Fines, in collaboration with Woodsworth's "Ginger Group" in Ottawa, had been preparing for twelve months, took place in Calgary.

It was the preliminary event before the CCF founding convention in Regina in 1933. But Douglas, attending an economics course at the University of Manitoba, had to skip the 1932 meeting.

The conference lasted only one day. It selected a name, the Cooperative Commonwealth Federation. It chose J. S. Woodsworth as its president, and Norman Priestley of Edmonton as secretary. A committee of westerners, Coldwell, Robert Gardiner, and George Latham, prepared an eight-point program containing some radical ideas:

1. The establishment of a planned system of the social economy for the production, distribution and exchange of all goods and services.
2. Socialization of the banking, credit and financial system of the country together with the social ownership, development, operation and control of utilities and natural resources.
3. Security of tenure of the worker and farmer in his home.
4. Retention and extension of all existing social legislation and facilities

with adequate provision for insurance against crop failure, illness, accident, old age and unemployment.

5. Equal economic and social opportunity without regard to sex, nationality or religion.
6. The encouragement of all cooperative enterprises which are steps toward the achievement of the cooperative commonwealth.
7. Socialization of health services.
8. The federal government should accept responsibility for the unemployed and supply suitable work or adequate maintenance.

The meeting set up a national council to prepare for the much bigger convention to be held in Regina the following year.

In Saskatchewan they carried on under the Farmer-Labour (CCF) title as they went into a provincial election in 1934. It was an interesting lot of men who came to the fore in this political struggle – as hardy a troop of non-politicians as ever felt the call of public duty. Among them were George Williams, John H. Brockelbank, Fred C. Williams and A. M. Nicholson.

George Williams, Douglas said, was probably the best organizer the movement had in those days. Digressing, he added,

J. S. (Woodsworth) you know had no concept of political work. He *taught* the people in his audience, with maps and charts. I used to kid him and say, 'How come you always have your nominating convention in a telephone booth?' He used to have it at his house, just call in a few friends. And he never appointed scrutineers for election day. He'd say, 'Who's going to cheat us?'

Well we knew we were being cheated in some elections. There was the time our man Benson came within a few votes of beating Gardiner in Melville. (Louise Lucas had given him a hard run in 1940, too.) There was a recount. The judge found that six ballots had been changed from Benson to Gardiner, but he ruled that this could have been done by the CCF to embarrass Mr. Gardiner! . . .

But Williams believed in organization. He was a veteran of the First World War, had been with the Strathcona Horse, and had his ankle badly smashed up. Ideologically, I suppose he was to the right of most of us.

Williams was also an irascible man, sometimes abrasive toward others, impatient when the right kind of effort was not put forward. Nevertheless his drive and strong convictions had put him in a position of leadership in the farmers' movement, and he successfully entered the first political contest for the Farmer-Labour party, in 1934. This put him in a difficult relationship with M. J. Coldwell, who did not get elected. Coldwell had been chosen party leader at the 1932 convention when Williams generously stepped aside. But Williams was *ipso facto* leader in the legislature, and was apparently not favourably disposed toward the idea of opening up a seat for Coldwell through the resignation of one of their successful candidates. Coldwell found the sarcastic Liberal references to "the leader in the public gallery" so galling that he turned the leadership over to Williams and moved into federal politics. In 1937 Williams antagonized the federal executive of the CCF by refusing to appear on a public platform with King Gordon, one of the leading intellectuals in the eastern section of the party, because he suspected Gordon of favouring neutrality in the approaching world conflict. Williams was probably the most militaristic man in the entire party in those pre-war days. He wasted no time in enlisting in 1939, and got himself posted overseas in spite of his mangled ankle. He died a few months after his return, in 1945.

John H. Brockelbank was a staunch friend of George Williams, a blunt sardonic man, dearly loved, who became one of the greatest ministers in the first CCF cabinet. His son, young John, is a member of the Saskatchewan legislature in 1974.

Brockelbank apparently never learned to dissemble, to say "Yes" in agreeable deceit. When he was asked a question he searched his mind for the answer, and if he found it he gave it, in perversely down-to-earth language, without any deference to either protocol or grammar.

He had come from Ontario with his family to a homestead near North Battleford when he was thirteen. He served in the First World War, and returned to find that even his grade ten education looked good in the scrubland of the north and he was asked to teach. "I guess I've got the only permanent Third Class Temporary Certificate in the province," Brockelbank said. Besides teaching, he began to break land on his own homestead in 1922, clearing the brush. "The so-called roarin' Twenties!" he said.

> Still, we were kind of making some progress, and then came 1930. In 1931, I remember a good crop, a slight frost blister but a good yield; it was graded 3 or 4 and it sold at 19 cents a bushel.
>
> I'd bought some cattle from my father when I started out and in 1924 I had cattle to sell. Four of us neighbours went together and made up two carloads to sell. I took them to Winnipeg. One of my steers brought top price for the whole two carloads – 4 cents to 4½ cents a pound. My total cheque for 14 head was $217. If things like that doesn't make you think, you must be awful dumb.

By 1924 he was actively involved in organizing the Saskatchewan Wheat Pool. He voted Liberal except when there was a Progressive running in his area, and in 1930 he voted for a Conservative, Robert Weir, whom he regarded a "left wing – or close to it." In 1934 the new Farmer-Labour Party sent in an organizer and Brockelbank immediately got into the campaign on behalf of the local candidate. He himself ran successfully in 1938 and was easily re-elected from that date on.

Fred Williams, for many years secretary of the Saskatchewan CCF and editor of its paper, *The Saskatchewan Commonwealth*, grew up in Creelman, near Weyburn, and shared some early political adventures with Douglas. He said he had been a socialist from about the age of fifteen, when he and other lads were instructed in its principles by a local carpenter who got them to read Bellamy's *Looking Backward* and *Equality*. His first job was in a bank, and the crippling of local farmers by loans they could not repay bore out the theories of the literate carpenter. Later he inherited and ran the *Creelman Gazette*, and as a sideline, with editorial contributions from Douglas, he began a small paper called *The New Era* which eventually became *The Commonwealth*.

A pale, thin-featured man with reddish hair, Fred Williams was addicted to composing poems about the prairie landscape, the drought, and social evils, as a vent for his feelings and a relief from the blunt realities of the printing trade.

Williams was pressed into taking the provincial nomination in Weyburn in 1938, even though he had to turn up at the meeting in a suit from a "relief" barrel. He recalls a 1938 visit to his Creelman printing shop by John Diefenbaker, then Conservative leader in Saskatchewan and intent on arranging to saw off certain ridings, including Weyburn, to defeat the omnipotent Gardiner regime. Williams was not averse to the proposal, since he was to benefit, but local Conservatives would have none of it. These Conservatives ran a local reeve who polled enough votes, 828, to ensure Williams' defeat to Liberal George Crane, 4167 to 4744. Williams did not try again, devoting himself instead to the penny-pinching tasks of a socialist editor.

A. M. (Sandy) Nicholson served the national party as its chief fund-raiser for a substantial period in the 1940s and 1950s, distinguished by a staccato voice and the message that CCF'ers could by that time toss folding money instead of "nickels and dimes" into the collection plate. But when Douglas was being drawn into the political arena in Weyburn, Nicholson was a United Church minister in the rugged northern bushland of Hudson Bay Junction. There he met straggling settlers who had trekked north from the blown-out south, settlers who thought wood for winter fuel, wild fruit, and wild game were a great bonanza and well worth the trip. Nicholson gave up his church in 1934 to campaign for the Farmer-Labour Party, and never went back to preaching, though his living was highly precarious even in good years.

The highlight of the 1934 campaign in Hudson's Bay Junction was a flying visit by M. J. Coldwell. Nicholson guaranteed to raise twenty dollars to help with his expenses, which included fuel for a light plane owned by a friend of Coidwell's who flew him around the province after school hours. Following a Friday night meeting at Melfort, Coldwell was scheduled to appear at Hudson Bay Junction at 2:00 o'clock Saturday afternoon. Saturday at noon Nicholson had a phone call from Coldwell at Crooked River, fifty-two miles west. That was as far as the pilot was willing to go. He had never seen trees so dense in his life, and he had no idea how he could land his plane if they had to come down. Coldwell told Nicholson not to worry, he had persuaded the CNR despatcher at Prince Albert to authorize section men to pick him up and take him the rest of the way on a jigger. He duly arrived, by open-air express, spoke to the waiting crowd at 4:00 p.m., and was driven on to his next appointment at Tisdale that evening.

Others Douglas was to meet with, plan with, journey with around the province, endure and triumph with, will no doubt have their yarns recounted in other form. In 1934 Douglas was only one of the first band of hopeful candidates, confidently predicting the end of the Anderson regime and privately convinced that the good sense of their appeal would immediately occur to voters as infinitely preferable to a return to the Gardiner machine.

Douglas, still undecided about running, had been encouraged by a huge meeting in the Weyburn rink immediately after the CCF national founding convention in 1933. Woodsworth, Joe Parkinson and Elmore Philpott went on to Weyburn and spoke to the audience about the goals of farmer-labour unity. Parkinson recalls the meeting chiefly because it lacked both light and music. The quartet of speakers stared from a lighted stage into total darkness. They also found themselves obliged to lead in the unaccompanied singing of the national anthem, with very indifferent success.

But by spring, 1934, with a provincial election in the offing, the party in Weyburn had still not found a candidate. The Conservative sitting member was the Speaker of the Legislature, E. C. Leslie, a one-time Progressive. Against him the Liberals were running the unbeatable, much-loved local family doctor, Hugh E. Eaglesham. Still, it was unthinkable *not* to enter the race, and Douglas was the obvious choice. Clarence Fines recalls the nomination meeting. He met Douglas for the first time, was invited to supper and met not only Irma but a new resident in the household, a baby daughter, Shirley. Fines says his chief recollection of the meeting was that there were at least twelve other people on the program and he came on last. In those days people expected three or four hours of oratory. Fines himself was not a candidate. He was to make his first break into municipal politics that fall.

Douglas, remembering 1934, scoffs at the innocence of his first campaign. "I went around to the little schoolhouses, talking like a professor, explaining our platform. We were lucky if the collection gave us enough for gas to get to the next place. We encouraged questions, and people would ask us if it was true we were going to take their farms, like the Soviets in Russia, and did we believe in God." A friend, Rod McLean, provided an office for their campaign headquarters, and J. E. Powers was campaign manager. And they were sure they were going to win, "like all CCF'ers running the first time."

The election was held on June 19. The Conservatives, bearing the blame for the plunge into the Depression, were annihilated, electing not one member. The Farmer-Labour Party elected five: Andy Macauley, Herman Kemper, Lou Hantelman, Clarence Stork, and George Williams. Douglas ran third in Weyburn, but saved his deposit, garnering 1,343 votes to Eaglesham's 2,281.

It was a sharp set back. Personally popular, he had found it too easy to accept his neighbours' cheerful "I hear you're running! Good luck!" as a guarantee of support. He had been confident of success. He had hinted that he had a fair chance to his father in Winnipeg, who had greeted the news of his nomination with approval. Annie Douglas had favoured his entry into the church, but Tom Douglas made no secret of his pleasure when their son turned to politics. That June night Tom was listening to the radio at the Legion Clubroom in Winnipeg. "You're taking a great interest in the Saskatchewan election," someone said. "Aye," Tom replied. "My boy's standing."

Irma was of course as let down as her husband, though perhaps more easily reconciled to continuing their Weyburn way of life, especially with a daughter to care for. Later she said, "It was unbelievable that we even thought he might win. But wasn't it a good thing that he was defeated provincially, as it turned out?"

What shattered the eager hopes of the new party was not only their inexperience but the determination of the voters to throw the Conservatives out. The CCF also suffered badly in the campaign because their farm platform was too easily misrepresented, and because of the hostility of the Roman Catholic Church.[3]

The Farmer-Labour Party had inherited their "use-lease" farm policy from the militant United Farmers. In the name of protecting the farmer from eviction, the government would assume public ownership of the land, paying off the mortgage companies in government bonds, and leasing the land back to the farmer. He could "use" the land but not own it, and security of tenure was promised to him and his family. It was the plainest piece of socialism in their platform.

But the farmers would have none of it. Liberal speakers had only to wave a title deed in the air, saying "This is what you will lose!"

The Roman Catholic Church had traditionally supported the Liberals, although in this election some breaks occurred with Ukrainian Catholics giving votes to Farmer-Labour in a few areas. In 1931 the encyclical, *Quadragesimo Anno*, had pronounced on state intervention, declaring private ownership to be a right which "the State cannot take away." It would be a long time before the CCF surmounted that wall.

A sharp blow fell on February 2, 1934, when the Archbishop of Regina, James Charles McGuigan, declared all forms of socialism to be contrary to tenets of the faith.

Douglas tried to counter in a statement in the *Farmer-Labour News*, May 11, 1934: "The program of the CCF is an honest endeavour to apply the social message of Christianity to life. It is complementary, rather than in opposition to the work of the church. For while the church is seeking to establish right relationships between man and God; the CCF is endeavouring to bring about a brotherly relationship between man and man. We must recognize that this cannot be done under the present competitive system."

When the next provincial election came around, in 1938, the CCF had got rid of the "use-lease" platform and came out as champions of "the family farm". They were less successful in winning Roman Catholics to their side, though even that was happening in a few instances.

But Douglas, after his 1934 defeat, was not consoled by explanations. He resolved that, having done his bit for the fledgling party, he would return to church activity and the completion of his Ph.D.

Chapter Six
The National CCF

Douglas, one year after his provincial defeat and his resolve to quit politics, ran in a federal election and won. Coldwell ran again and won in the same election. They switched easily to national politics because the CCF was a national party from the beginning: the objective was Ottawa. No one ever supposed that democratic socialism could be achieved within a smaller sphere. The party's 1933 founding convention at Regina had delegates from Ontario, British Columbia, and the three prairie provinces. The program, the Regina Manifesto, was a national program.

By a curious inversion the 1933 convention has been described as an event in which eastern Canadians gave direction and substance to western farm protest. This interpretation of events appears for example in a recent study by Walter Young.[1]

In fact, the principal leadership in the formation of the new party was western, including such men as Woodsworth, Coldwell, William Irvine and Bob Gardiner of Alberta, a number of others, and to a lesser extent Douglas. Woodsworth's tiny parliamentary group which had survived the demise of the Progressives was chiefly western. The keen young group of intellectuals who lent their support from McGill and Toronto, the League for Social Reconstruction (LSR), led by Frank Scott and Frank Underhill, included such westerners as Graham Spry and King Gordon who had gone on to study in England after graduating from the University of Manitoba.

Yet Young expresses a common bias when he says, "The League also provided the new party with at least a patina of eastern sophistication."[2]

There is a commonly-held assumption that agrarian people are conservative clods, that the true radical impetus comes from cities. This was hardly the case. The socialist conviction in Saskatchewan was deeply imprinted, and remained with the farmer long after he began to get a better price for wheat. The Saskatchewan CCF in fact sustained the entire national party to a very large degree, both financially and in proselytizing zeal, from 1933 onward. It was taken for granted that only on a national scale could economic solutions be found: the goal was a national party and power at Ottawa. The impetus from the west could hardly be called successful: it was rather like trying to make water run uphill. The east of Canada has always colonized the west, not vice versa.

Still, Woodsworth, Coldwell and Douglas, Irvine, and Gardiner, made an impact, and the party, with many reverses, held on and slowly made growth in Ontario, where other dedicated socialists like A. R. Mosher, Charles Millard, Larry Sefton, and Eamon Park were working hard within the labour movement.

The Ontario farmers had their moment of radical victory when they elected a provincial government in 1919, and their leader in parliament, Agnes Macphail, was a staunch colleague of Woodsworth's. She made a heroic effort to bring the United Farmers of Ontario into the CCF and (unsuccessfully) to keep them there.

Farther west there was a socialist group – or groups, for there were several factions – in British Columbia, more orthodox-Marxist and therefore regarded as more revolutionary than the prairie socialists.

In Canada it has always been easier to build a party with support from farmers than from urban workers, as both "old parties" had discovered at an earlier date in history. Their class loyalty is much stronger than the almost non-existent sense of labour brotherhood among urban workers in Canada. As Douglas has pointed out, it never has been possible to speak of a unified movement of industrial workers with strong bonds of loyalty and class consciousness. Industrial workers in Canada have middle class ambitions and would sooner lose themselves in the vast homogeneity of the city suburbs than build a "movement" of their own.

The farmers, on the other hand, have a common way of life they consider worth preserving, and this unifies their approach to social and economic problems.

Much of the national CCF bias in favour of a "labour" party, never much more than a profound desire even after the metamorphosis to the NDP, came from the dynamic national secretary of the CCF, David Lewis. Lewis was an urban socialist from Montreal and had little rapport with the Saskatchewan farmers, unlike Frank Scott who seemed to sense the genius of the province. Lewis' single-minded purpose from 1938 on was to recreate on Canadian soil a Labour Party similar to the Labour Party of Britain. He was never able to overcome the obvious disadvantage that in Britain the two had grown up side by side, the unionists had created their political party with zeal and fervour, while in Canada a fairly prosperous union movement, intent on gaining concessions from the old-line parties in office, never involved its soul in the creation of a political party, however much its various leaders might exhort it to do so. The CCF and later the NDP throughout Canada is not in any real sense a labour party, but draws its support from all classes, as the other parties do.

Young gives great credit to David Lewis for his zeal and determination in managing the party at the Ottawa headquarters. But when he says: "Indeed it is not an exaggeration to say that without Lewis the party might have subsided into nothingness altogether during the dark days after 1945, if not before" he is taking a myopic view indeed. The CCF had just been elected in Saskatchewan with a resounding majority and was launching an incredibly ambitious program "during the dark days of 1945".

Young comments only: "The pragmatic Saskatchewan section flourished, as the results of the 1944 election demonstrated."[4]

As it affects the career and the position in the movement of T. C. Douglas, Young's argument leads to an erroneous conclusion: "The CCF did not succeed as a political party"[5] when in fact it succeeded in Saskatchewan very well. And there is no mention of the leadership given by Douglas to the only part of the movement that was flourishing.

The experience in Saskatchewan under Douglas belies Young's thesis that there is something incompatible in a political "movement" – with a strong ideological base – and a political "party"; that a party cannot hope to succeed until it divests itself of the "movement" psychology. If Douglas' regime proves anything, it proves that a blending of both is quite possible, and was in fact the secret of the Saskatchewan government's success. The CCF in that province became increasingly effective as an administration and as a party, but it retained its ability as a "movement" to inspire the people's allegiance throughout its tenure of office.

J. S. Woodsworth set the national party on the course which found its first practical demonstration in Saskatchewan under Douglas. And Douglas, one of the young leaders at Regina in 1933, recalls the emotional pull of Woodsworth's address to the convention – a speech which also summarized party activity over the preceding year, since the Calgary conference:

> We are passing through a hitherto untravelled land . . . There are those who would frighten us with the horrible example of failure in England or Germany or captivate us by idealizing the experiments in Russia. The trouble is that we are inclined to think altogether too much in terms of Europe and in terms of the past . . . I refuse to follow slavishly the British model or the American model or the Russian model. We in Canada will solve our problems along our own lines. . . .
>
> The growth of the CCF during the past year, as indicated in the report of the secretary, is indeed remarkable . . . Last year, with one exception, the delegates were all from the Western provinces. This year we welcome many from the East . . . The organization is now almost Dominion-wide, yet our work has only begun.[6]

The presence in Regina of forty-five delegates from Ontario was proof of the proselytizing zeal of those appointed at Calgary to drum up attendance in 1933. Agnes Macphail, along with William Irvine, M.P. from Alberta, had successfully toured Ontario's rural areas, and the result was a delegation of fourteen members of the United Farmers of

Ontario. Aaron Mosher of the Canadian Brotherhood of Railway Employees (CBRE) had been charged with spurring union interest but had not done so: the five "labour" representatives from Ontario were not from the major trade unions but from small, doctrinaire "Labour Party" groups with questionable "labour" credentials.[7] The other twenty-six came from the third "section" of the democratic socialist movement in Ontario, those urban supporters from various occupations who had set up "CCF Clubs" over the previous year in a ready response to the meetings held throughout the province by Woodsworth, Elmore Philpott who was the Ontario CCF's first president, Agnes Macphail, and William Irvine.

The three-section structure of the Ontario CCF was an uneasy one, leading to chaos and crisis by 1935. At the founding convention, one of the UFO's leading delegates, W. C. Good, opposed the Regina Manifesto as too radical. His contention was that various electoral reforms had a higher priority than nationalization and economic planning by governments. The following year he wrote his own manifesto, "Is Democracy Doomed?" which he urged on the CCF without success.[8] He claimed that the UFO's participation in the new political movement came about largely because they had resented the conscription policies of both old parties during the war. At the opposite corner from the UFO were the "labour" delegates who talked in such radical and doctrinaire terms that their Ontario farm counterparts cringed.

But, says Caplan, " . . . the convention otherwise was remarkable for its unanimity on matters of socialist principle, its determination to be honest and frank about those principles, and its affirmation of a devout faith in democratic, constitutional methods."[9]

Douglas said that at the convention he liked and approved the Manifesto, a ringing document which denounced capitalism as unjust and cruel, stressed economic planning, and advocated public ownership of financial institutions, transportation, communication, and other services, along with export and import controls, more power to the national government (from the provinces), fairer taxes, socialized health services, law reform, and some other measures. He said, "To me it was a good, pragmatic document; I've often wondered what all the fuss was about."

The Manifesto had been drafted by the LSR and more specifically by Professor Frank Underhill. The LSR was a remarkable group of young men who had attached themselves in Ottawa to J. S. Woodsworth (who was their honorary president). They were intellectuals of considerable charm and perception and, as Graham Spry described them in 1974, very lively and high-spirited. "I am horrified," Spry said, "by what people write of the early days of the CCF. It was great fun – we didn't go around with faces of woe. It was a thrilling thing."

They almost all had had some association with Britain, at either Oxford or Cambridge. A significant number had studied with Keynes.

Graham Spry also recalls the strongly British background of many of the prairie leaders: Bob Gardiner, Henry Spencer, E. J. Garland, all with "distinct old-country accents". The links between Britain and Canada's CCF were many.

Graham Spry was the editor of *Canadian Forum* for a long period in its early life, having bought it from its bankrupt editor for one dollar. A varied career during the depression and war years took him to London and for a time he was employed by the California-Texas Oil Company which, he said, "was fascinated to have a socialist around". Later he served the Saskatchewan CCF government as Agent-General in London, pursuing the British (and other European) investor to interest him in Saskatchewan possibilities.

The LSR was gratefully adopted by Woodsworth as a "wing" of the new party. One of its first tasks was to produce the Manifesto for the founding convention. Scott described the document as "physchologically applicable to Saskatchewan", whose delegates were "some of the more radical members of the movement". Scott said, "The whole sentiment of the province was that capitalism was finished. The farmers found that fairly radical proposals fitted the actual situation."

But Frank Underhill was less satisfied. He wrote in *Canadian Forum* (September, 1934) that the new CCF was not the product of a "brains trust" but perhaps it should have been. It was his opinion that the new party ought now to concentrate more strongly on intellectual exercise, on intelligent research, rather than on "tub-thumping". Underhill said, "probably the CCF has attracted about all the votes that it is likely to attract by the mere emotional exploitation of our present discontents."

Going into the provincial election the following year, Douglas quoted from the Manifesto in his campaign, pointing out that it was a national platform, but "much could also be done provincially". That 1934 election put five CCF members in the Saskatchewan legislature.

The British Columbia section of the party had its first electoral test in October, 1933, and elected six CCF members to the legislature with a substantial one-third of the vote.

Back in Ontario, though, there was trouble brewing. The factious "Labour" section alienated many potential supporters. Strife over association with Communists at protest rallies brought on the rapid disaffection and withdrawal of the United Farmers of Ontario, and in a traumatic climax in 1934 the entire Ontario section was disbanded by Woodsworth. It took a long time to build again.

It was the first of the Ontario CCF "purges". The many that have occurred since have been less wholesale but similar in nature: a desperate few, convinced of their righteousness, have driven party officials to the end of their capacity to cope with them as a section of the party, and yet another expulsion has occurred.

At the polls in the provincial election of 1934 when Mitchell Hepburn's Liberals swept into power, the CCF elected only one candidate, Sam Lawrence in Hamilton East. And Lawrence was the only successful CCF candidate in Ontario until 1942.

By 1937 David Lewis was so concerned about the decline of the CCF in the most populous province that he wrote to Frank Scott: "I have become more and more convinced about the need for a Trade Union base for the party even though there are undoubtedly many political disadvantages in a Trade Union political set-up."[10]

In Caplan's account there is an attempt to explain the CCF's lack of acceptability in Ontario during the first decades. He suggests that the party was "beyond the political culture's mainstream", but he also says: "So far from being alien, the CCF was dominated by the United Church. Its leaders were Anglo-Saxon, Protestant, middle class, and highly educated; many belonged to the Orange Lodge. Its membership was overwhelmingly of British descent . . . " He feels that, "It had too many Oxford graduates. It had too many social gospellers. It had too many extremists even among its Christians."[11]

But there were prohibitionists, anti-Catholics, and other religious extremists in the Saskatchewan CCF too. There were doctrinaire Marxists who always found virtue in declaring that the party was betraying true socialism. Eccentrics of various kinds found their way into the CCF fold, and though some of them wandered out again many were tolerated. None were expelled, and it did not seem to matter. What was the difference?

It is quite possible that after the United Farmers pulled out, the Ontario CCF lost something in its lack of rural members, an imbalance that would have been more important in the 1930s and 1940s than in the 1970s. Andrew Brewin wrote: " . . . As for the farmers, well, we didn't know too many farmers. Of course we knew that as a democratic socialist party we had to appeal to the farmers and so we had a farm committee. The farm committee chairmanship alternated between a professor of classics who regularly read a farm magazine and a small manufacturer who knew a farmer – his cousin up Markham way, I think."[12]

The urban people who provided leadership in the Ontario CCF Clubs often gave the impression of being cranky and devious – very much on the defensive. They were not animated by the expansive good humour that seemed to light up the Saskatchewan members – particularly when they emerged from a Douglas meeting. Obviously democratic socialism was easier in Saskatchewan.

At least part of the answer is that the Ontario social landscape was not a simple polarization of extremes but a multiple-choice environment. Those who attempt to live by and impose any absolute thing fare badly in Ontario. The party in this large province had to find a place within a broader social tolerance, and what appealed to one element did not appear to appeal to the next. Neither the exploiters nor the exploited were single, conspicuous groups, though a great deal of exploitation was going on. Thus the Ontario CCF alternated between dazzling spurts of success when they caught the public fancy (but seemed unable to grasp and command that opportunity), and long periods of failure, frustration, and slow, hard inching ahead. When they gained a little with one group they seemed to lose with another.

The greatest single point of difference between the Saskatchewan and Ontario sections was the relation between political and religious commitment. In Saskatchewan a very strong original impulse was the "social gospel" in the pre-1930 period. But this social direction of the churches did not take place in Ontario.[13]

Ontario CCF members were much more likely to keep their religious convictions, if any, out of sight, as irrelevant to politics. They were more apt to describe their political faith as "scientific socialism". Allen mentions one meeting in Toronto when socialists discussed "Why a Socialist Cannot Be a Christian" and this was a widely prevailing attitude.

Young states that,

> Woodsworth was a western leader: he had little following in Ontario ... The psychology of the plains that emerges in the novels of Sinclair Ross is one which provides fertile soil for the kind of leadership Woodsworth provided, based as it is on bourgeois morality with its 'crabbed Protestant view of sensuality and emotion, emphasising strong patriarchal authority, a thriftness of feeling as well as money, a harsh sense of duty and compulsive restraint, order and methodicalness, enforced by a religious impulse which glorified work and an economic impulse for the rational pursuit of money.'[15]

This is an extreme and limited view of Woodsworth's leadership, probably not shared by many CCF'ers in any part of Canada. Yet Ontario socialists, if they did not totally reject the "social gospel" approach, were often embarrassed by it. It was more to their liking to see their politics as a "rational", even a "scientific" body of ideas. They were continually disappointed because, as they were forced to admit, men and women do not vote rationally.

It would probably have been more sensible from the beginning to accept and preach the ethical content of their chosen brand of politics. Frank Scott pointed out, "a democratic socialist party is held together by a group of ideals, which are essentially moral concepts."[15] But few in Ontario were bold enough to present their socialism in universal, moral terms. Given the mixed Ontario environment, it would have been extremely difficult to do so, and would have required heights of leadership that did not appear on the provincial scene.

Douglas believed that all people include in their make-up an inclination toward such moral concepts, so that his invitation to support the CCF was open and uninhibited. He was able to score considerable success by proceeding on this assumption.

Douglas' daughter, Joan Tulchinksy, said, "Oh yes, I thought the CCF policies were right. Everyone else was a fool! But – , but self righteousness annoys me a little really."

And that was the socialist's dilemma.

Douglas's genius is in surmounting that dilemma more successfully than any other CCF leader. By a deft, light touch, carefully paced to lead to a soaring eloquence, he is a moral persuader who avoids the pitfall of depressing self righteousness.

He learned how to practise this high art in his first successful election, in 1935.

His role in the party to that date was that of a youthful associate of the principal leaders. At the second national convention in Winnipeg in 1934, he was elected leader of the Youth Movement, the CCYM, established at that time. He contended for the office with a young Marxist from British Columbia, Rod Young, whose declaration of class war had the support of the Young People's Socialist League (YPSL), including a group from Saskatchewan.

Bill Davies, who was later to become Minister of Public Works in Douglas' cabinet, was one of those YPSL delegates in the party, travelling from Indian Head to Winnipeg by truck, with Fred Williams, the Creelman bank clerk. Davies said he rather favoured Rod Young's militant oratory, but Douglas won the office, and continued as head of the party's youth section until 1939.

Grace MacInnis, daughter of J. S. Woodsworth and with a long parliamentary career of her own, recalled that she first met Tommy at Winnipeg in 1934, and considered him "very youthful, full of enthusiasm. The young people were delighted with him," she said.

Rod Young went on to less brilliant adventurings; he was expelled from the CCF in British Columbia in 1954 for pro-Communist statements.

Though the CCF had made no more than a respectable beginning in the British Columbia and Saskatchewan 1934 elections, and had fared badly in Ontario, they entered the 1935 federal contest with great expectations.

The five years of depression under Bennett's Conservatives had brought the political pot to a boil. H. H. Stevens had broken with the Conservatives and had started the Reconstruction Party. Graham Spry, national secretary of the LSR and editor of *Canadian Forum* wrote in the magazine in August that Bennett's party deserved "a thorough and prolonged rest." One could foresee, said Spry, "not only the defeat but even the extinction of the Conservative Party." He reported that the CCF had shown surprising vigour, nominating well over one hundred candidates, though extremely short of funds: "It is certainly more than probable that the CCF will form the official opposition." His election prediction:

"The Conservatives will be crushed. King will hold 150 or more seats, Woodsworth and the socialists will get 25 to 50 or more, Reconstruction 20 to 25, and Communists, Social Credit and monetary cranks, independents and what not, a handful."

In Saskatchewan Coldwell was nominated at Sovereign, for the Rosetown-Biggar constituency, and Douglas was guest speaker. Coldwell recalled that he had three ministers of the gospel on hand for his launching, and he also recalled that, the evening having begun with a traditional prairie "fowl supper", Douglas' opening remark was that he had never before seen so many chickens entering the ministry. That sally was pure Douglas corn, tossed off in such excellent high spirits that the audience took it for the height of wit. He followed up, said Coldwell, with "a splendid talk".

Douglas was repeatedly asked by the Weyburn organization to run as their federal candidate, but he put it aside. He felt much let down after his 1934 defeat, even as late as the occasion of a visit with Stanley Knowles in Winnipeg early in 1935. Knowles had just been nominated (he did not make it) and he urged Douglas to get on the road to Ottawa with him. Douglas decided against it. He concluded that the better course for him lay within the Baptist church. He had a very tempting offer from a large church in Milwaukee, which would let him get on with his Ph.D. in Chicago.

But in the spring he had a visit at his Weyburn home from a superintendent of the western Baptist missions with a message from the church in Winnipeg. The church official asked Douglas whether he was considering entering the coming election, and before Douglas could reply he made it clear that if he did so he would not be able to obtain another Baptist church.

Douglas' response was predictable. "You have just got the CCF a candidate," he told his guest. And within twenty-four hours he had passed his decision to the Weyburn executive.

It was a turbulent summer. Douglas was in Regina to give a radio broadcast the day following the shameful riot of July 1, 1935. As he left the studio he heard accounts of the violence and he went to see an old friend, Dr. Hugh Maclean, who told him that for hours he had been kept busy patching up and extracting bullets from wounded young men. Maclean later gave evidence at the inquiry, contradicting police testimony that only a couple of the unemployed had been hurt. Two people were killed that day, and a number injured.

Unemployed trekkers, riding the freights from Vancouver, had stopped on their way to Ottawa, and had been in Regina several days. M. J. Coldwell had turned up in Weyburn with one of them in his car, taking him along to a Douglas rally.

"This young man," said Coldwell, "was in fact Charles Woodsworth, the son of J. S. Woodsworth, and a newspaper reporter at the time for the Winnipeg *Tribune*. I had gone to my home in Regina to find my wife Nora feeding this very disreputable looking chap, and I found out that he was doing a story on the trekkers for his paper, travelling with them, under the name of Shaw. So I took him down to Weyburn with me, and I introduced him to Douglas, who invited us to come back to the house with him for the evening. So I introduced the 'trekker' to Irma as Mr. Shaw, and later I told her he was Mr. Woodsworth's son, but she wouldn't believe me."

The riot occurred when the trekkers were attacked by Bennett's RCMP at a peaceful meeting in the Market Square. It was another bloody confrontation, like the one in Estevan, and it strengthened Douglas' resolution to do battle with "the system".

He was now a candidate. But he looked at the task he was facing in the Weyburn constituency and, still chastened by his previous failure, decided there was very little likelihood of winning. The Weyburn federal constituency encompassed four provincial seats that had all gone Liberal the year before, with three out of the four CCF candidates losing their deposits.

His pessimism was shared by Clarence Fines, who had come down to speak at his nomination meeting. "I didn't think Ed Young could be beaten," Fines said. Fines had, however, combed Hansard and discovered a statement by Young in the House of Commons that Canadians must settle for a lower standard of living. The statement played a significant part in the campaign.

E. R. Young was a prominent Liberal who had held the Weyburn seat even against the Conservative swing in 1930. He was slated for a cabinet post if King was re-elected, or so the hometown folks believed. As a member of the Stevens' Price Spreads Commission he had won attention with a minority report in which he defended companies like Canada Packers and the big retail merchants, Eaton's and Simpsons, against charges of unfair price fixing.

The CCF lads working in the campaign called Young "Old Socks from Dummer", because his favourite platform gimmick was to display two pairs of socks, one of US and one of Canadian manufacture, pointing out the price difference imposed by the Canadian tariff.

This time Douglas knew he must do more than teach CCF policy. To win, even not to fail ignominiously, he must attack. He put together a campaign and a fighting style.

"There was the man who bought a mule instead of a horse, and he couldn't get it to go. So he got his neighbour from down in the States who was used to mules to help him out, to get it started. The neighbour picked up a plank and hit the mule between the eyes. The man said,

'Wait! You're going to kill the animal!' The neighbor said, 'Oh no. The first thing you've got to do with a mule is get his attention.' "

So Douglas hit the electorate between the eyes.

He took into his entourage a colourful fellow named Dan Grant, who enlivened the campaign and taught Douglas a great deal. Grant was dapper in appearance, with a little bowler hat and high collar. He was a fountain of ideas, all of them attention-grabbers. It was before the days of "PR", but Grant had nothing to learn in that department. He had done some organizing for the Ku Klux Klan during the crazy days of its conflagration in Saskatchewan. When that passed he got a job with the Anderson government in charge of the Weyburn labour or employment bureau. When Gardiner beat Anderson, Grant was fired. Unemployed in 1935, he asked Douglas if he could drive for him in the campaign, and Douglas accepted the offer. Undoubtedly Douglas profited by the arrangement, though he always regarded Grant as amusing, but not very "deep".

It was Grant who seized on the quotation Fines had discovered in Hansard. Douglas must keep repeating it; their leaflets and posters must keep repeating it.

"The election had been expected in July or August but Bennett had a heart attack," Douglas said. "So there we were campaigning during harvest. The farmers were all in the fields, too busy to talk. One day I went up to one and I asked him if he'd like to come to a meeting we were having. He said he was too busy. I asked, 'Have you given any thought to whom you're going to vote for?' He said, never stopping his work, 'I know who I'm not going to vote for – that fellow who says we have to settle down to a lower standard of living.' I realized how effective that was, repeating that quotation of Young's."

He had discovered political shorthand. You cannot explain at length to thousands of people. You cannot tell them in detail how the Liberals, as he believed, were restricting the economy instead of expanding it to meet the challenge of the depression. One significant statement had to say it all.

He would be accused of being simplistic. He mastered the art of finding the one exciting circumstance that immediately transfers a whole body of fact.

He learned in 1935 that drama belongs in politics, that it is a political crime to be dull. He had been a fervent and compelling preacher, and he had been a skilled entertainer. He put the two parts together.

"I began telling jokes," Douglas said, "because those people needed entertainment. They looked so tired and frustrated and weary. The women particularly. They had all the back-breaking work to do. So I used to tell the jokes to cheer them up.

"And when they're laughing they're listening."

Grace MacInnis said, "He is a great story teller. The audience is afraid not to listen. Afraid they'll miss something. When they show signs of inattention he throws in another one."

People who have listened attentively to the Douglas style can testify to this genius. At a meeting heavy with statistics on inflation and monetary crises, there is suddenly a reference to hoarding: "Someone tells you there's going to be a shortage next week of blue pants with yellow buttons. And if you've never worn blue pants with yellow buttons in your life, you rush out and buy a supply of blue pants with yellow buttons." The ludicrous pants jolt the lulled train of thought. The audience is back on course with Douglas.

His car had given out. He did not know how he was going to get another one. Grant had the answer. He persuaded Douglas to finance a new Whippet which they named the Silver Bullet, to be raffled at the end of the campaign. Everywhere they went they sold one-dollar tickets on the Silver Bullet. They raised several thousand dollars, and the car was eventually won by a Creelman·farmer named Wiggins.

Douglas' followers began appearing at Young's meetings. They invariably sat up front and asked the chairman if there would be a question period. If the chairman said no, they walked out. If he said yes, the first question they asked was whether Young would agree to a public debate with Douglas. Young brushed off the question as beneath his notice.

But Douglas, attacking, was getting close to the bone. He discovered that Young had a rather important visitor, C. L. Burton, Simpsons president, who had arrived in Weyburn in his special railway car. Burton had just made himself notorious by telling a service club luncheon in Regina that the unemployed should be put in army training camps, as Hitler was doing. Douglas' friends, the railwaymen, brought Douglas word of Burton's arrival, and Young's visits to the private railway car, within hours of the event. Douglas made much of the meetings, joking that Young was reaping the reward of his kind words about Simpsons in his minority report to the Price Spreads Commission.

"It's an economic jungle, the survival of the slickest. How much is Mr. Burton putting into the Liberal campaign funds?" he asked his audience.

Young was on the defensive, telling *his* meetings that he would gladly make public every word of the conversations he and Mr. Burton had conducted. But this only confirmed that Young had in fact met Burton, that Young was in league with "the interests" down east.

The campaign was rough. Douglas put a lock on his gasoline tank after several experiences with sand or sugar poured into it. After arriving home one night he examined his car and found that all the nuts on the back wheels had been loosened. Another night an opposition gang broke into his meeting, shouting and jostling, elbowing their way to the stage. Douglas realized, first, that there was no rear door, and they were going to have to stay where they were and meet the fracas head on. He realized, next, that his Baptist deacon and campaign manager, Ted Stinson, had taken off his coat and was rolling up his sleeves. Douglas grabbed the nearest weapon, the water jug, smashed it, brandished it, and said, "If you come up here you're going to get hurt!" But through the door at the opportune time came a group of CCF supporters from Montmartre, marching in and up to the stage. " 'Having any trouble, Tommy?' they said. I said, 'Not now.' "

Then came Young's Watergate.

Douglas had rented a vacant print shop, where his workers turned out their own literature. They had planned a final leaflet, and while it was in production Douglas referred to it at meetings, " . . . this will be in your hands in a few days."

But Young, at his meeting one night, "exposed" the Douglas leaflet, reading an excerpt from it. Douglas knew it must have come from his shop. He would have ignored the matter, but Grant proposed that CCF committee officials go down to the RCMP and lay charges. Young, or someone on his behalf, had broken into their shop and stolen their leaflets. The police went to the McTaggart School, where the president of the local Liberal association was principal, and to the horrified delight of the students called him out for questioning. The Liberal president admitted that his people had broken into the CCF premises and made off with a half dozen pamphlets.

"It was a comic opera thing," said Douglas. "Totally unnecessary and stupid on their part. But there was a great furore about it."

Finally Young, stung by the prodding of his opponent, agreed to a debate.

It was held in the Weyburn rink. It saw one of the biggest crowds ever assembled in Weyburn. It was a raw October day, a little snow had fallen, and farmers in heavy coats, packed in the backs of trucks, were rolling in from miles away. The place overflowed with partisan spectators. It was a night Weyburn would remember.

Douglas spoke first. The crowd kindled his courage and his hope. His voice filled the hall. Now he believed that he could win, that the CCF could win – in his terms, that the people could win against the oppressive old-line party machine. He lit up the great bare stadium with his conviction.

In contrast, the weighty member of parliament was unable or untrained to send his words to the corners of the building. What he lacked in oratorical skill he tried to make up in anger. He produced the stolen pamphlet, which by now everyone had heard about, and launched into a sarcastic attack on its contents.

Douglas followed, with a few minutes for rebuttal. He made the pamphlet an issue. He said it had been prepared for "you – out there in this hall. I intended *you* to have it. But I object to this. I object to a political party breaking and entering other people's premises like common thieves. I'm saying to you tonight that any political party and any candidate who stoops to that kind of activity is not fit to represent you in the parliament of Canada."

The hall exploded. "And that," Douglas said, "turned the election."

A filched pamphlet or some other issue – it did not greatly matter. It was the fearless young champion slaying the old giant. It was pure David and Goliath.

One tactic in that election had serious repercussions later. Douglas was "endorsed" by the Social Credit party, which had just won a sweeping victory in Alberta under William Aberhart, and was striding into Saskatchewan. Their support, as it turned out, was negligible, but they were an unknown quantity.

The Liberals in Weyburn, when Douglas began to appear as a threat, decided to set up a dummy Social Credit candidate to split the "radical" vote. They approached Eric MacKay, a high school principal in Radville, who had lost the CCF nomination to Douglas and might conceivably hold a grudge, to run as a Social Credit candidate. However, MacKay phoned Douglas. They had offered him $1500 down, $1500 when nomination papers were filed, to run as "Social Credit". MacKay had refused.

Dan Grant, when he heard, was anxious to expose the story. The Liberals were sure to try someone else, and a split vote could ruin CCF chances. Grant paid a visit to Social Credit leader William Aberhart, who was speaking in Regina. Aberhart said that if a pseudo-Social Credit candidate ran, he would expose him as a fraud, and endorse Douglas. A candidate named Morton Fletcher subsequently entered the race as Social Credit. Quickly a "Social Credit convention", packed, it was said, with CCF'ers, was called to formally repudiate him and endorse Douglas.

Douglas never acknowledged the endorsation, and this saved his skin when George Williams got the provincial Farmer-Labour executive to agree to disown any candidates who had entered into an alliance with the monetary reformers from the next province. One CCF candidate, Jacob Benson, nominated in Yorkton, lost his Farmer-Labour credentials for this reason. Williams, hearing of the Weyburn situation, wanted M. J. Coldwell as provincial president to issue a statement also repudiating Douglas. Coldwell refused to do so.

Coldwell said,

We had quite a warm executive meeting. I remember Dr. Maclean was there and Clarence Fines, and George's friends were there and it ended in a rather unpleasant sort of atmosphere. I had to go on a speaking tour and I left Regina with this on my mind. When I got to Moose Jaw there was a telegram from George Williams saying there were criticisms coming in from around the province, and he would turn them all over to me to reply. Well I didn't get any of those objections and therefore I never had to reply to them. And throughout the campaign Tommy and I worked very well together, and Tommy and I were both elected to the House of Commons, the only two from Saskatchewan.

The confusion over Social Credit as a kindred or a hostile doctrine lingered for a few years – probably until John Blackmore began anti-semitic barrages in the name of Social Credit. In the beginning, several Alberta CCF members including William Irvine had been instrumental in bringing Major Douglas, head of Social Credit in England, to speak in Canada. Monetary reform was a strong mutual concern. But Woodsworth denounced Social Credit as one more capitalist party and Coldwell, at least at a later date, saw fascist elements in it. Douglas took a softer approach.

In a letter to Coldwell in 1936 he said:

> . . . I cannot altogether agree with your expressed strategy in dealing with the Social Credit forces. My experience throughout this province is that while there is a general admission that Aberhart is bound to fail, there is a feeling on the part of those who supported him that they want some place to go. The last place they are likely to go is to the people who have held them up to ridicule . . . Throughout my meetings I have consistently taken the stand that Mr. Aberhart has taken an economically unsound position but that he has endeavoured to give the debtor a fair break in his debt adjustment legislation, and that when those who have supported Social Credit come to realize its inherent weakness they will find a more comfortable home in the ranks of the CCF.[16]

Of Social Credit W. L. Morton later wrote bitterly: "Social Credit promised an easy and a sweeping reform, without socialism. The Albertans turned to it, and, aided by the war boom and the oil boom, achieved utopia. If it be objected that he did not thereby achieve a new society, it must be admitted that he has attained a new complacency. If one must travel to Nowhere, there is no more comfortable way than on a tide of oil."[17]

By 1955 it was clear to everyone that Social Credit was not a radical party, and those who turned to it were not radicals. But in 1935 Douglas, at least, was a grand optimist. Sooner, or later, by whatever route, everyone would go CCF.

It was something of a blow, in the 1935 election, when seventeen Social Crediters were elected across Canada, and only eight CCF'ers. Only the political analysts would note that the CCF had 300,000 votes in their first electoral try, Social Credit only 100,000 – while the short-lived Reconstruction Party actually polled more than either – 335,000 votes – but elected only one M.P. Such are the perils of a scattered rather than a concentrated vote in party fortunes.

But the Liberals smashed home to victory with one hundred and seventy-six and the Conservatives held forty-two. The two old parties were still the nation's choice.

Coldwell recalled: "After my own returns were in I remember I was driving back into Regina election night and I stopped for gas and the fellow told me Douglas had also been elected. So of course I got in touch with him. And I remember one of the first things I mentioned was that M.P.s have a free pass on the railroad and he thought that would be very fine. We joked about that, about taking trips."

In Weyburn they had waited for results through most of the night. Weyburn itself had a heavy Liberal vote; the outlying villages were late in reporting. But at last the results were clear. Douglas had won. When all the returns were in it was Douglas 7,280; Young 6,979; Berschal (Conservative) 1,557; Fletcher (Social Credit) 362.

"To turn around the defeat of a year ealier!" Irma Douglas said. "Our people came in from all over the country. They blocked off a whole street in Weyburn, in front of the Legion Hall, and people were jammed in there so tight you could hardly move for a block. It was such a great night.

I had no qualms. I guess I was so young. And there's no way you could live with someone who couldn't do what he wanted to do."

Yet Douglas said he still told himself that he would serve one term, and go back to his work in the church. He had learned how to win an election – but did he really want to be an M.P.?

Chapter Seven
Ottawa, 1936 to 1940

Douglas, his wife, and baby daughter Shirley spent the Christmas of 1935 with Douglas' parents in Winnipeg. It was a visit glowing with the success of Douglas' election to parliament, and he received some solemn counsel from his father about the trust that working men had placed in him, and his duty to them. It was also the last such occasion. Tom Douglas died of a ruptured appendix the following year, at the age of fifty-seven.

The Douglases followed the migratory pattern of most M.P.s. During sessions they lived in an Ottawa apartment; during the summer they were back in their small Weyburn house. When Shirley reached school age Irma enrolled her in a Weyburn school, and the journeys to Ottawa were less frequent for her.

Coldwell remembered Shirley in her pre-school years as a precocious child, who would call up a cab despatcher and inform him that Miss Douglas was to be picked up, and who usually had a ready retort, as when a condescending gentleman asked if she had ever seen a buffalo out west, and Shirley shot back, "Lots of times. On nickels."

The Coldwell and Douglas families were together frequently. Of Irma, Coldwell said, "No better wife or better person. She would never put herself forward, you know."

The bond between the two men was of lifetime quality. They had much in common, both old-country in their background, a preacher and a teacher, drawn into a political fight to lift the prairies out of dusty disaster, and to spread a new political creed across Canada. They had met and joined their not inconsiderable forces in creating the Saskatchewan Farmer-Labour party, accomplishing in that province the union of the two great working classes which were to be formally joined in the CCF. They were the only two successful CCF candidates, in that first electoral test, to represent Saskatchewan at Ottawa. For eight years they were Woodsworth's main support in the Commons, and shared the role of spokesman for western farmers. "My two agricultural experts!" Woodsworth teased them. Coldwell was by popular consent the successor to Woodsworth. With his role established in the federal field he would later urge Douglas to take the Saskatchewan leadership that led to provincial victory. There was loyalty and an impressive respect between them, despite the span of fifteen years in their ages.

When in 1973 a Regina seminar was held under the auspices of the Douglas-Coldwell Foundation, a message wired from the aging Coldwell read: "There has been no colleague over the years with whom I would prefer to be associated."

In August, 1974 when Coldwell died of a heart attack at Ottawa, it was Douglas' words, tight with emotion, that were most memorable. At the simple funeral service, attended by leaders from every Canadian political party, church dignitaries, academic and government figures of national reputation, and old friends, Douglas recalled that he had met Coldwell forty-three years earlier in his Weyburn church study, and expressed simply his "great feeling of sadness at having lost a lifetime friend."

"This was a man," said Douglas, "who gave himself unstintingly over a long and productive life to reducing wherever possible man's inhumanity to man." He quoted lines from a hymn Coldwell had liked:

"These things shall be, a loftier race
Than ere the world has known shall rise. . .
New art shall bloom, a loftier mold,
And mightier music thrill the skies.
And every life shall be a song
When all the earth is paradise."

Douglas' voice cracked with emotion, as no one listening had heard happen before, as he finished, "He didn't live, and you and I aren't going to live to see the day when every life will be a song and all the earth a paradise, but we can pay tribute by resolving that insofar as in us lies, we shall move the world a little closer, each in our own way, toward that goal when men shall live together in peace and security."

It was like a Saskatchewan late summer day, crisp and clear, and the sunset that evening was a marvel of flaming colour, like a last prairie salute to M. J. Coldwell on the day of formal remembering.

"A saint in politics," they called Woodsworth. "A gentleman in politics," they called Coldwell. How will Douglas be remembered? Perhaps he wondered, as he followed the casket from the chapel that day.

A preacher? An apostle? But he is a fighter, a ready antagonist, as those two were not; and he is a speaker to the blind hope of ordinary people, beyond the talents of either Woodsworth or Coldwell, and what English word is there to convey that kind of genius?

In 1936, Coldwell and Douglas joined the first group of eight CCF'ers in Ottawa. Woodsworth was informal about caucuses. "We used to pretty much go along with what he decided," as Coldwell recalled it. Agnes Macphail was ensconced in an office of her own, on the sixth floor corridor that historically has been Socialist Alley in the Centre Block of the parliament buildings. Other M.P.s doubled up, and drew on the stenographic pool for typing requirements. If there was a delicate problem involving a visiting constituent, the M.P.s roommate would tactfully absent himself and stroll about the corridors until the interview ended. Coldwell and Douglas shared an office. "We were right down at the end of the corridor next to the men's washroom," Coldwell said.

The research staff considered essential in later years was missing. Members of Parliament did their best to keep abreast of current developments. They relied gratefully on the LSR for basic direction; a first full-length publication *Social Planning for Canada* was a well-thumbed part of each M.P.'s equipment. When David Lewis appeared on the scene in the summer of 1936, his acute perception became invaluable to the political strategy of the group: after 1938, when his position as full-time secretary was confirmed, Lewis met regularly with the caucus.

The eight M.P.s were expected to cover the whole range of Canada's problems, to be on hand for every vote (no "pairing" was countenanced), and to be available for weekend and recess meetings anywhere in the country; the railway pass was an asset they exploited to the full. Their salaries were $4000 a year, plus $2000 for expenses, and they gave five per cent to the party in ordinary years, ten per cent in election years.

A. A. Heaps had been elected with Woodsworth from Winnipeg. Angus MacInnis and C. Grant MacNeil had been successful in Vancouver, and J. S. Taylor, who later left the party, in Nanaimo. William Irvine who had been elected with Woodsworth as one of the two original Labour men in 1921, had been beaten in 1935 and was out of the House of Commons until 1945. Agnes Macphail, in deference to the UFO's withdrawal from the party, sat as an Independent, but always close at hand.

A newcomer to parliament like Douglas and Coldwell, Grant MacNeil was much more in awe of the institution than his two prairie colleagues. Interviewed in 1974 when he was past ninety, MacNeil said he had had some dealings with government when he headed the Great War Veterans Association of Canada, the Legion's predecessor, immediately after the First World War, and had often called on Woodsworth for advice. But tackling parliament himself was a different matter and his first speeches were an ordeal. He described himself as, "always a rebel. I was active in the unemployed movement in Vancouver and never dreamed of going to parliament then. I went straight off the relief rolls to the House of Commons." He envied Douglas his easy way with the press; his quick recall of facts and figures. Douglas gave him encouragement when MacNeil was struggling to prepare a speech, painfully aware of the gaps in his educational background. "That's only a veneer," Douglas assured him. "You have nothing to worry about."

MacNeil considered Douglas "three or four grades ahead of me" with his "social work" training. Still, the thirty-one-year-old Douglas was regarded as a bit flippant and jocular by his older colleague.

But Woodsworth's daughter Grace welcomed Douglas' ebullient spirits and considered him "an indispensable member of that first group". Because of his lively interest in all issues she said he never seemed "just a prairie person. He was always a Canadian. Much broader than that: he had a world vision."

Her father, she remembered, had been very pleased with Tommy:

Father always enjoyed it when ministers who had been brought up in the traditions of the church suddenly got it into their heads that you had to build the kingdom of heaven on earth. J. S. had faith. I remember once he insisted on having one of his speeches sent to every minister of the United Church in the Maritimes. I had to address all the envelopes and stuff them, and I didn't share his faith in the redemptive potential as far as those ministers were concerned.

Father and Tommy shared the view about converting people. Father used to talk about the open-mindedness of the new people in the West, the immigrants from Europe. He said it opened our windows to new customs and new ideas, and *they* were open to socialism, in a way which didn't exist east of the Lakes.

Grace, who married Angus MacInnis in 1932, was already established in Ottawa helping her father with his secretarial and writing chores, including a weekly column to the *Western Producer*. She became secretary to the new CCF caucus, and undertook such assignments as arranging all the speaking itineraries for the eight members. She soon found Douglas much in demand across the country.

An admirer from this period wrote to Douglas in 1971:

The first time I saw you was in March 1938 when I went down to meet you at the Sherbrooke (Quebec) CNR station. A couple of us who were sympathetic to the CCF had persuaded the local YMCA to sponsor a "People's Forum". No CCF member had ever spoken in Sherbrooke . . . the first speaker (we had invited) was McNiven, the member for Regina City, who gave us a typical Rotary Club address. I wrote to Grace MacInnis and asked her if she would get someone from the caucus to reply the following week. She wrote back that you would be coming to speak on 'Canada at the Crossroads'.

You were just back from Germany, and the meeting was a tremendous success. My father was the Professor of Education at Bishop's, and he got the venerable Professor of Philosophy and Political Science (Father Burt) to come and chair the meeting. He took his politics from *Punch* and regarded himself as very advanced because he called himself a Liberal (though regretting that King was destroying the Empire). He was so overwhelmed by your address, in the witty and inspirational style with which we all were to become so familiar later on, that all he could say in thanking you was, 'Young Lochinvar has come out of the West!'

I next met you in Saskatoon in 1947 at a CCF convention while I was teaching summer school there. I was greatly impressed by the fact that although you were Premier of Saskatchewan you took the trouble to introduce me around as a friend of yours from Quebec.[1]

At first the CCF as a national party consisted only of the M.P.s on the Hill, linked by a common philosophy to the various provincial groups. That was the way Mr. Woodsworth liked it – a movement of volunteers across the country working toward socialism. Coldwell was appointed National Secretary to provide some liaison. When David Lewis came to Ottawa, immediately on his return from Oxford where he had worked with the leaders of the British Labour Party, he went to Woodsworth's office and was introduced to Coldwell and Douglas. He was seconded to "help Coldwell". But both Lewis and Coldwell felt this was not enough, and won over Woodsworth to the establishing of a national headquarters – a tiny shabby office on Wellington Street, with Lewis as a full-time secretary and a gentle, elderly man named Herbert Dalton as his helper.

Lewis recalled the first association with Douglas and the other westerners.

Ideologically, there was some difference in the source of one's faith, rather than the quality of one's faith. My root was the reading of Marx and Lenin (and I had totally rejected communism on the basis of those writings). Their approach was a moralist one.

I looked to the Labour Party in Britain as the origin of the CCF. My memory is that M. J. and Tommy did as well, but my link was a little more alive because of my previous three years of intense work inside the Labour Party. M. J. and Tommy were less convinced of the need for a labour base in Canada; they became fully convinced later.

Tommy was always of a very practical mind in regard to organization, which was our main preoccupation. I worked better with him than with J. S.

Douglas recalled of his first parliamentary terms: "I sat in the House with such charismatic personalities as Bennett, Lapointe, Woodsworth, Cardin and Chubby Powers. Life was never dull while they were around . . . Paul Martin and I entered parliament in the election of 1935. Later we saw a promising freshman take his seat, John Diefenbaker from Saskatchewan Lake Centre."

Douglas said he first met Diefenbaker during the 1940 campaign, when both appeared at a radio studio to record speeches. The Liberals were making things hard for him by mispronouncing his name to give it a German flavour, and Douglas was sympathetic. He considered that Diefenbaker did a great job during the war years in defence of civil liberties, ploughing through orders-in-council which were published by the yard under the broad provisions of the War Measures Act.

"In spite of our political differences I have counted many of these men among my friends," Douglas said. "Who can forget the irrepressible Gerry McGeer who said that the only person who ever approached parliament with the proper attitude was Guy Fawkes? Or when he followed Gatling Gun Manion in a debate and deplored the difficulty of 'trying to catch up with Irish suspicion travelling at two hundred words a minute.' "[2]

Douglas enjoyed the comedy of parliament to an extent not shared by his more serious colleagues. And he quickly earned a reputation for contributing some of its brighter moments.

A Wheat Board to sell wheat to the world had been set up by Bennett as one of the astonishing *volte-face* measures introduced – a reflection of Roosevelt's New Deal – in an eleventh hour attempt in 1935 to save his political hide. One of the first acts of the successful Liberal regime was to dismiss Bennett's appointee, John I. MacFarland, and appoint James R. Murray as Chairman of the Board. Douglas protested the appointment of Murray, who was head of a private elevator company, in his usual back-country style: it was like "putting a weasel in charge of the hen coop", he said.

His sorties into history were graphic. Winding up a lengthy reply to John R. MacNicol, the Conservative member for Davenport who had tackled the new CCF as a party that would "pave the way to communism", Douglas insisted that the reformers of history were the ones who prevented bloody revolution, and the reactionaires were the ones who brought it on. That's the way it had happened in France, he said. "When his ministers came to Louis XVI and asked him to make necessary changes he said, 'No. After me the deluge.' But the deluge came in his time, and Louis lost his head, not that he used it much while he had it but he was never the same after he lost it."

In January 1936 Gardiner had left the premiership of Saskatchewan to enter the federal house as Minister of Agriculture, though there was no doubt about his continuing iron control of the "machine" back home. Sparring between the two diminutive men – Gardiner and Douglas – was a special feature of the Commons. Gardiner was an inch or so shorter, barrel-chested and no mean speaker. Douglas was lighter, faster, always poised for a quick jab. When the Agriculture Department's estimates were before the House Douglas attacked government policy and was continually interrupted by Liberal hecklers, led by Gardiner. Douglas stopped short, turned and said, "If the minister will get back up on his chair and dangle his legs for a while, I'll get on with what I was about to say."

Gardiner scoffed at Douglas' championship of the farmer. "What does my honourable friend know about it?" he demanded. "He's not a farmer."

"No," Douglas retorted, "And I never laid an egg either, but I know more about omelets than most hens."

The press enjoyed him. In 1944 Austin Cross of the Ottawa *Citizen* recalled: "I have seen him tackle the formidable Minister of the Navy, Honourable Angus L. MacDonald, and flatten him. I have seen him push the Honourable Thomas Crerar around piteously."

Blair Fraser wrote, "At Ottawa he made a name for himself as a keen, aggressive debater. J. S. Woodsworth was CCF leader with Coldwell as his chief lieutenant, but most people ranked Douglas as Number Three, and he became Number Two when Woodsworth handed over active leadership to Coldwell after war broke out."[3]

The parliament of 1936 met on a sombre note. George V of Great Britain and the Commonwealth had died; there was official mourning in the capital. The House chose a francophone Speaker, Pierre-Francois Casgrain of Charlevoix-Saguenay. His beautiful wife Therese would be a political trailbreaker in their province, first to win votes for women, and then to lead the CCF. The Governor General was Lord Tweedsmuir, in private life an author, John Buchan, who singled out Coldwell and Douglas at a Rideau Hall garden party to tease them about their lack of true radical spirit. Buchan had been an independent member of the British House of Commons. Douglas discovered that a much admired writer, O. Douglas, was Buchan's sister.

Another newcomer to the 1936 parliament was a Conservative, Howard Green, elected in Vancouver South. In 1974 Green, retired, spoke of old parliamentary days from his study overlooking English Bay, where he watches ships of foreign registry come into port and never ceases to regret that Canada failed, after the war, to develop her own merchant marine instead of selling off her naval vessels. Green was Diefenbaker's Defence Minister in 1962.

He said that in their first parliamentary term, in 1936, Douglas was well-liked, and was a particular friend of Green's room-mate, Denton Massey. "They were two of the brightest young men in Parliament," Green said. He considered himself on the left wing of the Conservative Party – some distance from his leader, R. B. Bennett, leader of the Official Opposition.

"Bennett," said Douglas, "was quite brilliant – the Conservatives have produced some brilliant men. He had an amazing memory. I've seen him sitting in the House writing letters, but with one ear open. A minister was stumped when a question was thrown at him about the capacity of a certain harbour. Bennett growled out the answer – the size of the harbour, when it was built, the tonnage of the ships that could be accommodated. The press boys suspected he was bluffing and went and looked it up, and he was right.

Bennett had no capacity for making friends; neither had Meighen. Both would pass through the Members' Lobby and they might nod, or might not even speak.

But I was sort of the baby of the House and Bennett was very kind to me. He asked if there were any books I needed. He gave me a book once, *England Before and After Wesley*, by a Winnipeg professor. Bennett had helped him get it published.

He was a tragic figure. He died alone in England years later, an embittered old man. I talked to him in England after he became Lord Bennett, but he had lost any interest in Canadian affairs. He had great vanity and he couldn't take defeat. And his party was very unkind to him after their defeat. The Conservatives' favourite game – *swallow the leader*, once he's been beaten at the polls.

I went down with Howard Green and Ernest Perley from Qu'Appelle, to see him on the train the morning he left for England. I believe it was 1938. We were the only ones there."

Green also recalled that morning.

The train left for Toronto very early. It was snowing. I had said goodby to Bennett the night before; I felt very badly about his leaving. I happened to wake up early and I didn't want to think he might be leaving with no one there, so I went down to the station. Bennett just came down from the shadows and shook hands with us, didn't stay to talk. He felt he was being driven out of his native land. It wasn't the case, of course.

As for Prime Minister Mackenzie King, Douglas said,

I wasn't impressed with him at all. Agnes Macphail called him 'a fat man full of words'. He was the spider spinning the web. He never moved unless he had to. He allowed public opinion to build up, and when it got to the place where it was apparent that a majority of the people were demanding some reform, King seized the flag and ran to the head of the parade. The great reformer!

Agnes Macphail said one night that she had sat in the House with two prime ministers, and they had somewhat different attitudes toward poor people: we had a lot of poor people in Canada in those days. She told us that one day Bennett, looking out from his office in the East Block, noticed some unemployed fellows sitting around on the parliamentary lawn. He ordered the RCMP to chase them off. He didn't want to look at them. King would never have done that, Agnes said. He would have gone over to the window and pulled down the blind.

With King, everything was a little step at a time. Take the Bank of Canada. In the depths of the Depression, both Social Credit and the CCF wanted monetary reforms. *We* wanted to socialize the Bank of Canada, and *they* wanted a bigger printing press – . But between us we had managed to convince a large part of the public that leaving control of currency and credit in the hands of the chartered banks wasn't working. In those days they even printed the currency, their own bank notes. And in good times they let the money flow and at the first sign of a depression they called it in, thereby hastening the depression.

So in the 1935 election King was saying, 'Usury once in control will wreck the nation. Currency and credit must be issued in terms of the public good.' It sounded very forward-looking.

Bennett had already set up a privately owned central bank. So King brought in legislation to make it 50-50. Half public and half owned by the private banks! J. S. moved an amendment to have it one hundred per cent publicly owned but that was voted down. Later on, of course – it was so unworkable – it was made one hundred per cent government owned. When they were sure of public support for the idea.

But King was very kind to me. He got the idea I looked like his brother Bruce who had died. I couldn't see any resemblance in the photo he showed me, except the hairline was pretty far back.

And he told me he had visited Gladstone in Britain when he was at the London School of Economics. He accepted the Gladstonian principle that that government governs best that governs least.

His attitude to conscription was very typical. First he pledged there would be no conscription. He knew he faced the possible resignation of certain cabinet ministers if there was conscription. But eventually his military advisors demanded overseas support. He waffled for months, and brought in conscription only for home service. Then by order-in-council he sent sixteen thousand conscripts overseas. When certain ministers resigned *both* because of opposition to conscription, *and* because not enough men were sent overseas – Powers and Ralston – he concluded his policy must be the right one.

He told me once that he never got over the traumatic experience of Laurier and the conscription crisis of 1917 that split the party down the middle. He made up his mind that the strength of the party lay in Quebec and he must never again allow a split between French and English. He always chose a first-rate French lieutenant and left Quebec to him – Lapointe, Cardin, Chubby Powers.

Powers was a real Tammany Hall politician; he knew every trick and dodge in the game. He loved the in-fighting. But he was a good administrator. I was on the War Expenditures Committee – we couldn't discuss military expenditures in the House but we got all the information we wanted in the Committee, and then passed the expenditures in the House by voting a dollar or so, so as not to give out information about the extent of our arms. I would raise a matter in the Committee. Ralston, when Defence Minister, would make copious notes and an hour later there would be a Brigadier-General in my office followed by about six corporals carrying loads of material – or Ralston would send me a five-page letter dictated by himself with two or three postscripts – answering my questions. Powers on the other hand would go back to his office and tell someone there, that son-of-a-bitch Douglas wants to know so and so, will you see that he gets it. He would give the job to somebody. But Ralston was tied to his desk; he broke down under the strain.

The House of Commons of the 1930s was a much narrower and more provincial world. MacNeil recalls it as racist, anti-semitic, to an extent that would be unacceptable today. He said that one day he had two overseas visitors from India, and he asked them to go to lunch with him in the parliamentary dining room. He called Angus MacInnis, who said he was tied up, but Grace was free to join him. "Did I catch it afterwards! A very prominent Liberal was the worst. He said, 'The idea of taking a white woman in there with those Indians!' "

Sometimes it was rowdy, MacNeil said. "Tommy didn't drink, not compared to the rest. One time a big bunch of ex-servicemen met, a non-partisan group, and we came thundering down the stairs. I went into the Chamber just as Woodsworth led a terrific attack on this sort of thing going on in the House of Parliament."

MacNeil and Douglas worked together on problems related to the unemployed. Once they led a parade of trekkers from the west up Parliament Hill. No demonstrations were permitted on the grounds of the parliament buildings then; an M.P. must escort a delegation. It created a stir when the two CCF'ers brought the shabby lot of single unemployed men up to the ministers' offices. King wasn't in, but they arranged an interview with Norman McLeod Rogers, Minister of Labour. Nothing came of it: the days of confrontation politics were far in the future.

Grace MacInnis recalled those trekkers, and that the leader of the group became ill, and she found out where he was staying and took food to him in his room. "There were many transients," she said. "They found out where we were living and would come for handouts. The trekkers were trying to convey the needs of the unemployed to King and Bennett, but the government floundered around, not knowing what to do."

There was no unemployment insurance. The CCF pressed for it in repeated resolutions, and the first measures were introduced by the Liberals in 1940. There were no family allowances: the CCF was also the first advocate of this income-support idea, but it would have to wait until

1945. There was no concerted plan of "social assistance" in the modern polite phrase; "relief" was granted in niggardly fashion by local administrators, backed up by provincial grants and, in a series of traumatic and reluctant steps, by Ottawa money.

It was an era when traditional politicians still believed that the government had no direct responsibility for either social security or employment.

Assistance to the unfortunate poor was left to churches, benevolent societies, neighbours, and kin. Yet in the background lay the revolutionary concept of England's Poor Laws. In the last resort, people could not be left to starve. The state must see that they were fed. So had been set in motion all the fiercely contested legislative developments of the modern welfare state.

As for employment, the notion that governments should somehow make available a number of jobs sufficient to match the number of workers was unheard of, and had no Magna Carta. Only in the 1950s would parties begin to talk of "the right to a job", and the duty of the government to provide "jobs for all".

The first line of attack of the new CCF party was on the desperate economic conditions of the 1930s. They proposed welfare measures, at the same time making clear that what they were really after was a full-scale transformation of society to a "cooperative commonwealth". Each year Woodsworth introduced his resolution. In 1936 it read,

> Whereas the concentration of economic power in the hands of a comparatively small and irresponsible group has failed to provide security and a decent standard of living for large numbers of our people; therefore be it resolved that, in the opinion of this House, industrial, commercial and financial organizations and undertakings that are failing to function in the general interest should be taken over by the appropriate public authorities and operated as public services or cooperative enterprises.[4]

Conservative J. R. MacNicol commented that it was "just as communistic as last time".

Douglas said that if everyone who condemned capitalism was a communist Bennett would have to be included since, in one of his astonishing "eleventh hour" broadcasts in January 1935, Bennett had inveighed against "this capitalist system". Even the United Church, in those chaotic times, had come out with a statement at its 1933 General Conference which said, "It is our belief that the application of the principles of Jesus to the economic conditions would mean the end of the capitalistic system."

Douglas divided his first contribution to Commons debate, on February 11, 1936, between the frightening developments in pre-war Europe and the desperate poverty of his constituents. "There is a family of eleven persons living on relief. They are getting $8 a month." A 1932 study from the University of Saskatchewan of the debt structure in one municipality near Weyburn had showed an average farm debt of $14,700 – many times more than the farm could be sold for. "Is the law of economics the survival of the slickest?"

When he followed other CCF speakers in the debate on Woodsworth's motion he drew heavily on the new LSR publication, *Social Planning for Canada*, with its wealth of ammunition dealing with wage rates, the concentration of corporate wealth, and the price spread between producer and consumer. He made clear that the public owner-ship he and the rest of the CCF talked about was not a blanket takeover by government of everything commercial. He had designs only on "monopolies", not on "a little shoe store here and an ice cream parlour there." It was a distinction he would have to continue making to every fresh set of ears throughout his lifetime. He challenged the old-party critics not to wave the CCF solution aside "by stating that it is anti-religious or communistic or going to hurt individualism. Honourable members should realize that today we are faced with the greatest tragedy in human history. There are millions of people in the civilized world with no gainful employment, and yet there is a great abundance of goods not being consumed."

On March 9, 1936, protesting the demoralizing work camps set up under Bennett, he was saying, "Some sociologist has said that every nation gets the criminals it deserves. We shall get the criminals we de-serve; we shall have the tramps, the transients, the vagrants we deserve, if we continue over a period of years to allow the young men and women, from whom we might create the finest Canadian citizens, to drift gradually into a state of dry rot."

He had included "women" at the end of his peroration after re-peated vocal prodding from Agnes Macphail, who objected to the calam-ity of the depression being described in terms of damage to "young men". She rose to speak immediately afterwards, and remarked "I should like to see Canada composed entirely of young men, and see how they would get on."

For the western farmers, the battle was for fixed prices under a strong Wheat Board. Bennett had set up the Board; the Liberals emascu-lated it by making it inoperative except when wheat fell below niney cents a bushel; above that price the private market operated and the Grain Exchange, that "den of thieves" in the farmers' eyes, took its percentage, manipulating the price through advance bidding. Only during the war was full control returned to the Board. At the same time the government imposed maximum prices so that no unpatriotic farmer could gouge a war-torn world.

In 1939 Douglas wanted a 5 per cent profit limit imposed on muni-tions manufacturers: the government at first agreed, then abandoned the idea in the face of manufacturers' resistance. Some are required to be more patriotic than others.

The open trading in grain in the United States has never been subjected to the control of a Board. In January, 1974, Otto Lang, a very late-comer in recognizing the value of the Board to the nation's economy, pointed out in an interview with Canadian Press that while Canadians could count on enough grain for domestic use before any was exported, US citizens had no such guarantee. "The minister said the US has some philosophic resistance to establishing a wheat board-type operation and 'I appreciate how useful it is to have our type of system'."[5] Still the battle goes on, with the Liberal administration and Otto Lang in the 1970s fighting against the inclusion of feed grain under Wheat Board operations.

Wheat was a universal yawn in Ottawa. Coldwell described how the agricultural debates were scheduled for the late hours on Friday, so members could be on their way home for the weekend and avoid the dull topic – it was only the nation's bread, after all.

A much livelier debate was sparked in the first session over the design of the new Bank of Canada currency. Bennett had had some bills issued in English and a smaller number issued in French. Now the Liberals, ever mindful of Quebec's concerns, were proposing two languages on all bills. The Conservatives claimed that bilingual currency would create disharmony across the country.

The CCF group felt remote from the controversy, and scornful of what they considered a trivial and irrelevant issue. Douglas suggested a bill that simply said, "Canada". He expressed himself as "a little pained to see this House spending a day and a half discussing what to many people in Canada is a very trivial aspect of this bill. There are hundreds of people across the prairies today who would be very glad to get money, no matter in what language it was printed ... If honourable members would use as much energy and heat in getting money into the pockets of the people."[6]

The fatal flaw in Douglas' performance as a national leader was apparent during these early years of his career. Economic problems basic to the lives of all Canadians were to him the one great issue. Matters of language were mere divisive tactics employed by those who refused to take the magnanimous route toward an egalitarian society.

His emphasis on depression issues was reinforced whenever he spent time in Weyburn. In the summer and on weekends throughout the year he was busy with meetings, local radio talks, party organizing. He was a tireless worker. Occasionally the strain showed: he developed duodenal ulcers during that first term as an M.P., and was packed off to hospital for treatment in 1943. There were other bouts later, though Douglas, never inclined to spend much time describing his state of health, dismissed it all as "nothing serious".

He never let up. The pace was described by M. J. Coldwell:

It was in 1937, I think, and Nora and I and our children were driving out to Vancouver but we stopped to visit Tommy and Irma at their summer cottage at Carlyle Lake. We were to meet Tommy at Weyburn and go on out. Well he suggested that Jack (Coldwell) take Nora and Margaret on to the lake, and he would take me. So I got into his car. I had no coat or hat, I remember. I'd left them in my own car. And Tommy suggested that we should go to a picnic where I would make a speech. So we did that, and afterwards to my surprise he drove me back to Weyburn to stay overnight. The next morning he took me off in another direction to speak at another picnic at Strawberry Lake. Well, finally, after that, we headed for Carlyle Lake, but he turned off again to go to an evening meeting where we both spoke. So it was very late the second night, about two in the morning, before we got to our families at Carlyle Lake. Nora never quite got over it – I had missed our wedding anniversary.

Irma Douglas recalled one of the country meetings in winter. It was scheduled as a box social and dance. Their great friend and campaign worker Charlie Broughton drove with them to a wind-swept, icy schoolhouse, where they were the first arrivals. They wrestled with a box stove to get some heat, and used a rug from the car to plug a broken window. The dance orchestra didn't quite make it through the snow, but Irma played the piano, Charlie the violin, and someone else hit the drums. "We found her pretty dismal, but we left her in a blaze of glory," Charlie said.

Douglas was not permitted to confine his efforts to his own riding. The Saskatchewan organization had begun calling on his services throughout the province. Far in the north in Mackenzie constituency Sandy Nicholson talking to the dried-out farmers who had arrived to start a second homestead, heard about the celebrated big debate with Young in the Weyburn arena. Sandy proposed to the provincial executive that he raise two hundred dollars to bring Douglas north for a week, for a series of six meetings. Nicholson said:

Those were the best meetings we ever had. The two hundred dollars came in, and a great many memberships. We had very heavy rain that week, but people came many miles over ungravelled roads to see and hear Tommy again. They were feeling wonderful about being part of the organization that had sent Tommy to the House of Commons.

Tommy had great skill in getting the audience in a good humour. He had a wonderful collection of yarns, though he never spent too long on them. And he was especially good handling hecklers, drunks. I've never known anyone else who could say the right thing without hurting, and leave the audience in a good mood after the incident.

Fred Williams recalled travelling with Tommy in the Weyburn district during the record heat of the summer of 1938, when one July day reached a level of 114 degrees, and at a picnic near Stoughton the potato salads were foaming when the waxed paper covers were removed. William said he and Douglas were mutually embarrassed one evening, after tramping and travelling through the heat and dust, and sharing the hospitality of a single bedroom in a farm home discovered they had two of the dirtiest pairs of feet in the province. "Of course there was no question of *baths*," Williams said.

Up north at Tisdale, J. H. Brockelbank had become secretary of his constituency association, and agreed to spend the winter organizing. The party paid the wages of a hired man, $25 a month, to look after Brockelbank's farm for three months, and paid Brockelbank $15 a month for his services. He lived "off the land", accepting the hospitality of supporters, and he travelled in a small covered "caboose" drawn by a horse, and fitted out with a small stove with a stovepipe through the roof.

Brockelbank had been trained for his work as an organizer at a school run by the party the preceding November. There he met Tommy Douglas for the first time. Douglas no doubt was a valuable instructor at that school, but Brockelbank remembers him for a side-splitting performance at a social evening, when he presented an impersonation of an eight-year-old girl reciting "The Charge of the Light Brigade".

During that period Douglas was also a household authority, though he could hardly have been aware of the influence he wielded. John Burton, later M.P. for Regina East, still carries a grudge because the amorous exploits of Rhett and Scarlett were denied him after Douglas, visiting the Burton home near Humboldt one weekend, remarked to John's parents that he considered "Gone With the Wind" inappropriate reading for a boy of ten.

"A year later when the movie came to town *they* went to it, but I still wasn't allowed to," Burton said ruefully.

Chapter Eight
War

Overriding all public concerns in the 1930s was the march toward war.

Douglas was perhaps the single most realistic member of his party in those dark dramatic times.

The CCF contained many people in addition to its leader, J. S. Woodsworth, whose opposition to war was an absolute tenet of faith. Violence was wrong and accomplished nothing; passive resistance was moral victory. Wars were a diabolical farce that exploited the young and innocent for old men's vanities. Wars were imperialist weapons for economic advantage against primitive peoples. To break from a moral position so passionately held was a wrenching experience, achieved only after much evasion and dodging and qualification and pretence. It was not an experience that split the party, since the outright opponents of war and the very reluctant accepters of war were mixed in every CCF group across Canada, and eventually almost all conceded that fascism was the greater evil. Perhaps it was an experience so filled with common anguish that the party members passing through it developed even stronger ties among themselves. Certainly no rancour remains between those who held back from war, and those, like Douglas, who urged that the fact of war be recognized and met. And after 1942, when Coldwell advised an affirmative vote in the plebiscite to permit conscription, the party wholly supported the war effort.

The League of Nations, the first "world parliament", was idealized by the CCF. But Douglas was one of the few who wanted force behind the League, who claimed that the League was useless unless it was prepared to back up its demands, in the last resort, by collective arms. Initially he equivocated about *Canada* contributing armed forces to back up the League, but he thought other countries should. (He might have gone further but for the inhibiting policy passed at party conventions.) Canada should bear down hard with economic sanctions, which would stop most acts of aggression, he claimed. And Canada stood condemned in his eyes when economic sanctions against Mussolini were withdrawn by the nations of the League, and Canada concurred in that retreat.

The rift between Woodsworth and his followers on this issue was apparent at a very early date.

The Speech from the Throne in 1936 commented on the seriousness of the international situation, and the importance of "adherence to the aims and ideals of the League of Nations". Douglas spoke in the debate, five days after the opening of the session, and launched immediately into a sharp denunciation of Canada's action in repudiating Dr. Walter A. Riddell, her League representative, who had been one of the chief initiators in the proposed oil sanctions against Italy.

"In signing the covenant of the League, for the first time in the history of the human race over fifty nations gave up their sovereign right to wage war" for a guarantee of collective security. "That after all is the only way that you and I can ever hope to live in a law-abiding and peaceful world."[1]

He approved the declaration of the League that Italy must be charged with aggression for its attack on Ethiopia, and he approved the King government for its professed support of economic sanctions. "We will not trade with a murderer while he is murdering." But what commodities was Canada withholding from Italy? Canada had had second thoughts about the vital one, oil, and decided not to deny oil to Italy. "But Italy can get along without Christmas trees, Christmas candles and teddy bears." He saw the hidden hand of the Anglo-Persian Oil Company of Great Britain and Standard Oil of the United States, in the knuckling-under of the League, and of Canada.

In March Douglas introduced a resolution and initiated a debate on the League. He urged "sincere and complete fulfilment of all obligations assumed under the covenant of the League of Nations", and asked that Canada initiate a collective reduction of armaments, open and collective diplomacy with reference to international disputes, revision of peace treaties and a just settlement of economic, territorial and racial problems. On the touchy question of going to war, Douglas deferred to his leader by proposing that "Canada will refuse to participate in any foreign war no matter who the belligerents may be," but *only* if she were convinced the League of Nations had not made sincere efforts to forestall the conflict. It was a proviso, slender at best, but moving slightly from the adamant pacifist position.

The thrust of his speech was to regain lost ground by imposing "effective sanctions".

In the summer of 1936 Douglas went to Europe and saw the situation for himself. He had worked actively to organize a Canadian Youth Congress, a massive affair with young participants from all the large churches, the Ys, the political parties, groups of all colours. The objective was the sending of a Canadian delegation to a World Youth Congress in Geneva. Thirty-five young people were delegated to attend, under government auspices. To act as counsellors, three youthful Members of Parliament, Paul Martin from the Liberals, Denton Massey from the Conservatives, and Douglas from the CCF were designated to go along. Massey was renowned for his enormous York Bible Class in Toronto.

Even with such respectable credentials, the occasion was used as a "Commie smear" against Douglas in later years. In 1961 a four-page gutter press pamphlet issued by the "Canadian Intelligence Service" ran an article by the police "stooge", Pat Walsh, who had been used by the RCMP to infiltrate left-wing groups in the fifties. Digging back in old files, Walsh found a misty photograph taken on the deck of the S.S. Aurania of the group bound for the Congress. It included several young men (William Kashtan, Roy Davis) later identified as communists, and in the front row, large as life, were Paul Martin and Tommy Douglas.

"Paul Martin was much more embarrassed by that article than I was," Douglas laughed. But the pamphlet was in fact used against him, and other NDP candidates, in the general elections of the 1960s.

The peace movement of the 1930s certainly included some very vocal Communists. It was a "United Front" epoch, when Communists, card-holding or clandestine, exhorted the world to awake to the perils of Fascism. The Front collapsed very quickly with the German-Russian pact which helped launch Hitler into war; it was ressurrected even more shrilly, under various names, once Hitler broke the pact and attacked the USSR. These reversals, tuned always to the fate and the well-being of Russia, were regarded with vast contempt by the CCF. Yet each turn of the wheel meant new embarrassing associations. At the 1936 national convention of the CCF there was a loud clamour for a united front with "other left-wing" groups, which Woodsworth turned back with a firm hand. The Canadian League against War and Fascism, formed in 1935, enlisted a cross-section of churchmen and others, and was headed by A. A. Macleod, a communist, as president, and Tommy Douglas as vice-president.

Douglas was not defensive about such activities. "I have never made a practice of abandoning a good cause merely because the Communists were in it. In Canada, they were like fleas on a dog, they had to have a host to live on. But if you stayed with the purpose of a movement, and they found they couldn't manipulate it, they often picked up their marbles and went home."

Douglas met an interesting cross-section of people at the Geneva conference, including some Spanish students passionately pleading for aid in their Civil War. Douglas went with them to the frontiers of Spain, seeing the boldly emblazoned German and Italian fighting planes in support of Franco forces against the beleaguered government. From there he went to England in the company of young Labour Party members. He was by now convinced of the enormity of Baldwin's non-intervention policy which had refused support to the Spanish government forces. In London, at Transport House, he met Arthur Greenwood, one of the few Labour Party seniors on hand while a party conference was taking place in Edinburgh. He was appalled to hear from Greenwood that the conference was expected to pass a resolution supporting the non-intervention stand. With his young companions he hurried on to Edinburgh, and was relieved when, after hearing the on-the-spot reports of the Congress delegates, the British Labour Party changed its position, voted support for the Spanish loyalists and launched a drive for funds for ambulances and other supplies.

Before returning to Canada, Douglas visited Nuremburg and witnessed a vast military display put on by Hitler youth. Now he was convinced that Germany was preparing for war, and that Spain was a prelude to a larger conflict.

When parliament met again in January, 1937, the painful shift in the CCF position was apparent. On January 25, Woodsworth, still adamant, brought in a resolution stating flatly "that under existing international relations, in the event of war, Canada should remain strictly neutral regardless of who the belligerents may be." The rest of his resolution asked for a prohibition against profit-making in war munitions, and "that the Canadian government should make every effort to discover and remove the causes of international friction and social injustice."

Douglas, significantly, referred to his leader's resolution only by commenting that Mr. Woodsworth had rendered a distinct service in having the issue discussed. This, however, was more than a polite remark. Parliamentary debate on foreign policy had been almost totally lacking. As Howard Green said of that parliament in which both he and Douglas sat for the first time: "There was very little discussion of external affairs; Mr. King discouraged discussion; he seemed to be of the opinion that if there was discussion in the Canadian parliament it might start a Second World War. He took a very peculiar attitude."

After his brief nod in Woodsworth's direction, Douglas launched into a ringing denunciation of the government's head-in-the-sand stance. "Europe is an armed camp", he said. Canada might soon be "inundated in a world war". He went back to the sins of Mackenzie King in failing to stand by Dr. Riddell to stop Mussolini with oil sanctions. Cutting off her oil would have stopped the fascist advance in Ethiopia, he said, quoting from the newly-published memoirs of General de Bono, commanding the Italian forces in Africa. What happened at the League of Nations was "collective duplicity, collective cowardice, collective evasion of our responsibilities," Douglas told the House. "While peace was preserved in the Mediterranean, it was preserved at the expense of a primitive people who, possessing only obsolete weapons, were wiped out."

He accused King of moving toward a position of "armed isolation" which he believed would be impossible to maintain. King had appeared at the League table to urge "mediation and conciliation", – but "he overlooks the fact that we are dealing with nations not all of whom are equally interested in peace ... One cannot talk about conciliation with a mad dog. One cannot talk about mediation with a megalomaniac who says that the idea of peace is abhorrent to him ... A League such as envisaged by the Prime Minister would be an international debating society that would be as effective as a Ladies Aid meeting . . . To take from the League all capacity to enforce its decisions, is to make the League of Nations null and void."

Still hedging on the sore point of committing armed forces, restricted by the position of his leader, Douglas said that Canada had always, under the League, claimed some reservations about being obliged to impose military sanctions, partly because of her distance from any likely scene of conflict, partly because she herself was unlikely to have any territorial or other disputes but would merely be stepping in to support another nation considered to be in peril, and partly because of her own mixed population, many of whom had come from Europe on the understanding that they would be exempt from military service.

But economic sanctions were another matter. Douglas urged not only a return to such a policy under United Nations auspices, but unilateral action against Japan, whose successful invasion of Manchuria had been an even earlier instance of flouting the inadequate League. He pointed to vast exports of Canadian nickel the previous few years. "It does not take a very fertile imagination to conceive the possibility that there are young boys in Canada tonight, whose bodies will be torn to pieces by the very nickel we are now exporting,"[2] he said with grim prescience.

In the same address to the Commons, Douglas analyzed the mood of the country in those pre-war days. There were the imperialists, he said, who would promptly commit Canada to war in the event Great Britain became involved. Many Conservatives were in that camp. There were also the isolationists, and he was inclined to put King in this category, though King's speeches, as he said later, were like a feather pillow, you could punch them into any shape, and there was always a paragraph to gratify every turn of opinion. The third category was the collective security crowd, who still banked on the League of Nations or, failing that, on concerted action of some kind to stem the fascist advance.

Isolation, continental security, was very popular in the United States at that period, and Douglas accused King of catering to it. "For a long time I have suspected that the honourable gentlemen opposite were pro-American in their trade policy, but it is becoming increasingly evident that they are also pro-American in their foreign policy."

But among the leadership of his own party the three elements were almost as clearly represented. George Williams, the leader in Saskatchewan, was among the most militant, the most ready to adopt a pro-war policy. There was also a good sprinkling of isolationists, whose primary concern, like King's, was that Canada should extricate herself from Great Britain's apron strings and demonstrate independence in world affairs. As late as January 1939 Frank Scott was writing that Canada ought to maintain neutrality in the event of hostilities involving Great Britain.[3] Frank Underhill had influenced the LSR to insert a completely isolationist section in the CCF guide, *Social Planning for Canada* in 1935; and in 1937 in *Maclean's* he wrote an article titled "Keep Canada out of War". David Lewis said that his position had been close to Scott's: both had protested the long tradition by which Canadian foreign policy was made in London, Canadian troops were considered to be England's troops, and any declaration of war by England was considered automatically to speak for Canada too.

At the 1938 national convention of the party, a resolution moved by M.P. Grant MacNeil had stated: "If collective action should fail and war break out, the CCF believes, that our decision as to participation must be based on the determination to keep Canada out of any war whose purpose is really the defence of imperialist interests; recognizing that in future, as in the past, an attempt will be made to dress up imperialist wars in a guise acceptable to the general public."

The pessimism in much of the country was reflected in a *Maclean's* article by Arthur L. Phelps in September, 1934: "Except by a miracle, Canada can no more stay out of the next war than she can stay out of the rain."

But many Canadians were not so convinced. They had clutched to their hearts the 1919 promise of a War to end War. They had gone through a period of de-bunking of war that had been quite unique in history. Pacifism had gained credence as a moral, defensible philosophy.

Coldwell said that he was strongly influenced to change his position by Douglas in 1937. But Douglas had no luck with Woodsworth:

> I said to him, 'Suppose we impose economic sanctions by, say, putting a blockade on to stop oil going into Italy, and someone runs the blockade and fires on the ships, what do we do?' He said, 'We withdraw.' I said, 'That's no blockade!'
>
> When we came to 1938, when Hitler invaded Czechoslovakia, the majority of us took the position that this was it, we must take our stand. J. S. refused to go along with it still, but the rest did. I said to him in jocular fashion because we were always good friends, 'What are you asking us to do? Put a gun to Hitler's head provided it's not loaded? We can't just *protest* now.'

When the momentous events of 1939 unfolded, the CCF was still divided. In March Hitler took Austria, and Neville Chamberlain, Great Britain's Prime Minister, went off for further talks with Hitler, returning to assure his country and the world that peace had been assured "in our time".

"J. S. was in Edmonton and I was in Victoria," Coldwell said. "We issued different statements. King had sent a letter to Chamberlain congratulating him, and J. S. approved. I didn't; I denounced Chamberlain. The position J. S. took was that war was *always* against the common people."

The final stand was Poland. Hitler had assured Chamberlain there would be no aggression against Poland. When the German armies marched into Poland on September 1st, England declared war.

In Canada, King sent a message to members of the House of Commons to reassemble on September 9, 1939. The CCF caucus and national council met for an emotion-charged three-day meeting in a room in the Centre Block of the parliament buildings.

It began with Woodsworth handing in his resignation, which was firmly rejected. Whatever else might happen, the CCF was incapable of abandoning the man who was not only the founding leader but the light and soul of its existence. So it was agreed that Woodsworth (who had suffered a slight stroke prior to the meeting) would speak first, for himself only, in the House debate. Coldwell would speak for the party, and thus the tacit transfer of leadership took place. The Council's job was to manufacture a statement for Coldwell that would reconcile the varying opinions in the party. By this time the collective security group would have supported the war. Angus MacInnis spoke for them, and Douglas, though pressing his view less strongly in the Council circle, was close to MacInnis' position. Other delegates were pacifist. Eventually Frank Scott and David Lewis, as on so many other crucial matters, were given the job of drafting a statement.

"We recognized the need for collective security," Lewis said. "But we resented all-out support because we disliked Canada saying, 'Ready, aye, ready.' We were probably wrong. We thought, 'Why go to war now, when only Europe is at war? We should go at the same time as the rest of the American continent.' Finally, we got together in a committee and drew up a policy advocating only economic support – a very untenable position! But we were also impressed by the need for a policy that would not split the party. It wasn't long before we extended our policy to full support."

Stanley Knowles recalled that he supported Woodsworth's position, which was a minority in the Council.

I remember there were three of us from Manitoba, S. J. Farmer, Beatrice Burton and I, all of us on J. S.'s side. I remember the session vividly. I remember the deathly silence of the night when he in very simple language said he had spent his life as a pacifist and if this party was going to support the war he would have no option but to resign as leader, and possibly should resign from the party as well. We pleaded not to have the decision that night. There were discussions overnight, and next day the compromise had been worked out.

There were to be no overseas commitments, only defence of

108

Canada, protection of civil liberties, and concern for the post-war period. Our leaflets also emphasized this.

I remember my last conversation with J. S., before his death in March, 1942. It was his last trip to the West, in November, and he was in bed in a compartment of the train. Harry Chappell and I and others went aboard in Winnipeg. His speech was difficult. He was a realist. He said, 'If you have any influence with the party in Ottawa, get them to concentrate on the post-war. The others will fight the war. We must be concerned with the future.'

Grace MacInnis, daughter of J. S., understood her father's position but supported her husband's reasoning. "Tommy and Angus were the same. They both realized what was happening. Under fascism all the forces for progress like trade unions and civil liberties associations were being destroyed. Fascism besides the destruction of legitimate governments and private property and private lives, was destroying institutions painfully built up over the centuries for the preservation and advancement of human rights. This just couldn't happen – humanity would be the loser."

Coldwell said, "We finally agreed, in the speech I was to give, that while we must support the people of Britain and France in their fight against a dictator who threatened freedom in all its forms, still we had no confidence in the leadership of Chamberlain and Daladier."

Grant MacNeil recalled only, "We were sorry about J. S.' position on the war. We were in agony on the whole thing. There was no ill feeling. We just loved him, felt we should protect him, but we couldn't go along with him."

So the matter was resolved. Only Woodsworth, speaking for himself, to a hushed House, and Coldwell, speaking for the party, represented the CCF in the debate of the emergency session of September 1939.

Douglas later told Ralph Allen, editor of *Maclean's*:

Only a few people knew it then, and only a few have heard of it to this day. But a few days earlier Woodsworth had had a severe stroke. When he rose to speak he could scarcely see and one side was partly paralyzed. The night before Mrs. Woodsworth had made a few notes at his dictation – a cue word here and there – and put them on cards in thick crayon letters at least an inch high. I slipped into the seat beside him and handed the cards up to him one by one while he made his moving but hopeless plea for peace. I knew that in a few minutes I would be voting against him, but I never admired him more than I did that day.[4]

Douglas immediately tried to enlist. On his return to Weyburn he found the first battalion of the South Saskatchewan regiment already filled. "The boys were coming off the boxcars and into the recruiting

109

stations," he said. He joined the Second Battalion, enlisting as a corporal, and was later commissioned.

"Actually," he said, "I had had some military experience. In Winnipeg in the militia, the 79th Cameron Highlanders, I played a clarinet! I say I played it: my mother and sisters had other names for the performance. Oh yes, I went to band practice once a week and wore kilts on parade. I got *paid* for it."

But his training sessions in the real war had to be interspersed with parliamentary duties. King summoned parliament again in January 1940, only to dissolve it immediately for a new election in March. The catastrophe for the back benchers was that they were caught short without the sessional indemnity they had counted on.

It was fierce, snowy weather, the worst possible time for an election. Douglas had accepted his second nomination. The campaign was difficult. Instead of calling door-to-door, contributions had to be rasied by mail.

And there was concern about how badly the CCF would suffer for its anti-war policies. It was not a crystal-clear situation. The Communists, forsaking the United Front and the League against War and Fascism were now on Hitler's side, ranting against the Allies as imperialists, passing out leaflets proclaiming the CCF were war-mongers and betrayers of mankind.

In Weyburn there were many German settlers who were anxious, fearing internment or deportation.

In other spots in Saskatchewan, pro-Hitler groups had been active; there had been gatherings of a *Deutschbund* to greet a visiting German counsel, and a photo of such a group in Holdfast showed a swastika prominently displayed, while Dr. J. M. Uhrich, Gardiner's provincial Minister of Health, stood by. Douglas liked to keep that photo handy when the Liberals accused him, as they did, of being a "National Socialist (Nazi)."

Striving to concentrate on economic matters, Coldwell and Douglas had proposed an amendment to the Defence Production Act at the previous session, to limit profits on arms production to five per cent. C. D. Howe, Minister of Munitions and Supply, had accepted it. During the brief September session Douglas had questioned Howe about contracts let under the Act and had been told that the five per cent limit was removed by order-in-council, since no manufacturer was prepared to accept it. Howe told the House: "I can say to my honourable friend that from that day to this the Defence Purchasing Board has done its very best to place contracts on that basis, and has used every pressure that could be brought to bear in the form of patriotism and so on, but to date it has not succeeded in placing a single contract on that basis."

"It was scandalous," Douglas said. "The arms manufacturers actually

110

went on strike. If the workers, or the soldiers, had taken such a position, think of the outcry!

"We were saying, 'Let there be no conscription of men without a conscription of wealth.' Let there be some equality in sacrifice."

In this vein the CCF fought the 1940 campaign, and in a fearful country facing the unknown terrors of war they held their own remarkably well. They had seven Members going into the election; they emerged with eight, five of them from Saskatchewan. Saskatchewan also sent to Ottawa a "National Government-Conservative", John G. Diefenbaker.

In Ontario, however, the CCF made a dismal showing, running only twenty-four candidates and drawing only 3.8 per cent of the vote in that province. The CCF strength was still in the West, where they elected MacInnis in British Columbia; Woodsworth in Manitoba; Coldwell, Douglas, Nicholson, Wright and Castleden in Saskatchewan. But added to the group this time was a Cape Breton miner, Clarie Gillis.

Douglas won his seat with a vote of 8,509 to 7,554 for his Liberal opponent. The Conservatives failed to run a candidate in Weyburn, but if the strategy was to polarize a winning vote against Douglas they were not successful. Douglas was to prove unbeatable for the next twenty years. There was no question now of a quiet return to the pulpit of a little church, or to an academic life.

In the summer of 1939, George Drew, later Premier of Ontario, wrote a series of articles for *Maclean's* on Canada's defence position, and in one of them broke the story of the questionable manner in which a highly lucrative contract to manufacture Bren Guns had been given to a little company in what looked like a straight patronage deal. Douglas, with Howard Green of the Conservatives, took up the matter in the House and insisted upon and got a committee of inquiry. It was a tempestuous business, with Gerry McGeer, the mayor of Vancouver, acting as chief defence counsel for Ian Mackenzie, the Minister of National Defence, and Drew appearing as star witness. The upshot was that Mackenzie was switched from his post, to make way for J. L. Ralston as Defence Minister, and defence contracts thereafter were handled with more circumspection.

One of the events of the war that roused Douglas most was the ill-fated Hong Kong expedition. In October 1941 two Canadian units, the Royal Rifles of Quebec and the Winnipeg Grenadiers had been moved under Brigadier J. K. Lawson to reinforce the British Hong Kong garrison. The Japanese attack caught them totally unprepared and Hong Kong surrendered on Christmas Day. Many Canadians were killed and others held in concentration camps until the war ended.

In no time there were ugly reports that the Canadians were badly equipped and untrained. In January R. B. Hanson, leader of the Opposition, asked for an enquiry, and on February 12 Douglas rose to accuse the government of stalling in setting up the enquiry.

One hundred officers and men from Saskatchewan units had been transferred to the Winnipeg Grenadiers for service in Hong Kong. Douglas had been one of six officers in that group. After several weeks with the unit he had been turned down because of the osteomyelitis condition in his leg. From that point his war service was that of a training officer in the militia.

He said in the Commons, "Last year I lived in barracks with some of these men, and I know just how little training some of them had. Five of the officers who went to Hong Kong are men with whom I had lived and worked for weeks. One expects to lose one's comrades in war time, but not through incompetence and negligence."

The inquiry was set up as a commission under Chief Justice Lyman Duff, the proceedings were held in camera, and the five-and-a-half page report, when it appeared in June, infuriated Douglas because he believed much evidence had been suppressed. He had testified before the Commission, and he maintained that his evidence, including conversations with the five fellow officers about their inadequate training and their concern about their readiness to lead men into a potential war theatre, had been completely misinterpreted in the report. He moved a resolution calling the report inadequate.

Douglas said later,

The morning the debate was to begin on the report, King's secretary sent me a message asking if I would come over to see him. I said I wouldn't go unless accompanied by Mr. Coldwell. I didn't want any private conversations. He agreed. When we got there King opened an important looking file and informed us that the reason the Winnipeg Grenadiers had been sent was that he had the written assurance of British Intelligence that there was no prospect of Japan entering the war. Our men were going only for garrison purposes and could do their training while on duty in Hong Kong. And he said, 'It's apparent that their intelligence was deficient but it's not our fault. I hope you won't press this matter this afternoon.' I said, 'Mr. Prime Minister, I appreciate your position. But if you want to be a bomb-proof shelter for British Military Intelligence – ! The fact is that constituents of mine went into battle, some untrained, all without adequate arms, and if you want to explain it to the House of Commons you do that. Certainly I propose to go ahead with my motion.' An attempt was made in the House to cloak the report in judicial immunity because Sir Lyman Duff was the Chief Justice, but I refused to accept that. I said that when he was acting as the head of a Commission he was not immune.

In 1971 in Hong Kong Irma and I put flowers on the graves of those men I had known.

Douglas' address in the House that day was reproduced in full in the *Globe and Mail*. He said that if the men of the Winnipeg Grenadiers were in the galleries instead of in Japanese internment camps they would not want to see the investigation turned into a whitewash. He defied the government to go ahead and "make the most of it" if they considered he was transgressing judicial immunity.

The report had said that in October "the best informed opinion available to the Canadian authorities was that hostilities would not arise in the near future." But Douglas said the Pearl Harbour investigations showed that on October 16, US Intelligence knew hostilities were likely to break out in the Pacific. Did British Intelligence know this or didn't they? Did they convey it to the Canadian government or didn't they? "The people of Canada will not permit Canada to be treated as an overgrown colony." If relying on other military intelligence was inadequate, Canada should set up facilities to find out such matters for herself.

He painted in detail the inadequacy of preparation of the officers and men, due to short training periods, lack of training arms, and lack of ammunition. "Men in both units had never fired a two-inch mortar, a three-inch mortar, an anti-tank rifle, an anti-aircraft machine gun, a sub-machine gun, or a rifle grenade; nor had they thrown a live hand grenade."

But the "saddest" part of the story was the preposterous arrangement for shipping the units over without their equipment, which arrived much later and never reached them. Canadians had relied on British naval vessels, but the *Arvatea*, equipped for only five hundred men, had been sent to carry over two thousand men and 125,000 cubic feet of equipment. As a result only 10,000 to 15,000 cubic feet of equipment went with the units. Douglas denounced the words of the Commissioner that the lack of Bren Gun carriers was not too important, since, "a truck would serve equally well where there are roads." Said Douglas, "The Japanese were ungentlemanly enough to fight where there were no roads."

He was criticized later for calling public attention to the fiasco. He replied, "If there was inefficiency and incompetence at Hong Kong there was no point in trying to keep it from the Japanese. They knew all about it."

Again in 1942 Douglas took an unpopular stand by mounting a criticism against the handling of the Dieppe raid. *Why* had aerial and naval bombardment been called off and men sent in to be butchered? He pressed the question so hard that at one point Defence Minister Ralston rose with a folder in his hands and said that if he really wanted that information he could have it. King silenced him before he could continue. Douglas was convinced that effective command of Canadian troops had been taken out of Canadian hands, and the much-prized independence of Canada's war effort was demolished by the British attitude toward its former colony.

As one of the government's sharpest critics during the war, he protested the signing of the Teheran and Yalta agreements which he saw as a repetition of mistakes of the Versailles treaty – dividing the spoils of war without reference to the wishes of nations and peoples.

"I was called a doctrinaire socialist by those on the right and a fascist by those on the extreme left. I took the position that the great powers had no right to sit down and divide up the world like a pie."

Douglas was undoubtedly in a position to assert himself as a leading figure in the CCF federal caucus. With the retirement and death of Woodsworth, he was Coldwell's obvious lieutenant. But before the war ended he resigned his federal seat. He yielded to party persuasion in doing so, but it was a decision he did not regret.

Chapter Nine
Time of Triumph

During the first four years of the war the growth of the CCF almost kept pace with the high hopes of its founders. It was a nation-wide advance. Even the Quebec legislature had a CCF member for a brief period. Nova Scotia elected three in their 1941 election, and British Columbia elected fourteen CCF members and became the official Opposition, the same year.

In 1942 the first breakthrough in Ontario occurred with an astonishing upset in a York South federal by-election, when a CCF schoolteacher, Joe Noseworthy, defeated the Conservatives' great man, Arthur Meighen. The Ontario CCF was jubilant.

In July 1942 the party celebrated its first decade at Toronto's Royal York Hotel. Tributes were paid to J. S. Woodsworth, who had died in March. The anniversary program carried the words of Bruce Hutchison: "He lit a fiery torch which burns with increasing light and, more than any public servant of his time he gave everything, gave himself entire, to his beliefs and to his fellowmen. He was the saint in our politics. Our politics, and all men who knew him, gained a certain purity from his presence and lost a vehement flame in his passing."

But it was no time for sadness. Excitement rippled through the party, and for the first time it felt itself on course with the Canadian people. Curiously, the party that had dragged its feet so reluctantly in entering the war, found itself with the most to gain by war's experience.

Few indeed were the Canadians who went through the years of the Second World War in a spirit of blind patriotic zeal. The jaunty marching songs and the bustle and glory of the 1914-1918 conflict were absent. Canada was committed to its course, but the nation, shocked and sickened by the atrocities of the Nazis, deeply sympathetic toward the stubborn English in their trials through the blitz, shouldered rationing without much complaint, and was sobered, even faintly embarrassed by its own wartime prosperity: the new jobs (the first jobs for many), the higher prices for wheat and bacon. They would have liked a moral justification for the new industrial pace that was completely changing Canada; they pondered the irony of being rescued from the depression by war. In this national mood the fervour of the CCF, and particularly the party's dedication to a better future, found a response.

At the 1942 gathering Coldwell, now leader, said, "Our convention this year, celebrating the tenth anniversary of the Cooperative Commonwealth Federation and building further on its sound democratic foundation, meets in the critical hours of a grim world struggle. Our movement, born in struggle, sees at once in this tragedy a symbol and a challenge: A symbol of the destruction and chaos, misery and suffering that follows lack of social planning; a challenge to men embroiled in immediate striving to refashion the world for living."

In the report written by the secretary, David Lewis, "The CCF Today", this bold statement appeared: " . . . the CCF is able to celebrate a record of progress and consolidation which has established it in the minds of most Canadians as the only post-war alternative to the present government."

And he said: "The experiences of this war have underlined the correctness of the principles of democratic socialism. The people of Canada, like the people everywhere, have not failed to learn the lesson. They are determined that if the resources of our country can be organized effectively for war, they can and shall be organized for abundance and security when peace comes. This is the reason for the tremendous growth of the CCF at the present time."

The same analysis of success appeared in Coldwell's Foreword to a joint David Lewis-Frank Scott production, *Make This Your Canada*, published in 1943. Coldwell said the lesson of the war was the effectiveness of national planning. "If we can do these things under the pressures of war, why can't we do them for the even nobler purposes of peace?" He described the efficiency of such creations as the Foreign Exchange Control Board, the War Industries Control Board, the Wartime Prices and Trade Board and he pointed to an eight hundred million dollar direct government investment in new plant and machinery.

Douglas' quip was briefer: "In the dark days of the depression I used to ask the Minister of Finance why the government couldn't get industry moving again, develop our resources, provide jobs for the unemployed, and his answer to me was, 'Young man, money doesn't grow on gooseberry bushes.' And I used to tell him, that if it was a gooseberry bush or something else, if the government was really concerned with achieving these results, the money problem wouldn't stand in the way. Well – then came the war – and they found the bush!"

The cry for social justice never flowed more easily from CCF pens. *Make This Your Canada* presented the brave new world in such terms as: "Every man is the equal of every other in that he has a life to live. The inequalities of men are superficial and physical; the equalities are profound and spiritual."

The Gallup Poll showed CCF support rising in a high curve: 10 per cent in January 1942; 21 per cent in September 1942; 23 per cent in

116

February 1943, and a delirious 29 per cent in September 1943, at which point it topped the poll, a percentage point ahead of the Liberals and Conservatives.

Two wins in federal by-elections in Saskatchewan and Manitoba in 1943 brought the Ottawa caucus to ten. Douglas was very visible in both campaigns. Joseph Burton was elected in Humboldt, Saskatchewan. In Manitoba they were able to elect William (Scotty) Bryce in spite of newspaper reports of a particularly inept statement by Harold Winch, leader of the British Columbia section of the party, to the effect that "when we become the government, we will institute Socialism immediately," and "those who defy the government will be treated as criminals. If capitalism says no, then we know the answer – so did Russia."

Stanley Knowles wrote to the national secretary: "A few weeks ago Brandon looked to be ours with a bang, but the capital made out of H. W. was terrific and as one (along with Tommy) who clarified and explained H. W.'s position, and ours, to the satisfaction of our audiences, perhaps I can be frank enough to say that the tempest over H. W. almost cost us the Brandon (Selkirk) seat."[1]

In Ontario, the 1942 victory in York South by Joe Noseworthy had fired the organization with new spirit. E. B. Jolliffe was elected provincial leader and an intensive membership and financial drive, along with avowals of support by union leaders and unprecedented affiliations by union locals completely changed the mood of the Ontario section.[2] In the provincial election of 1943 they moved from no seats to thirty-four in the legislature, with Jolliffe as leader of the Official Opposition. It was a high-water mark.

Caplan points out that Ontario, unlike Saskatchewan at the same period, had a typical "North American attitude of passivity and quiescence towards political participation," so that even at this peak of public acceptance the number of CCF party members in Ontario was only 15,000: in Saskatchewan's terms it should have been 150,000. The base of support was far less durable.

But the CCF across the country enjoyed a blissful epoch when its proposals and its warnings about averting a post-war slump, were seriously echoed by journalists, and every election showed a dizzy increase in its share of the vote.

In this euphoric state the question of assumption of power seemed an immediate concern. It was only a matter of where it might happen first. Eyes turned to Saskatchewan, and the question of leadership there became, in a sense, a national problem.

In 1941 the CCF in Saskatchewan had been the Official Opposition for three years. Its chances were clearly better than most, though in 1941 the British Columbia section elected a larger number – fourteen to Saskatchewan's eleven. But people were aware that Saskatchewan was nearer to a breakthrough. "The mood was better," David Lewis said. Unfortunately, Saskatchewan's leader, George Williams, had riled more people than he won, and now was off to war.

Many also had been disturbed by the decision in 1938 to run only thirty candidates, arranging saw-offs in other constituencies. It was a "terrible schmozzle", Douglas said. "Williams got the idea that the government was impossible to defeat and the only way to save the CCF from annihilation was to enter into saw-off relationships with Social Credit and the Conservatives." When the Liberals romped home with thirty-eight seats, leaving eleven to the CCF and one each to a "Unity" and a Social Credit candidate, it was clear that Williams' strategy had gone awry.

Williams, however, had strong support in the province. He had been a determined and tireless leader of the farm movement. Beatrice Trew, who became the only woman M.L.A. in the Douglas government in 1944, wrote: "The leadership contest between Tommy and George Williams had me on the side of George Williams for several reasons. I thought Tommy's place was in Ottawa. George Williams was the farmers' man. He was overseas, and I just did not like the manoeuvering that was displacing him. Probably you could say I was voting for the underdog, and against the party establishment."

Williams had enlisted in January 1941, and had gone overseas as Quartermaster with the Princess Louise Dragoons. In February, the caucus had chosen Brockelbank as House Leader. Among the M.L.A.s there was considerable support for continuing the arrangement. New M.L.A.s like O. W. Valleau and Myron Feeley backed the Williams and Brockelbank combination against what they saw as intrusion by the "federal boys".

Who first broached the subject of leadership to Douglas is not clear. It apparently was not the national secretary, David Lewis, who later acquired a mystique as grand manipulator of all party affairs. Lewis kept out of it, although, he said,

> I recall dissatisfaction with George Williams as leader. I didn't get around the country very much, but there was criticism of various traits or actions. Some key people might have chosen M. J. as first choice, but he was now interested in the federal field. Tommy was the other choice, with an immense reputation as a speaker, a very attractive young man, who had championed Saskatchewan agricultural interests in parliament. He wouldn't have expected to win, when he took the leadership. It was to his credit. My observation would be that he took the leadership partly because of commitment to the party, partly because he was flattered to be asked to be top man.
>
> I remember being much in favour. We were sure he would galvanize the party, though we really didn't expect Saskatchewan to win in a couple of years.

118

Coldwell said, "I advised Tommy to take the leadership. I never organized support for him, but I didn't think George Williams could do a good job. I urged Tommy. He was more interested in federal issues – but if the party wanted him, he felt he should take it."

Douglas was candid:

I was looked on with some coldness as being Coldwell's man. I was literally dragged into the provincial movement because the organization was going down so badly. We had the lowest membership in years, and when Williams went overseas things went dormant.

I wasn't that enthusiastic about going back into provincial politics. I was not too familiar with the scene. What influenced me really was that farmers came to me and said, 'A lot of us are losing our farms. The prices we're getting aren't adequate to pay off the huge accumulation of debt. Farms are being foreclosed, there are evictions, machinery is being repossessed – . If you can't do anything else but get us some type of debt adjustment, some security! You can make speeches in Ottawa but you can *do* at least this much because we can form a government here.'

The replacement of leaders was accomplished in two stages. In July 1941 the office of president, held by Williams, came up as usual for election. A resignation came from George Williams, and Douglas was elected in his place. Fines became vice-president, and immediately plunged into the task of rebuilding the organization.

But Williams was not out of the picture. He was still regarded as "leader" and his photo appeared in the 1942 national convention souvenir program in that capacity. It was expected that his resignation would be submitted to the 1942 Saskatchewan convention, and that Douglas would take over.

Some heavy in-fighting was taking place. Williams had M. A. Macpherson, a lawyer in Saskatoon, draft a letter which was sent to the provincial executive members and other officials charging that Douglas was unworthy of trust because of the Social Credit support he was said to have received in 1935. Williams' own "arrangements" in 1938 were apparently to be overlooked.

"I disagreed with Williams completely," Fines said. "The Social Credit organization had endorsed Tommy unknown to him. He had nothing to do with it."

"At a Council meeting," Nicholson said, "Tommy had to stand up and say, 'If I'm this sort of person, Council certainly shouldn't choose me as a leader.'

"Even George's best friends felt this was an unfortunate letter."

The party's newspaper editor, Fred Williams, recalled that when he went to Regina to take up his job, "I was immediately asked by the man I succeeded, 'Whose side are you on? Are you for Douglas or Williams?'

No one thought Tommy was out for the leadership himself. But some thought the so-called intellectuals from the East were wielding too much influence, and thinking, 'Tommy is our boy.' "

Nicholson recalls the 1942 convention.

The House was still in session, but Tommy and I went to Saskatoon. The understanding was that Brockelbank would be challenging Tommy for the leadership. Williams' resignation was second on the agenda. Brockelbank spoke and said he wanted this left until the election of officers. I then knew something was cooking. I asked Fines who was sitting behind me, 'What's behind this?' 'Haven't you heard? George has withdrawn his resignation and is contesting the leadership.' When Tommy heard that he said, 'I can't stand against George while he's overseas. It would be suicide.' We said, 'You must. You let the convention decide.'

Williams, Brockelbank, and Douglas were nominated. Brockelbank read George Williams' telegram promising to return immediately if an election was called. Brockelbank said, "I let my name stand so I could talk for George Williams because he wasn't there. But my speech had little effect. I would have to admit, future events proved me to be wrong."

In this acrimonious fashion, in July 1942, Douglas became leader of the Saskatchewan CCF.

The rapidity with which the smell of gunpowder died away is due entirely to his skill.

Said Brockelbank: "I worked 'agin' him at that convention. Tommy never showed the slightest bad reaction to that. And he never had anything but the best relations with George Williams. Tommy was a diplomat; George wasn't."

Douglas said of his defeated rival,

Right after the election (1944) I told him, 'You've got your pick of any portfolio you want.' I thought he would select Finance. But he said, 'Minister of Agriculture. That's what I want.' And I said, 'You've got it.' He died within a very few months. He would have been a very good Minister of Agriculture.

There were rumours that we didn't get on well, but I got on better with him than most people did. I understood him – his abrasiveness, his impatience – because I've a good dose of it myself; I conceal it better than George. I had tremendous admiration for his ability, and for the fact that a man his age who didn't need to go into the Army pulled every string to go overseas.

Beatrice Trew admitted: "Once Tommy became leader, I really think there was not much dissension. The success the party began to have helped, and Tommy is quite good at keeping a group together. His humour helps so much."

120

Of Douglas as diplomat, David Lewis said, "He went out of his way to avoid offending anyone in the party. I don't necessarily agree that that is the way one should act, but undoubtedly it has its advantages. It is important in a party that had as little money, that had to depend on human effort.

"That undoubtedly no one else could have given, that kind of spirit."

Significantly, as an indication of the way Douglas worked, the one M.L.A., Jake Benson, who had most openly backed him, was left out of the cabinet. He was left out because he was not good cabinet material. Rewards and punishments were not Douglas' style. Benson quit the party in 1945. A crusty individual, he had been first elected in 1943. Nicholson said, "He would never leave those cattle of his, his farm. He missed Council meetings. So Jake wasn't asked to join the cabinet, and his nose was out of joint."

The CCF had more time to prepare for an election under its new leader than it had expected. The normal lapse of time between elections is four years. The CCF breathed a sigh of relief when 1942 passed without an election call. But 1943 was the legal limit.

On Gardiner's departure to Ottawa, the Liberal administration had been taken over by Premier W. A. Patterson. He had won handily in 1938. But he was nervous about taking the plunge again. In 1943 he had two Independent M.L.A.s introduce a bill, which the government accepted, prolonging the Legislature's life to six years, because of the exigencies of war!

Douglas commented:

If he had called the election in '42 or '43 we would have had a close call, either way. By the end of '43 the tide had turned and nothing could save him.

Mackenzie King told me privately he had written to Patterson warning him, saying he ought to go to the country: he was violating all the democratic principles we were supposed to be fighting for, and every day he was inviting more disaster.

Gardiner was still premier in absentia. But his machine was gradually breaking down. What patronage could you have during a war? Jobs were plentiful. Nobody needed welfare. There were no clubs with which you could beat people into line.

Brockelbank recalled the dying days of the Liberal regime: "During the war it became very popular to talk of building a new order. It had people thinking of a new heaven on earth. Then, when they contrasted this with the Liberal government in Regina – it didn't fit! They were guaranteed to do nothing. Patterson was a nice fellow – but when you said that you said the works. Never had a new idea politically or economically since his mother took him out of three-cornered pants."

Clarence Fines had become provincial president. Jack Douglas, who had helped elect Coldwell in 1935, became organizer.

The provincial executive began to function as a cabinet. Fines was in charge of the office. Carlyle King looked after the youth section. "Everyone got a job, and had to report to meetings," Douglas said. "I told them, if you don't want to work on this executive then get off. It's not a roosting place.

"Sandy was in charge of raising funds. He could raise money like nobody I've ever known."

Sandy Nicholson became a legend. The party was in debt. It starved its employees.

> We had to raise money! I went after $4000, right away. I put it to the executive – we need ten people to give $100; 20 to give $50; 50 to give $20; 100 to give $10. Mrs. Lucas said people shouldn't be asked to give $100, but I pointed out she had given a lot herself, and couldn't her neighbours do it once?
>
> There were the Logans in Yorkton, they always gave ten dollars when I went in their drugstore. So I didn't pick up the ten dollar bill; I said 'I need nine more like that.' Well, Logan had been impressed by Tommy and he made out a cheque. I went to a railway conductor in Kamsack for my next $100. Even farm labourers getting $25 a month boosted their contribution.
>
> I didn't talk about paying off debts. This was a Victory Fund. I said, 'Tommy Douglas is our new leader, we have to do what we haven't done before.' And the way we got that money was the indication to me that we were going to form a government.

Nicholson said that as he went through the country, if he saw a farmer with a good herd of cattle he asked, why not give one of them, or her cash equivalent, to the CCF? He explained, "If one of the cows dropped dead overnight the farmer would carry on, so why not let the CCF have her?"

Within two years the CCF had an organization in every constituency, had candidates nominated in most of them, and workers were canvassing door-to-door and farm-to-farm, exhilarated by the response of the people they called on.

Beatrice Trew was nominated in Maple Creek in 1941, in anticipation of a 1942 election. She had many qualms; she had young children and they had no money. The choice resolved on her husband or herself. Albert Trew decided it made more sense for her to run so he could keep the farm going and raise money for her campaign. In two years she had called at almost every home in the constituency, taking to the road for three or four weeks at a time. When her husband needed the family car she set off with a driver, who was required to find her another driver at the end of his stint.

122

In 1944 the Liberals at last called an election. Knowles had Douglas' resignation prepared and ready to hand to the Speaker of the Commons and Douglas hastened to get himself nominated in Weyburn and launched his campaign.

T. H. McLeod, who later became deputy minister under Clarence Fines, had been a high school student in Weyburn and had worked in Douglas' 1934 campaign. After further education at Indiana State University he was teaching at Brandon, when the 1944 election was called. He said:

> During the summer break I went to Weyburn to manage the city campaign, more out of friendship than out of conviction that the CCF was going to sweep the province. Fairly early, the light began to dawn. I remember going into that campaign – well, the CCF had about eleven M.L.A.s; mathematical progression would suggest we'd come out with a good-sized Opposition, a good, large group looking like a real alternative.
>
> Then I saw the Liberals were vulnerable, tactics bad, organization weak. The publication they put out: 'Please Give Us Another Chance'! So we moved in with total ridicule. We were facing a bunch of tired old men.

In Patterson's final session the Speech from the Throne took a distant look at federal promises for the post-war period, but promised nothing of much interest at Regina. The Honourable Hubert Staines referred to the CCF as "a proper cesspool and a political sewer", a party which "fails to conform to its Hitlerite prototype only in its lack of the swastika and the goosestep."[3] The Liberals put out a four-page campaign bulletin pointing out that the CCF would take away the farmer's land, the people would lose their insurance policies, the CCF would close the churches, and Douglas would close the beer parlours. On January 27 it said: "There has emerged out of the Coldwell fog the true character of national socialism, its statism and its sameness with the Communism of Tim Buck's Labour-Progressive Party." It was a unique situation to be identified as fascist and communist in the same sentence.

The three big city dailies, Liberal supporters all, passed the point of persuasion. People gave up believing them; they drew laughter at public meetings.

"Why does not Mr. Lewis come out frankly and say that the CCF socialists will use democracy to obtain power, but will scrap it as soon as they get into office," the Regina *Leader-Post* wrathfully demanded after a campaign speech by the national secretary. Since the Liberal Administration was the only one in the country to illegally prolong its own life without going to the country, such editorials were fuel to CCF public speeches. Douglas gave a solemn promise to hold an election every four years in the month of June, a promise he carefully observed.

Five days before the election, the *Leader-Post* ran the results of an unidentified poll – "The consensus of opinion of a number of electors" – predicting that Premier Patterson would be back in office. It was greeted with skepticism on the streets.

The Gallup Poll had predicted a CCF win, but Saskatchewan papers neglected to print it. The CCF brought in papers from outside the province, and displayed them at public meetings.

On the eve of the election the *Leader-Post* warned gravely that the election result "would affect vitally the way of living of every individual, will affect the right to own and use property . . . " and would decide whether a "stultifying dictatorial system" was to be imposed. A CCF victory would "start Canada on the road to strife and devastation that has been followed by European countries."

Douglas campaigned in 1944 on a short list of promises, chief among which was an immediate moratorium on farm debt, along with hospital and health care on an insurance basis, under public control, as soon as it could be introduced. He promised a fall session of the legislature to move immediately on the farm security and other issues.

But his message was in much broader terms. The choice was between conditions "as they were before the war: a period of free enterprise and all the poverty it caused, or a change to a commonwealth of social justice."[4]

He drove from meeting to meeting, non-stop. At night in his hotel he wrote broadcast scripts by hand; the War Measures Act required that texts be submitted to radio stations in advance of delivery.

There were picnics in the afternoon and meetings in rinks and halls at night.

"A politician's cross," he said, "is that what he needs is sleep and what he doesn't need is food, and everyone wants to give him food and not let him sleep."

But T. H. McLeod had a different version of his eating habits: "Tommy had the health of an elephant. Then and later. Sometimes I drove him to those three-meetings-a-day he was holding, and the last one would end at an ungodly hour in a remote corner of the constituency, but then the candidate wanted to get back to Weyburn to sleep in his own bed. We arrived at four or five a.m. Then Tommy wanted something to eat – like a piece of pie. My stomach rebels at the memory."

CCF'ers from other provinces had swarmed in, as usual, to campaign. Those who came were unanimous in believing that Douglas himself was central to the victory. Grace MacInnis saw Tommy as all-important, the "living symbol" that people needed in their hope for a better post-war world. "And of course," she said, "in 1944 the media couldn't create a leader as they can now. He had to do it himself."

Grant MacNeil was sure they could not have won without Tommy. "He was head and shoulders above everyone out there."

Stanley Knowles agreed. "Tommy was the man. Fines couldn't have done it. No one else on the scene could have. Saskatchewan was ripe for the CCF in 1944. But would they have won it with George Williams? I don't think so."

Nicholson said the same thing. "Oh no. We couldn't have won the election without Tommy. I don't think so."

But Brockelbank was of a different mind. "Sure. *I* could have won that election. Campaigning in 1944 I just couldn't believe it. I figured 'There's something wrong.' It couldn't be true. I couldn't find anyone who was going to vote Liberal."

And Clarence Fines said, cautiously, "I was confident we would be elected. You could just feel it wherever you went. But I don't think we would have got anything like that majority without Tommy. We might have squeaked in. The enthusiasm generated by his leadership made the difference."

Those who were there are sure they will never again experience anything quite like Douglas in the 1944 campaign. His presence, his electric vitality and the sheer eloquence of his voice as he set out to win Saskatchewan were scarcely more remarkable than the open joy of the people who heard him.

The stories he told were parables, delighting his listeners.

In Regina City Hall, packed to the rafters, he talked of the white cats and the black cats. Every four years in Mouseland, it being a democratic country, the mice held an election. One year they would elect the black cats. And conditions – for mice – were terrible. So after four years they rose up in protest, threw out the black cats, and – elected white cats. The white cats preyed on the mice even more terribly than their predecessors had. So next time – back in went the black ones.

Until one day, a small mouse stood up in his corner and proposed, "Let us elect *mice*." They called him a radical, a Communist, a National Socialist. But the idea spread. Mice got the message. The day came. . . .

The story of the cream separator was even more beautifully apt. What Douglas did with this story is a perfect example of his skills for it was apparently derived from a paragraph by Lewis Mumford:

"During the age of expansion, capitalism gave cream to the few, whole milk to the middle classes, and a blue watery residue to the majority of farmers and industrial workers, agricultural labourers and slaves. The highest hope of capitalism, its most sacred incentive, was the hope that a fractional few of the skimmed-milk drinkers might, by elbowing and pushing, claim a place for themselves among the cream drinkers. In an age of economic balance, on the other hand, we must look forward to a widespread distribution of whole milk for everybody."

That, for Mumford, was well said.

But Douglas began it with a homely lead-in, with Douglas visiting around at the farms, toward meal-time, and finding himself stuck to assist with the farm chores. Because it was easy, he got the job of turning the handle of the cream separator. He usually whistled "Onward Christian Soldiers" to keep from being bored. "But gradually I began to think how much the cream separator resembles the economic system of Canada. There were the farmers, pouring in the good fresh milk. There were the city workers, turning the handle. And out of two spouts came blue milk for the workers and farmers, cream for the guys who owned the machine. When those guys got a bellyache from too much rich cream they held up a hand and said, 'Stop! Hold it! No more milk. This is a Depression!'"

By the end of the campaign he had so caught the ebullient mood of the people that his first words from a table behind an elaborate floral display: "This is little Tommy Douglas behind the gladiolus," were enough to set them off in paroxysms of laughter.

His voice was gentle when he spoke of farm women working without the benefit of electric washing machines or stoves, of young people unable to get an education or a job, but trying on their first good clothes, going to a dentist for the first time, when war needed them. He left out harsh or bitter lines. He led his listeners up a shining spiral of shared hope and high resolve, all there, all theirs.

"It was a good campaign." That was how Douglas spoke of it, thirty years afterwards. "There was such tremendous interest.

"The war was coming to an end. The Allies landed in Normandy on June 6, and we went to the polls on June 15."

The CCF won forty-seven seats, the Liberals five.

The Liberals were not prepared for defeat. Their organizers, whether from reluctance to relay bad news or genuine misjudgement, had produced confident reports right up to polling day.

The only surprise for the CCF was the size of the win.

"I didn't think we would do as well," Fines said. "I didn't expect personally to be elected. Regina was the capital, with so many public servants; I thought it would be the last seat we would win."

Another person surprised at her own success was Beatrice Trew. "No we did not expect to win," she said. "There were very conservative-thinking ranchers around Maple Creek, and a heavy German Roman Catholic population in the whole area." But win she did.

Credit for their success must be shared between leader and party. Douglas was the man, as his followers said. But Saskatchewan went CCF that day with a kind of inevitability that everyone who understood the province, understood.

Douglas had ended his campaign with a meeting in Stoughton before driving back to Weyburn. All election day he moved about the riding, checking the polling stations. When they closed he returned home to eat, and the returns were spelling success before he could shave and leave the house. He went down to share that night with his workers –

there was no time to drive to the mammoth celebration that filled the streets of Regina with people marching and people dancing.

McLeod said,

Clarence's final estimate before the election was that the CCF would win 48 of 52 seats; we accused him of insanity. (In fact they won 47). Tommy's most optimistic guess, once he began counting on a victory, was 35 seats.

We had set up a fairly elaborate telephone network in the Weyburn committee room, pulling in all the results from our constituency and the whole province, so I was about the first to know. I remember Shirley dashing in and out wanting to know if her father was the premier yet. We knew by ten o'clock. There was a big victory rally in the Legion Hall.

It was a terrible shock to the Liberals. There were people on the street, Liberals I knew quite well, *crying*. Many believed their own propaganda, the tales that if the CCF was elected they would take over your insurance, all you'd paid in would be confiscated. If you were a farmer the CCF would take over your land – all the work you'd put in improving your property would be lost. Very few people in their right minds believed that – but there were very few Liberals in their right mind at that time! Those grown men standing there crying! What the hell had produced this state of mind in those people?"

Douglas said:

I watched the results in the committee room in the Weyburn Legion Hall. I was fully conscious of what we were starting in to. A province with the second highest per capita debt, the second lowest per capita income! Patterson had said we were a bankrupt province: we hadn't been able to borrow a dollar on the open market since 1932.

I had no illusions that I was starting on a honeymoon.

But I wasn't alarmed. When you're young you think you can lick anything.

I kept remembering what the farmers had said. If you can just save our farms; if you can just do that much.

Shirley Sutherland, interviewed from her Los Angeles home, remembered, "I was ten. I stayed up late. None of us could believe it was happening. Was Dad excited? Oh, you could see it in his eyes. Though he was quite calm when he spoke. Afterwards he and I went to call on an old friend, T. H. Hillier, a lawyer in town, a good supporter, but quite deaf. He hadn't been well enough to go to the committee room."

Irma described the vast crowd, the dreamlike excitement, the fact that she had washed that day to have something to do, and that Shirley had stood up to the microphone and wowed everybody when she said, "It's been a great victory for all of us."

In Weyburn, Douglas got 5,605 votes to the Liberal's 3,489. The two old parties united against him and continued to do so in every election he contested in Saskatchewan.

The votes of the men and women in the armed forces went heavily to the CCF, which took 60 per cent to the Liberal's 28. The same trend would show up in the federal election the following year. Mackenzie King lost his seat in Prince Albert in 1945, his advantage wiped out by the service vote. Prince Albert put up a sign on its outskirts, a souvenir of European battles: "This town liberated by the Canadian Army."

Douglas had established "a beachhead of socialism on a continent of capitalism." The event was played down by the press of eastern Canada as an aberration, inexplicable, a folly confined to the hinterlands. Those CCF spokesmen in other provinces who tried to impress voters with the Saskatchewan achievement found little response: the average Canadian living in Ontario or points east was not quite sure what the difference was between Social Credit and the CCF, which belonged to which prairie province, or why it should interest him.

A national convention was set for Montreal in the fall of 1944. Lewis had it postponed a month to accommodate Douglas, who was completely absorbed in his first whirlwind batch of legislation. Douglas was to be the star attraction. It was therefore devastating to be informed that Douglas had decided to accept a chance to visit Canadian forces overseas. "I received your letter of October 24, and almost literally wept," Lewis wrote.[5] Douglas had said to Lewis on an earlier occasion, when an officers' training course kept him from attending the 1940 gathering, "You know that I dislike conventions anyway." It seemed he was glad to escape this one, where he would have been lionized.

Clarence Fines presented the five-month record of the first democratic socialist government, in Douglas' stead. In spite of the premier's absence, the 1944 convention was a jubilant one for the party. It had been a year of triumph, the peak of the sudden success the CCF had enjoyed during the war years.

But the war was nearly over, and the CCF bubble was about to burst. Saskatchewan would be isolated over the next sixteen years, working out within its borders new concepts of government management, scarcely noticed by the rest of Canada.

Chapter Ten
People, Party, Power

How socialist was the CCF government of Saskatchewan?

Anyone answering will begin, "It depends on what you mean."

And so it does. If the interest is in economics, and if this leads to an analysis of the CCF regime in terms of government intervention in the free market, the answer is disappointing. One of the first enquiries into the 1944 experiment was made by Seymour M. Lipset, who subsequently, in a book titled *Agrarian Socialism*, concluded that agrarians are not socialists.[1]

In a book by another American published the same year, the party and the Saskatchewan government were assigned their place on the world scene: " . . . a new Canadian political party, built in part on the pattern of the British Labour Party, yet adapted to the needs and aspirations of North America. The CCF is to this continent what the 'third force' is to Europe – a middle way between the extremes of reaction and revolution."[2]

A Canadian writer, political scientist Evelyn Eager, also saw a lack of radical socialism in the CCF:

> Distinctive features of CCF policy from the time it assumed office in 1944 until its defeat by the Liberals twenty years later did not represent the sharp departure from the practices of its predecessors or of neighbouring provinces which was sometimes pictured. Enthusiasm and a reforming spirit were evident, administrative innovation occurred, there was early socialistic experimenting, changes were made and new policies and services were introduced; but these occurred within the framework of the existing economic and social order.[3]

All three writers noted particularly that the policy of land nationalization, the "use-lease" idea put forward first by the United Farmers of Canada (Saskatchewan Section) had been lost along the way in the political progression through the Farmer-Labour Party, the CCF at its first national convention in Calgary, and the CCF bidding for election in 1944. Not only was the ownership of agricultural land, the biggest natural resource, to remain private, but the socialist inclination to expropriate existing enterprises didn't get much beyond utilities such as power and bus companies, and the takeover of one small ill-starred box factory in Prince Albert. Some new enterprises were initiated as crown corporations, notably insurance, but the total did not impress those who saw socialism solely in terms of uprooting capitalism.

The wave-of-the-wand believers were sometimes unhappy. These disillusioned followers conveyed their reproaches to the new government, as in this sample from a member of the great unwashed, who found himself, ten months after the "takeover", still without a bathtub:

"The petty bougoisee (sic) who have taken control think they have solutions for social problems. Because they have made a success of their lives they believe the rest of us can and must. They have pat answers to most problems, such as soap and water for B.O., forgetting that a person cannot take a bath in a room at 60 degrees nor is a basin of water sufficient."[4]

Douglas replied: "I believe a man of your experience will realize the limitations of a provincial government. In establishing socialism it is extremely difficult to build a complete and watertight unit within a provincial area."[5]

The core of the apple is financial policy. In this, the Douglas government was orthodox, even conservative. It was its boast that the budget not only balanced but recorded a surplus in each successive year of the CCF regime. No government debts were repudiated; on the contrary a frugal policy of debt repayment was consistently followed. A pay-as-you-go policy for public works was maintained, despite every longing plea for extra expenditure. There was no attempt to circumvent the money system or substitute "social dividends" or other "funny money" tokens – that approach belonged to Social Credit.

The government stayed within the constitution of Canada. No breakaway, separatist tendencies developed. In fact, Saskatchewan pressed for greater federal control, beginning with the 1945 federal-provincial conference when Douglas took a strong position for the retention of wartime centralization of power. It showed up repeatedly in pressure on Ottawa to take over such programs as hospital insurance, initiated by the province. Being Canadian was essential to the economic survival of Saskatchewan, and the CCF wasted no time on sovereign pride.

In economic terms, the socialist thrust of the CCF government was directed toward planning in place of ad hockery, toward more and larger crown corporations and government services, and, in the exploitation of new natural resources such as oil and potash, toward tighter control, and a greater diversion of wealth through royalties and taxes into the public purse.

If this seems less than socialist, it is clearly in line with experience elsewhere. An interesting parallel took place in France, as Michael Harrington describes it:

Finally, in 1936, capitalist collapse and working-class militance forced Blum to accept the exercise of power. In a legislative whirlwind – twelve laws were voted in ten days – the Popular Front established paid holidays for the workers . . . the forty-hour week, the reform of the Bank of France, the extension of compulsory education from 13 to 14 years of age, the nationalization of war industries, social security, the organization of state markets and much more . . . But these reforms, as Andre Philip, a participant and observer, writes, were as far as 'distributive socialism' could go . . . As a result of this rethinking, a concept that was to become a key to socialist programs after World War II came to the fore – economic planning.[6]

Harrington contends that socialism in this era became a system of planning, and directing the uses of capitalist economic growth.

H. S. Lee, Douglas' executive assistant for a number of years and now on the faculty of York University, contends that innovative measures *were* taken in Saskatchewan: "The laws of contract, so long sacrosanct, became items that were negotiable and changeable, and they were changed. Governments in Canada are now doing it every day, but it started with Tommy and the people around him. Old-fashioned rules of the market were challenged."

But it seems clear that Douglas, on the whole, accepted the limits of provincial jurisdiction as a framework for his government. He was convinced that much more would be possible through federal power, with the full resources of the nation to command, and was eager to see this happen. But to some degree he accepted the constitutional reasons for avoiding drastic action in one province. In other words, he was practical, he was a realist.

But within that framework he presented revolutionary concepts in ways that seemed normal, sensible, and obvious. He did much to change the economic direction of the province without appearing to do violence to normalcy.

Frank Scott said,

It was his sagacity, his sense of how people react. That was part of his real greatness. The ultimate policy of the CCF is revolution. The method of persuasion, criticized by some people, can only succeed if Tommy Douglas' belief is right, that you can win enough people over to move the thing along. The philosophy of gradualism.

This means that the people you want to accommodate are always on your right. But if you don't talk to *them*, you're left with nobody to talk to but yourself. The people with wrong views, wrong as you see it, must be respected.

You have at the same time to make the people behind you believe you're not selling them out, and make the people you're inviting in believe you haven't got some horrible thing up your sleeve, and once you've got them in you're going to eat them all up.

The CCF might have squeaked into power in 1944 without Douglas. It held power through four successive terms because of Douglas. The economic change in Saskatchewan did not test the bounds of the familiar too violently, but it did move always, and with energy and despatch, toward wealth more broadly distributed among the people of the province and toward economic growth to produce a bigger pie. And this was Douglas policy throughout.

To cite the degree of new government economic control is not a thorough analysis of a socialist regime. Socialism has always had a dual meaning. In economic or materialist terms it asserts that there are simple, rational ways by which people through collective action can manage and distribute the earth's abundant resources. This assumes a moral content in the limiting of man's acquisitive nature to spread the benefits more evenly; thus the creed allows a man personal economic freedom only to the extent that he does not exploit others.

But the significant other half of the socialist philosophy is that the advent of this moderation is not to be reached except by popular will. Harrington has devoted a solid volume of research and exposition to the essentially democratic nature of socialism, with a re-interpreted Marx as his mentor. He defines socialism as "a movement of self-emancipation of the people that uses democracy to make the economic system as classless as possible."[7]

Neither of these two tenets of socialism: rational distribution of abundant wealth, or the will to cooperate, with the necessary degree of mutual trust, to achieve an egalitarian society, seem particularly applicable to the present world scene. Instead of abundance there are shortages or severe limits to vital resources. Instead of a basic belief in trustworthy fellow humans, there is an unmistakable trend toward hostility, distrust, and self-preservation in the dense crowding of over-population. It is perhaps too soon to say that socialism is irrelevant, and socialists will plead even more passionately that their way is the only way that bears thinking about for the future of mankind. But the pessimists have never had so large a load of evidence on their side.

In Saskatchewan in 1944 this was not the case. It was believed that greater wealth could be achieved and distributed by determined government action. And, more important, the concerted will toward public action that would benefit all was uniquely present. In this respect the CCF regime was profoundly socialist, and Douglas the ideal exponent.

A very large part of the population was ready, with a deep emotional predisposition, to participate in the program of cooperative achievement expounded by the CCF. A considerable number of the uncommitted were persuaded to "wait and see", or to "go along", largely on the strength of Douglas' own determination to convince them.

132

There are many stories to illustrate how Douglas won over groups who objected to his policies. A. M. Nicholson described a first meeting after the 1944 election with the College of Physicians and Surgeons. Douglas had taken the Health portfolio. It was a strained atmosphere. Douglas omitted the jokes. He said. "You are disappointed not to have a doctor as Minister of Health. It's a pity no doctors ran. I think we should have more doctors in the legislature; I hope some of you will run on future occasions. But you'll have to put up with me, and there is a place for laymen in the administration of health services." After outlining concisely what the government had in mind he told his audience the story of the osteomyelitis he had suffered as a child, and his experience in the public ward. "He got a very very warm reception," Nicholson said. The initial contact with the medical profession was in fact cautiously favourable.

Blair Fraser, *Maclean's* prestigious Ottawa correspondent for many years, once wrote:

He is probably the most effective stump speaker in all Canada, one who can win even his enemies to a reluctant admiration.

One of his government's first acts when he became premier of Saskatchewan in 1944 was to raise the licence fee for commercial trucks in the province from a very low figure to a range of very high ones. The truckers were furious. About a thousand of them converged on Regina for a protest meeting which they invited, or rather commanded, the Premier to attend.

'When Tommy walked out on the platform they were howling at him, hissing and booing,' said a man who was there. 'I honestly think if they'd got their hands on him they'd have lynched him. But Tommy just stood there smiling until the noise quieted down and then he started to talk.

'He told them how much he sympathized with them, all the trouble they'd had trying to do business on Saskatchewan's roads, the worst in all Canada. He told them how the government was going to fix things for them, give them decent roads and a chance to do business with the same advantages as other provinces. He told them about the cheap insurance his government was going to bring in. He told them some funny stories too.

'At the end of it they were laughing and applauding him. I drove away with a bunch of them, and halfway home we were talking about what a great speech he'd made and what a wonderful guy he was. Then somebody interrupted to say, "Yes, but what about the licences we came here to squawk about? The little son-of-a-gun never even mentioned them."[8]

Another person recounted the story of a delegation of small-town merchants who met Douglas to protest taxes, particularly as they related to an extensive program to bring water to the villages and towns of south Saskatchewan. Douglas told them about the brisk trade they would be doing in tubs, toilets, taps, and other gadgets, and left them quite convinced that they stood to gain, along with the householders.

At meetings he was good-natured and tolerant with hecklers. He managed more often than not to turn the vituperation aside with a mild joke: "I once held similar views but my wife talked me out of them." To put the man to shame, to make him look foolish was to make an enemy. That was not his objective.

His letters now in the Saskatchewan Archives include an occasional rebuke to those who, for purely selfish reasons, objected to such programs as hospital insurance or compulsory car insurance. They ought to be willing to pay into a scheme that would benefit others, he suggested, quite apart from the possibility that they might someday need to draw on the benefits themselves. When one gentleman threatened to withdraw his political support ("It isn't my intention to donate any further, until I am rewarded for service rendered in the past,") he got a lengthy reply which began:

> Dear Lou: Thank you very much for your letter of November 11, which I was pleased to get although a little mystified at its contents. I am not just sure what reward you have in mind. I took it for granted that the reward you wanted was better government, and I am quite prepared to demonstrate to you at any time that you are getting better government; that you are getting better social services, better roads built and better health services than you have ever had before.[9]

He entered into a personal dialogue with people to an extent that would probably have been impossible in a larger province but which, even in Saskatchewan, was previously unheard of.

Eleanor McKinnon, his personal secretary, said that when they moved into the Premier's offices they discovered cabinets completely cleared of files. She said, "It was just as well we were starting from scratch. We were so busy. There was mail up to the ceiling. Farmers filled the office. They sat there day in and day out. There were some party people there to make sure the government got off on the right foot, but mostly it was farmers. It was difficult keeping things on schedule, it was such an open-door office. Tommy would greet them as though he was prepared to devote the whole day to them. We had to screen people after a while."

In February 1945, a burly, impoverished free-lance writer, Jim Wright, sent a long letter to his friend Clarie Gillis, the Glace Bay M.P. in Ottawa. He thought Gillis was probably not getting much news of the new government, and proceeded to fill him in.

In Saskatchewan the two daily papers in Regina and Saskatoon are owned by the Sifton Liberal interests who suppress and distort each day the news concerning the CCF government and party. They play up bickering criticism by Patterson the Opposition Leader, and when Tommy takes Patterson properly over the road in the Legislature there is not a mention of it. Furthermore, they control the news going over the Canadian Press wires so that no daily paper in Canada or elsewhere in the world is getting anything worthwhile about the CCF side of the story. . . .

We spent a week in Regina prior to coming to the farm. And I believe history will record the CCF premier and cabinet as the most honest, conscientious, hardworking, forward-going government that has taken office to date anywhere in North or South America. There is, besides, a refreshing lack of personal intrigue and political patronage. I saw no evidence of either, and believe neither exists. (God has taken care of George Williams who is ill at the West Coast and has recently resigned as Minister of Agriculture). Tommy, able, trusted and popular, needs more help . . . The 'commodore' is much overworked, and where the hell they'll find a commodore as good as he is if his health gives out, I don't know . . . I did mean to make an appointment with him for a longer visit, but instead of intruding on his time I feel more like guarding him against intruders. There are the usual well-meaning individuals trying to see him about some detail that looms large in their life, and including their life history and what their grandfather died of. First time I saw him was a Saturday afternoon when instead of being home resting he was in his office struggling with a reply to Ilsley on the seed grain.

Eleanor McKinnon recalled one startling occasion shortly after Douglas took office when a man appeared in the office with a gun, a pocketful of cartridges, and the announced intention of "shooting the bastard". She was alerted by Jack Douglas' secretary, to whose office the would-be assassin had gone first by mistake. In a weird succession of events the secretary had redirected him to the Premier, but at least had had the wit to phone that he was coming. Eleanor, reminding herself that she had worked in a mental hospital and must keep calm, got Douglas' executive assistant on the inter-com and instructed him to call the police. She handled the man herself, persuading him to go away and visit a doctor who was head of the government's mental health services. As he left Douglas emerged from a cabinet meeting and his staff shooed him back, but instead of retreating he popped into the corridor to see where the man was headed. He had disappeared. Much later the police picked him up on a train near Moosomin. "It was so bizarre," Eleanor said. "We never thought of such things really happening. There were no security precautions of course." She said she never did find out what his complaint was.

On more peaceful days the staff was waist-deep in personal letters. The "Dear Premier" letters were usually from devoted admirers, like this one, hand-written on ruled paper:

> . . . I see my paper The Commonwealth is a bit in arrears . . . Please find enclosed ten dollars . . . I am an old chap 81 next July 21 but have not been on my feet since a year ago early Jan. from Gangarine trouble. I had my right leg amputated above the knee, and have not got my crutches going yet . . . Election day is drawing near. I think we are safe. I wonder how you can hold yourself when talking to or about Tucker. (Leader of the Opposition) . . . I may go to the poll in my wheelchair but I'll get there. We have had light crop for three years. Hope we get a good soaker soon. Wishing you the best.[10]

Douglas wrote the editor of the party newspaper asking that special mention be made of the contribution, and answered his correspondent, "I really think this is too much money to come from you . . . I want to thank you especially."[11]

Another letter said:

> . . . Tommy, I like to think that you really have remembered me. I mind the last time I shook hands with you here in Shaunavon and you remembered me and also my former wife whom you mentioned as having met down Montmartre way . . . Just as a layman and through a layman's eyes there have often been little things that I would have liked to draw to your attention; then at other times I have wanted to congratulate you for your courage and tenacity of purpose.[12]

An excruciating example of original spelling, and a heartfelt comment on the Liberals' political ways:

> . . . for my expericence CCF government of Saskatchen $2^{1/2}$ years don more security farmer and worker Saskatchen than ever liberaly party and conservwhat party for 25 years. I could prove it myself. I'm sorry lot of high word I diding spell right. When I was going to school that the time liberaly and conserwhat party in power in Saskatchwen lot of time there was no teacher because district coulding aford it. Not enough money for teacher and low wages for teacher. There was no road to school or town. Everytime before laction liberaly party bring graderese and caterpiller to show people if they come back in power they will make the roads. Couple days after laction dispear altoghter.[13]

The letters poured in. "I had to stand up to open them, especially after he made a major speech on the radio," Eleanor McKinnon said. "And it was an absolute rule that every piece of mail must be answered."

The devotion of many people to the movement is illustrated in the example of one woman whose will contained a bequest to the party, along with the instruction that her CCF pin was to be fixed to her dress when she was buried.

There were some critics who felt Douglas spent too much time travelling about the province, away from Regina. "He was criticized," it was said, "because he didn't give attending a sub-committee of the cabinet priority over meeting ordinary people in some little village forty miles away."

And there was skepticism. "I don't believe in painting people as angels," one leader at the national level said. "It was only partly that Tommy was tolerant. It was also because of a deliberate policy – he would be extremely friendly to people even though he might not think very highly of them. Undoubtedly there were people whom he considered stupid or intractable or troublesome. But he never lost sight of the importance of keeping them friendly and avoiding a confrontation which led nowhere."

But Grace MacInnis was deeply impressed by Douglas' warmth. He seemed, she thought, to see himself in the same perspective as everyone else, "finite in an infinite universe". She said, "I've seen him so often when the little old ladies crowd around him, and he is as genuinely interested in them as in anyone, while he keeps the big shots waiting on the fringe."

"Yes, he has faith in people," Allan Blakeney, Saskatchewan's present Premier, said. "But not in the simplistic sense, that if you got one hundred people together their consensus would be right. But he felt if you put the arguments to them and appealed to their essential better nature, that they would respond and could be convinced that they had an obligation to their fellow man. He never gave up on that."

Douglas seldom took a church pulpit once he entered politics, but one late August day in 1946 he preached a morning service to a little group of forty cottagers at Carlyle Lake, where he and his family spent their holidays. A visitor from Ontario, Elizabeth Trott, was there that morning, and wrote about it later in an article published in the Regina *Leader-Post*:

> I confess that I had been half dreading a minister given to flights of fancy and self-conscious oratorical effects. Those fears were groundless. The premier's eloquence was pure, brief, direct and untainted by any hint of the flowery. When he led the congregation in the reading of the thirteenth chapter from Corinthians – 'Though I speak with the tongues of men and of angels. . . ' – more than one in the audience, like myself, must have reflected that seldom if ever could they hope to hear those beautiful lines delivered so effectively again in any church.
>
> I forget the text completely, but I remember the sermon was something I had wanted to hear from a Protestant pulpit for many

years. There was that sense of a message about it. The theme was the Christian spirit.

Premier Douglas preached without notes. Service and brotherhood were identifying characteristics of the Christian spirit, according to his definition ... The central need of our time is to assess accurately the real meaning of Christ's message ... He deplored racial discrimination as practised by our big hotels in Canada, even within the borders of Saskatchewan.

Suddenly, in the next paragraph, Elizabeth Trott is writing not about Douglas but about Saskatchewan, as if the transition was scarcely felt:

There is a greatness here – even in the unpainted small towns. It is a greatness not easy to define or describe, yet one feels it deeply. It has something to do with the strength that comes from the soil. Something to do with the domination of land and sky, the sweep of fields, the high cloud formations. And in the inescapable preoccupation of the people with the weather, and change in season, and growing things – in other words, a preoccupation with life.

As we walked back along the stony path, I recalled Spengler's prophesy that the world might look for its future leaders to the Mongolian steppes or to the vast North American prairies. Here, on these open plains, men of vision would rise, men unafraid of the Spenglerian view. I began to think that there was much virtue in this idea. Saskatchewan was different, somehow, – people seem to think more clearly, to be more aware of essentials.

"They were the greatest people to work for in the world," said Tim Lee who had come to Saskatchewan from the west coast to become Douglas' executive assistant. "We were never inventing policy for a disinterested public. They were active, informed people, from every ethnic group. They were always on top, making their own constructive demands."

The same sense of a democratic force quite new to his experience was described by Frank Scott:

I was present at what we called the 'takeover' of the legislative buildings. After the election in 1944, we all marched up – I was beside Tommy as we walked up the steps to take over the vacated offices of the old Liberal regime. The new Minister of Agriculture didn't know where the office of the Minister of Agriculture was. It was very inspiring and amusing. I use the word 'takeover' that the Communists made symbolic, moving in to take over when the old state collapses, and here we were legitimately, with proper authority, moving in to take over this great legislative building.

Had Douglas been in the least arbitrary or autocratic toward the people of Saskatchewan he would not have succeeded. He was singularly sensitive to the public, and he gave first priority to meeting with people on every possible occasion, at meetings, picnics, gatherings of all kinds in every corner of the province. No matter what the size of this audience, he pulled out all the stops, like a trouper too proud to give less than his best.

Eleanor McKinnon said,

Not long after I began work, Shumy asked me, 'Have you ever heard Tommy on the hustings?' I hadn't. I'd never been to a political meeting, though I'd heard him in the pulpit. He was speaking that night in Radville, which isn't far, so we went down without letting him know we were going. It was just a rough hall, the farmers and their wives. Well, Tommy got up to speak. I got so excited, I clapped and laughed at his jokes and eventually I put five dollars on the collection plate – an absolute fortune in those days.

It was wonderful to hear farm people laugh. Farm women – the way they laugh.

To open the doors of communication wider, Douglas had Hansards, the debates of the legislature, made available in printed form from 1948 onward. Later he began radio broadcasts of the proceedings during the session, the first legislature in Canada to adopt the practice.

Douglas said,

The provincial network thought no one would listen. So we said we'd pay for time for six weeks to see how it went. We put it through the Estimates. On the last day, I told Fines to go up to the booth in the gallery and say goodby and thanks for listening, as we closed it off. When I got home for dinner the phone was ringing. It was the radio station, saying their phones were lighting up like a Christmas tree, people were blaming them, wanting the broadcasts to go on. I said we couldn't, we had no more money budgeted. Two hours later the chap phoned back and said they would carry it on their own.

After about a month I was having lunch with a constituent and I ask him, 'Does anyone ever listen to those debates on the radio?' He said, 'One day I took a load of grain to town. I wanted to get home by three when the Legislature opened. When I got part way home I realized I wasn't going to make it so I pulled into a farm yard and asked if they had a radio. There were four other trucks there, all farmers who had pulled in to listen to the broadcast.'

It delivered us from the tyranny of the one-party press. All the dailies and the private radio stations were owned by the Siftons, and all of them were Liberal. We divided the time in the debates very fairly, and people could listen and hear it all.

In the sense that many people were involved, in a common spirit of "self-emancipation", and if this is a criterion of socialism as Harrington contends, socialism had in fact "established a beachhead on a continent of capitalism". It may indeed have been a unique experience in any society in modern history.

When a political party elects a government, a delicate relationship must be established between party and ministry. Should the government assert complete independence and impartiality, in the name of responsibility to the whole electorate? No government does. The most common, if somewhat crass, relationship is through patronage: the dispensing of government jobs and contracts to party supporters.

The CCF government was certainly not free from this kind of preferential hiring, though it did endeavour to keep free of the notorious patronage that characterized the Gardiner regime. In Weyburn, for example, there was complaining from disgruntled CCF'ers because the employees at the mental hospital, all Liberals, were not fired, and the same situation turned up in road contracts, especially in the north, where outraged CCF'ers reported sabotage by Liberals who had been kept in their government jobs. Still, the upper ranks of the civil service filled up fairly rapidly with "people who share our philosophy", if not with "people who deserve a reward".

But, quite apart from patronage, this government had a different kind of relationship to establish – the degree to which it carried out the policy decisions of the party. All party conventions pass resolutions on policy. In the case of the national Liberal party they are usually far in advance of government policy – for state health insurance in 1919 and for a guaranteed annual income in 1970. The Liberal government pays them scant attention: they are not the real business of a party, which is to act as a power base.

But the CCF was not that kind of organization. It believed earnestly in the resolutions it passed and the policies it adopted by majority vote at its conventions.

The CCF maintained an open membership, meaning that anyone could join who was not a member of another political party. Members were zealously sought, year round, because the membership fee was the basis of party finance. On the local level, members met in a constituency organization which had great autonomy, to choose a candidate, to run a campaign, and to send delegates to the annual provincial convention. The convention made policy. It also elected a provincial executive and provincial council to meet several times a year, and it elected its party leader for a one-year term. Every year, Premier Douglas appeared before the CCF convention to ask for re-election. If the convention had rejected him he would have been obliged to resign not only as leader of the party but as Premier of the province.

Douglas believed in this procedure. He had been one of those early CCF members elected to Ottawa who signed an agreement to resign, placing it in the hands of his constituency executive; the "power of recall". If he had displeased them, they were empowered to call a convention to replace him.

The CCF policy-making process worked in Saskatchewan, but met with difficulty elsewhere. Speaking of the national party Young says:

> . . . members had to be found and kept. It was not difficult to sustain this kind of organization in Saskatchewan, but elsewhere there was not the same social basis for it. It assumed a high level of political orientation and interest on the part of a large portion of the Canadian population, and yet the only evidence for the assumption was the interest shown in the West during the twenties and thirties. Only those people who were prepared to involve themselves wholeheartedly in politics became active CCF members and these people were not, as a rule, typical of the Canadian electorate except in Saskatchewan. The Saskatchewan conventions have been described as 'a representative gathering of the province' and those in Manitoba and Ontario – and one could add British Columbia – as more 'like meetings of special interest groups, sprinked with malcontents and radicals.'[14]

Young, as mentioned earlier, found the people of Saskatchewan almost incomprehensible, and ignored them for the most part in his examination of the CCF party as a whole.

Another writer, Desmond Morton, speaks in the same vein: ". . . the CCF in Saskatchewan managed to maintain the unique grassroots organization which had carried it to power and, probably to a greater degree than any other democratic socialist party, the CCF in government remained accountable to its members and supporters."[15]

In November 1944, the Saskatchewan CCF party had 25,180 members, according to provincial office records. The total population of the province was less than 900,000.

After discussions between Douglas, the party president, Dr. Carlyle King (then as now with the University of Saskatchewan), and others, a Legislative Advisory Committee was set up by the party's provincial council. It was empowered to meet with the caucus. A report by King to the provincial council on December 2, 1946, notes for example that the Committee had met and prepared recommendations for caucus on provision for the physically incapacitated; reducing government insurance rates on old trucks; developing the sodium sulphate industry under government ownership; and selling the products of government industry (a) direct to retailers or (b) by mail order.

Douglas said,

> Before we took office, we discussed how we would keep the government and the party on parallel lines – social democratic governments in almost every country in the world start out together but end up

going in different directions. We amended the constitution to require the setting up of a Legislative Advisory Committee by the provincial council. It would report back to the Council which reported back to the Convention.

The Committee had five members, including the president and vice president. Some of them always sat in with caucus when we were preparing the budget, or drafting the Speech from the Throne. They took those drafts to the Council, on which there were representatives from every constituency in the province. *Yes, before the budget was released*. I didn't believe that nonsense about having to fire the Minister of Finance because he's told people about the budget. If we were going to put on a tax from which somebody could make some money, of course we wouldn't tell them. But in a province like Saskatchewan there was no need for that. You were either going to raise the income tax or sales tax or property tax or liquor tax, or borrow large sums – why not discuss it with people?

We would say, 'Here are the various programs that need to be improved. Here is the cost. Now, on the revenue side – shall we raise this tax? What do you think?'

Only once in all that time did we have a 'leak'. It was an M.L.A., not one of the Council members. The manager of Simpsons phoned me and said, 'Somebody's left a document and I'm looking it over. I'm sure it must be a confidential document.' I said, 'It certainly is. Thank you.' I sent someone over to get it and it was the outline of the budget. After that I numbered the copies, so if one turned up we'd know who dropped it.

The system had two advantages. The Council had representatives from all over the province, and they were identified with the CCF in their communities, so they had to know what we were going to do and why. Then when a new tax was introduced and the neighbours started phoning, they could say, 'It's because we plan to do this and this.' It's not fair to your people to throw facts out to them through the media, without any prior explanation.

And second, it gave us a reaction. If those people said, 'No way!' We'd say, 'That's fine. Let's vote on it.' You put the responsibility back on them.

The great mistake governments make, and socialist governments are no exception, is that we keep talking about things we'll do for people, without saying that somebody's got to pay for it. As a socialist you'd have no objection to paying for it – but you want the burden of payment to be equitably distributed.

I remember discussing this with Harold Wilson and he said they ought to be doing it in the Labour Party.

After conventions the Legislative Advisory Committee went over the resolutions that had been passed with the Cabinet, before each session. We had to account to them. If we couldn't do things in full, we had to justify the changes.

At party conventions the members separated into panels to debate the policies of their choice, and to each panel was assigned the appropriate cabinet minister, to explain and listen and discuss. In June 1945 a letter from the provincial secretary to the premier set out the panels for the coming convention, commenting that the "Ministers will no doubt be in attendance." The five panels were: Agriculture and Cooperatives (Hon. L. F. McIntosh); Rehabilitation and Labour (Sturdy and Williams); Municipal Affairs, Natural Resources, and Highways (Brockelbank, Phelps, J. T. Douglas); Health, Social Welfare, and Education (T. C. Douglas, Valleau, Lloyd); Legal, Taxes, and National and International Affairs (Corman, Fines).

Evelyn Eager described the process:

The CCF during the Douglas regime in Saskatchewan achieved a unique juxtaposition of two opposing principles: the operation of party democracy while in power and adherence to the traditions of parliamentary government." Douglas, in an address to the 1953 convention, was quoted as saying, "It should never be forgotten that CCF provincial policies are made here by this sovereign body and it is to this convention that your elected members must report regarding the progress they have made in carrying out the policies you have laid down. . . ."

Against this intensity of feeling (for party control), any discernible effort in 1944 and succeeding years to diminish rank-and-file control could have served only to tear the party apart. To maintain the form and reality of party democracy sufficiently to satisfy the doctrinaire and the suspicious, while at the same time to dilute it enough to enable a strong and independent government to function, represented a rare and delicate feat of political accomplishment.

Furthermore, this was essentially the achievement of one man, Mr. Douglas. He satisfied both the doctrinaire and the realist by upholding the principle of party control of government . . . His strategy to prevent conflict between party and government was simply to keep them moving in parallel lines, without sufficient divergence in policy for them to clash. The tactics employed were mutual consultation and explanation. . . .

This dependence on one man's skill establishes high requirements for succeeding leaders.[16]

Tim Lee, as executive assistant, heartily endorsed this process. "The party was quite vigorous and effective. Tommy and the Caucus and the Cabinet were highly responsive to it – it was one of the measures of their success."

It may have made for harmony between a vigorous government and an equally determined party. But was it in fact democracy at work? Douglas said, "Of course the Liberals and Conservatives said the party was running the province, and under the British system of government only the government did this. But I said, 'This is not just an ordinary political party. This is a democratic socialist movement – not just socialist, but democratic. And the people are going to have some input.' "

Evelyn Eager saw a "paradox" but no basic conflict in the elected government's responsibility to the people at large and also to the party. Within the legislative chamber, the government was still subject to the will of all the elected members, and governed only by consent of the majority. And if it took its cues from an organization with 25,000 members – always open and on the search for new members – it was as broad a base as any governing power could look for. "The safeguard against this exclusiveness was the presence within the party of political realists who, whether from principle or expediency, kept a shrewd political eye on those who outnumbered avowed party supporters many times over."[17]

Which begs the question. The invitation to membership, with a real input to government policy, is an invitation to "join if you think as we do". Left outside was the other Saskatchewan, the anti-socialist Saskatchewan. The polarization within the province was not dispelled by CCF methods, but intensified. Only, for the time being, the socialists were the majority and were mindful not to rile too seriously that other group, who would never admit they were benefiting by anything that Douglas did.

The men Douglas chose as ministers included several of outstanding ability. His first approach had been to George Williams, who served as Agriculture Minister for a few months until his death. Clarence Fines came in immediately as Provincial Treasurer and as the minister in charge of government organization. "The hero of the civil service," Tim Lee described him. "He was organized, systematic, thorough, fair – and then decisive, and then communicative."

A former alderman who had interested himself in Regina's financing, Fines had no extensive training or experience for his portfolio, but a ready aptitude. He was admired as a "wizard" for his handling of Saskatchewan's treasury, a somewhat exaggerated claim that indicates the bafflement, not to say disapproval, with which many regarded the success of an avowed socialist in the traditional money markets. But he did operate with panache.

"My first job was to build up Saskatchewan's credit to finance our programs," Fines said. "The province hadn't been able to borrow a nickel since 1932.

"I had some Victory Bonds of my own, and I borrowed $15,000 from the bank. I made it very clear to all within hearing that I wanted the money to buy *Saskatchewan* bonds. Then I went to three of the leading investment dealers and bought the bonds. It worked. The news was flashed to eastern Canada."

Douglas recalled: "He said to me, 'Those bonds that are now at 83 to 84 cents are going to be a bargain. I'm going to buy some myself. Why don't you go down to the bank and borrow $50,000?' I said, 'Clarence, I was raised in a Scottish home where we never in our lives bought anything until my mother had the money in the sugar bowl to go and pay for it. I wouldn't sleep nights if I owed the bank $50,000.' But he went ahead, and he went on the radio urging school boards and municipalities to buy up those bonds, because they were going to go up.

"Then we took a trip Down East."

"The financiers were scared to death at first." Fines related. "One of the first things I had to do was get Down East to try to reassure them. Tommy Douglas came with me, to Toronto, Montreal, and New York. I'll never forget some of them. I visited the Prudential Insurance Company, I told them I'd come because they had five or six million dollars in Saskatchewan bonds, and I wanted to assure them that those bonds would be repaid with interest. They said, 'You're mistaken, Mr. Fines. We did have five million in them. At present, we haven't any, When you people were elected, we sold them.'

"I said, 'I resent that, not as provincial treasurer but as an individual. I had some insurance policies with your company and I had hoped you were looking after investments better than that.' They sold at about 92 cents on the dollar. A year later the bonds were 102."

"We had the highest per capita debt in Canada. We were 178 million dollars in debt. When we left office it was down to 18 million, and the next year it was paid off entirely from our sinking funds. The province has been free of debt ever since.

"We did it by setting aside ten percent of the annual budget to retire debts as they came due. It was hard, but we did it."

The tough policy adopted was to put money "in the sugar bowl" for public works that were non-revenue-producing. Only developments which would generate revenue were undertaken with borrowed money. Schools, hospitals and roads had to be paid for out of current taxes – there was to be no more of the financial quagmire which saw the province still loaded with debt for old buildings that had been paid for two or three times in terms of their original value.

After 1947 Fines was in charge of the Government Finance Office, the holding company for all crown corporations. By 1960 the biggest of these, the Saskatchewan Power Corporation, was worth $314 million and Government Telephones worth $92.5 million. Other corporations under the umbrella were the Saskatchewan Government Airways, the Timber Board, the Fur Marketing Board, the Government Insurance Office, the Saskatchewan Transportation (bus) Company, and a variety of others.

"People said he wasn't a socialist," Douglas said. "but he helped in taking over all the small power corporations in Saskatchewan, and he put the Corporation into natural gas: Saskatchewan is still the only place in Canada where the government is the sole purchaser and distributor of natural gas. He got us into the steel industry. Nobody thought we could have a steel industry in Saskatchewan!"

The Interprovincial Steel and Pipe Company, located in Regina, makes pipe, among other products, from scrap. One of the biggest western industries, it has thousands of people on the payroll. It remains part private, part public, financed originally with the help of a government guarantee of ten million dollars – for which the company handed over 140,000 shares of common stock.

Fines had a cool image, a pale oval face, dark hair brushed smooth to his head, dark eyes that were hard to the interrogator, with a tendency to amusement, dapper in appearance, a man who might be expected to wear rings, tie-pins, cuff-links, and well-shined shoes. He wore a neat bow tie in early photographs, but his most flamboyant bit of haberdashery was the salmon pink brocade tie he sported on budget day. For sixteen years he brought in a budget with a surplus, and his signal to the press that he had "done it again" was the eye-popping tie, which featured a design of cornucopias spilling forth fruits and sweetmeats. It had been purchased when the Atlantic Charter's "Four Freedoms" had brought on a rash of pictorial images, including ties, and this one represented "Freedom from Want".

When Fines retired in 1960 the *Leader-Post* was cautiously complimentary about his most recent $148 million budget. "This is the same Mr. Fines who shocked the province with the audacity of a $40 million budget in 1945 and a prediction that some day, before long, provincial revenues and spending would be on the order of $60 million."

Fines became the most controversial of the Douglas ministers. When he retired at the age of fifty-five to enjoy a private life, he was a wealthy man, though perhaps not as wealthy as rumour and his own confident manner would suggest. He had acquired his wealth by shrewd investment in the stock market; he bragged that he never sold for less than he bought throughout those years. Inevitably, (in Saskatchewan) there was talk of improper use of his government position, but no accusations were ever made and the suggestion was denied with some heat by everyone interviewed on the subject.

John H. Brockelbank first took on the Department of Municipal Affairs, later of Natural Resources. Universally admired as tough, honest, and fearless, he was one of the great assets of the Douglas ministry. Particularly in the latter post, when the discovery of oil and some minerals brought a swarm of fly-by-night promoters to the province, his solid sense undercut blown-up expectations and kept the government calmly on course. With rugged features, thick dark hair, a slight stoop, and deliberately "backwoods" speech, he was the minister described by David

Lewis as "a really remarkable man" and by T. H. McLeod as "a very rare person; there aren't too many of him around". His signature in the government files is attached to memos such as one disclaiming responsibility for air travel by cabinet ministers at election time, and referring the account, firmly, to party headquarters. And he appears to have pulled the government out of the woods on a grandiose semi-commitment of vast resource rights to a private company in the north of the province.

The "Foxy Grandpa" of the cabinet was Jack Corman. Brought into the ministry because he represented the city of Moose Jaw, where he had been mayor for a number of years, Corman was, as the only lawyer, promptly handed the key post of Attorney-General. As Attorney-General he was eulogized by CCF'ers for the way he "outfoxed" city-slick legal adversaries, but his other major contribution to the Douglas team was political sagacity. Douglas said,

> He would put on his straw boater and take his cane and amble up and down the main streets of Moose Jaw, and he would know more about how people thought on any particular issue than the Gallup Poll. He was responsible for a lot of our success in the first two years because of what he kept us from doing. Somebody would bring in some great idea, quote a lot of statistics and argue for a long time, and Jack would sit there puffing on his cigar and then say, 'If I were Joe Lunchpail I would want to know this and this.' And he'd just puncture the whole thing.

Corman was a popular radio broadcaster on behalf of the government. His talks generally ended: "You are born either a Liberal or a Conservative, but you have to think your way into the CCF." He claimed that all Liberals are double jointed so they can sit on the fence and keep an ear to the ground. On January 2, 1948, he told his radio audience, after refuting the standard Liberal charges of dictatorship and regimentation; "Our Cabinet meetings are informal affairs. I understand that at Ottawa ministers before taking their seats bow low from the waist and say, 'Good morning Mr. Prime Minister' to Mackenzie King. If any of us tried that on Tommy Douglas he would think we had a stomach ache."

After a breezy run-down of cabinet posts he concluded with an outrageous disclaimer: "Tommy . . . knows people and human nature; he loves people and wants to help them; he could no more be a dictator than could the great Saviour of mankind."

The one minister Douglas sought out before the election was Woodrow Lloyd, at that time president of the Saskatchewan Teachers' Federation. Mindful of the local organization's pride in its autonomy he approached with caution.

> I went up to see the executive of the Biggar constituency in 1943. I asked if they had any candidates in mind for their nomination con-

vention and they named a couple of big farmers. So I said, 'I've got a problem,' and looked kind of helpless. They said, 'Anything we can do Tommy?' I said, 'I don't know. I've been visiting all the constituencies and I have farmer candidates coming out of my ears. I don't know where I'd find a minister of education if we won the election.' They asked if I had anybody in mind and I said, 'There's a fellow who's very well thought of. He's only twenty-seven or twenty-eight but he's been head of our task force on education.' They asked where he was, and I said, 'He's just come to Biggar. He's the high school principal.' And then I dropped it. About four nights later they approached him to run.

If I'd told them I want you to nominate Woodrow Lloyd they'd have told me to go to hell. But I left it with them. And later I used to kid Woodrow about doing that spadework for him.

The occasions when the Premier interfered with the prerogatives of the local organizations were rare. He was lucky to find among his forty-seven locally-elected members a cabinet that functioned, as well as that one did.

A standout from the generally harmonious group was Joe Phelps, who became the first Minister of Natural Resources. He was an impetuous man who stomped into town in high boots from his expeditions in the north, needled Fines for new program money, and flared into temper over alleged breaches of the socialist faith. He was impatient with the parcel of civil servants he had inherited, and at one cabinet meeting when he was forbidden to chuck them all out he threatened to rent a room downtown, crowd them all in with one blank piece of paper a day, and run his own show elsewhere.

Eleanor McKinnon saw Joe Phelps as a fearsome presence. She recalled an occasion when Douglas became worried about interruptions during the serious planning sessions the cabinet was holding. (Every fall there was a revision of one-year and five-year plans.) The ministers had gathered in the Council Chamber and Eleanor had instructions to hold all messages. "But Joe wheeled in, late, and hung up his coat telling me, 'I'm expecting an important call. Let me know the moment it comes.' So it came, and I went in and whispered to Phelps. Tommy beckoned to me and said, 'I told you not to call anyone out.' I just said, 'I know you did, but I'm much more afraid of him than I am of you.'"

There was some relief when Phelps did not make it back to Regina at the 1948 election, but Douglas was well aware of his value as a farm leader and at a later date he urged him, unsuccessfully, to run against Gardiner.

Douglas created three new departments: Labour, Welfare, and Cooperatives. O. W. Valleau, a handsome silver-haired farmer from Melfort headed Welfare and "Lochy" McIntosh from Prince Albert got

Cooperatives. There was one obvious choice for Labour, Charles C. Williams, mayor of Regina, who was a former telegrapher. Williams was the only minister who has been described as inadequate for his job, and he was shored up by a succession of carefully chosen deputy ministers whom Williams regarded with suspicion. In spite of this Williams retained a high popularity in Regina and topped the polls at each successive election.

John H. Sturdy took on a Reconstruction and Rehabitation Ministry, a super-scrounging enterprise to turn the redundant equipment of the armed forces to peacetime community use. Even before the war ended he was in Ottawa asking C. D. Howe where to apply with a bid for the extensive inventories at the air bases in Saskatchewan and in the north, along the Alaska highway. Douglas followed up that visit with a letter to Mackenzie King:

> The feeling is abroad that some war materials are already being sold to private individuals and corporations. Mechanical equipment has been moved to Winnipeg . . . army trucks have been seen in second-hand car lots. . . .
> A great many airports have been closed on the prairies. Most of those airports have excellent hospital equipment, road machinery and some very fine buildings, also quantities of training planes, army trucks and other mechanical equipment.[18]

The Canadian taxpayer had already paid for it; why should a private entrepreneur move in to buy the stuff for a song and resell it to the public? Sturdy purchased all of the war materials located in Saskatchewan, plus as much more as he could lay his hands on. Howe charged him six to eight per cent of the assessed value. What the provincial government was unable to use, it turned over to municipalities, school boards, hospitals, and non-profit community groups at ten per cent of its value. Little Saskatchewan towns got $25,000 fire engines for $2,500. The metal airforce hangar became the architectural norm for community skating rinks. Paint spraying outfits, manned by veterans, brightened 80,000 farms.

Toby Nollet took over Agriculture. "I never pay much attention to so-called 'left wing' and 'right wing'," Douglas said. "It's mostly rhetoric. I suppose Toby was our most vociferous socialist. Sometimes he wasn't too clear on details, but fortunately he had a great respect for Corman's judgment."

Jack Douglas became Minister of Highways. At later stages new men who came in were Robert Walker as Attorney General after Corman's retirement, Bill Davies in Public Works and briefly in Health, and Allan Blakeney, in 1960, as Minister of Education. Blakeney, a Nova Scotia lawyer, had been brought to Saskatchewan first to untangle a snarled situation in resource development as Commissioner of Securities and then, under Fines, to head the Finance Office. He was persuaded to run in the 1960 election, served under Douglas and Lloyd, and in 1971 led the party (now the NDP) back to power as Premier.

"One of the first things we did in cabinet was to knock $1000 off our salaries, from $7000 down to $6000," Fines said. "I suppose it was the stupidest thing we ever did, but I was one of those who advocated it.

"The cabinet was a good cross-section of people. Average people with a lot of enthusiasm and devotion. We had a vision; that made the difference."

Over this group Douglas presided with finesse. "His leadership was beyond dispute. No challengers. No questioners," T. H. McLeod said.

If Douglas is to be faulted in his management of the administration, it must be on the basis of his hesitation in dispensing with the services of people who turned out to be wrong for the job. A few "weirdies" wandered into the government service, self-styled "adult educationists", for example, who wanted to reshape the thinking of the people along proper lines, and it took some time to send them on their way. "In decisions affecting other persons, he slowed down considerably. He lacked the killer instinct that people like Mackenzie King were famous for. He never had it," McLeod said.

Tim Lee, executive assistant, said, "He was an ultra-democrat. When I was drawing up the agenda for cabinet meetings I put the items down in the order they came in – very rarely did I change them. Tommy never rearranged them. *In cabinet* they might decide to rearrange them if it was needed, to deal first with urgent problems."

Bill Davies thought Douglas demanded a lot of his ministers. They were given the best staff he could provide, and they were expected to produce. The premier himself had extraordinary energy and ability to get things done. "He was moving all the time."

Douglas had the intellect, nimble yet retentive, to keep ahead of a vast daily agenda. His staff was awed and often hard-pressed, but inspired. Blakeney saw him as uniquely an "energizer".

> I saw him as a truly great leader. He had a quick mind, able to assimilate substantial bodies of fairly technical information with speed. He had very strong views of essential right and wrong. And he was a great motivator of people.
>
> I used to hear people around the government say, 'What are we doing all this for?' Working night and day as they habitually did around here. And one would say 'Go and hear Tommy and get your batteries recharged.'

"If someone had wanted to replace me it wouldn't have broken my heart," Douglas said. "I never relished being able to say to this man 'Come' and to that man 'Go'. We were a group of happy warriors. People

150

talk of an efficient office – I want a happy office. We had that, at that time."

In Ottawa there is in 1974 a group of perhaps a dozen and a half very senior federal executives who have dubbed themselves "the Saskatchewan Mafia". They are ex-civil servants of the Douglas regime, and they are friends still, united by a bond that has to do with an epoch they remember somewhat wistfully as "a golden time". Three of them are now deputy ministers in the federal administration, others hold senior directive posts.

Thomas H. McLeod, now a senior administrator in the federal Public Service Commission, had grown up in Weyburn and had joined the boys' club which Douglas, as minister of the Baptist church, had organized. The program consisted of one sports night, one night for debate and public speaking, weekly. McLeod, while he was a high school student, took meetings for Douglas in the 1935 campaign which he vividly remembers. Later he went on to university and was teaching at Brandon when the 1944 election campaign took him back to Saskatchewan.

The morning after that triumphant night he took a visiting Brandon friend with him to call on Douglas. The introductions and congratulations were scarcely done when Douglas asked, "How would you like to work for the new government?" McLeod made a rather tentative indication of assent. "That's fortunate," said Douglas. "I wired your resignation to the President of Brandon College this morning."

Within forty-eight hours McLeod was at work in the old CCF office in downtown Regina. The swearing-in ceremony was scheduled for July 10. He began developing position papers for the first cabinet meeting, "with a chart the size of a barn wall". He acted first as economic advisor to the cabinet, later as deputy minister to the Provincial Treasurer.

McLeod was instrumental in recruiting a number of people who proved their value, Tom Shoyama, Meyer Brownstone, Al Johnston, Tim Lee, and a list of others. Shoyama had just been mustered out of the Canadian Intelligence Corps with the rank of sergeant when he visited a friend, George Tamaki, in Regina, and met McLeod. He was persuaded to join the Saskatchewan Planning Board.

Besides the incentive of freedom to innovate within a new government, these young men were offered an early sabbatical at half pay, in return for a pledge of two years' employment. It was a radical idea thirty years ago, though more familiar today. Under Saskatchewan government auspices a half dozen keen young professionals attended Harvard, McGill, or Wisconsin, and returned to Regina, most of them to work for extended terms with the government. Ken Bryden was also recruited in Ottawa to serve as Deputy Minister of Labour, and George Cadbury, an older man, at the peak of his career but entranced by the Saskatchewan experiment, went in at David Lewis' suggestion to act as head of the Planning Board.

When Walter Gordon travelled Canada as head of the Royal Commission on Canada's Economic Prospects in 1955, he told an Ottawa acquaintance that the best civil service in Canada was at Regina.

"The best tribute they could have," Douglas said, "was that when the Liberals took over here in 1964 and Thatcher fired some and others quit, about seventy of them were grabbed by the Liberals in Ottawa."

Douglas gave all Saskatchewan civil servants bargaining rights, inviting them to form a union, instead of their "tea party and bowling club" Association. Job classification, superannuation, promotions, salaries, and conditions of work all became negotiable. It was many years later that other Canadian public servants secured similar rights.

Douglas' secretary, Eleanor McKinnon, was the daughter of a Weyburn merchant, and was secretary to Dr. Campbell, superintendent of the Weyburn Mental Hospital in 1944 when Douglas began casting about desperately for someone to manage his office. "No one knows what it means to have someone who can deal with things intelligently," he said gratefully, recalling the chaos of the first few weeks without Eleanor. She worked for him throughout the sixteen years of his term of office in Regina and moved to Ottawa when he became leader of the NDP. Eleanor said,

> There was never a *normal* working day. You'd start in at 8:30, expecting to get a lot done. By nine the phones were ringing. . . .
>
> But every day I admired him a little bit more. He never criticized his colleagues, or any of the people he worked with. He never nagged after he asked you to do something.
>
> His itinerary was killing. He never drank coffee during the day. He got more mileage out of the oatmeal Irma served him in the morning, and his poached egg at noon. If he had to go without a meal, out in the country somewhere, he had a double milk shake with a raw egg in it.

She recounts delightful stories.

> Things were always happening. Once returning from a Federal-Provincial Conference, TCA called Tommy and me for pre-boarding. I asked Tommy how he managed that. He said he wanted us to get aboard so he could start some dictation, so he told the stewardess he was escorting a mental patient back to Weyburn.
>
> I was always having trouble with *other* Tommy Douglases! There was one in Weyburn who was the sanitary inspector. One day Tommy got a phone call from an outraged party in Weyburn blasting him for the poor burial job that had been done the day before – the carcass of the horse wasn't covered . . . It took a few minutes for Tommy to get that cleared up, especially since he had preached a funeral service in Weyburn just previously.

And once there was a mix-up in Calgary. The CCF secretary phoned me and asked if Tommy was there, and I said, no, he was in Europe. Liesemer said he *thought* there was something wrong . . . An operator had connected him with a Tommy Douglas somewhere in B.C., and he had asked the chap to be guest speaker at their banquet, and it seemed to take him a long time to decide, but then he said he guessed he could. I got Lochy McIntosh to go in place of Tommy, and I hope Liesemer got in touch with that B.C. fellow. . . .

Once Tommy had to ride a horse in a parade. He got a particularly wild one, and he was no more good on a horse! But he managed alright, and we asked him how he did it. He said he just leaned down and whispered to the horse that if he didn't behave he'd get sent to our horsemeat plant at Swift Current. We *laughed* . . . "

There was no question in Eleanor's mind that Douglas' office was the "happy" place he wanted it to be.

The subject of political patronage in the civil service was never entirely free of argument. Brockelbank said,

Not many civil servants had to go. A few ran before they saw us coming. There were some non-supporters who stayed, and I got a little hell from our own people for keeping them on, but I'm still convinced to this day that they got their work done and kept their noses clean. Vote how you like, but don't prejudice your work by political action.

I caught a few things going on. For example, in one northern settlement I got complaints that a Métis family was getting relief, and the officer of the department had the woman come in and do his washing and paid her with the relief ticket. I investigated personally with an interpreter. I asked the woman how much she got for relief, and she told me, and then I asked her how much she got for her work. She said, 'I get my relief for doing that.' So he was another one who got it.

Jack Sturdy took a strict position on the subject of patronage. In a memo to Douglas in regard to a young man who put in a claim for a job, Sturdy wrote, "I have been connected with the movement since its inception, and never at any time have I informed anyone that he would be given any position if and when I was elected."[19]

It was Sturdy's opinion that ideology took second place: "It's a damned sight easier to make a socialist out of an engineer than an engineer out of a socialist," he once told Douglas.

But there were complaints from CCF'ers, especially after a loss of seats in the 1948 election.

Another reason we lost votes is, too many ungrateful Liberals working in and for our CCF government. They are undermining our good cause. I have listened to you speak many, many times, Mr. Douglas, as far back as the very early thirties. I remember in those days and again in 1944, you said that any civil servant that done his work efficiently and honestly, need not fear being fired. Quite fair – But we have had over four years of CCF government now, and we have enjoyed it, but we find Liberals still working for the CCF government, and who are doing dirty work against the CCF government! I think four years are plenty long enough to be fair with them?[20]

In an article published in 1968, C. E. S. Franks, former Assistant Clerk of the Saskatchewan Legislative Assembly and later on the faculty of Political Studies at Queen's University, wrote of the long tradition of political patronage in the province:

In the first six months after the Liberals returned to power in 1934, for example, over one-tenth of the public servants either resigned, were dismissed, or were under notice of dismissal. . . .

To implement its programs and carry out its reforms the CCF Government greatly increased the size, quality, and administrative competence of the public service. The incidence of patronage was reduced . . . . The change from CCF to Liberal government (in 1964) meant almost as significant a change to the public service as that of 1934. However, most of the public servants who left (and most left voluntarily) were in the senior ranks rather than the lower ones which are normally considered as patronage appointments. The Treasury Department, for instance, lost almost its entire budget and administrative analysis groups, both of which had contributed to the analysis on which the plans for reforming the organization of financial administration had been based. Largely, the exodus of senior public servants was not because they were patronage appointments, but because the Liberal Government had a quite different attitude towards professionalism in the public service and planning in government. In comparison, the CCF Government in 1944 had kept many of the old Liberal appointments, although this had slowed down if not handicapped the implementation of its program of reform.[21]

Where did the backbencher, the ordinary elected M.L.A., fit into the power picture? Beatrice Trew, the only woman Member who sat in the first Assembly, from 1944 to 1948, gave this account:

We met in caucus almost every morning, and often evenings. We were given every bill in draft form after we had agreed to the cabinet proposal to bring it in. We went over it clause by clause and after it was amended or agreed to it was then prepared for the House and we went over it again. We were free to oppose any part or all of it in the House as long as we told caucus we were going to.

154

For instance I moved an amendment to an Act which had failed to exclude 'discrimination on account of sex or marital status' in the employment practices of the civil service. I was really ashamed of our government's attitude that time. There was a hue and cry against married women working. . . .

Each cabinet minister had an advisory committee of private members – we could choose. I acted on Natural Resources, Social Welfare and Health. Some ministers made more use of their committees than others. On the whole I felt these committees were not of much use. Even then, the expert advisors were taking over from the private member. We didn't mind it so much for there was opportunity in caucus. . . .

The private members also proposed resolutions and if accepted by caucus then prepared their speeches on them. We were expected to speak either on the Throne Speech debate or Budget. Because of our numbers we were not encouraged to speak on both.

Then of course we all had lots of correspondence from our constituents and problems to take up for them with various ministers or departments.

I was secretary of caucus, and on several Standing Committees of the House, so I was very busy, but so were most backbenchers of that House. You must remember we were bringing in some far-reaching new legislation and we all felt we were its authors, not only the Cabinet.[22]

Premier Douglas was a slight, quick-paced man of thirty-nine when he set the CCF government in motion. His height was a modest five-foot-six; his weight varied from one hundred forty-five pounds in summer to one hundred forty-eight in winter. His light brown curling hair rose in an obstinate lock above his high forehead, the features were small, the nose a pug, the mouth laughing. He seldom wore a hat, his suits were fastidious but not extravagant. When weather and his leg permitted, he walked from his Angus Crescent home to the legislative building, fortified with oatmeal porridge. Usually he took lunch – a poached egg – in the civil servants' cafeteria, joining the queue.

At night there was dinner at home, and there Irma and his two daughters provided the quiet he needed. They seldom entertained. Douglas had been seeing too many people all day to welcome visitors.

Joan, their second child, was six years younger than Shirley, quieter by nature, and closer to her mother. Shirley adored her father, thought other girls' lives were dull, and fought political battles among her peers. Their neighbourhood was, as luck would have it, Liberal. Irma counselled Shirley to ignore the remarks of other children, and regretted her helplessness to defend her daughters. Politics in Saskatchewan was a partisan affair, even in the schoolyard.

Their happiest times were at the simple cottage they owned at Carlyle Lake. Joan remembered the annual first launching of a massive rowboat, and picking berries, though sometimes they bought the berries the Indians brought to the door. The lake lies within an Indian reserve, and was leased by the town, but in later years run by the band council. They seldom saw the Indians, except when they brought berries, and they rather liked a story that a chief had died in the lake, his heart had been buried on nearby Heart Mountain, and the water after that was shunned by his people. "But perhaps," said Joan, "they only stayed away because of the white cottagers."

"Dad seldom talked about politics at home," Joan said. "He read mystery stories, or walked in the evening at the cottage. He wasn't interested in cards. He drank very little, and both Mother and he watched their diets – they didn't like big meals. He has oatmeal every morning forever! He doesn't worry about his health, but he has a respect for keeping fit."

Almost every fall Douglas had a bout of osteomyelitis, which sometimes took him to hospital, or to bed at home. He stayed in bed with bad grace. His response to solicitous letters after these attacks was a brisk, "Am now completely well, and . . . ". On to the next day's work.

His doctor once advised a hobby, a suggestion which baffled him, until Clarence Fines hit on the idea of a mink farm as a joint enterprise. They purchased an establishment close to Regina, and spent a few days banging together wooden cages and planning the biological succession of their minks. "Sometimes I think we'd get two males in a cage", Douglas said. In any case it was not a profitable hobby, and they sold it presently at a loss of about a thousand dollars.

Their next project was an interest in a drive-in Theatre Under the Stars, a first in Regina. Unfortunately a co-owner, Phil Bodnoff, was discovered by the Liberal Opposition to have formerly arranged a government loan for another venture, and there was a row in the legislature until Douglas and Fines sold out. The Opposition referred to the Theatre Under the Stars as the "Premier's passion pit". Douglas said it was healthy outdoor entertainment, where families could go for an evening, and it always showed religious films on Sundays.

These brief adventures were apparently Douglas' only efforts to seek out leisure time activity. Nor did he find time for close friendship. Of his colleagues each was inclined to say, "I don't know him very well personally."

He was well aware of the need to do what the public expected of him, but it is hard to regard him as vain.

There are too many instances when he was obviously totally unaware of his own importance. Yet he has a sense of human dignity – and of his own dignity.

I've never heard Tommy talking about his rights, never once, his particular *right* to do anything. His interest is in the rights of other people, and this is his way of expressing himself. If you were to accuse him to being 'unselfish' he wouldn't know what you were talking about. It isn't part of his lexicon. Unselfishness means having some estimation of his own rights, which he hasn't got! It isn't there. In this way he is a very uncharacteristic kind of person.

Tommy McLeod was musing about the man who in Saskatchewan, "had a million friends, but not very many really close." He said, "He's a very proud man. That's a Scottish characteristic – they're not an open people. Self-contained, reluctant to let their guard down. Tommy certainly had that whole thing ingrained in him. Don't argue with where God had put you. Accept that as a fact and move on."

His lack of personal vanity left him free to pursue social objectives with only secondary attention to the antagonisms that are bound to be set in motion. It was this spirit that distinguished the CCF regime, kept the staff working eighteen hours at a stretch, kept cabinet and party moving "in parallel lines", kept the private members pulling together, kept the public impressed and applauding, kept his personal life subordinate to his job.

Tim Lee, considering it all in his Toronto living room in 1974, said,

His approach is valid.

It is worth it to pursue the Tommy Douglas method – to make social, economic and political policy paramount. To set goals and proceed toward them whether you risk losing public office or not. I have no patience with people who say the primary job is to gain office, the second is to retain office, and the third is to preserve as many of your policies within the framework of the first two as you possibly can. I reject that. Number Three is more important. That's what I learned from Tommy Douglas. . . .

That's his strength. That's the measure of that man.

Chapter Eleven
Premier 1: Farm Politics

The cyclone that ripped through the town of Kamsack on August 15, 1944 provided a roaring start and an opportunity for the government to turn in a virtuoso, a *bravura* performance. The ministers were still settling in and learning the first names of their deputies. McLeod's big chart was on the wall. Innumerable conferences were putting together the seventy-odd pieces of legislation slated for enactment before Christmas. When the news of Kamsack's devastation hit Regina the Executive Council chamber was turned into Emergency Measures Organization (EMO) headquarters. Charlie Williams, in what may have been his finest hour, set up telegraph equipment in the chamber and manned it for three days around the clock. Sturdy had National Defence send in the army; emergency relief kitchens materialized overnight; the premier took to the radio to ask for private contributions to match government aid; and Chief Justice Martin was appointed head of a relief fund. Douglas wired C. D. Howe for war-scarce building materials, got carloads en route to Vancouver rerouted to Kamsack. Kamsack was rebuilt in jig time, the citizens were compensated for losses, there was even a surplus in the fund after the dust settled which, after due deliberation, was turned over to the money-starved University of Saskatchewan.

But the cyclone was only part of the general commotion. The official opposition behaved as though a natural calamity of first magnitude had befallen the province.

T. H. McLeod said,

> In 1944 when there were only five Liberals elected they were sure that the design of the Almighty had been frustrated and all the world should resent that fact. The whole thing had an unreal atmosphere for quite a period of time. It is a national characteristic of the Liberal party, the belief that it is born to govern, and when they are not governing then society is in the hands of the devil. It's almost a theology with them.
>
> At times, they are almost frightening people. Many of us felt that if there was a kind of nascent, authoritarian, quasi-fascist element in society, it was to be found in that particular group. It purported to be on the side of business, yet I'm convinced that the attitudes of the

more substantial business community would be far to the left of them. A red-neck element.

Douglas used the same phrase. He said, "The Liberals in Saskatchewan represent the right wing of the party in Canada. Farther right than the Conservatives. They are not liberals at all in the classical sense, they're reactionary rednecks."

The legislative chamber was uninterrupted bedlam. A. T. Proctor, who had been Liberal Minister of Highways, took one occasion to call Douglas a "stinking skunk" and was escorted from the chamber when he refused to withdraw the remark.

Douglas said,

That particular row arose when we found some of the old files, and revealed their contents in the House. One had a letter of instruction to a government field officer telling him to 'put the heat on' to get the Liberal vote, or take the consequences. Another pointed to some strange transactions in the manufacture of the purple dye we used in Saskatchewan to identify the cheaper gas used for farm equipment. We wired the company for their correspondence file and we discovered there was a dummy company, existing on paper only, operating between the manufacturer and the government and taking a mark-up which went into Liberal party coffers.

In my own office the filing cabinets were empty, absolutely stripped bare. We couldn't believe it. Even the invitation to attend the federal-provincial conference on reconstruction was missing. I had to write Mackenzie King for another copy of the agenda.

They were not gracious losers. I met Dr. Uhrich shortly after we took office and I asked him if he had any good advice for me as Minister of Health. He said, 'You made all the promises, you know all the answers, so you go ahead and see how you make out.'

Few governments have assumed office with legislative plans so well in place. The party had during the previous year set up task forces under chairmen who, in many instances, became the cabinet members. Legislative proposals had been studiously examined by the party's provincial council and even by a special meeting of the CCF national executive the previous December. Many bills were close to a final draft even before the election was called. Two more departments, Welfare and Cooperatives, were immediately established under separate ministers.

The priorities of the new government were predictable: much attention to health care, particularly its administration as a public service under Douglas as Health Minister; increases in old age and blind pensions and mothers' allowances; initiatives in larger school units and the free provision of text books in public schools; help to cooperatives; and, above all, protective and supportive programs for farmers. The four successive terms saw advances in all these areas, particularly in health care. In the late fifties increasing attention was given to economic growth. Advanced labour laws were also put on the books, the first in the first legislative session in 1944.

But farmers received top attention, and furious battles ensued with the federal government over farm issues.

Douglas had pledged an end to the wholesale foreclosures by mortgage companies that were turning farmers out of their farm homes (one hundred eighty evictions in 1943; forty-five in the first two months of 1944). Those who continued to farm were buried in debt beyond the remotest possibility of repayment, condemned to a meagre existence while their interest payments stretched ahead forever.

One of the first bills passed in 1944 was the Farm Security Act. It protected the home quarter section against foreclosure, and suspended mortgage payments during years of crop failure, defined as those years when, for reasons beyond the farmer's control, he received a cash return of less than six dollars per acre sown to grain. But the Act went beyond that. It wiped out interest payments for those years of crop failure.

There were precedents for exempting from seizure the farmer's home and his means to continue in business. Such action was not particularly popular with the mortgage companies, but it was difficult to challenge. What drew blood was the cancellation of interest on debt during a bad year.

Douglas, brash and full of fire, argued that mortgage companies ought to share the farmer's precarious fortunes. If all the farmer's gains were wiped out by frost, rust, or drought, so should the mortgage company stand to lose its profit for that year.

Mortgage companies argued against such legislation on the basis of its interference with the "sacredness of contract". In the fall of 1945 the federal government announced hearings to consider disallowance of the Farm Security Act, along with two other bills which had to do with taxation of unused mineral rights in the large holdings of the CPR (which had been granted ten million acres of Saskatchewan land as partial payment for building the first trans-Canada line) and increasing the powers of the Local Government Board to enforce debt adjustment in municipalities. The Dominion Mortgage and Loan Association along with the CPR, had prevailed on the federal government to initiate disallowance.

The federal government's right to disallow provincial legislation has been used at irregular intervals. The cases when it has been employed are noteworthy for two reasons. Disallowance has always been used against a provincial government of a different political stripe. Secondly, the legislation in question has generally had to do with business and financial interests. Human rights infringements, even breaches of the constitution (as when the Liberal government of Saskatchewan extended

160

ts own life by an unlawful twelve months) went unremarked and unchallenged. Aberhart's attempt to manipulate credit in Alberta was swiftly quashed; Duplessis' infamous Padlock Law in Quebec was ignored, and left to the action of private citizens and the courts.

In September 1945 the Douglas government was informed that it had three weeks to prepare a defense of its legislation before the Ottawa hearings.

On September 25 Douglas spoke by radio. He had been denied the provincial network of the CBC; he made do with local stations and regional re-broadcasts, but he roused the people of Saskatchewan in one of the most powerful fighting speeches of his career. He told his radio listeners.

We have just finished a war which was fought, we were told, for the preservation of democratic institutions. It would appear that the war is not finished. We have simply moved the battlefields from the banks of the Rhine to the prairies of Saskatchewan.

If corporations can have these laws disallowed then there are no laws passed by a free legislature which they cannot have set aside. Where then is our boasted freedom? Why elect governments if Bay Street and St. James Street are to have the power to decide what laws shall stand and what laws shall fail? We have reached a time of supreme testing in this province.

He mocked the Liberals who had spread campaign propaganda: the socialists would take away the farms, they had said. Who now was taking away the farms? Who was defending the rights of the big financial institutions, which every year took more than eight million dollars in interest out of the province?

Let me issue a word of warning to those who are moving heaven and earth to have this legislation disallowed. I want to tell them that they are not dealing in this case with a government of tired old men who are merely holding onto power for the spoils of office with a hope of finding a final resting place in the Senate. They are dealing with a government fresh from the people with a mandate to carry out the people's wishes. Those wishes will be carried out. If these vested interests succeed in persuading the Federal Government to disallow this legislation we still have other resources at our disposal and we will not hesitate to use them. . . .

My object in speaking to you tonight is to let you know that the government is not prepared to retreat one single inch. The one thing we must know, however, is that the people of this province are behind us in our determination to fight this invasion of our democratic rights by the financial barons. The legislation in question has not yet been disallowed. We still have three weeks – three weeks in which to write your members of parliament – three weeks in which to send resolutions from municipal councils, city councils and various farmers', labour and businessmen's associations. . . .

We are prepared to lead that fight if you are prepared to follow us into battle.

Follow they did. The government at Ottawa was deluged with the protests of aroused citizens. Mass meetings were organized throughout the province and enraged demands against disallowance were levelled at Ottawa.

Attorney-General Corman presented Saskatchewan's case at the October hearings. The federal decision in November was not to proceed with disallowance.

But the action against the Farm Security Act moved to the courts and was eventually taken to the Privy Council of Great Britain. The only clause in dispute dealt with cancellation of interest during a crop failure year: interest was claimed as an exclusively federal matter of concern under the British North America (BNA) Act, and *ultra vires* of provincial legislation. The federal government employed a former cabinet minister J. L. Ralston, to plead its case against the clause.

Throughout the period of the court action Douglas answered anxious letters from farmers with the assurance that they had "the full protection of the law" until a final decision was reached. Crop failures in 1946 reduced the return on many farms to three dollars an acre. Douglas wrote directly to many mortgage companies who were claiming that the law was *ultra vires*, and were pressing their mortgagees to pay up: "I is the law of the land and must be regarded as such."

The Liberal Opposition in the Legislature saw the act as "confiscatory". Opposition Leader Patterson said, "It is best to leave to individuals the nature of their business transactions." A fellow Liberal, Herman Danielson, contended that the law would destroy credit and double interest rates, and moreover "will be an inducement to honest people to become dishonest. It is an invitation to a debtor to practise deceit and fraud. It is a bill that will have the effect of lowering the morals of the people of the province."

In 1947 the Supreme Court ruled the bill *ultra vires*, with a dissenting judgement by Mr. Justice Taschereau. The federal government took the unusual step of opposing Saskatchewan's application for leave to appeal to the Privy Council, and Saskatchewan proceeded on its own, but with declining hopes.

Corman now turned his attention to the power of the Mediation Board to intervene in debt disputes. In August, 1947 every rural municipal office was supplied with a notice to be posted on its wall and with application forms for farmers who had suffered crop failure. The notice said:

The Supreme Court decision, holding the Crop Failure Clause of the Farm Security Act to be beyond the power of the Provincial Government, prevents the enforcement of the protection given by that clause pending an appeal to the Privy Council. The Provincial Government is determined, however, in view of adverse crop conditions in many parts of the Province, to protect farmers suffering a crop failure from pressure by creditors whether under a mortgage or an agreement for sale. The Province possesses the power by moratorium to prevent the collection out of this year's crop of both principal and interest and is prepared to use such power in cases of crop failure as defined in The Farm Security Act.

Application should be made to he Provincial Mediation Board, Government Insurance Building, Regina. To facilitate such applications forms have been supplied to the secretary-treasurers of all Rural Municipalities.

If you have suffered a crop failure, that is a crop less in value than $6 per sown acre, and wish protection see your secretary-treasurer or write the Mediation Board, Regina.

In November 1948 the Privy Council upheld the Supreme Court, and threw out the clause that would have tampered with the sanctity of interest.

Corman introduced a stronger Moratorium Act in 1949, threatening "to do by Order in Council what we can't do by legislation". The Moratorium Act would allow the province's Mediation Board to stay proceedings in the collection of debt in meritorious cases.

But the same fate befell the Moratorium Act. In 1954 it was challenged in the courts of Saskatchewan and appealed to the Supreme Court of Canada. Though the act had originally been passed, in 1943, by a Liberal government and under the supervision of Saskatchewan's Attorney-General, J. W. Estey, who later became a Supreme Court Judge, it failed to pass the scrutiny of the Court. Pressing the case before the Supreme Court were the Canadian Bankers Association, the Dominion Mortgage and Investments Association, and the federal government represented by the Justice Deputy Minister, Mr. Varcoe. The Act was seen as an interference with federal jurisdiction over bankruptcy and insolvency.

Thrown back on other devices, Corman outlined to Douglas in a 1956 memo the protection they could still offer the insolvent farmer. The judgement had not affected the other provisions of the Farm Security Act, nor did it prohibit the use of an updated Exemptions Act, or prevent the operations of a very sympathetic Mediation Board.

We have made the Mediation Board an active, sympathetic agency to mediate and negotiate settlements. . .

The (Farm Security) Act provides that in event of a crop failur
the farmer shall not be required to make any payment of principa
under any agreement of sale or mortgage during that year, and th
life of the agreement or mortgage is extended for one year for eac
year of crop failure. . .

The Exemptions Act prescribes what may be seized under a
execution. The Liberal Exemptions Act gave the farmer only toke
protection; he could be pretty well cleaned out.

Under the CCF Exemptions Act, a farmer may now retai
sufficient of the crop to provide a living allowance for himself an
his family, to provide necessary costs of farming operations and t
provide seed for all his land under cultivation. . .

A farmer may also retain now against an execution all farn
machinery, implements and equipment reasonably necessary for h
agricultural operations.

Each sheriff has a copy of the new CCF Exemptions Act and i
the discharge of his duty will see that farmers unfortunate enough t
have executions against them are not stripped clean as they wer
back in the good old Liberal days.

Corman contended that the original intent of the BNA Act in th
distribution of powers between nation and province had been altered b
the judgement. He quoted Sir Frederick Haultain, an early Chief Justic
of Saskatchewan:

The Legislature has exclusive jurisdiction to make laws in relation t
property and civil rights in the province and in relation to the ad
ministration of justice in the province, including the constitution
maintenance and organization of provincial courts of civil jurisdic
tion. It creates the courts, and bestows and prescribes their jurisdic
tion, and may at anytime enlarge or circumscribe, or otherwise alte
that jurisdiction. It may, in my opinion, abolish any existing right o
action, or postpone it by moratorium, under its power to legislate i
relation to property and civil rights.

But Haultain had obviously not foreseen a CCF government pre
pared to intervene and suspend payment of all drought-stricken far
mers' debts in penurious seasons. Faced with this challenge to the sacrec
laws of contract, judgement came down to save the money-lender.

A second row with Ottawa developed when the federal governmen
suddenly decided to withhold revenues to clear off an old debt incurre
in supplying seed grain during the thirties.

Douglas had scarcely moved into the Premier's chair in the summe
of 1944 when a demand was received from Finance Minister Ilsley fo
repayment of the 1938 seed grain debt, incurred – of course – by th
Patterson government.

164

The bankrupt province had been forced to appeal repeatedly for federal guarantees to obtain credit during the depression. The year 1937 had been the most devastating of all – almost a total crop failure – after many successive years of poor crops sold at low prices. The meagre crop went to the elevators at rock-bottom prices of about eighty cents a bushel. In the spring of 1938 wheat had to be bought for seed at a price almost twice that amount. The farmers had no money for the purchase, and their borrowings from municipalities had to be backed not only by the provincial government but by the federal government as well before the banks would furnish the required funds. Over time, the debt to the federal government had amounted to sixteen and one-half million dollars. Though deferments had been regularly arranged for the provincial Liberals, the loan was called in when the CCF took office in 1944, and Douglas was informed that this time treasury bills would not do.

Douglas negotiated hard to prevent this catastrophic and unexpected drain on the treasury – and he had dark suspicions that Jimmy Gardiner had engineered the move – when in February 1945 J. L. Ilsley, federal Minister of Finance, played a trump card. He informed Saskatchewan that he would withhold the payment due to the province under the wartime tax rental agreements. The amount would be set-off against the seed grain debt.

Special arrangements had been made during the war by which Ottawa "rented" certain taxation rights (income and corporation taxes) which constitutionally belonged to the provinces, and paid the provincial governments annual sums in compensation. Saskatchewan was to get $5,830,471.29 annually, paid in four instalments per year. The payments came through in 1942, 1943, and 1944, but in January 1945 the instalment failed to arrive. Saskatchewan found itself short by fifteen per cent of its anticipated annual revenue.

Douglas urged arbitration to determine whether such a procedure was lawful. Professor Frank Scott from McGill acted for the Saskatchewan government, on a three-man tribunal set up in Ottawa. Scott's judgement was that the two financial agreements were distinct and separate, the taxation payment being expressly designed to let provincial governments carry on during the years of tax-sharing; there had never before been an attempt at set-off, though many millions of dollars were owed by the provinces for various borrowings. Scott said, in 1973, "It was one of the dirtiest things the federal government did. I was convinced they had no power to do this. But I was outvoted two to one. It was a brutal piece of dealing."

Even though Saskatchewan was far from prosperous in 1945 – some crops were going at nine bushels to the acre and some at less than five – the province had to agree to pay up. They would pay Ottawa over seven million dollars over the next eleven years, the balance to come from rural municipalities and the farmers.

Their battles over farm questions with Ottawa usually encompassed a row with the Saskatchewan Liberals as well, and these Liberals had a difficult time defending the federal position.

The dichotomy of Saskatchewan attitudes about the economy is nowhere more apparent than in the split between *open market* and *stable price* philosophies for getting rid of the annual wheat harvest.

The Ottawa Liberals only very grudgingly acceded to farm demands for marketing boards and government handling of bulk sales abroad.

Douglas and the CCF, as might be supposed, came down hard on the side of stable, long-term, government marketing. They supported the farm organizations and the wheat pools. The federal wheat board should make long-term deals, barters if necessary; the international wheat agreement should extend globally. The farmer should know what his income would be next year.

On one occasion it looked as though they and the farm organizations had pressed this philosophy to their own disadvantage. The post-war agreement with Great Britain came to an end in 1951 with the final payment disastrously less than the prevailing world price, and less than the farmers had hoped. Somehow Douglas managed, through sheer oratorical skill, to turn deftly aside any aspersions on the valiant British and cry shame on Gardiner for such aspersions, to fix blame on the federal government for niggardly dealing while it let farm costs soar, and to come out of it all to a drum beat of applause.

All political parties had feared a slump in prices after the war. In 1946 a large wheat sale contract with Britain, to extend over four years, was welcomed. Canada received $1.55 a bushel under the contract during the first two years; $2.00 a bushel during the second two years. However, by 1951, the United States was giving away huge proportions of its crop to maintain high prices on the remainder, and Argentine wheat was selling at five dollars a bushel. In Canada, the consumer had been paying an artificially low price for domestic flour at the expense of the farmer. And during the period 1946 to 1950, according to *The Economic Analyst*, the Canadian farmer's cost of production had gone up 51.5 per cent.

Farmers were not pleased when Prime Minister St. Laurent announced, in 1951, that the Anglo-Canadian Wheat Agreement would be wound up with a final payment of 8.3 cents per bushel. Resolutions from farm organizations, and in parliament by CCF M.P.s, protested the amount and asked the government for 25 cents.

Jimmy Gardiner hurried to London at the eleventh hour, apparently to ask the British to increase the final figure, and was coolly turned down.

The Searle Grain Company, in their March 7, 1951 bulletin, saw these dealings as a rebuke to "the glittering airy promises of stability and price security assured by those ardent planners, the leaders of the Wheat

Pool and of the Federation of Agriculture . . . The fundamental cause (of the loss of revenue) is involved in Compulsory State Marketing itself."

Walter Tucker, leader of the Opposition in Saskatchewan, preferred to blame the CCF, claiming that the party's lenient statements about war-torn Britain had led to the British rejection of Jimmy Gardiner's appeal.

A Saskatchewan farmer put Tucker in his place: "I wonder if Mr. Tucker will ever grow up and realize the people are not fools and know different . . . It's contemptible in a grown man. No doubt he will swear he was misquoted again. I never saw or heard of a more persecuted man, even his own Liberal papers are always misquoting him."[1]

Douglas gave a radio address on "The Wheat Fiasco", and his speech in the Legislature on the subject also went out over the air waves. A sampling of the mail he received in the following week testifies to the effectiveness of his defence of Britain, castigation of the federal government, reproach to Gardiner, and sympathy to the farmer:

"One of the best speeches in defence of the Canadian farmer and in defence of Canada's best export market that has yet been made in our country. . .

"Very masterful. . .

"I would have given a great deal to have been in the House this afternoon and seen the leader of the opposition squirm when you were speaking. . .

"Tremendous. . .

"Your speech today covering the wheat payment, agreement with the British, etcetera, in my opinion (was) one hundred percent perfect. Was sorry when the announcer said time was up. . .

"I cannot find words to express my feeling of satisfaction with your address this afternoon. Luckily, I knew in advance what you were to speak on and was able to let a lot of farmers around here that do not usually listen in, know about it. I have already had the opportunity to speak to some of them and they agree with me that you were perfect. . .

"What Jimmy Gardiner and Tucker had said about British Government not living up to their wheat contract had made me very unhappy. I still believe that the Old Land, in spite of what she has gone through in the two wars, is still as sound as ever. . . ."

Douglas correctly gauged the pro-British sentiment of Saskatchewan, a surprising phenomenom in a province where people of other ethnic origins outnumber those of English and French stock. Throughout his regime he stressed trade relations with Britain, urging in 1954 that British imports be encouraged, and that Canada accept part payment for exports to Britain in sterling. It was a bias he shared with that other Saskatchewan politician, John Diefenbaker.

Official Opposition Leader Walter Tucker might have fared much better without the guiding hand of Jimmy Gardiner at Ottawa, but in fact his term as leader was bedevilled from the outset. The Liberals had not been satisfied long with mild-mannered former premier William Patterson. Immediately after their 1944 defeat they began to search for a replacement. Gardiner persuaded them to reject the able and articulate lawyer, E. M. Culliton, later Chief Justice, in favour of Walter Tucker, a federal M.P., at the leadership convention in 1946. Douglas, keeping an eye on the convention, hoped Tucker would win. Culliton would have been a much more dangerous opponent. He considered the Liberals had done him a favour, but had made a poor choice. "Just like the Liberal party," he said, "blowing its brains out."

Tucker proved to be all too easy a foil for Douglas' lightweight rapier style. He was no newcomer to politics; after graduating in law he had entered the House of Commons as M.P. for Rosthern in 1935, the same election that took Douglas to Ottawa. The Rosthern constituency included a Mennonite colony, and it was unshakably Liberal, deriving no doubt from the aid received from a Liberal federal government in emigrating. Tucker's local campaign speeches were heavily weighted with denunciations of communism, which carried a very direct message to the former victims of Russian persecution. His preferred method of attack was to charge that the CCF were communist in ideology.

There was an incipient rebellion in Saskatchewan ranks against Gardiner's domination, and Tucker was persuaded by Culliton to launch, finance, and organize a more independent provincial party. When Gardiner's organizers discovered what was happening there was a confrontation, and Tucker backed down.

Tucker had been one of only two Liberal M.P.s from Saskatchewan, the other being James Gardiner, and had been appointed parliamentary assistant to the Minister of Veterans Affairs. In Ottawa he was regarded as a man of considerable promise. Wilfred Eggleston, from the parliamentary press gallery, wrote: "He ought to become a dominant figure in the Saskatchewan Legislature because of his skill in debate and his thorough grasp of economic affairs."

Eggleston saw the move as an indication that the Liberals were taking Saskatchewan very seriously: "A man of Tucker's capacity and promise, with the post of parliamentary assistant already under his belt, and full Cabinet rank an early probability, isn't likely to throw it all up on a hopeless gamble." Eggleston wrote that the party was determined to regain Saskatchewan and recover its prairie support. There had been a time when Mackenzie King could count on sixteen M.P.s elected from Saskatchewan. "So far nothing has happened to Premier T. C. Douglas from which they can gain much satisfaction: but they evidently propose to stiffen up the Opposition and make a bid for a much larger representation in the next legislature." And he concluded, "If Tucker fails then the Liberals may as well write that province off their slate, because it is difficult to conceive of a stronger candidate."[2]

With so much riding on his success, Tucker believed his only hope was to strike hard. His 1948 election campaign slogan was "Tucker or Tyranny". He had proclaimed on assuming the leadership: "Socialism is a pathmaker to totalitarian Communism".[3] He pursued this theme, warning farmers: "When it suits their purpose, the socialist CCF government will not be deterred by His Majesty's seal on their title to land from trampling on the farmers."[4]

Well in advance of the 1948 election Douglas and Tucker tangled in debate, the most widely publicized occasion being a huge afternoon rally at Crystal Lake when each man spoke for an hour from the canvas-covered back of a truck to a throng of 1,500 people. Here the charge of CCF "communism" was not well received, according to *Leader-Post* reporter Ken Liddell: "Brightest interest the crowd took in the proceedings came during Mr. Tucker's rebuttal when, answering an allegation by Douglas that he was the servant of big interests, Mr. Tucker said that Premier Douglas' group was receiving the support of the Communist party. The crowd booed this no end."

The writer described the pair as a "frisky young colt" and a "plodding work horse", and the difference in size – Tucker was a very large, heavy-set man – led to one of the most frequently quoted exchanges between the two men. As Liddell heard it: "Mr. Tucker had said the Liberals had introduced mothers' allowances when Premier Douglas 'was just a little fellow' and the premier countered with the remark that 'I am still a little fellow. Tucker is big enough to swallow me but if he did he would be the strangest man in the world because he would have more brains in his stomach than he has in his head.'"[5]

CCF supporters were gleeful about such encounters. Tucker must have become aware that he was no match for the Premier, yet his only tactic was to continue his outright attack, whether from conviction or as the political strategy approved by his party, or a combination of both. Reporters in the legislature after his election would describe Tucker as "losing all control of himself if jabbed at the right moment. He was highly emotional; he would become completely incoherent."[6]

The 1948 election campaign was enlivened by a suit for slander brought by Tucker against Douglas. Douglas had in his files the circumstances of a case in which an elderly couple in the Rosthern district had lost their farm to the Rosthern Mortgage Company. They had signed a quit-claim deed on the understanding, they said, that they could continue to live on the farm. Later the farm was purchased from the mortgage company by the man who had acted as interpreter for them (they knew little English) when the quit-claim was signed. The couple had subsequently, unsuccessfully, filed a statement of claim to recover their former home, and the lawyer acting for that mortgage company had been Walter Tucker.

At a meeting in Caron, south of Moose Jaw, Douglas was questioned about Tucker's accusations that the "communist" CCF planned to take title to the farmers' land. Douglas said he was tired of such accusations, the real threat to losing title was through actions such as those of the Rosthern Mortgage Company.

The men clashed on the issue at a meeting soon after, in Rosthern. Tucker challenged Douglas to back up his charge, and Douglas produced his documentation. Tucker filed a slander suit for $100,000.

"Where will we get a hundred thousand dollars?" Irma asked her husband.

Tucker lost the suit, but on appeal it was referred back for re-direction by the appeal judge. It was clearly not a case of slander, the judge said, since the facts were as Douglas had presented them. It could however be brought forward as a suit for libel; the charge would then be that the presentation of the facts by Douglas had been deliberately malicious and harmful to Tucker's career. Tucker did not proceed with the libel charge, and it was dropped.

"It cost me a bit of money," Douglas said, "and I was worried. I knew the statements were accurate but maybe the whole thing was undignified and would reflect badly on the CCF. Scots always believe that decent people should stay out of court!"

The 1948 campaign was a rough affair. The Liberals and Conservatives ran joint candidates in 28 seats. The daily newspapers not only devoted their editorial space to attacking the CCF, but frequently interspersed editorial comment in their news stories, pointing out in parentheses their disagreement with the statements of CCF speakers. The Canadian Underwriters Association supported the Liberals, set up headquarters in the Saskatchewan Hotel in Regina, and even schooled insurance agents throughout the province to campaign against the CCF which had set up a government insurance office and was in active competition with private companies. Short canned radio talks extolling free enterprise and denouncing socialism – but claiming to be non-political – were prepared by Ontario research offices of the Canadian Chamber of Commerce and supplied to Saskatchewan stations. Higginbotham in 1958 said. "There was enmity in the air. It was almost like a civil war."

The CCF used a small pink card called "Promise and Performance" listing nine promises made in 1944 and how they had been carried out. The slogan was "A Government Which Keeps Its Promises is a Government to Keep".

PROMISE	PERFORMANCE
1. Security in your home.	1. Farm Families protected against eviction under mortgage from home quarter; city families may obtain protection from the Mediation Board.

2. Real debt reduction	2. Province's debt reduced $72,000,000; farmers reduced own debts $212,000,000.
3. Increased Old Age Pensions	3. Old age pensions increased, plus free health care; exemptions on earnings increased; caveats removed from property; no claim against estates under $2,000.
4. Medical, dental and hospital services, irrespective of the ability of the individual to pay.	4. Free health care to 30,000 citizens. All others share in hospitalization plan. Six Health Regions organized and working toward complete health care for everyone. Free treatment of cancer, tuberculosis, polio, venereal disease and mental illness.
5. Equal educational opportunity for every child in the province.	5. Forty-five Larger School Units organized. In these areas school costs are equalized. Grants to poorer districts increased by $1,000,000. In some parts Government pays 75% of school costs. Authorized text books for first eight grades. Many children assisted to attend High School.
6. Increased Mothers' Allowances, Maternity Grants and care for the Disabled.	6. Mothers' Allowances increased, and free health care for mothers and dependents on allowances, Income exemptions increased. Hospitalization plan provides for large share of maternity costs. Disabled fathers also eligible for grants. Increased pensions and free health care for the blind.
7. Freedom of Speech and Freedom of Religion.	7. Bill of Rights guarantees freedom of speech, religion and association, and that no person shall be discriminated against on grounds of race, colour or creed.
8. The Right of Collective Bargaining.	8. Trade Union Act guarantees Right of collective bargaining.
9. Encouragement to the Cooperative Movement.	9. A new Department encourages coop development. Assistance given to Horse Marketing Coop and Matador Coop Farm. Government loans to coop enterprises. In three years Saskatchewan coops gained 197 new organizations and 180,000 new members.

The CCF promise for the next term of office was economic expansion to sustain the increased welfare and health services which had seemed urgent in 1944, along with rural electrification as a new priority.

Douglas feared that the election would be close in many seats, and in fact lost more than he expected. The CCF dropped from forty-seven to thirty-one, with the Liberals moving up from five to nineteen. A consoling letter from Professor Harry Cassidy, head of the Department of Social Science at the University of Toronto, suggested that there was no cause for disappointment; the miracle was that the CCF was re-elected. It would never be quite so difficult again. In 1952 the CCF was back to forty-two members; in 1956 they elected thirty-six; and in 1960, thirty-seven.

Douglas believed he lost ground in 1948, not because of the Liberals' strong attack, but rather because so many new programs had been introduced in a short space of time. "Only a small minority might have their toes stepped on, but they tend to remember," Douglas said. "The many you have helped tend to forget."

It was during this 1948 election that Douglas added to his repertoire a rueful story borrowed from Winston Churchill. A candidate calls on an old friend to ask how he intends to vote, and is told that the old friend is undecided. "What?" says the candidate. "How can you say that? When we were boys together we went skating and you fell through the ice and I pulled you out. When you wanted to get married I loaned you two hundred dollars. When your house burned down I signed a note for you at the bank. When your child needed an operation I lent you the money you needed. Isn't that so?" To which the voter replied, "That's all true. But what have you done for me lately?"

One of the more conspicuous efforts of the government radically changed the countryside in the two decades of CCF administration. The roads – the long miles of road past great squares of tilled and empty earth – were brought up to modern standards and out of the quagmire era. In 1944 there had been only one hundred thirty-eight miles of black-top in the province.

And rural electrification transformed country living. Trans-Canada Air Line passengers flying over at night were impressed by the patterns of twinkling lights below, where darkness had once stretched endlessly. The rural program, started in 1949, had brought power to 47,000 farmers by 1958.

In the late 1950s a determined effort was made to bring water and sewer systems to the small towns. Wells and pumping units were financed jointly by three levels of government. And, triumphantly, after decades of promises of a new source of irrigation and power, the Saskatchewan River Dam was undertaken in 1958. The work began with an opening ceremony addressed by Douglas and Prime Minister Diefenbaker. There were skeptical shrugs on completion when Prime Minister

Pearson named it "Gardiner Dam". Diefenbaker told reporters, "There never would have been a Saskatchewan Dam had it not been for my government. The Liberals never thought Saskatchewan was worth a dam, and I don't care how you spell the word."

It was small consolation when the backed-up water was named Diefenbaker Lake and the surrounding area Douglas Park.

In his direct dealings as premier with successive governments at Ottawa, Douglas' attitude was generally of *rapprochement*, despite his volleys of wrath on the hustings. He and his government in fact fought a rearguard action to preserve the wartime ties, when the shift in federal-provincial relations took place after the war. His was not the fist-on-the-table provincial-rights stance at inter-government conferences. He made attempts to interest Ottawa in taking over on a national scale such programs as hospital insurance and old age pension supplements; provincial power was not pursued as an end in itself. He challenged the federal jurisdiction in the matter of mortgages, in the hope of protecting the farmer from heavy debt, but having lost that round he kept a careful eye on constitutional limits. He had quite enough to do in his own sphere; what he became concerned with was more of the wherewithal, from the total of Canada's wealth, to carry out his obligations in Saskatchewan.

At federal-provincial conferences when tax-sharing arrangements were debated, Douglas pursued the belief that Ottawa should collect taxes on wealth that derived from all Canada (though head offices, and secondary industry, might be concentrated in Central Canada) and Ottawa should then pay out to the provinces the money needed to bring up services such as health, education, and housing to a common standard across the country. He was quite prepared to accept joint administration with Ottawa, if Ottawa would join in. He was angry and disappointed when Drew in Ontario or Duplessis in Quebec thwarted such agreements.

He went about negotiations without bluster, and without a parochial view.

Frank Scott said, "Saskatchewan was the only province speaking *as Canadians* at these conferences. Other provinces were finagling for power, wanting things for themselves. Saskatchewan wanted certain things, but especially wanted *Ottawa* to assume its proper responsibility."

The assumption of wartime power by Ottawa was rapidly dissipated during the fifties. The brief interval of Conservative administration did nothing to check the Liberal course. Strident provincial voices, politically out of tune with the federal government, demanded a return of tax powers to the provinces, blocked and obstructed conference meetings, and forced their point of view on Ottawa.

Professor Frank Scott of McGill University was consultant for Saskatchewan in many of these negotiations. He was a strong advocate of federal leadership, and he found the Saskatchewan ministry entirely sympathetic. He recalled the conference of 1960 in a chamber that seemed symbolic of the balkanization that had happened in the post-war decade. "Every provincial delegation sat with its name before it at the table," he said. "But the word 'Canada' was nowhere in that room. There were federal ministers present. But it seemed nobody dared use the word 'Canada'. I was struck by that. What had happened to our country!"

It had begun back in 1950, Scott thought, when Prime Minister St. Laurent opened a conference by saying, "We are just here for you gentlemen to tell us what you want." The federal government had not come with a single proposal. "They were not prepared to give leadership. It was a complete abdication," Scott said.

Douglas' view from the outset was clear in an inter-government memo[7] which reviewed the advantages to Saskatchewan of continuing under the kind of agreement that operated during the war. Getting back the sole right to tax personal incomes, corporations and succession duties would not do much good when there was so little to tax. (As Douglas pointed out in another paper of the same period, even succession duties meant little because so many people of means left the province for an easier climate in their old age – and died somewhere else.) What Saskatchewan would seek at the coming conference would therefore be: increases in payments to meet growing needs in social services, education and health and, in addition, *federal* action to implement a new scheme of crop insurance or an extension of the Prairie Farm Assistance Act.

The rationale was: "The centralization of industry and commerce in two or three provinces resulting in a greater tax-paying capacity in those provinces should not operate to deprive the citizens of other provinces of equal social benefits. Such concentration is largely dependent on (a) favourable federal policies and (b) the existence of a hinterland for the purposes of trade."

The "hinterland" wanted equal shares.

With Premiers Drew, Duplessis, and Hart all intractable, the best that could be salvaged were bilateral tax-sharing arrangements, and Douglas was usually one of the first to sign with the Prime Minister at Ottawa as successive five-year agreements came up for negotiation.

The cooperative approach lost another round in 1956 when, after an inconclusive April conference, Ottawa announced its intention to go ahead with taxation of incomes and redistribute the proceeds arbitrarily, leaving the provinces free to impose additional taxes if they wanted to.

Beland Honderich, editor of the Toronto *Star*, queried the Premiers for their reactions and got the following answer from Douglas:

(The announcement) almost completely disregards all representations and evidence advanced by the provinces, supporting our need for a more adequate share of receipts from direct tax fields jointly occupied by both levels of government. 1) The level of payments is much too low to relieve increasingly serious financial strain on provinces and municipalities with pyramiding costs of education, road building and social services and urban growth. 2) The proposals are related solely to revenues from direct tax fields. They make no provision for the fiscal needs of poorer provinces struggling to achieve minimum services despite scant revenue from alternative tax resources. Instead of seeking cooperation of provinces in maintaining an efficient, coordinated tax system, the new proposals encourage double taxation and may seriously weaken the fiscal powers of Ottawa in combatting a major economic crisis.[8]

The Toronto *Star* ran an editorial commending the federal proposal as "much more flexible". The advantage was that "it satisfies Quebec; on the debit side it involves the risk of double taxation and the weakening of the federal government's taxing authority." The *Star* thought the proposal might have allowed the provinces fifteen per cent of the income tax take, to meet their growing needs, instead of only ten per cent.[9]

The insistence of Quebec, a new and overpowering factor, outweighed "the debit side", and Saskatchewan's plea for an easing of its position was acknowledged as just – and dismissed.

Douglas made some attempts to find common cause with Premier Campbell of Manitoba and Premier Frost of Ontario in urging conferences as a regular feature of the fiscal life of Canada. A. W. Johnson as deputy minister of finance sought agreement from his provincial counterparts for annual meetings. Both initiatives bore fruit in later years.

Professor Scott said, in an interview in 1973, that the CCF had been centralist since its beginning, and Douglas, though he strongly concurred, was also helpful in reminding the national party of the responsibilities the provinces carry under the constitution, which meant a quite legitimate and sometimes desperate need for funds. "One of the things Tommy did was to put a little more balance into the total CCF view of federalism, to show how important the role of the provinces was, how many things they would have to do, and we began I think slightly to modify our approach. Today I think the pendulum has swung far too far the other way. We are practically a number of little states all fighting with each other."

Some of Douglas' sharpest exchanges on federal-provincial tax-sharing were with Donald Fleming, Minister of Finance under Prime Minister Diefenbaker, whose crusading conquest of Ottawa had yielded few practical results.

When the Conservatives advised farmers to switch from wheat to beef as a remedy for export losses, Douglas ridiculed the "solution" in a major address to a CCF banquet in Winnipeg. He was in sympathy with Diefenbaker's aim to switch Canadian trade from the United States to Britain, but he questioned the Conservatives' genuine commitment to the idea. Douglas' consistent views on the Canadian approach to trade are visible in this 1957 speech, and have their relevance in 1974. The meeting was reported in the Winnipeg *Tribune* by Peter Desbarats:

Premier T. C. Douglas of Saskatchewan drew his best brand of 'Tommy-gun' oratory from its holster Wednesday and aimed at Canada's new Conservative government.

Using wit to whittle his statistics into sharp missiles he fired away at Tory efforts to increase trade with England and reduce the wheat surplus.

A CCF dinner audience of 250 people, celebrating the party's 25th anniversary, gave him a standing ovation at the end of the speech.

Premier Douglas said the Conservatives blithely suggested shifting fifteen per cent of Canada's trade to Britain and then reacted like 'maiden aunts at an indecent proposal' when the British suggested dropping all trade barriers.

The Canadian trade situation is worsening steadily, he said, and the Canadian government has never indicated it has the remotest idea what to do about it.

Mr. Douglas said he believed free trade with the U.K. would benefit Canadian manufacturers in the long run by giving them a larger market for their products. But free channels of trade aren't the only solution. Equally important is the removal of monetary restrictions.

'Canada's share of the world wheat market has dropped from 43 per cent in 1951 to 22 per cent in 1956,' he said. 'We must be prepared to accept the currency and goods of other countries in return for our wheat. We are in a new trading era.'

Premier Douglas unloaded both barrels at a recent Conservative proposal to cut back wheat acreage and devote more land to cattle.

'Our meat consumption is already at an all-time high and we can only look to a slow increase due to population (growth). The only effect of the proposal would be to give us a livestock surplus instead of a wheat surplus.

'A great act of statesmanship,' he said acidly. 'It is criminal folly to suggest we curtail wheat production in a world crying with hunger.

'Inflation is one of Canada's greatest problems,' Premier Douglas said. 'Even the Liberals have admitted it since June 10. It's amazing how a kick in the pants makes the brain work.'

Chapter Twelve
Premier 2: Some Days are Better than Others

Douglas brought in a succession of measures on behalf of organized labour which paralleled his farm legislation. The industrial workers in the province, outside of construction and transportation, were a very small group. His concern for their welfare was based on the primary objective of his party to work for "farmer and labour", and more especially was designed to impress the federal party's potential supporters in eastern Canada, in the ranks of the trade union movement.

At the 1944 session his government passed the most advanced labour code in the country, guaranteeing the right to organize, as underpinning to bargaining procedures. The bill was the handiwork of a federal M.P., Andrew Brewin of Toronto Greenwood. The CCF Labour Minister, Charlie Williams, went to Ottawa in August 1944 for a round of talks with Brewin, A. R. Mosher of the Canadian Congress of Labour, David Lewis, and others. The bill that Williams brought back was a "showpiece".

Even before it was presented in the legislature in October there were irate reactions from business groups. The Saskatchewan Employers Association said in a statement: "Up to now, Saskatchewan has enjoyed industrial peace . . . Saskatchewan is to be a guinea pig for the East where labour is much more important politically; for the sake of party fortunes in the East, legislation will be forced upon Saskatchewan which its small labour population does not need. The draft Bill is discriminatory, class legislation of a coercive and punitive nature."

What the Trades Union Act provided was the still controversial closed shop and universal check-off of union dues. There was also a concurrent Annual Holidays Act which guaranteed two weeks holiday with pay per year of employment, with part-time workers permitted to accumulate work credits to the same ratio, – this bill also met with some opposition; it put Saskatchewan workers far ahead of other Canadian employees.

Once union organizers secured a majority vote among employees, under the Trades Union Act, certification would follow, and employers were compelled to negotiate in good faith with the union. That was standard stuff. What raised the hackles of employers was the provision that all new employees must join the union within thirty days, and their union dues would be automatically deducted from their pay cheques.

Of particular significance was the provision that civil servants were included. The government put itself in the same position as all other employers in the province. Its employees had full rights to bargain on every aspect of their jobs, they were entitled to the full gamut of negotiating procedure, and they were not denied the right to strike.

Despite the generous provisions, labour men in Saskatchewan were irascible and critical. Douglas found some of them hard to take. The Trades and Labour Congress (T.L.C.) was not publicly allied with the CCF and in fact supported Liberals frequently, both on the national scene and in Saskatchewan. But most of the disgruntled conduct came not from the T.L.C. but from the Canadian Congress of Labour (C.C.L.), which was officially the party's friend. Communist sympathizers in some key posts nagged and attempted to bully the new government, and Douglas, exasperated, had to write to David Lewis to "set Pat Conroy (C.C.L. Secretary Treasurer) straight", since he was apparently getting misinformation from his Regina lieutenants. "Tactless and offensive" was the way Douglas described the C.C.L. Regina representatives.

"What I would like you to make clear to Conroy," Douglas wrote, "is that I am not perturbed about the welfare of the Saskatchewan government. We have a solid basis of support whatever the C.C.L. does and, if M – continues for another month on the same basis that he has followed for the past few weeks, the C.C.L. will be through in Saskatchewan for many years to come. The labour movement in this province is essentially made up of railway workers and the Trades and Labour Congress. Of the sixteen trade union locals affiliated with the CCF in Saskatchewan only five are C.C.L. We are prepared to give the latter every possible assistance in getting underway, but their own tactics are alienating public support every day and, if continued, will make it impossible for us to help them even though we want to do so."[1]

The letter brought results. Some friction between Charlie Williams and the C.C.L. continued, but David Lewis and other CCF leaders in Ottawa confronted national labour men with Douglas' charges, and quite abject letters to the Premier were forthcoming. Douglas replied somewhat stiffly to the promise that, " – will be told to apologize for the embarrassment he has caused you," with this comment: "There is no need for him to do any apologizing. He has not caused me any embarrassment. But I am quite convinced that if he continues his undiplomatic actions he will do a great deal of damage to the cause of the Canadian Congress of Labour."

Douglas had difficulty in accepting the unions' interpretation of the "maintenance of membership" clause in the Act his government had passed. In the spring of 1950, in an effort to rid themselves of communist "infiltrators", some unions were threatening to refuse membership to undesirable individuals. They claimed that such a refusal would, under the Act, mean that the worker must be discharged from a "closed shop" place of work.

"The claim is that since the employee must be a member of a union, if the union expels him or refuses to accept his membership, management cannot employ him . . . It certainly was not the interpretation the Government put upon it when they placed it in the Trade Union Act," Douglas wrote to one labour official.

He proposed a new clause in the Act: "Refusal of admission to or being expelled by the union should not be considered as a failure on the part of the employee to maintain his membership."

The proposal brought a flood of protests from unions.

In a letter to Pat Conroy, Douglas expressed his concern:

It was never our intention that such a power should be given to the union. We recognize that there are instances in which an employee who has been brought in for strike-breaking purposes or as a stool pigeon for an employer should be denied employment. On the other hand, however, to give the union the power to deprive a man of his bread and butter without any right of appeal seems to us to have very serious implications . . . It has been agreed that we will leave this matter over for this Session and that during the next year we will try to work out some formula.

The unions petitioned Douglas, and warned that the amendment would open the door to destruction of the "closed shop" principle. They saw an ever-present threat by management to destroy their union, and were convinced that if an employee could stay on the job after being expelled by the union the loophole would be exploited to the full, with all management's persuasion brought to bear on dissidents to have the union expel them until the union was undermined.

The Saskatoon and District Labour Council even threatened that if the amendment went through "the policy of the C.C.L. endorsing the CCF as the political arm of Labour will not remain long."

Douglas decided not to pursue the matter.

Bill Davies, a former cabinet minister, and later secretary-treasurer of the Saskatchewan Federation of Labour, said in a 1973 interview, "Tommy had difficulty with the labour movement from time to time . . . It was a rather serious question of union security. What we did was a stand-off. We let the legislation be broadly interpreted. We needed the provision there, though actual cases didn't arise."

If there had been a feminist organization in Saskatchewan of the kind that arose in the early seventies, Douglas would have found himself deep in hot water over another labour matter. In a 1945 letter to a worried gentleman in Prince Albert, the Premier assured him that in the currently difficult times no married women would be allowed to take employment from a male breadwinner:

It is this government's policy to employ those persons who are supporting a family, or who are single, in preference to married women. This policy was carried out in 1945, when an amendment was passed to the Public Service Act, at which time it was stated that, except in cases of emergency, married women shall not be appointed or continued in the public service, and then only when she has had special training and has technical or professional qualifications required for the performance of the duties of her appointment.

It is, however, wellnigh impossible to impose a similar standard upon other employers in the province.

The restriction was withdrawn a few years later, and in 1951 Douglas redeemed himself somewhat in feminist eyes by bringing in legislation requiring equal pay for equal work by men and women. A letter from Margaret Hyndman, Q.C., well-known Toronto exponent of women's rights, said: "It seems to me better than the Ontario Act in some respects and I shall look forward with interest to seeing how it works out in practice."[2]

The most serious rift between Douglas and the trade unions operating in his province occurred in 1954 and 1955, when employees of the Saskatchewan Power Corporation threatened strike action.

The year 1954 was one of the worst crop years in the two decades of the CCF regime. Both drought and rust took a heavy toll; the crops that survived were of low grade and the farmers faced heavy losses.

In this situation Douglas issued a general restraint dictum to the managers of crown corporations. Contract negotiations were not to include general wage increases, though particular categories might be allowed to catch up. An agreement signed with the Civil Service Association was to set the pattern. There had been a change to a five-day work week and some salary adjustments but no general wage increase. In a press statement on December 1st Douglas laid it on the line: farm income had declined by $285,000,000 or $2,500 per farm family. In these circumstances other workers, who had received pay increases "almost every year" since unions were organized, must be content with normal annual increments and some adjustment of inequalities. "We are simply stating that we cannot give what we haven't got . . . Under present economic conditions no group in the community is entitled to a larger slice of a smaller cake."

Two weeks later Douglas had a visit from two international representatives of the Oil Workers International, Union Congress of Industrial Organizations – Canadian Congress of Labour (OWIU, CIO-CCL), Alex McAuslane and Cy Palmer, who asked him to reconsider. In the current negotiations between Local 649 of their union and the Saskatchewan

180

Power Corporation, no "meaningful discussions" could take place under such a dictum.

A mid-January meeting of Local 649, attended by the OWIU's Canadian director, Neil Reimer, condemned the government's "anti-union" attitude. There was talk of strike action. The union said it had begun negotiations with a 17 per cent wage increase demand and had reduced it to 5 per cent, but the Power Corporation made no counter offer, claiming it had no authority to negotiate wage increases that year.

Douglas had in fact laid down a firm line for the top union men: the Saskatchewan Power Corporation was already paying rates comparable to other power employees on the prairies, but would consider increases up to the level of other Saskatchewan crown corporations if inequalities existed. He was angered by a suggestion from McAuslane, which he quoted in a letter to Reimer:

> Mr. McAuslane advised the two ministers of the Government whom he met last fall that the farm electrification program should be scrapped since it was this expensive program which had reduced their surplus to a nominal amount and was preventing an across-the-board wage increase. These two ministers also informed me that Mr. McAuslane advised them that if they could not make bigger surpluses than they were now getting they should turn the power operations of the province over to private enterprise who could probably show a much better profit.[3]

Douglas was so incensed by the language and tactics of union representatives, as reported to him by the Corporation's negotiators, that he sent a reporter into the bargaining room and later sent a transcript of the proceedings to Reimer, saying he was "not prepared to submit them (government negotiators) to ill mannered abuse." Reimer replied that the government men had shown themselves "pompous and devious".

When the union made public threats of strike action, Douglas first asked them to accept voluntary arbitration and, when that was rejected, threatened compulsory arbitration. Explaining his position in a letter to C.C.L. President A. R. Mosher, he wrote, "It is 25 degrees below zero this morning in Saskatchewan. Thousands of homes are entirely dependent on power and gas to operate their heating facilities . . . Much as we would dislike making arbitration compulsory, I think you will agree that it would be an act of complete irresponsibility for us to stand idly by and permit a strike."

At its national office in Ottawa, CCF leaders were appalled at the thought of compulsory arbitration, that most detested of union bogeys, imposed by the Saskatchewan government. "It would mean the end of CCF support in the labour movement for years to come," National Secretary Lorne Ingle wrote to Douglas. Ingle reminded Douglas of the discussions for merger of the two giant union congresses, a move that would be a prelude to closer alliance with the CCF, and the long-hoped-for national support.

But at the end of March Douglas was drafting an anti-strike bill for the legislature, calling for compulsory arbitration. Cy Palmer and his team, Douglas believed, were banking on the government not daring to proceed because of pressure from the C.C.L. and the national CCF.

Two days later a mediator had been appointed, and the legislation did not have to be introduced. The mediator was David Lewis, at this time practising as a labour lawyer in Toronto. Lewis recalled the phone call:

> I was in Windsor. I got a call from Tommy who informed me Neil Reimer was on an extension, and they both wanted me to go out to mediate the dispute. I asked, 'Why me?' and there were two laughs on the line. It was probably Tommy's idea. He told me, 'You're the national president of the CCF so you can't possibly do the CCF in, and as a labour lawyer acting for the same union in Ontario you can't possibly do the union in, so we think you're the right guy.'. . .
>
> It was typical of Tommy's acute judgement. Most people would have said I was impossible for the job because of my double role. But I did settle it. I met with them for eight or nine days, and there was no strike. Exactly what Tommy predicted did happen. I was able to get away with saying to labour, 'Stop being bloody fools' and I was able to tell management, 'you'd better go back and tell the government this isn't acceptable.' It worked out.

In June there was an exchange of letters between Douglas and Lewis. Lewis presented his bill for expenses as mediator, and commented sadly on the CCF's failure to make progress in the Ontario election just past. "What the future holds, it is at this moment difficult to conjecture," Lewis wrote.

Douglas replied that he could not anticipate any better results in the pending Alberta election. "The one thing you have to admire our supporters for is their ability to take defeat after defeat and still come back for more . . . Moreover, I believe some day their tenacity will pay off."

The letters were amicable, philosophical, and commiserating. Douglas would bend as far as his position in Saskatchewan would allow him, out of regard for political consequences across the country, even when it seemed the rest of the country could not care less. Lewis recognized and respected that attitude.

Douglas had, at this date, survived two elections and was well into his third term. The 1952 campaign had been hard-fought, but gratifying in its results: the slight setback of 1948 was reversed and the CCF came through with forty-two seats to eleven for the Liberals.

But immediately after that election the government was embroiled in the one serious scandal of its twenty-year history, an episode referred to in party circles as "the Rawluk affair". Douglas was profoundly shaken, and fought the implications of wrong-doing with bull-terrier tenacity.

Douglas has recalled that it was normal procedure during campaigns for solemn affidavits to be brought forth to support preposterous charges – once he was accused, he said, of advising people not to sing "God Save the King" and the charge was supported by a sworn affidavit – but politicians seldom bothered to pursue such campaign theatricals in the courts.

However, the government had scarcely settled down to what promised to be a peaceful legislative session in 1953, when Walter Tucker dropped a bomb. It was an affidavit charging Provincial Treasurer Clarence Fines and M. F. Allore, head of the Government Insurance Office, with taking kickbacks. This time the Liberals were trying to make the charges stick. Tucker raised the matter in a meeting of a committee of the legislature, and moved for an inquiry, which Fines seconded. The proceedings of the committee inquiry were conducted publicly, and attracted such a vast audience of fascinated spectators that they were moved to the Legislative Chamber, occupying that large hall every morning and evening for four weeks.

Joseph Rawluk, a collection agent, had set up a small insurance firm with the help of Phil Bodnoff and Morris Shumiatcher, who had resigned as Douglas' executive assistant in 1949 to practise law. Rawluk wrote some government insurance, but his business affairs did not prosper and his agency was suspended by the Government Insurance Office which claimed he was in arrears by about $3000. On the witness stand Rawluk was discredited by his admission of various petty misappropriations of funds and passing bad cheques.

But he had put together a tale of kickbacks to the head of the Government Insurance Office, and one somewhat bizarre story of an assignation on a street corner for the purpose of handing over one hundred dollars to a gentleman who he believed was Clarence Fines. This was the tale that emerged in the affidavit produced by Mr. Tucker and sworn before a lawyer, Darrell Heald (later Attorney-General in the Thatcher administration). Rawluk had worked for the Liberals in the 1952 campaign, and had tried to tell his story at that time without success. After the election Tucker had, according to Rawluk, sent for him and decided to make the charges public. He may have been influenced by the fact that a federal election was due that summer, he probably believed there was some basis for the charges, and he was also desperate to bring down his CCF opponents.

The charge against the cabinet minister, Fines, seemed particularly far-fetched, as though it had been added to an involved story almost as an afterthought, but it was, of course, the charge that drew widest attention. Fines said, "At first I looked upon it as nothing very serious at all. It was all so stupid that I didn't think anybody could possibly have believed anything that was said. When I realized there were some people who actually believed the statement it shook me up quite a bit. I think the greatest consolation I got was when members of the Opposition would come to me and say, 'Clarence I don't believe a word of it as far as you're concerned.' "

Attorney-General Corman, who was in ill health, was shocked by the affair and wrote to Fines:

I don't know just how to say this but I do want you to know that no one who knows you believes a word of the charges being made. They will boomerang. You have a reputation for integrity that cannot be shaken.

If from a sick bed I might make a suggestion it is this: Keep your defence separate from the defence of others. Good luck.[4]

A prominent Conservative lawyer, E. C. Leslie, was engaged as counsel by the government and in the end prepared a report finding the charges against Fines to be false and recommending that the entire case be dismissed for lack of evidence.

Douglas took an active part in the proceedings, cross-examining witnesses, as one observer said, "like Clarence Darrow", and at one point asking Rawluk if he would consent to take a "truth serum". He said he believed Rawluk was being used, and was "mentally sick". When the report was brought in he delivered a blistering two-and-a-half hour speech denouncing the Liberals and Tucker in particular. To the amazement of the House, the Opposition Leader did not rise to reply. Other members with speeches ready on their desks found themselves voting on the motion without debate.

Shortly afterwards Tucker resigned from the Saskatchewan Liberal leadership, a defeated man. He was elected again to the federal House, though the promise of a bright future as a cabinet minister was never fulfilled.

Asmunder Loptson of Saltcoats became temporary leader after Tucker's departure. Chris Higginbotham wrote: "Another exponent of absolute opposition, he would make preposterous charges against the government in a low monotonous voice. By the time the government members realized he had accused them of allowing their friends to make $200 million on oil concessions and rise in protest, he was forging ahead with accusations that the Wheat Pool had been founded by Communists."[5]

Loptson's desk-mate was a die-hard old-timer, Herman Danielson. Douglas called them "the Dead End Kids".

In 1954 a Liberal convention was held in Saskatoon to choose Tucker's successor. There was a fierce battle between the Gardiner forces and a more independent provincial group, who believed their only salvation lay in some disassociation from federal Liberal policies, and who wer tired of the strong ruling hand of Jimmy Gardiner. Gardiner was hoping that his son Wilfrid would move toward provincial leadership, and pressed for the election as interim leader of the elderly Dr. L. B. Thompson who was well known through his association with the Prairie Farm Rehabilitation Act (a federal program which did much to restore the ravages of drought in southern Saskatchewan). The recalcitrant Liberals would not accept this proposal, and elected instead a personable and successful young farmer, Hamilton McDonald, who had been elected in 1948 as a Liberal-Progressive Conservative. McDonald was an able and less vituperative Opposition Leader, and some of the storm and tumult in the provincial legislature died away.

The CCF in Saskatchewan during these years was indignant as the press in the rest of Canada mocked their efforts to attract industry to the province. This was the nub of socialist behaviour, and fair game for charges from left and right.

The most acceptable tactic they pursued was to improve the climate for cooperatives, which are generally regarded with approval in Canada (except when they are disregarded as of little consequence). The CCF encouraged cooperative growth. In 1941 the percentage of the population that held membership in cooperative organizations was 5.7; by 1946 it was 15.4, and by 1960 it had become 23.2. It has continued to increase since that time, to 32.3 per cent in 1971, with membership in credit unions a substantial 36.7. Farm products marketed through cooperatives in Saskatchewan were valued at $413,000,000, with Alberta next in line with only $260 million, and Quebec following with $225 million. Cooperatives sold supplies and merchandise to the value of $141 million in Saskatchewan in 1970. The development of cooperative enterprise received its greatest impetus under the CCF administration. There were, on the other hand, obstacles in the path of cooperative growth in federal legislation, which for many years arbitrarily classified the associations as "corporations" under tax laws.

The projects varied from marketing agencies for fish and fur, to an oil refinery. The cooperatives that looked most promising at the war's end were groups of young farmers, who arranged, with some difficulty, for joint parcels of land under the Veterans Land Act, but only one of these ventures lasted and most of the holdings were sold back to individual owners.

The Liberal newspapers tried to promote conflict between cooperatives (which represented "freedom") and socialism (which represented "slavery"). This kind of jargon made little sense to Saskatchewan people, because in most cases the staunchest supporters of the coops were also stalwart members of the CCF. When cooperatives and government agencies occasionally overlapped, the problems were settled amicably.

Douglas declared from the outset that three kinds of industrial enterprise would be encouraged: cooperatives for whatever function citizens might wish to organize; private business where its activities were competitive; and government corporations where private enterprise had failed to fill a social need.

It became a tenet of faith to diversify – to build up industry – so that the economy would be less dependent on agriculture and so that Saskatchewan's old capricious enemies of drought, frost, or plagues of insects would have a smaller impact. In 1944, Douglas would point out, non-agricultural production was only $277 million; just before he left the province in 1960, it was $948 million. It had been only 25 per cent of the gross production value in 1945; it had become 62 per cent in 1960. The biggest new non-agricultural producers were oil, minerals, and manufacturing. Whenever Douglas used such figures he could refer to agricultural catastrophes that would have devastated the province and piled new debt on rural communities if wheat had continued to be the only source of wealth: in 1954 in a single night, August 6, a hailstorm wiped out $250 million worth of grain; in the spring of 1960 there were 50,000,000 bushels of grain still lying in the fields under the snow which had come too early for the 1959 harvest.

The most direct route for the government to take in diversifying the economy was through public investment and ownership. Crown corporations are of course nothing new, and Saskatchewan, like Ontario, had a government power corporation as well as a government telephone service. Both, but especially power, were vastly expanded in the CCF regime. The government also moved with alacrity into the insurance field, taking a special satisfaction in channelling into the public purse substantial funds which private insurance competitors would have transferred to head offices in Toronto. In 1946 they introduced the first "no fault" accident plan in North America under their compulsory automobile insurance scheme. Later they moved into fire and other forms of insurance, forcing private competitors to reduce premiums drastically. They took over the bus companies which always claimed to be losing money, invested in new buses, maintained service to remote small towns, and managed to operate with a profit. They developed a northern airways service, and a number of marketing agencies, some of which were transferred to a cooperative structure at a later date.

In all these service industries a triple goal was carefully kept in balance: the crown corporations must provide good service wherever needed in the province; they must keep charges down (and in fact car insurance and telephone rates became the lowest in Canada, while power rates were reduced several times); and they must, if possible, make a profit for the government, over and above their costs. This they managed to do. Year after year the crown corporations brought in extra revenue to boost the general accounts. It was due in part to Clarence Fines' hard-headedness, as well as to other remarkably efficient men like David Cass-Beggs who was head of the Power Corporation for some

years, George Cadbury, and later Thomas Shoyama who were succes-
sively head of the Planning Board, and a number of others who saw the
triple goal as a challenge in administration. The concept as it applies to
crown corporations and government agencies in other parts of Canada
often seems much less well defined. The federally-run post office is an
unhappy example, and one minister's declaration that it must "pay its
way" had disastrous consequences for employee relations and hence, for
service.

A government printing plant also turned out to be a revenue-
producer in Saskatchewan. But most of the processing and manufacturing ventures, mercifully on a small scale, were not destined to flourish.
One box factory in Prince Albert was taken over by the government
when the manager refused to comply with labour relations laws. The
government ran it for a few years, usually at a loss. Competition from
cardboard and plastic containers led to a declining market for wood
boxes and to inevitable failure of the factory. Efforts to manufacture
shoes, to run a tannery, and to operate a woollen mill, similarly floundered and were finally abandoned. Saskatchewan was too far from large
markets; small-scale industry could not compete. Allan Blakeney, Saskatchewan's present Premier, defends the attempts by pointing out that
the Department of Regional Economic Expansion (DREE) spends considerably more money to produce jobs in out-of-the-way places, and with
the federal government's blessing. But Saskatchewan CCF'ers were thin-
skinned about the ridicule their luckless factories brought them. Douglas'
private secretary, Eleanor McKinnon, sighed, "No *good* news ever got
past Fort William."

Much as the government tried to divert the attention of journalists
and editorial writers to the flourishing state of the government insurance
office, it was the red ink of the box factory's books that appeared in
newspapers down east. Even some entirely sensible and ingenious projects were the butt of anti-socialist wit. Douglas said that in 1947 he
happened to be in New York discussing oil with a New York
businessman, who seemed highly skeptical of the government's good
sense and at last referred to a little piece written by Harold Kritzweiser
and published in *Barron's Weekly*. It joked about the ludicrous venture of
the Saskatchewan socialists in processing horse meat. Horse meat! In
Canada!

Douglas said, "I asked him if he wanted to end the interview or if he
wanted to hear the actual story. He said he wanted to hear it."

The story as Douglas related it was of herds of wild horses running at
large in the southern ranch areas, and the problem of the ranchers who
didn't need them, couldn't get a price for them, and wanted to be rid of
them. Cabinet minister John Sturdy made a trip to Belgium and secured
a contract for horse meat. He got a further contract with the United
Nations Relief and Rehabilitation Agency (UNRRA). Back in Sask-

atchewan they rented inexpensive premises at Swift Current, equipped them for a temporary business venture, employed a number of local people, got the ranchers a decent price for their surplus animals, and even cleared a little money. They wound up the business and sold the premises to a large Canadian firm as a pet food plant. A businessman would hardly fault the government for that operation, and the New York executive's skepticism faded.

"I could tell one man the true story," Douglas said ruefully, "but how about the many hundreds who read that article and decided Saskatchewan was the last place in the world to invest their money?"

Attracting private investment was essential to Saskatchewan. The province was obviously unable to raise local capital to develop mineral and oil resources, or to develop the large-scale iron processing and cement plants which were set up as joint public-private ventures. Discoveries of oil and potash offered new sources of wealth.

During the last three terms of the Douglas administration, from 1948 to 1960, there could be no arguing with the rapid growth of the province. Despite adverse publicity, capital *was* moving into Saskatchewan. In 1961 the federal Department of Trade and Commerce, in its report on "Private and Public Investment in Canada, Regional Estimates", gave Saskatchewan high marks for performance. From 1948 to 1960 it had shown the highest rate of growth for private plus public investment per capita of any province. Its increase had been 140 per cent, almost double that of British Columbia at 74 per cent.

The Liberal Opposition followed an ambiguous line of criticism in the matter. It argued that investment was being chased away from the socialist province, yet professed to see numerous shady deals which permitted disreputable operators to exploit the province's resources for vast sums, with gross kickbacks to the CCF ministers. Political charges of scandal and corruption were the daily conversation of the out-of-power Liberals. There was patently malicious gossip concerning Swiss bank accounts and private fortune-hunting. Provincial Treasurer Fines was the favourite target. He could have bought and sold Las Vegas, and was just the type to do it, if a quarter of the rumours had been true.

Douglas in fact imposed conflict-of-interest guidelines, insisting that no cabinet minister should own any shares in a firm doing business with the government. As far as he was concerned, he lived on his official salary, without private resources.

Douglas had hoped for complete public ownership of the potash find near Unity which in 1946 opened up immense prospects. The province had been able to develop sodium sulphate deposits by government funds alone, with an assured Canadian market. But the potash not only called for more capital but for the cultivation of export markets. Douglas tried to get federal government participation – he had gone personally to Sir Stafford Cripps in London who would have favoured an inter-government agreement – but Prime Minister St. Laurent and his Minister of Mines and Resources, Alison Glen, turned it down. So private investors were invited in. By 1964 when the CCF regime in Saskatchewan ended, the plant at Esterhazy was producing four million tons of potash annually.

The discovery of considerable quantities of natural gas brought the province another major asset. Gas distribution became a government monopoly, and this fact had some repercussions in the great pipeline hassle which precipitated the downfall of the Liberals. C. D. Howe's crude haste in preventing debate and ramming a bill through parliament to meet his personal commitment to an American company jolted the nation that spring, and launched Diefenbaker on his successful campaign for the Prime Ministership. But privately and in public the CCF had been fighting the pipeline battle for the previous five years. They had fought for an all-Canada route, in which they were joined by Conservative Howard Green in 1952 but opposed by Conservative Carl Nickle in 1955. (Nickle said that insistence on an all-Canadian route was based on "denial of economic sense in favour of nationalism".) The CCF was even more deeply concerned that the pipeline should be publicly-owned, instead of merely publicly subsidized. The roughest and costliest sections were being constructed by the government but the whole thing was to be handed over to the private company, Trans-Canada Pipelines. In this aspect of the battle the Conservatives lent some qualified support, inducing Trade Minister Howe to invite them sarcastically to "stand up and be counted with the party on their left, who at least advocate public ownership out of intellectual conviction, not out of intellectual confusion."

C. D. Howe was the architect and prime mover of the piece, " . . . this sinister man," as a *Globe and Mail* editorial called him on May 26. William Kilbourn, who chronicled the whole affair, called Howe: "the member in a different orbit from the rest, C. D. Howe, who was by turns bellicose, bored, impatient and jovial, but always obedient as he could be to whatever plan would end all the palaver and get him his bill by June 7."[6]

But it was to Prime Minister St. Laurent, who remained silent and withdrawn through most of the affair, that Douglas addressed his request for consideration of a scheme to finance and build the pipeline through joint federal and provincial government ownership.

The request was sent in November 1955, when there had already been innumerable delays in reaching an agreement with Trans-Canada Pipelines. The federal government had set up a "temporary" crown corporation through joint action with the Ontario government as the only means of getting the line through the unprofitable stretch of northern Ontario. It was to be turned over to the company as soon as other links were completed.

Douglas was being pressed by Trans-Canada to sign a contract taking gas from the still-to-be-built section from Alberta to Winnipeg, for distribution through the Saskatchewan Power Corporation. He was reluctant to do so if the signing would be construed as approval of the privately-owned line. Saskatchewan had already constructed some northern transmission lines of its own directly from its own gas fields and neighbouring Alberta. There was every indication that Trans-Canada would, eventually, go through the southern section of Saskatchewan, in which case the sensible course was to buy gas from them instead of building duplicate lines. But how soon would Trans-Canada be operating? Douglas decided to press his proposal for joint government ownership.

> In repeated public statements I have made it clear that the Saskatchewan Government is of the opinion that the Trans-Canada Pipeline should be a public utility with the Government of Canada building the main transmission lines. From press statements I gather that your government is opposed to such a policy. I would like to suggest that as an alternative you might sound out the provinces involved to see if they would be prepared to enter into an arrangement with your government for the joint construction and operation of the Trans-Canada Pipeline.
>
> Your government has already expressed its willingness to enter into an agreement with the province of Ontario for the construction of the unprofitable portion of the line which runs through Northern Ontario. It would seem to me that having accepted this much responsibility there are sound reasons for proceeding one step further and constructing the entire line as a publicly-owned utility. By doing this the people of Canada would retain control of a vital natural resource and would have power to direct its usage in such a manner as to best advance the interests of the Canadian economy.

Douglas might have claimed the people of Canada seemed to favour public ownership, as the Gallup Poll and a number of leading newspapers indicated. But he chose to be deferential:

> So far the Government of Saskatchewan has not been asked for any expression of opinion on gas transmission by your government and it may be that I am displaying undue temerity in placing my views before you. May I assure you, however, that I am motivated by a desire to cooperate with your government and the provinces concerned in working out a policy which, I believe, will in the long view be beneficial to the future development of our country.[7]

He sent copies of his letter to the Premiers who might conceivably share in such a scheme, Campbell of Manitoba, Frost of Ontario, and Duplessis of Quebec.

But it was brushed aside by St. Laurent:

190

This matter will undoubtedly be the subject of discussion early in the next session of our Parliament. In these circumstances, I feel it would be improper of me to attempt in correspondence with you to anticipate the substance of that discussion. I have no doubt that the points you raise will come up in the debates in the House of Commons and those speaking for this government will be quite prepared to explain the reasons why a course of action of the type you suggest was not followed.[8]

Douglas discussed the matter fully with the CCF leader in Ottawa, M. J. Coldwell, expressing the dark suspicion that Trans-Canada was pressing Saskatchewan to sign a contract with them well in advance of the line being built, chiefly to give the Liberals in the Commons a weapon to silence the CCF critics of Trans-Canada: "I am not completely convinced that the favourable contract now before us is entirely motivated by the need for Trans-Canada having this contract before it will get permission to build the line to Winnipeg. I fear that Trans-Canada and the Federal Government would like to have Saskatchewan's signature on the contract so that they can use it to answer criticisms of the CCF in Parliament and elsewhere."[9]

His suspicions were well founded. In May the following year, when the violent debate erupted in the Commons, Walter Tucker, Saskatchewan's Liberal leader, suggested that Douglas was on good terms with the private company his federal leaders were attacking. Douglas countered by making public his correspondence with St. Laurent, and insisting that he had always advocated that gas distribution be a public utility. He added that the federal government had now found it necessary to advance a great deal of money to support Trans-Canada's prairie section of the line and, "If the people of Canada are going to put up 95 per cent of the money to build the gas pipeline then surely it is only common sense to put up the other five per cent and retain ownership and control of this resource which is vital to the economic development of Canada."

Kilbourn records that "federal officials" were sensitive to the public's interest in having government ownership of the line which their taxes were so heavily supporting. At the conclusion of the 1955 agreement with Ontario to build the northern section,

> The federal officials left the meeting with the promise that government ownership of the whole line would not be ruled out, at least until it was discussed at the October dominion-provincial conference. But as Premier Douglas of Saskatchewan later remarked in a letter to Prime Minister St. Laurent, 'the federal government had really made up its mind long since.' Neither he nor Premier Campbell of Manitoba were effectively consulted about the possibility of a multi-government crown corporation.[10]

Trans-Canada Pipeline was completed in October, 1958. Eventually Home Oil became the biggest shareholder.

The big break-through in the diversification of Saskatchewan industry was oil – not in the gushing abundance of Alberta's fields but in very satisfactory annual totals. From 1948 on there was a rush for exploration and development rights. Who owned what mineral rights in the province had to be sorted out. Very early homesteaders were lucky; they had acquired mineral rights with their land up to 1890. Homesteads taken up after 1890 at first ceded their mineral rights to the federal government, but after 1930 rights were transferred to the province, which became a very large holder of the mineral rights within Saskatchewan borders. Large private holdings still belonged, however, to the CPR, which had been given the mineral rights to the vast acreage the company had acquired with the building of the first rail lines.

In the lands where it owned the mineral rights, the provincial government kept control through a checkerboard pattern of leasing, which let oil companies lease alternate sections. It offered variations in conventional royalty arrangements, under which companies make a bonus bid for a fixed royalty percentage. Companies were offered an option of bidding at a lower figure with the government retaining a larger royalty. Saskatchewan has retained and increased its direct interest in its oil, a situation that becomes increasingly important, and which has prompted the province's present premier, Allan Blakeney to praise the "good decisions" of the 1940s and 1950s. Blakeney has not been tempted to renege on original contracts, as he claims Alberta's government has done by increasing royalties beyond agreed-upon ceilings. Douglas, he says, left the fixing of royalties open to future governments, within "reasonable" limits. Blakeney contends that today's royalties are "reasonable", a contention that is not quite the view of the companies involved, but which cannot be described as a violation of earlier contracts.

It was interesting that Blakeney sought and found a sympathetic federal ally in Tommy Douglas in 1973 when the "oil crisis" brought furious charges from eastern Canada that Alberta and Saskatchewan were holding up eastern consumers for ransom. Some Ontario members of the NDP had difficulty accepting Blakeney's Saskatchewan-first position. Douglas met for hours with party leaders at Ottawa, at Blakeney's side. Those long years of uneven-handed battle with the more prosperous provinces were clearly etched in Douglas' mind: he pressed for a position that would not exploit the situation but would clearly favour Saskatchewan's treasury.

The messiest aspect of the oil exploration period in Saskatchewan had to do with the small land holders who still retained their mineral rights, and were in danger of being fleeced out of them by fly-by-night operators. Not only mineral rights, but surface rights to permit drilling were being sought, and some highly questionable deals were signed and bitterly regretted by rural people, until a housecleaning was undertaken by a tougher Securities Commission (under Blakeney).

A few on-the-spot journalists sang the praises of Saskatchewan's economic growth under the CCF. Notable among them was Chris Higginbotham who said that Douglas "presided over the province's leap into the twentieth century."[11]

Higginbotham said that though God and good weather might get some credit, "there was nothing fortuitous about the building of the first modern highway system, extended education, extensive public and private industry, a twentieth-century public service, farm and rural electrification, farm home sewers and water."

Average personal income in the province during the Douglas years remained slightly below the national average. (In 1959 it was estimated at $1,302 per capita compared to a national figure of $1,492.) It was still, in the national picture, a resource-poor province, but development and industrial growth had left the old agrarian homestead economy far in the past.

In the distribution of wealth, it is significant that the greatest emphasis was on public services, like health or low-cost insurance, along with less tangible emphasis on educational and employment opportunities. Cash handouts were never very prominent in the CCF gamut of government benefits. But the outlay in health services, in housing for the elderly, and a considerable range of other programs was extensive, and the attention to economic growth was tied closely to awareness of those growing costs.

Chapter Thirteen
Premier 3: Jubilee

. . . reflect with me on the health and welfare of the CCF movemen
as it has developed through the years. It seems appropriate to do thi
in our Province's Golden Jubilee Year. The Province was born ir
1905; the CCF dates from the Regina Manifesto of 1933. That is, the
CCF has been an active force in Saskatchewan for nearly half of the
Province's life – more indeed than that if we consider, as we quite
properly may, the beginnings of the CCF idea in the Farmer-Labour
and Progressive movements of preceding years.

We can take a great deal of satisfaction in what our movemen
has achieved in that sweep of years. We have established a patterr
of cooperative living, we have enhanced the quality of life in thi
Province.

The speaker was Carlyle King, CCF president, addressing a provin
cial convention on July 20, 1955. Did he invent, for the politician'
phrasebook, "the quality of life"? He was talking of it forty years before i
became a federal election slogan.

There were cultural achievements – in this province poor in re
sources and with less than a million people – years ahead of similar gains
in other parts of Canada. The Arts Council to assist performing artist
was established a decade before the Canada Council at Ottawa. The Bil
of Rights was fourteen years ahead of the federal proclamation. Th
Archives established in 1945 became a model imitated elsewhere. A
second university campus grew at Regina – to serve less than a millior
people – while at Saskatoon was developed a College of Medicine and a
first-rate department of agricultural research. There were nev
museums, travelling libraries, local auditoria, and art galleries. The ar
galleries were small but selective; theatre groups were parochial bu
enthusiastic; and travelling companies of artists increasingly reached
Regina and Saskatoon.

For many the greatest cultural interest was always hockey and curl
ing. Every tiny village had an ice rink for each. In the 1940s mammotl
arenas replaced open, board-fenced rinks. And other sports flourished
the Douglas family were Regina Rough Rider fans, as was the rest of th
province.

Society "opened up" from more puritan days. Saskatchewan retreated by slow and awkward stages from the prohibition era. Until the end of the war public drinking places were labelled "licensed premises", screened from the street, and restricted to male customers; no food or entertainment were allowed within those profane "premises". Douglas opened cocktail lounges and beer parlours to both sexes, and licensed restaurants and dining rooms to serve liquor with meals – except on Sundays.

Making a second series of changes in 1958, Douglas said, "I would prefer that people not drink at all. But I recognize that in a free society I have no more right to prevent another man drinking than he has the right to force me to drink."

He had taken to heart the observation of Chief Justice Armour: "I do not think drinking intoxicating liquor makes a man criminal any more than eating oatmeal makes him a Presbyterian."

Until the war's end, school children in Saskatchewan purchased their own books and scribblers. Under the CCF textbooks were provided free. The rickety frame country schools were abandoned for reorganized, larger units of school administration.

Parks were included with the development of the Saskatchewan River for power and irrigation. "Pioneer trails" encouraged vacationists – it was odd but no doubt commendable to see septuagenarians celebrating "the past" in which they had played active roles. Quite a grand concept developed, once the province felt it could afford it, around the legislative grounds in Regina. Douglas in his last year as Premier initiated plans for Wascana Centre, where among extensive parks and waterways a large new theatre, music hall, and buildings of the Regina Campus (now Regina University) imposed a "centre for government, education, arts and recreation" on the flat stubble of the prairie landscape.

Elitism was treated with scorn in Saskatchewan: Douglas tried to abolish the Lieutenant-Governorship in 1944 and when Prime Minister St. Laurent insisted on the appointment as a federal prerogative, the Premier took His Excellency's house away from him and converted it to educational purposes, billeting the gentleman in a hotel.

Despite its protests, Saskatchewan was not averse to a bit of royal pomp. Douglas' audiences loved to hear about his encounters with the Royal Family, particularly those stories in which a plain sort of guy said something outrageous to His Majesty.

Archie McNab, who left office in 1945, had been a popular Lieutenant-Governor, a genial, unpretentious man, short, round and jolly, wearing a derby hat pushed well back and resembling no one so much as a London cab driver.

Douglas said,

When I went to him with my list of new ministers I approached him very properly and began, 'Your Honour' . . . But he tapped me on the shoulder and said, 'Call me Archie.' We got along famously.

In 1948 I was in London as a guest of the United Kingdom Parliamentary Association. Parliament was opened while I was there by George VI. It was followed by a buffet dinner at Buckingham Palace. A footman came up to me and said, 'His Majesty would like to see you.' I was led to where the king and queen were standing and after the king shook hands he asked 'How is my friend Archie McNab?' I said with regret that McNab was dead. He told this story: after a state dinner in Regina when the king and queen were visiting in 1939, they had coffee together at Saskatchewan House and Archie invited King George to take off his coat, which he did. When it was time to retire Archie fussed around looking for the coat, and the king, right behind him, heard him say, 'Where in hell is the king's coat? The bugger wants to go to bed.' Queen Elizabeth said it was her husband's favourite story for years.

In 1951 Princess Elizabeth and the Duke of Edinburgh visited Regina, on a particularly cold and austere October day, and the preparations were a mixture of loyal desire to do the right thing, and a determination to "be what we are." First the cabinet decided not to present a gift. Why get into competition with other provincial capitals, and spend a bundle of money on yet another diamond pin? Later they relented. A tasteful group of paintings by a Saskatchewan artist, along with Indian leather work, were considered appropriate.

In addition, the city of Regina presented the Princess with what must have been one of her least likely acquisitions, a certificate for five hundred bushels of Number One Northern Wheat. Fortunately she was not required to take delivery. A special sale was arranged which realized $14.14 a bushel, and the sum was bestowed by the Princess on a crippled children's hospital. The wheat itself eventually went to Greece.

A Saskatoon artist, Robert Hurley, had the good luck to sell four paintings to the government for presentation. Hurley's water colours already had achieved some fame, and his fortunes soared after October 1951.

A close-at-hand description of preparations for the big day was written by Eleanor McKinnon to her sister in Montreal:

Monday and Tuesday the office was a madhouse. At one time in our outer office I counted three CBC engineers, a commentator, a rug mender, a window cleaner, two electricians, a carpenter, a painter the Public Works housekeeper and two of his staff. Each had a ladder or a vacuum or a pail of varnish and confusion reigned. One fellow while vacuuming the tapestries knocked down and broke the vial of oil which was the first to come through the Inter-Provincia Pipeline and which Tommy treasured. I haven't yet told him. All th while the phone was ringing at thirty-second intervals. One woman called long distance to say they had a son named Duke and she thought he should have a special invitation and be presented to the Duke. I could hardly refrain from telling her a lot of people had called their dog Duke too. . .

In all this mess I had to place the fifteen watercolours by Hurley around the office and try to decide which four were the best. We peered at them through ladders and moving men, and once we had made the selection I had to rush them downtown, arrange to have them remounted and find a bookbinder who would make a leather folio to fit them in time for the great day – which incidentally was the next day. . .

The four Hurleys represented prairie scenes during each of our four seasons and were a happy choice, I think. In addition we sent a rush call to the far north for Indian leather work. Our pilots dropped down in every settlement, and radio operators and the entire northern population cooperated beautifully. At ten p.m. Tuesday I called at the back door of the Regina Post Office to pick up the parcel which had been flown some eight hundred miles. Mar and Mrs. Sinton were standing by ready to wrap them. From what was sent we selected embroidered white caribou gauntlets for the Duke; fur-trimmed, embroidered caribou slippers for H. R. H. and the same for the children.

At 9:45 Wednesday morning our driver called for me and the Royal presents. I had a lot of last-minute things to do and I had just rolled the red carpet out for the balcony appearance (off our office) when Their Royal Highnesses walked into the Council Chamber. I was presented to them first, then Tim. They were invited to sign the book and I handed the pen to Princess Elizabeth. Tim handed the pen to Philip and to my horror it didn't work. I had tested it but a moment before. He looked a bit annoyed and amused at the same time. His reaction is beautifully registered in a newspaper photograph which I'll send if I can pick up an extra. I'm moving over to hand him the other pen . . . I had on my new Blanche Buchanan suit for the first time and it's really a darb and I was all spit and polish but the picture records my long nose. . .

That situation over, I was asked to escort Princess Elizabeth to CD's office to remove her wraps and as I told you, I lifted the mink coat from the royal shoulders. The lady-in-waiting was there too and the three of us chatted for some time. Princess Elizabeth seemed in no hurry to face the throng again and powdered her nose twice. We discussed the weather which was plain awful – penetratingly cold and very dull – and they both laughed when I said a polar air mass had just moved in. I kept forgetting to say 'Ma'am' at the end of every sentence but I'm sure she'd forgive me. . .

197

I slipped into the Speaker's Gallery for the presentation of the 300-odd farmers and dignitaries. The curtseys of some ladies were something to behold. When the guests were assembling earlier one of the ladies fell down the steps on entering the Legislative Chamber. The husband in question was beast enough to glare at her, but she picked herself up from her belly position on the floor and walked away with dignity. One story I particularly liked: a reporter at the Stadium where the kids, rural and urban, had congregated, stopped a little girl who was looking after a younger brother and asked where they came from. 'He's just come from the bathroom,' the little girl replied.

Mr. and Mrs. Douglas attended Queen Elizabeth's coronation in 1953, as almost every inhabitant of Saskatchewan would have wished them to do, and there was a later visit to Saskatchewan by the royal pair in 1959 when Queen Elizabeth turned on the switch for a newly-completed power station near Saskatoon. Princess Margaret flew by helicopter to visit farms near Prince Albert in 1958. Royal visits in Saskatchewan were always a homey blend of excitement and local pride, and their effect was to heighten the province's determination to demonstrate its own special brand of democratic progress.

The Bill of Rights, prohibiting discrimination on grounds of race, colour or creed, was considered advanced legislation in 1946. Request for copies came from B. K. Sandwell, chairman of the Committee for a Bill of Rights in Ontario, from points in the United States, from Port Louis on the island of Mauritius.

Its influence was felt almost at once. In September, 1947, a black CNR porter from Winnipeg, Charles A. Blair, wrote to Douglas. He had heard of the Bill of Rights, and he had just been refused entry to a dance hall in North Battleford. The dance hall, ironically, was the "Uncle Tom's Cabin". Attorney-General Corman followed up the case and received a candid letter from the proprietor, Tom Cabourn, who said he was an American and it had always been the custom of white people to bar negroes from the establishments they patronized. It was no longer the custom in Saskatchewan, he was told, and he was let off with a warning.

Saskatchewan had a population of mixed racial origin. In 1941 the census showed thirty-three nationalities within the province. There were 168,917 English, 108,919 Scottish, and 95,852 Irish. There were only 50,530 French. There were 130,258 German; 79,777 Ukrainian; 27,905 Poles; 25,933 Russians; 14,576 Hungarians, and 35,894 Dutch. From Scandinavia there were 39,213 Norwegians, and 20,961 Swedes. The Chinese population was only 2,545, the Negro population only 403. Those who listed themselves as Jewish numbered 4,149.

When Angus MacInnis, the CCF M.P. for Vancouver East, raised the issue of west coast Canadians of Japanese descent who were expelled

rom their homes during wartime, Douglas alone among Canadian
1eads of government offered refuge to them. Grace MacInnis wrote in
1945:

"I see by the weekend papers that you have been the only province to
ay that you are willing to accept your share of these Canadian citizens
. . It is good to know that one can become a Premier and still be able to
vithstand the kind of pressure that race prejudice creates."[1]

Douglas answered, "We are finding a considerable amount of bitter-
1ess, especially among the Canadian Legion, in regard to this matter . . .
The flames of racial prejudice have been fanned so long . . . If there is
1ny one thing which the CCF owes to the memory of your father, it is
hat they should defend the rights of minority groups, and befriend
hose who are the victims of racial and religious persecution."[2]

Douglas, for his action, incurred the wrath of some Sask-
1tchewanites. A gentleman named Joseph Tucker, speaking as a rep-
·esentative of Sub Rosa (a locality which does not appear on the highway
nap, though we have Mr. Tucker's letter for proof that it exists) told
Douglas: "Maybe your acceptance of Japs for the rest of the province
goes, but not for Sub Rosa. We have now a peaceful and well-conducted
:ommunity at Sub Rosa, and we want to keep it so . . . If a public meeting
vith a unanimous anti-Jap vote is necessary it can be arranged."[3]

In 1947 Douglas was criticized by the Vancouver *Sun* for hiring
Thomas Shoyama (now a deputy minister at Ottawa) in a senior adminis-
rative post. The newspaper carried a headline: "CCF Government
Opens Posts to Japs", and began:

Socialist Premier T. C. Douglas has named three Canadian-born
Japanese to high advisory posts in the Saskatchewan government
service. One is on the provincial cancer commission. The other two
are on the government's economic advisory staff.

Similarly, one of the most important positions in the entire public
service, that of legal advisor to the Labour Relations Board, is held
by a member of the Jewish race. His post makes him almost the
dictator of labour policy in the province.[4]

The darkest problem facing Douglas, and the one he was least able to
olve, was the degradation of the Indian people of Saskatchewan. The
olains Indians were perhaps the least lucky of any native groups, for the
videness of land had been as necessary to their hunting as it later became
o successful farming by white settlers. Saskatchewan farmers acquired a
ection or more, as rapidly as possible, because any smaller acreage
vould not "pay". Yet the dispossessed Indians, corralled on small re-
erves, and with no agricultural tradition were expected to farm tiny
1creages of not more than forty to eighty acres per family, an amount
hat could not begin to support them except by the most intensive mod-
·rn cultivation. Indian people on the reserves were barely sustained

from one generation to the next by handouts from the federal government whose "wards" they had become.

The 1941 census counted 13,384 Indians, and 9,160 "halfbreeds" in Saskatchewan. The "halfbreeds" were the Métis, and because they were not Indian by paternal lineage they were outside federal responsibility; they were Saskatchewan citizens, they had the right to vote, they had the right to whatever "quality of life" was made generally available under CCF government. Because most Métis were brought up by Indian mothers and lived in fringe areas close to Indian reserves, they were regarded as Indian by the white population. This meant that they were ignored, for most purposes. The epic story of Saskatchewan as it has been told was a white man's story.

Larger numbers of Métis lived in the northern bushland, and the CCF government's first contact with them was the attempt to regularize and stabilize fish and fur marketing through government agencies. It was not an immediately acceptable or workable arrangement: some Métis trappers suspected they could get more through private sales and sometimes the government cheques were slow in arriving. The government tried to foster cooperative stores for general supplies, in competition with the ubiquitous Hudson's Bay Company. But a cooperative enterprise is not to be imposed on a nomadic and unsophisticated people, and development was slow.

The northern Métis had organized a Saskatchewan Métis Association in 1943. But the southern Métis were harder to organize, suspicious of the northern group: they had a different way of life, and not much of a life at all.

In July 1944, earlier reports by the provincial health department which had been brought to Health Minister J. M. Uhrich's attention in 1942, landed on Douglas' desk.

The 1942 report was brought to Douglas' attention, as Minister of Health, by J. H. Brockelbank. He had been told of its existence by a woman of Yorkton, a member of the Métis Association, who had approached Brockelbank with a request to purchase a large farm of three hundred ninety-five cultivated acres for resettlement by Métis. The land could be bought for $20,000. The woman thought eight or nine of the families mentioned in the report could be maintained there.

The report was exhumed from the files. It had been written in December 1942 by Dr. F. C. Middleton, director of the division of communicable disease, and it accompanied and confirmed, after Dr. Middleton's own investigation, the report of two other doctors of the department earlier in the year.

Within twenty miles of the little city of Yorkton was a community of some twenty-two Métis families, twenty of them squatters and, as nontaxpayers, denied assistance by the municipal authorities. Forty or fifty children of school age had never been to school; some had begun school and had been refused admission to the classroom because trustees and ratepayers objected to their filthy condition. Ten young men had been rejected by the army because of illiteracy and health problems. Within the community were advanced cases of trachoma and tuberculosis, some waiting for admission to hospital, some not previously diagnosed. Scabies and impetigo were prevalent. Métis with venereal disease had been turned away by doctors who said they did not treat veneral disease. All of them lived, Dr. Middleton said, in "filth and squalor".

From Lebret, Leross, and other points came similar accounts. Métis families were living on nothing but potatoes. Métis people were treated at a hospital but the municipality refused to pay for them; the bill was forwarded to the government at Regina.

Fred De Laronde, president of the Métis Association, persisted in his letters to the Premier and to the Minister of Welfare, O. W. Valleau. He thought it was probably "against the law" to talk about V.D., but conditions were very bad. The answer to that was that the CCF health department had set up five free clinics to treat venereal disease – all of them in the cities.

A first conference was arranged to bring Métis together, but Fred De Laronde, when he asked for assistance to get to Regina, was told that delegates must pay their own expenses.

De Laronde wrote, in March 1946, saying that a cash surplus might be found, if the government looked for it, from a grant of $10,000 under the Patterson government, earmarked for research and for a delegation to Ottawa to determine responsibility for Métis rehabilitation. A law firm had been paid $7000 of the money to prepare a brief, and the brief concurred in the federal government's position: Métis were a provincial responsibility. Surely the balance could be used for current organizational needs of the Métis Association?

An inter-government memo to Douglas on the matter stated: "After we took office a Treasury Warrant of $500 was given to the Métis Association to allow them to take a trip to Ottawa to satisfy themselves that there was no possible chance of the Dominion assuming responsibility . . . My information is that the balance (about $3000) reverted to Treasury at the expiration of the year since it was unexpended . . . It cannot be assumed that a balance is owing to anyone."

De Laronde was sent a copy of a brief which had recently been prepared on the problems of the Indians. He replied, "Just to thank you for the Indian brief which I just received. It contains valuable material for the Indians.

"Now we will go on for the Métis."[5]

That year, 1946, a first Métis Convention was held at the Court House Building in Regina. It was held during Regina Fair Week, when many native people made their way to the city, and were in fact encouraged to set up tents on the perimeter of the fair grounds as a colourful added attraction.

It was the first time a Premier had met with them, and Fred De Laronde was jubilant. Valleau had begun a cooperative farm at Lebret; some initiatives were underway in vocational training for Métis youths. Slowly a start was being made.

Two Métis organizations clashed at the conference, to the frustration of Morris Shumiatcher, at that time executive assistant to Douglas, who was bent on achieving a prompt solution. A variety of briefs were presented. The Métis population was said to have reached well over 50,000, an indication not so much of an ascending birth rate as of completely unreliable statistics (the 1941 census had put the number at just over 9,000). The cheating of the Métis by issuing them worthless "scrip" in payment for their land, a fraud exposed in 1922, was related again. The action of the Anderson government in cancelling Métis fishing rights in the Qu'Appelle waterways in the midst of the depression was described. The expulsion of a Métis settlement at Willowfield by the passing of a herd law on behalf of ranchers was reported. The plea was for land-lease, equipment for farming or small industry, building materials for homes, vocational training.

Douglas spoke to the group with less than his usual resounding confidence. No one anywhere, no government, had accepted responsibility for these people of mixed ancestry. He did not want to be paternal. He did want to give them a chance to do things for themselves. The Lebret cooperative farm might prove worthwhile, and if the Métis wished, others could be started. The government was still trying to work out what assistance was most needed.

Fred De Laronde said: "I was glad when I got a letter from the Honourable Mr. Douglas. One night I got that letter. I read the letter over and over again. It kind of more or less surprised me. I didn't believe it was possible until I read it over and over again."

O. W. Valleau reported that a school had been opened in the district near Yorkton which had been the subject of the 1942 report. In fact that school, under a particularly dedicated teaching couple, became a source of some satisfaction to the Premier, who visited it for its first graduation exercises in 1951. The top girls in the graduating class had received no schooling at all until 1946, when one of them had been nine and the other twelve years of age.

Under Shumiatcher's purposeful guidance, a Métis Advisory Committee to the government was appointed at the 1946 Regina Conference. By November that Committee had presented its first report:

> The Métis in and around the Welby District wants a certain piece of road to be fixed in that area;

The Métis of Lebret wishes for a Market Gardening project to be started in the Lebret District;

The Regina and Saskatoon Métis wishes for long-term housing loans to be made available to them;

The Métis in the following districts wishes for assistance in acquiring certain blocks of land to build homes on: Willow Field, Lestock, Jack Fish Lake, Cochin on Midnight Lake, Tweedsmuir, Big River, Carrot River Valley, etc, etc;

In the Estevan district the Métis wants a Cooperative Coal Mine to be opened up in that district;

A very large percentage of the Métis of Saskatchewan are not satisfied with the present Fur Trapping and Fur Marketing provincial laws;

The Métis Advisory Committee agrees with the Provincial Government that the only way to iron out Métis problems, especially problems needing government attention, is through an effective provincial organization;

"Therefore we request a cash grant of $1000 to be used for living and travelling expenses of organizers.

The request for $1000 was turned down. Caution, still mixed with strong doses of paternalism, was apparent in the government action.

By 1948 the Métis were included under the free hospitalization program of the province. By 1949 a group of one hundred Métis had been moved from a southern area near Lestock to Green Lake, some miles beyond North Battleford. Farming and a saw mill were initiated, land and home-building supplies were granted. One of the tactics used by the saw mill operator, Douglas said, was to see that every Métis woman received the Eaton's mail order catalogue, to keep the men at work. The experiment met with at least moderate success, as did similar rehabilitation efforts at Duck Lake, Glen Mary, and Lebret. A single season could not transform unhealthy, uneducated, and uncertain people into hardy pioneers. The government, hard-pressed for funds on every hand, found some discouraging reports hard to take, and was particularly sensitive to Liberal attacks on the projects in the Legislature.

In 1953 Douglas wrote to anthropologist V. F. Valentine who had reported on conditions among Métis in the north: "My own observation compels me to admit that we have so far failed to come to grips in a realistic manner with their basic problems."[6] In a further letter he admitted the government was only "scratching the surface".

Later in the 1950s, as more money and effort continued to be directed to assist Métis to establish farms and other projects, more hopeful reports came back from Green Lake and Lebret. But the rapidly expanding birth rate, and the seemingly uncontrollable poor health and destitution had led Douglas to conclude that no real solution was possible without federal and provincial help in a program for all native people: "Our Department of Social Welfare is convinced that we cannot clean up the Métis problem unless something is done simultaneously about the Indian problem."[7]

The Métis had tried in vain to persuade earlier governments that they should have the same "rights" as treaty Indians. Those rights were pathetically meagre, and the fact that Métis regarded Indians as favoured in relation to themselves is a particularly depressing commentary on the lot of each.

Douglas found that his difficult and frustrating efforts on behalf of the Métis were considerably easier than his efforts to help the Indians. The Indians were the victims of jurisdictional conflict – clearly, under the constitution, to be cared for by the federal government yet in fact disgracefully neglected and ignored, and at the same time clinging to their treaty rights and their holdings on the reserves.

The practical, obvious "solution" to Douglas (as it was to Trudeau twenty years later) was to do away with the reserves and the degradation that went with "wardship" and integrate the Indians with all speed into Canadian society. He worked to assume provincial jurisdiction, with the federal government paying the cost for the indigent, to incorporate the Indians into provincial health and welfare systems. He wanted Indian children bused to white schools, and fought the objections of white parents to that integration. Until 1960 when he left Saskatchewan, progress for Indians was measured in terms of integration, The more recent militancy, the nationalism of new Indian groups was a product of the seventies, when Indian parents would protest integrated schools and insist on restoring education to Indian communities.

What Douglas did for the Indians of Saskatchewan was to give them the vote, and the right to drink liquor like white people. The first benefit was offered repeatedly and accepted reluctantly; the second was eagerly sought, and was granted with misgivings. Those misgivings were in fact shared by many older Indians, and Douglas could only fall back on the broad truth: "If liquor is bad for us, it is bad for the Indian. But there has to be the same law for all."

The period of CCF administration was the time of sudden, unexplained revival among the Indian people of Canada. The population had dropped steadily. The popular white assumption was that Indians were a "dying race". In 1941 the Indians made up little more than one per cent of the population of Saskatchewan. A decade later they were more than two per cent. All over Canada the native birth rate shot up and the hopelessly overcrowded reserves sent more and more Indians to skid row districts in the cities. Pressures mounted and produced a revision of the federal Indian Act in 1951, the first important change since 1860, and there were drawn-out negotiations to use provincial social services, health and education facilities for the federal "wards".

204

In July 1945, a year after taking office, Douglas had his first important encounter with the Indians when he was invited to a Pipe of Chiefs ceremony on the Assiniboine Reserve near Montmartre. There he was named Chief Red Eagle, We-a-ga-sha. Those present recall his wife Irma's amusement at the enormous feather headdress above his small, spectacled face, and how Shirley danced with delight. "I took part in their dance," Douglas said. "It's comparatively simple. You just do the Highland Fling as though you had a ten-pound weight on each foot."

"But I told them," Douglas said, "that I intended to take the honour seriously. And we tried hard."

The Assiniboine chief with whom he felt most at ease was Dan Kennedy, whose eloquence marked him as a gentleman of the old school, and who visited him shortly after the Montmartre ceremony and later wrote of the "cordial reception accorded to our delegation". Chief Kennedy said, "I am at a loss to say which impressed me more, the matchless splendour of the architectural beauty of the noble edifice of the Parliament building with its marble colonnades and lofty dome, or the spiritual pre-eminence of the Noble Chief Red Eagle who sits in honour in this sanctum."[8]

Progress was hampered, as with the Métis people, by factional disputes, and Chief Kennedy said, "I was particularly pleased with your readiness to help smooth over the differences of the Indian organizations in Saskatchewan and of your quick appraisal of the chief source of our weakness."

Douglas had invited Indians to visit the legislature and discuss their problems, and many came, to sit quietly in chairs, to exchange a few words, presently to leave. There were few as gifted in speech as Kennedy.

Eleanor McKinnon expressed the frustration of the Premier's staff. "Our problem with them was that they would just sit all day in the office. It was hard to get out of them what they wanted. I don't think they were too sure at times . . . Chief Dan Kennedy was a very intelligent leader . . . There were a lot of delegations. But they were not articulate."

Across a cultural abyss so vast, what could an Indian delegation say they wanted? A new road past their reserve? A new deal? A new society?

Again the effort was made to bring Indian representatives together to form a single provincial organization. At least three groups existed, the Indian Association of Saskatchewan, the Protective Association for Indians and the Treaties, and the Saskatchewan wing of the more militant North American Indian Brotherhood. A succession of meetings early in 1946 resulted in the Union of Saskatchewan Indians with an executive drawn from all three groups. Trouble rose in Lebret, a predominantly Catholic district, when a brief drafted by Shumiatcher and directed to the federal government recommended an end to parochial residential schools. The *Indian Missionary Record* said the Lebret Indians would turn down the proposed organization "drafted by Mr. Douglas" they feared Chief Red Eagle was trying to use them to his own political advantage and impose a "pagan" rather than a Christian education. In fact the federal government was soon to phase out the residential schools after a number of unfavourable reports on their operation.

There was expressed resentment also by some Indian leaders against the active presence of government officials, M.P.s and M.L.A.s at meetings, and Douglas was asked to restrain their participation.

Douglas held out for total federal responsibility for old age and blind pensions for Indian people, and replied to an enquirer (A.J.E. Liesemer a CCF M.L.A. in Calgary) that he was extending an argument over pensions into broader discussions with the federal government:

> I don't need to tell you that handing out family allowances and old age pensions to Indians and Métis doesn't even begin to solve their problems . . . we asked the Federal Government to join with us in setting up a Royal Commission to study the Indian and Métis problems with a view to bringing down recommendations which would be carried out by both governments . . . not only did the federal government refuse to take any action, but Paul Martin was extremely curt and apparently uninterested in grappling with the problems in question . . . In all probability we shall end up by paying our share of the old age and blind pensions to the Indians.[9]

Martin's disinterest reflected the federal feeling that having revised the Indian Act in 1951 after a parliamentary committee had investigated the subject, native matters could rest for a time. In fact the problems accelerated in urgency over the next few years, as economic disparity increased between whites and Indians.

In 1955 a report by the Legislative Librarian, John H. Archer showed 16,308 Indians in the province. The largest group, 8,402, was Roman Catholic in religion, and a surprising 1,035 retained their aboriginal faith. Every report showed that poverty, illiteracy, and economic dependency were facts of life on most reserves. Douglas wrote to a friend in 1956:

> I sometimes think that Canada has the worst record of any civilized country in the handling of its aborigines . . . I have thought for some time of making an approach to Ottawa suggesting that we take over the responsibility for the Indians if they would undertake to pay us a lump sum or a set amount per year for a period of ten or twenty years. At Green Lake and a number of other points we have already demonstrated among the Métis people what can be done by a well planned rehabilitation program . . . (we have organized) cooperatives in the north and while it is uphill work because they are not familiar with the cooperative movement, I think we are making considerable progress.[10]

In 1957 Welfare Minister Sturdy had a meeting with Jack Pickersgill in Ottawa and a move to set up a full-scale enquiry, involving the University of Saskatchewan, was begun. The objective was to turn over some responsibilities from the Department of Indian Affairs to the Regina government, along with some financial aid. But the move died in the Diefenbaker regime and was not revived.

Two major conferences were required before the Indians accepted the franchise. They feared it would interfere with their treaty rights, and they required considerable reassurance. John Tootoosis, president of the Union of Saskatchewan Indians, opposed the franchise as "the thin edge of the wedge", but later supported it. One northern Indian cautioned Douglas:

> To send the Northern Indians to the polls you might as well send a green Englishman to the traplines . . . You must realize this, that there are two thirds of the Indian people in Saskatchewan Roman Catholics and these Indians are pretty well dominated by their priests and you can be sure that those Indians if they were told to vote they would vote the way their Father the Priest told them to vote and you can be sure it won't be CCF either.[11]

In 1960 the Saskatchewan Elections Act was revised to extend the vote to all Indians. Their first opportunity to use it was in a provincial by-election in Turtleford in March, 1961, and Douglas wrote ruefully: "The Indian vote went badly against us. This is somewhat ironic since it is only last year that we gave the Indians the vote but while we were appealing to their hearts and heads our opponents were appealing to their pockets by almost every form of bribery in the book. This is something which we are in the process of investigating."[12]

The restrictions against selling liquor to Indian people were removed in 1960. The reserves retained the local option regarding prohibition of liquor within their boundaries. The government hired two Indian workers to counsel the importance of sobriety among those who frequented the hotels and beer parlours, with some initial success.

The natives' position in Saskatchewan remained in 1960 as it had been in 1944, a sore – wide open and unhealed. An indigenous development among people with an even earlier affinity to the province is still needed to bring "quality of life" to all citizens of Saskatchewan.

The high point of the Douglas era in Saskatchewan was 1955, the year of the Golden Jubilee. That celebration lifted the province to a new level of self-confidence, as "Expo '67" would for Canada.

The CCF – always the planners – set up committees in 1952, and every conceivable avenue was explored to excite the population to a year-long festival. Advance planning, for example, booked sixty national conventions and competitions into Regina and Saskatoon that year, everything from the North American Figure Skating Championships to the Dominion Drama Festival to the annual meeting of the Postmasters Association.

Comparisons have to be made. 1955 was also Alberta's fiftieth anniversary. Alberta marked the occasion by building two very large auditoria, in Calgary and Edmonton, costing two million dollars each, and, after a predictable clamour arose from smaller places, further per capita grants were handed out in compensation. An Alberta broadcaster on CBC radio, Brenda Parsons, commented unhappily in December 1955 that in contrast to Saskatchewan, *their* planning coordinator had resigned; *a professional square dance caller was imported* to assist in local celebrations although Alberta was supposed to be famous for its square dancing, and other plans continually misfired. The illuminated scrolls for senior citizens were late in printing and ceremonies went ahead without them; a provincial song writing contest was called off when the Alberta Music Board decided no entries of sufficient merit had been received; the "day of prayer" was cancelled.

Alberta just didn't have the same spirit. The Saskatchewan events were all home-grown and locally inspired. Four hundred and thirty local committees informed the provincial director about their projects. There were hundreds of pageants performed, hundreds of local histories compiled, old-timers were honoured in ingenious and touching ways – in Wakau school children raised money for a banquet in their honour. Cairns were erected, picnic grounds were opened, trees were planted, main streets were cleaned up, painted, and given new streetlights, people who had moved to other provinces were invited home. There were barbecues, boat parades, Indian dances, Maypole dances, Highland dances. Unity baked a Jubilee cake. The oldest pioneer woman was crowned the Princess of Esterhazy. When an elderly gentleman named Thomas Fisher executed a number of paintings and offered them to the Western Development Museum (located in a vast unused airplane hangar in Saskatoon) they were received with grace by the curator, George Shepherd, who described them as having a certain "down to earth" quality. The newspapers accepted poems from inspired homesteaders, now in their nineties.

One of the happiest events of the year was a short-lived but much-admired Jubilee Choir of high school boys and girls from Regina. They had practised three evenings a week for more than a year, under the direction of Neil Harris, who toured with them throughout the province, and as far away as Chicago, Toronto and Ottawa for special concerts. They received one hundred dollars apiece for their efforts – forty-five teenagers, the girls in navy blazers, calf-length skirts, and saddle shoes.

The Saskatchewan Homemakers compiled a cookbook which had sold 22,000 copies by the year's end.

"The provincial government didn't run the show," Douglas said. "We just set up a committee and helped things along."

208

Douglas had already been Premier of Saskatchewan longer than any previous holder of that office. In 1955 he was praised even by the Sifton press for his contributions to the province, and in particular for the verve he brought to the celebrations that year. He had spoken over the radio on New Year's Day, 1955. In February, when the legislature opened, he reminded the Members: " 'Jubilee' has a deeper meaning. It is a people's prayer of thanksgiving to God for His abiding presence and continuing goodness to the children of men."

In May he welcomed the Governor General Vincent Massey, who opened a new natural science museum at Regina, and fired the first gun of the year's celebration.

It all wound up on September 5 at a formal ceremony in Regina when four former Premiers were assembled, along with Prime Minister St. Laurent who spoke in his best Uncle Louis style to crowds of children, enjoining them to recognize the value of good homes and good citizenship. There was a presentation of beribboned early settlers to the distinguished guests, there was a motorcade with an RCMP escort, the Jubilee Choir made its last appearance, and there was a commemorative banquet.

A week later Douglas received a letter from the manager of Radio Station CHAB at Moose Jaw:

Mrs. Boyling and myself had the pleasure of attending the Saskatchewan Jubilee banquet, an occasion that will long remain with us. And while the occasion was important because of its historic significance, it was a personal incident that we will remember most.

The Head Table that evening featured a great number of people who, amongst their abilities, were required to express themselves competently during their careers; even so, while you were speaking, we noticed a completely new reaction from the audience. I am sure you must realize it, but despite the business I am in, I have seldom seen such warm reaction to a speaker.

While we have always enthusiastically admired your speaking ability, that evening we had the pleasure of experiencing a new insight to the amazing influence you exert over the people. I think it's a wonderful thing.[13]

The following year was another election, and another CCF win. Under Hammy McDonald, the Liberal party increased its seats from eleven to fourteen, but no one even whispered the possibility of an upset.

In 1959 McDonald resigned. A new Liberal leader had appeared, epitomizing the most adamant right-wing element in the province, and the Liberals under Ross Thatcher began a comeback that would take them back to power as soon as Douglas had left the scene.

But it was still in the spirit of the Jubilee, with the successful 1956 election past and many of his goals for the province achieved, that Douglas wrote:

> The CCF is an adventure in idealism. It is a movement composed of ordinary men and women drawn together into a political organization because they share a fundamental belief in the moral potential of individual human beings and of human society. We do not agree with those who insist that the destiny of human beings should be settled in the competitive jungle of the market place. We contend that once man's eyes are opened there need be no limit to what might be achieved. . . .
>
> Within Saskatchewan itself the ethical idealism of the CCF has been the main and vital dynamic inspiring the whole of the provincial government's policy . . . Our first concern in Saskatchewan has been the good life of the multitude. . . .
>
> If these common ideals and common faith have been shown to work in one small province of our country, are they therefore appropriate to a vastly larger scene? I am convinced they are.[14]

Chapter Fourteen
Premier 4: Outside the Province

The peak of popular success for the CCF party on the national scene was near the end of the Second World War, closely linked to a vision of a "new order". It was above all a national vision. In Saskatchewan as elsewhere the party looked ahead to what "we as Canadians" might achieve.

For Douglas, while Saskatchewan was the job at hand, a national government was the only objective that made economic sense. Only the resources and power of the whole country could establish a cooperative commonwealth.

For this reason one can find no record of actions taken to benefit the Saskatchewan wing of the party at the expense of the federal CCF. Douglas contributed to the work of the federal party and turned up in every province (even Quebec) to fill as many requests as his timetable would allow.

It was a period when the Liberal government at Ottawa was making every effort to attract United States capital and development. The other, more conspicuous post-war trend was the introduction of welfare programs. While the industrial growth under foreign capitalist ownership might have identified the governing party as rightist, the welfare programs – pensions, unemployment insurance, family allowances – were much more obvious to the average citizen and persuaded the country that the Liberals were "going left". Together – the American investment because it brought rapid industrial growth and affluence, the welfare programs because they took care of people – the Liberal strategy of those years effectively spiked CCF chances.

Echoing Britain's Beveridge Report, the Ottawa Liberals commissioned a study by Leonard Marsh, completed in 1943, which promised a cushion of security to Canadians, doing much to erase the fears of a post-war depression. The Family Allowance scheme, a direct payment of five to six dollars a month for each child, was the top attraction. There was also a "Veterans' Charter" of benefits to men from the armed forces, on a much more generous scale than any rewards after World War One. And there was a new federal Labour Code, PC 1003, which for the first time recognized the rights of organized labour, and won the approval of both labour congress presidents, A. R. Mosher of the

C.C.L. and, even more enthusiastically, Percy Bengough of the T.L.C.

The 1945 Dominion-Provincial Conference on Reconstruction brought out solid federal government proposals which showed a remarkable readiness to follow the new gospel according to Keynes. There would be deficit budgeting to prime the economy at the first hint of a depression, with a shelf of public works ready for attention to relieve any hint of unemployment. There was even a breakthrough in what had been solely a socialist preserve – government economic planning. The Liberals called it "indicative planning", and it was to take the form of helpful research and suggestions to industry.

All this may have measured the extent of the scare the Liberals had received from the sudden CCF successes in Saskatchewan and Ontario. The Conservatives were also infected. They cast around for a successor to Meighen, and chose a westerner, John Bracken of Manitoba. They added "Progressive" to the name of their party, acquiring a schizophrenic combination that has been characteristic of their party position since that date: they continue to number in their party ranks libertarians well to the left of the Liberals, and old-time Tories well to the right.

As though all this were not enough to contend with, the CCF was plagued by communists intent on tacking together a "United Front" as long as Russia remained in good standing with the western allies. In some instances the Communists passed over the CCF as too reactionary (at least their adamant leaders, Coldwell and Lewis and Douglas) and linked arms with the Liberal Party. Their support went to the Liberals in the 1945 general election.

It was a disastrous election for the CCF; it could hardly have been otherwise. On top of all the political shifts that threatened it, a scurrilous advertising campaign was subscribed to by hundreds of business firms in 1944. This campaign was run by B. A. Trestrail, with newspaper and radio advertising and a pamphet, *Social Suicide*, mailed to households across Canada at a cost of hundreds of thousands of dollars. The object of the campaign was to vilify the CCF and paint a lurid picture of "socialism".

But no one in the CCF was prepared for the dismal showing in 1945.

In the summer months of 1944, after the CCF win in Saskatchewan, three other provinces held elections. The party's mood was to expect further victories, without any of the organizational groundwork that had made success possible in Saskatchewan. Even in New Brunswick in August the party faithful were worrying about the possibility of a win, with some consternation about their lack of preparedness for the task of government. A party organizer wrote to Douglas: "I urged the executive to plan their campaign with the view to being reasonably sure of electing *some* members. What they are in fear of, is that they may find themselves leading the polls. Joe Noseworthy suggested in that case they'd better ask for a recount."[1]

The Quebec wing of the party was ecstatic at having won a seat in their legislative assembly, an achievement not duplicated since. Alberta in July managed to elect two – one each in Calgary and Edmonton. Alberta's CCF'ers were disappointed; they had expected to do much better. David Lewis wrote to Douglas for a *post mortem,* and Douglas summarized the problem:

> First, lack of organization . . . We were doing in the campaign what should have been done one year ago . . . Secondly, the failure to departmentalize their work in such a way as to get each person doing the job he can do best . . . Roper, who has a first-class style with city people and Rotarians, was out rousing the countryside . . . I don't think pigs were mentioned once until the Saskatchewan men hit Alberta. Whoever heard of an election in the West without pigs?[2]

One of Douglas' immediate plans after his election was to travel overseas to visit Saskatchewan regiments in European battle areas, and he was determined not to let either the demands of his new administration nor the many calls of the national party, in anticipation of a general election, interfere. His first attempt to travel overseas in November 1944 ended abruptly in Ottawa. He took ill as he travelled by train from Regina; he was taken off the train in Ottawa and put in the care of Dr. Paul Telner, David Lewis' brother-in-law, who packed him off to the Civic Hospital. It was a difficult case of embolism; antibiotic treatments were still experimental in 1944. There was a brief period of convalescence in Ottawa before he was allowed to return to Regina, and one of the highlights of that occasion was an evening at Mackenzie King's home, with a private dinner and a great deal of confidential chatting. Douglas was somewhat embarrassed by the confidences. He was told the whole story of the conscription-if-necessary-but-not-necessarily-conscription incident. When Defence Minister Ralston returned from Europe demanding conscription of troop reinforcements King refused, in order to hold the support of the French-Canadian members of his cabinet, and accepted Ralston's resignation on the issue. But to meet the criticisms from English Canada and the Army, he eventually sent the 16,000 draftees overseas (they had been conscripted for home duties), thereby inviting the resignations of Quebec ministers Powers and Cardin. King had persuaded others, but he did not attempt to persuade Chubby Powers that there was danger of military *coup d'état* if the draftees were not despatched to Europe. King told Douglas that he neglected to discuss the matter with Chubby Powers prior to the cabinet meeting, because he was prepared to dispense with Powers' services in the belief that a resignation on *both* sides of the conscription issue would leave King – and the country – safely in the middle of the road.

When Ralph Allen, editor of *Maclean's* in 1961, noted a photo of Mackenzie King on Douglas' office wall bearing a warmly-worded autograph, he recorded Douglas' comment: "He was a very lonely man, with a need to unburden himself now and then . . . In 1944 he kept me up half one night to tell me the whole incredible and devious story of his manipulations and intrigues in and out of his cabinet and frequently behind the cabinet's back . . . He used to tell me that I looked like his late brother and, mystic that he was, this might have given him some special confidence in me."[3]

Douglas could only marvel at the crafty old master of Canadian politics. That winter evening he listened to the usual blandishments – Douglas could surely have found a place in the party of Gladstone and Lloyd George; King was a great friend of British Fabians like Beatrice and Sydney Webb. But there were no hints of what King had up his sleeve for the next year's general election.

Douglas returned to Regina, cheerfully informed all sympathizers that his "health was now completely restored", and promised E. B. Jolliffe of Ontario, head of the Federal Election Steering Committee, that, "I think I can fulfil any itinerary the National Office draws up for me without doing myself any harm."[4]

Douglas went on to Europe at the end of March, flying into Brussels and Germany, making his way to military hospitals and bases wherever there were Saskatchewan units to visit. In Germany he wangled a ride up the line in a jeep with Lieutenant Les England of the South Sask-atchewans, but on the way back they crashed with a truck and Douglas was thrown out. The jeep was smashed. Lieutenant England said he could account for the loss of the jeep more easily than the presence of Premier Douglas in his vehicle, so Douglas offered to find his own way back, which he did, rather warily, clad in his civilian clothes and on foot.

He had hurt his knee in the fall from the jeep. The old osteomyelitis started up again, and there was a recurrence almost annually from 1945 on.

Douglas was back in Manchester when war came to an end on May 8. A general federal election was imminent. He flew back to Canada in an unheated Lancaster bomber which called for oxygen masks above 18,000 feet, accompanied by several prospective candidates.

The discontent with the Liberal government showed up strongly in the servicemen's vote, which went against the Liberals and defeated King personally in Prince Albert, Saskatchewan. But for a variety of reasons, Canadians at home voted the Liberals back into power, in what turned out to be King's final election. The Liberals won handily in Quebec, but their vote across the country dropped from 53 per cent in 1940 to 34 per cent in 1945. West of the Great Lakes the CCF polled the largest vote and elected the most members of any party. Saskatchewan returned eighteen CCF M.P.s and only two Liberals. But elsewhere the wily King was able to turn back a CCF tide which had appeared a year earlier to pose a genuine threat. The Liberals had a new lease on the future.

The CCF's ecstatic hopes of 1944 were dashed. Their new group in parliament was only twenty-eight members, a "splinter party" still.

Factionalism and dispute began to plague some sections of the party. Douglas refused to be drawn into such party strife. His policy was to mind Saskatchewan's business. When friction showed up in Alberta over provincial leadership, he declined to take sides, and advised a correspondent to work through the organizational structure to resolve the problem: "In a social democratic party no one ever gets all the things they want, but we have a right to fight for those things and to try to persuade others to support our point of view. If, however, those who do not get exactly what they want pull out of the CCF then, of course, we are simply playing into the hands of the reactionary forces who are seeking to continue an economic system which you and I both believe to be inhuman and unjust."[5]

As Canada moved steadily away from that momentary madness when it had almost seemed that a democratic socialist party could aspire to power, it was of considerable comfort to CCF'ers to keep an eye on Britain's performance under the Labour government. Douglas visited Britain in 1948 as a guest of the Commonwealth Parliamentary Association, when he was much impressed by Nehru, and again in 1953 when he and Irma Douglas attended Queen Elizabeth's coronation. He formed vivid memories of Britain's first democratic socialist ministry.

Clement Attlee was not a "mousey little man, a sheep in wolf's clothing," as Churchill had described him. He had a London-bred toughness and tenacity. Sir Anthony Eden had described him to Douglas as "amazing". Eden's impression of Attlee was that most people had a wrong impression. "All through the war he was deputy prime minister and presided at cabinet meetings. Churchill did the talking but Attlee kept all the committees working and fed the stuff to Churchill. If Churchill presided we didn't get any work done but got a marvellous resume of military strategy for two hours. When Attlee was presiding we heard little about military strategy but we got the agenda cleaned up."

Douglas said,

Attlee said a strange thing to me one day. He said, 'You know I was pretty well tossed in here by the accident of events. But this man Coldwell of yours, if he hadn't left England and gone off to Canada he could have been prime minister. He'd have made a better prime minister than I've been.' I think that was true. Watching those men and working with them, able as they were, I still don't think there was anyone either intellectually or in terms of communication with people who could exceed Coldwell.

Douglas attributed to Attlee a story about Tom Williams, his Minister of Public Works immediately after the war. Priorities, for the rebuilding of factories and homes, were stringent. "A part of Buckingham Palace had been bombed. Tom Williams went personally to view the damage, and was shown about by George VI and Queen Elizabeth. When the inspection tour was finished the Queen inquired when the work might be done, to which Williams, like a kindly Lancashire uncle, replied, "Tha turn'll come, lass.' "

The warm personality of Herbert Morrison impressed Douglas, and he found Jim Griffiths "a lovable man".

He admired Aneurin Bevan's brilliance, but not his personal ambition. Douglas visited Bevan and his wife Jenny Lee while in London, and later they were hospitable to his daughter Shirley during her brief years in London theatre. Bevan, he said, "was in the great traditions of orators. He was the only man in the Commons who could stand up to Churchill. Once he began a speech on economic shortages by saying, 'Mr. Speaker, this country is a lump of coal set in a sea of fish and only a man with the organizing genius of Mr. Churchill could arrange to have a shortage of both of them at the same time.'

"An old Welshman told me Bevan was on a par with Lloyd George, which was saying something. I heard Lloyd George myself when I was a boy in 1918, speaking in St. Andrews Hall in Glasgow when he was at his peak, and he had the crowd in the palm of his hand."

Sir Stafford Cripps, Douglas described as "Woodsworth without a beard. He looked like a schoolmaster but he was the greatest corporation lawyer in Britain. He never bent his views to suit the crowd, he said the hard things that needed to be said. As Chancellor of the Exchequor he carried out an austerity program that no one but the British would have put up with. But he was not so austere personally."

On his 1948 trip, Douglas also attended a commemorative occasion at Pourville in France, where a plaque was unveiled to honour the South Saskatchewan men who had landed there in the abortive and devastating Dieppe raid in 1942. Douglas went to the ceremony with journalist Bill Boss, who coached him in a few French phrases, and Graham Spry, the Saskatchewan Agent-General in London. The party decorated the graves of Jimmy Gardiner's son and several other RCAF men who had died there. Douglas complimented the mayor on the well-kept cemetery and was told that care was maintained by the people of Pourville through voluntary work. He met the little old teamster who had insisted on taking out his cart to carry away the bodies of the dead left on the beach, for decent burial on the hillside, and he met the Sister Superior from the convent who had also disobeyed German orders to stay inside that day, and had opened her doors to the wounded.

The young son of Pourville's mayor had been born the night of the Dieppe raid, and expressed a vast interest in Canada and its *cowboys*. Douglas decided to get a cowboy suit for the youngster, and arranged for it through Eleanor McKinnon in Regina.

Eleanor told the story: "Shumy (Morris Shumiatcher) and I went to work. There were still shortages, and all we could get in Regina was the lariat. But Shumy got a complete outfit from Calgary – boots, chaps, a gun in a holster, and a cowboy hat. I noticed that the hat had a 'Smithbilt' brand name inside. Anyway we sent the stuff over and everyone was pleased, especially the little boy. But I thought it was a funny sequel – a year or so later I was travelling East with Tommy, Dr. Mott and Shumy and when we stepped off the train at Broadview I noticed a lot of Alberta kids with 'Smithbilt' hats. Shumy said that was his uncle in Calgary. I said 'Smith?' and Shumy said, 'Can you imagine Schumiatcherbilt?' "

Douglas visited Falkirk in Scotland after the ceremony at Pourville. It was a delight to find his aunt, Maggie Stewart, still vigorous and in good spirits. "Come in," she greeted Tommy. "We heard about you on the wireless."

The 1949 election saw the CCF group in parliament reduced painfully to thirteen from twenty-eight, with the Liberals under St. Laurent advancing strongly to a majority position with one hundred ninety members. It was the end of the post-war dream. In Saskatchewan only five instead of eighteen CCF'ers were elected, accounting for almost all of the total drop. Douglas felt that he had been wrong in spending so much of the 1949 campaign in other provinces, at the urgent request of the national committee. As it turned out the party might have benefited more if he had campaigned at home.

In 1952 he put a restriction on the number of meetings he would take in Alberta during their provincial election, limiting himself to one day in Calgary and one in Edmonton:

"I think this is all I ought to take, first because I am completely fagged out by the Saskatchewan campaign, which in reality has been going on for almost two years, and also because I doubt the psychological effect of me being in Alberta too much . . . People somewhat resent the premier of another province coming into their backyard."[6]

Certainly the Calgary *Herald* felt that way, referring editorially to Douglas as the "meandering messiah from Saskatchewan . . . Alberta is up to its ears in messiahs already . . . there is such a thing as too much salvation." The paper defended the free enterprise economic system Douglas was attacking: "People are ambitious, which is a nicer way of saying they are selfish, and they set out in the world to do as well for themselves and their families as they can. Some of them have always done better than others . . . We can't revolutionize human nature."[7]

Douglas' neighbour to the east was also in constant need of aid and advice. In late 1952 Douglas and M. J. Coldwell considered the problem: "The CCF organization in Manitoba has reached an all-time low . . . I am convinced that Manitoba could be won by the CCF if it had some aggressive and dynamic leadership . . . We must rack our brains, or Manitoba will go by default."[8]

Coldwell's reply was despondent. He was on the point of going into hospital for surgery, and the question of leadership worried him: "I wish Stan (Knowles) were well enough to take the task, but his physical condition would not allow it . . . I am convinced that if we had the kind of leadership you have given in Saskatchewan, the province could be won. Our problem in so many places is the development of leadership . . . Take care of yourself – there are so few of us upon whom this Movement can rely."[9]

Douglas was less downcast. Though Manitoba was "fraught with difficulties . . . I can't believe that in the whole province we haven't some person who could take on this job with some hope of success."[10]

In April the following year he was urging his cabinet ministers to help in other provinces: "CCF organizations in B.C. and Manitoba are badly in need of some assistance for their respective election campaigns. I know that it is very difficult to get away but a serious setback in either province will adversely affect our chances in the coming federal election campaign and leave Saskatchewan more than ever a lonely beachhead."[11]

Douglas' mail bulged with pleas for his appearance at meetings, which would invariably "mean the difference in winning this riding". He accepted when he could, and he even recorded short speeches for use in local areas where he was unable to appear in person.

Prior to the 1953 federal election there was another trip to the United Kingdom, to attend the Coronation. The Douglases remember the ceremony as something of an ordeal. They were booked into a hotel not far from the Abbey ("It was on the route of the procession and after we left the window space was rented to someone else," Irma recalled.) but they were required to be present in their formal attire at seven in the morning. The ceremony was to begin at eleven.

"Irma," Douglas said, "had managed to put some sandwiches in the cuff of her fur jacket. And Joey Smallwood who was standing next us had some chocolate bars in his hat, so we managed.

"But it was British pageantry at its best," Douglas said. "The Duke of Norfolk, who was in charge of arrangements, told some of us that the crown was actually placed on the Queen's head thirty-one seconds ahead of schedule."

"Some of us got a bad case of stomach flu," Irma said. "I was in hospital over there for about three weeks. Jimmy Gardiner got it too – but he was sure his was cancer."

Douglas was determined, in August, 1953, to win back federal seats in his province: " . . . as I pointed out to Lorne I think I should spend practically all my time in Saskatchewan. If the provincial organization feel that I should go to Toronto or some point outside of Saskatchewan because of the national publicity I have no objection to doing so, but I am against a long itinerary such as I had in 1949 when I felt my time was largely wasted and when I could have done more effective work here at home."[12]

218

When he did sally forth to take meetings elsewhere Douglas was invariably a hit. Judith Robinson, *Telegram* columnist, described his performance at a Toronto collegiate auditorium. Local candidates had spoken, presently Douglas "took over":

> The Premier of Saskatchewan is a small slight man with light brown hair on end, too much forehead for the rest of his face, a look of unconquerable lightheartedness and no platform majesty whatever. Nevertheless he took over. He made a couple of old jokes while he took off his coat and a couple more while he undid his cuffs and rolled up his sleeves. After the fourth joke, with both sleeves well rolled, he changed pace and swung into his speech. . . .
>
> There are several politicians in Canada who make more eloquent political orations than T. C. Douglas. None can put more sense in fewer words or more conviction into what he says. None this reporter has heard makes a campaign speech with as much fire and bite to it. . . .
>
> He can also speak simply and directly of the hopes and faiths that simple people hold.[13]

His more intensive campaign in Saskatchewan paid off. Saskatchewan's number of seats in the federal House had been cut from twenty to seventeen by redistribution, but of these the CCF this time won eleven, instead of their previous five. These six new Saskatchewan M.P.s, with four additions from other provinces, restored the parliamentary group to a more respectable twenty-three.

"The CCF made the biggest gains, boosting their number to twenty-three from thirteen chiefly on the strength of a Socialist onslaught in Saskatchewan that overthrew the Liberal majority from that province" wrote Canadian Press journalist John Leblanc.[14]

The strategy was particularly useful. By increasing their representation from Saskatchewan the party gave an appearance of increased strength, even though (as Canadian Press failed to observe) their percentage of the vote across the country dropped in this election to eleven per cent from thirteen per cent in 1949. The party was in poor shape outside Saskatchewan. Membership had fallen by half between 1949 and 1950, and had not been regained by election time in 1953.

St. Laurent had campaigned quietly "on his record". The country was in no mood for upsets. The Liberal formula, importing large chunks of American capital (and ownership) was still working, with advancing growth and prosperity at least in the most populous provinces.

The federal CCF party was labouring to produce policies to fit the times, but the policies attracted little attention. Their 1953 election platform said that "our vast resources are being plundered by profiteers" and urged "new agencies of economic planning and investment", adding "where necessary for adequate economic planning some key industries, such as primary iron and steel, will be publicly owned" in the CCF program. The document was anxious but not fiery. It asked (once again) for nation-wide health insurance, higher pensions, and family allowances. It also pursued such matters as the need for more holiday facilities for the masses, a "Canadian Council to support arts, letters, humanities and social sciences" and a Canadian Bill of Rights.

But it is significant that the election program stressed international problems first, in 1953. The Cold War was in full frost. The position of the federal CCF was that communism could only grow where there was hunger and privation, and it was Canada's duty to "give leadership for peace, to eliminate the hunger and poverty on which communism thrives, and to build collective security and support of the United Nations and its principles." But the North Atlantic Treaty Organization (NATO) caused some problems.

The statement confirmed CCF support for NATO, with some slight qualification, and this reflected a rift in party thinking in which Douglas and Lewis had taken different routes. The qualification put NATO "within the spirit and framework of the United Nations", and urged that the United Nations be strengthened so that "regional pacts will become increasingly unnecessary".

In May 1950 David Lewis had been disturbed by a report that a visiting Saskatchewan cabinet minister had discussed with M. J. Coldwell a foreign policy statement put forward in Regina which opposed NATO. Like Coldwell, Lewis was alarmed. He fired off a letter to Douglas with a copy of a policy statement carefully drawn up by the National Executive, to go before the next national convention. He hoped the Saskatchewan people weren't putting forward a "kind of foreign policy confusion that is inherent in a combination of pacifism and sentimental pro-sovietism."[15]

There was no question of where Lewis stood in the Cold War. Not only for Canada but on behalf of socialist parties in Europe which had experienced communist terror, he was determined that the CCF should go on record in support of the "free world".

Douglas took a less absolute position, one that still sought a more independent stance, and he was far more skeptical of United States' good intentions than Lewis was prepared to be at that time. The Regina document, which Douglas forwarded to Lewis, put its faith in the United Nations and its various instruments and agencies, and expressed disappointment that the North Atlantic Treaty Organization "has so far been only a military alliance that has increased suspicion and ill-will, and (we) urge that instead it become a cooperative measure for the social and economic betterment of the nations." The document saw war between Russia and the United States as the ultimate catastrophe, and declared that the greatest need at the time was "the easing of international tension."

The National Executive document on the other hand, which Lewis presumably had been instrumental in drafting, expressed more support for US-initiated organizations, and particularly NATO, although it would oppose any policies "contrary to the principles of the UN Charter" and would "stand on guard against the policies of greedy capitalist forces in Canada, in the United States and elsewhere".

The two statements were not greatly at variance, but the correspondence between the two men indicated the distinctly different philosophical approach. Lewis feared that a "woolly" pro-Soviet attitude among some CCF'ers (he did not number Douglas among them) would unwittingly serve an "increasingly more evil cause."[16]

Douglas sought to reassure him, and revealed his much greater tolerance for woolly-mindedness. It should be brought out in the open and sharpened by debate. The Regina resolution wasn't perfect, but it wasn't bad, Douglas thought. The debate had been instigated by the Regina executive and cabinet because "(1) We found that the communists and some of our own woolly heads were going to bring in 'ban the bomb' resolutions. We felt that there had to be something fairly positive in order to counteract such a move. (2) We wanted some statement in general enough terms that our people could have a discussion and air their views and begin to crystallize their own thinking with regard to this important subject."[17]

If Lewis thought the Regina statement was too soft in not outrightly condemning Russia, Douglas thought there was a "Pollyanna" flavour to the national executive statement in regard to the United States.

"I am still convinced we have to stand with the western democracies against Soviet aggression," Douglas wrote, "but while we are standing with them we don't have to be dumb and blind . . . When a man like John Foster Dulles comes back to the United States and says that any sudden ending of the cold war would cause a dislocation in our economy, it makes a lot of socialists wonder whether the cold war is designed to defend freedom or to preserve capitalism. For that reason I don't think we should get too excited about some of the honest and sincere criticism of foreign policy which is taking place in our own ranks. This does not mean that we should *condone* for one minute the fuzzy-minded fellow travellers who are being deceived by the communists and inveigled into joining some of their peace front organizations." Douglas thought the National Executive statement was not very clear in regard to what was meant by collective security: "it is in danger of becoming not so much a policy of collective security, but of American security."

In a further letter, Lewis felt that the Regina policy statement should have supported NATO clearly, and expressed his conviction that the national convention that summer must be explicit on the point. It was impossible to equate the US with Russia, he maintained, for while capitalist policies "hinder the forces of progress", they are not in the same class with the ruthless aggression practised by Russia. He thought hopes for cooperation with Russia were somewhat impractical, in the light of Russia's refusal to that date to join in UN organizations. But he conceded that there had to be a certain amount of "wishful thinking" in any such statement.

The result of the exchange was the policy that led to the 1953 program, supporting NATO but hoping that a greater reliance on the United Nations would soon make such regional pacts unnecessary.

It was one of the few occasions when Douglas and Lewis put their thoughts on paper in discussion of party policy.

Recalling the period, Douglas said in 1974,

> There was some division in the party. M. J. and a majority of the caucus and party supported Canada going into NATO. Others wanted us to stay out, especially the Alberta group. They formed the 'Woodsworth-Irvine Socialist Fellowship' which still exists and is somewhat anti-American and isolationist.
>
> I had seen enough – in Nuremburg with Hitler's great military display before the war, and in Spain – to know that you *have* to stop aggression, even though you may not always be happy about those you join with.
>
> It was the same thing with NATO. M. J. did criticize it in the House because its main function was military and Article Two, which called for economic cooperation, was never used. But with Russia after the war, Germany prostrate, the tremendous Russian army in Eastern Europe, gobbling up Czechoslovakia, there had to be a group of nations prepared to stand up to Russia. At that time we needed the military alliance.
>
> The situation is totally different now. Germany is strong. Canada is maintaining an army in Germany that doesn't make sense any more. We feel there is no need for NATO now.

Douglas was too blunt for some of his eastern colleagues when in 1955 Quebec finally wrecked the federal-provincial tax-sharing arrangements carried over from the war. As he saw it, to step into the income tax field as Quebec was doing, with Ottawa's acquiesence, was to shatter the supreme right of the central government to direct the economy through fiscal policy.

Arthur Blakely, writing in the Montreal *Gazette* (February 5, 1955) saw a pattern of hostility against Quebec in statements made by four CCF M.P.s – Hazen Argue, Harold Winch, Angus MacInnis, and Erhart Regier. For these, Blakely said, national secretary David Lewis had felt obliged to issue a "statement of regret". Blakely added: "Premier T. C. Douglas' vicious attack on the tax deal . . . his caustic references to the arrangement itself and to Quebec's provincial rights position were even more offensive than those of Hazen Argue." He said that none of the M.P.s, despite Lewis' intervention, had offered to retract and as for disciplining T. C. Douglas "who heads the world's one and only CCF government out in Saskatchewan, it is just not in the books . . . Without the Quebec wing, the CCF might lose any pretensions it has of being a national party. But without Saskatchewan and Premier Douglas, it might as well cease to be a party at all."

Therese Casgrain, the indomitable leader of the Quebec CCF, wired her concern to Douglas: "On account recent statements in Ottawa House, situation in Quebec worse than bad. Am afraid complete foldup and *en masse* resignation of provincial council if nothing dynamic done soon. Kindest regards with much sorrow."[18] Douglas the same day wrote a long explanation to Mme Casgrain. He urged that

> the workers of Quebec have as much at stake in this issue as any other group of Canadians. I would hope that they would join with us in insisting that Mr. St. Laurent has no right to toss overboard the welfare state and the planned fiscal program which he outlined in 1945, merely to please Mr. Duplessis.
>
> In my radio speech last week I went out of my way to repeat what I had said before, namely, that the Saskatchewan Government was prepared 'to do anything within reason to assure the people of Quebec that we have no desire to encroach upon those rights of race, language and culture which they hold so dear.' I pointed out that I objected to favouritism being shown any province, even Saskatchewan. I feel certain that the people of Quebec do not want preferred treatment and I think it would strengthen national unity if our movement in Quebec were to speak out at this time in criticism of what is clearly a political dodge designed to outbid Mr. Duplessis but which will in the long run hurt not only Canada but even the people of Quebec because it will sow ill will and discord between the provinces of Canada.[19]

Therese Casgrain may not have been wholly reassured by the letter, and it was not designed to promote vigorous growth in the CCF wing. In a letter two months later she, with great tact, requested the privilege of being on hand as a possible consultant during a federal-provincial conference in Ottawa, adding, "Pierre Trudeau whom you have met and who is one of our extremely promising young Canadians is willing to accompany me."[20]

Looking ahead to the next federal election in 1957, there was a dominant trend in the Ontario CCF to moderate radically socialist views. Canada was prosperous. The workers had much to lose besides their chains. It was impossible to sell "a new order". The feeling led to the 1956 Winnipeg Declaration, which was regarded as an updated version of the Regina Manifesto of 1933.

It is interesting that the greatest move toward this change did not come from Saskatchewan, where a party in power for twelve years might have been expected to develop some cautionary views. Instead, the president of the Saskatchewan wing of the party, Carlyle King, denounced the less revolutionary and less upsetting position: " . . . the main business of socialist parties is not to form governments but to change minds. When people begin to concentrate on success at the polls, they become careful and cautious; and when they become careful and cautious, the virtue goes out of them."[21]

A committee to prepare a new "manifesto" was set up at the 1950 national convention. It included Douglas, Hazen Argue, Andrew Brewin, Clarie Gillis, Lorne Ingle, Francois La Roche, David Lewis, Grace MacInnis, Joe Noseworthy, and Frank Scott. Numerous drafts were circulated and discussed, no one was satisfied with the product of the unwieldy committee. Grace MacInnis said, "It was supposed to be democratic; it was only chaotic." At a National Executive meeting the Saskatchewan people wanted the whole project abandoned and attention given instead to the 1953 election platform. But many, particularly M. J. Coldwell and David Lewis, felt that a new, less terrifying statement was needed, and eventually David Lewis, Morden Lazarus, Omer Chartrand, and Lorne Ingle were designated to prepare the Declaration which was passed at Winnipeg. It was a far less resounding piece of prose, and Douglas pointed out in a radio address following the convention that it was no great change from the Manifesto. He had never regarded the Manifesto as too radical.

Grace MacInnis described the Declaration as "a messy kind of document", and it appeared to serve little purpose except to convey to the public a general impression of a modification of radicalism. Grace MacInnis said that Douglas did not take an active part in the Winnipeg debate.

> He never got too involved in the fierceness of party controversy. He knows what you can do and what you can't do with a crowd. He would go into controversies like medicare, backing the party against the enemy outside.
>
> But within the party – Tommy has always had a remarkable ability to defuse argument, to make people see things from the sensible down-to-earth point of view instead of from the heights of prejudice.

Douglas' relations with David Lewis and other federal officers of the party were on the whole amicable. He had a particular respect for Frank Scott, to whom he once referred as "an architect of all this".

Douglas was a different man from David Lewis – in personality, in approach to party management, and occasionally in his point of view on public policy. These two men of approximately the same age, both totally committed to the cause of democratic socialism in Canada looked at each other across a considerable gulf of family background and training, but each, through many years, was realistic enough to recognize the ability of the other and his importance to the party.

An early piece of correspondence reveals the potential for antagonism that existed. David Lewis could be heavy-handed in his dealings; in 1939, shortly after he took on the job as national secretary, he circulated to national executive members a rather officious and formal letter requiring them to signify by return mail their vote for or against the ratification of the appointment of E. J. Garland as national organizer. Douglas fired back the letter, with a flip inscription penned across the bottom of the page: "Aye, aye, sir! T. C. Douglas."[22]

Professor Walter Young has commented on the number of "condescending" letters of advice sent by Lewis to Douglas in the early days of the CCF government. For example:

> I would, however, emphasize that within the next few months, particularly after the session of your Legislature and before the federal election, it will be important for the national movement to give the people of Canada a coherent and dramatic picture of what the CCF has undertaken and is contemplating. Such a picture we have not yet received. I am going to write to the Saskatchewan CCF Office some organizational ideas on this point. But I also believe that you yourself ought to receive some help of a professional nature in the field of information and publicity.[23]

In July he had written about the need to get a Labour Bill drafted: very few things are of equal importance at the present moment."[24]

Lewis of course considered the Saskatchewan victory only a prelude to the success at the federal polls that seemed imminent. When the 1945 Ontario and federal elections had sent hopes plummeting, he wrote a considerably chastened letter wondering if it would be alright to drop in at Regina on a trip west. He wondered if Regina should organize a public meeting for him to speak: "Sandy Nicholson has suggested that in view of the rather widespread attacks which were made on me during the recent campaign, it might be a good thing to have me make some public appearance in the not too distant future."[25]

Lewis had suffered in the anti-CCF Trestrail propaganda, which attacked him as a "Russian Jew".

An illuminating incident occurred at the 1950 national convention which was held in Vancouver. A west coast member of the party, Mrs. Eve Smith, had been assigned the task of managing a literature table, always a prominent feature at CCF conventions. But Mrs. Smith had her own – possibly Trotskyite – views, and added a large mix of pamphlets that were clearly not CCF-approved. There were protests from other delegates, the national officers of the party instructed her to desist, but she continued on her dedicated course. Douglas sought to persuade her but in the midst of a rather fruitless argument with her David Lewis arrived on the scene and issued an order. Mrs. Smith said she was not taking orders from him; only the entire convention could rule on her behaviour. Whereupon Lewis interrupted the proceedings of the convention to raise the matter and *get* their approval – and incidentally to get some lively stories in the press.

In the aftermath, Mrs. Smith's constituency association sent an aggrieved letter to Lorne Ingle, then national secretary, arguing, "We feel Mr. Lewis' action is to be condemned for bringing this matter up in such a way as to cause a disturbance when it could have been done quietly through the national and provincial officers."[26]

To which Lorne Ingle replied that quieter methods had been tried without success. The local organization, still unsatisfied, appealed to Douglas.

Douglas backed up Lewis without hesitation:

> The statements in Mr. Ingle's letter insofar as I am connected in any way with the incident are completely accurate. I found several people taking strong exception to the books Mrs. Smith had on display. I thumbed through one or two of them and drew Mrs. Smith's attention to several statements which were not only offensive but were deliberate falsehoods. When I asked Mrs. Smith by whose authority such literature was being displayed she became very belligerent and wanted to know whether or not we believed in democracy and why opposing points of view should not be available to the delegates. To me such an argument is preposterous. If we were to carry it to its logical conclusion we should also have literature issued by the Liberal and Conservative parties and by the Chamber of Commerce. Certainly they would not be any more out of place at a meeting of Canadian socialists than would literature of a Trotskyite nature making scurrilous attacks on the British Labour Party.
>
> Instead of criticizing the National President, I think your club ought to be asking itself where Mrs. Smith's allegiance lies and whether she is in fact loyal to the CCF or has given her allegiance to an organization bent on the destruction of the democratic socialist movement.[27]

It is highly unlikely that Douglas would have handled the incident in the manner of David Lewis. But he had no hesitation in coming down hard on the misguided Mrs. Smith and her local group, in Lewis' defence.

Lewis had run several times for parliament, unsuccessfully. In the 1950s he withdrew from full-time work as national secretary to build up a law practice in Toronto, though he remained on the National Executive.

When Joe Noseworthy died, the party sought a candidate to replace him in a by-election in York South. Douglas urged Lewis to run. "Your debating skill and wide knowledge of public affairs will increase the effectiveness of our group by fifty per cent," he wrote. "I think your election to the House of Commons could be the turning point for the CCF in Canada and I know you will respond to the challenge if it is at all possible to do so."[28]

But as Lewis explained in a letter on May 16, he decided he must continue for a time to practise law and establish his family's finances on a more secure footing before seeking a way into parliament. "When one is faced with two competing moral obligations, the choice is always extremely difficult." The York South seat was lost in the by-election, but it was here that Lewis campaigned successfully in 1962 and finally moved out of the role of back-room adviser and party official and into parliament.

When the general election of 1957 was called Douglas was again under considerable pressure from Ingle to take meetings across the country. "I think all of us are agreed that every seat we can win in Ontario this election would be worth perhaps two in western Canada if we are at all serious about our attempt to establish ourselves as a national movement."[29] Ingle asked Douglas to take meetings in four important centres; Oshawa, Hamilton, Timmins, and Toronto, and also, if he could, in Montreal. "David Lewis," Lorne wrote, "unfortunately will be tied up with the Railway Royal Commission all through the election period."

There may have been some asperity in Douglas' reply that he would agree to the four Ontario meetings but thought Lewis, who could speak French, could surely get a day off from Commission hearings to go to Montreal. Douglas wrote:

> I don't see how I can take any more time away from the campaign in Saskatchewan. Our people are still a bit weary from the provincial election, and the Liberals are playing on the theme that the CCF are disappearing in other parts of Canada and that Saskatchewan might as well throw in the sponge and vote Liberal. We could lose some ground here, and I feel that I ought to put all the time I can into stimulating our organization and preventing a repetition of 1949.[30]

In that election Saskatchewan lost one CCF M.P., dropping from eleven to ten. Across the country they gained, moving up from twenty-three to twenty-five. This was the election following the pipeline debate, when the Liberals had over-reached themselves in arrogance. And it was the year of Diefenbaker's first strong break-through, carrying the Conservatives from fifty-one seats up to one hundred twelve.

It was a development that could bring no comfort to CCF hearts, though Eugene Forsey was pleased with the balance-of-power position in which the CCF group found themselves in the Commons: "As we couldn't get a majority ourselves, the next best thing was a new Government in leading-strings to us."[31]

Predictions had been put forward from many quarters for many years that Canada's three-party grouping would peter out. Liberals and Conservatives expected the CCF to fade away, and the country to return to the comfortable old Grit-and-Tory politics of earlier times. The CCF, on the other hand, confidently predicted the fading-away of one of the old parties, and the concentration of all the anti-socialist forces under one right-wing banner. This had happened in Saskatchewan. But the resurgence of the Conservatives, and the competing populist appeal of Diefenbaker, shattered their hopes.

Diefenbaker had won personally in Saskatchewan by virtually ignoring the rest of his party, and building his fortunes solely on his own magnetism. It was a kind of campaign that many CCF'ers viewed with scorn. J. H. Brockelbank said, "Some people love to believe in a god, a saviour, someone who will promise to fix things all up, and without any effort on your part. This was the Messiah, this was Diefenbaker. I have thought ever since I knew Diefenbaker that he was the top champion phony that we ever had in Canadian politics. I went to school with him except that I was in Grade 9 and he was in Grade 12, and Grade 12 didn't speak to Grade 9 especially when you're in from the country. I remember at a meeting in 1957 I said, 'Diefenbaker has no more chance of being P.M. than I have.' Did I get that rubbed into me afterwards."

Douglas was more generous, wiring his congratulations to Diefenbaker and declaring his success was a "great honour for Saskatchewan."

The CCF congratulated itself on having survived the Conservative upsurge, and on having elected more M.P.s in the western provinces than any of the other parties. But they were anxious, as Diefenbaker walked the tight-rope in the dangerously poised minority government.

A letter to Douglas from an astute old CCF politician, John Wellbelove, expressed his alarm at the possibility of a new election with a shortage of funds and a possible Conservative swing. "A section of our support, as I suppose is the case in most constituencies, comes for original supporters of the Conservative party. They stayed right with us and elected our sitting members, but if there should be another appeal to the country in a comparatively short time, they might be influenced by the appeal to support Diefenbaker to get a stable government."[32]

Douglas agreed: "We could quite easily be hurt in this squeeze-play. Our best tactics are to refrain from entering into any coalition arrangement with any other political party, but at the same time to make it clear that we will support any legislation which is in the best interests of the Canadian people."[33]

A year later their gloomy predictions came true. The Diefenbaker forces won a vast majority across Canada, picking up votes in Quebec where the Progressive Conservatives had been all but obliterated for ears. In the wake of that cross-country sweep the CCF was demolished. Saskatchewan had sent ten CCF M.P.s to Ottawa in 1957, but in 1958 elected only one, Hazen Argue in Assiniboia. All the rest of the Saskatchewan seats went Conservative. Coldwell and Knowles were both defeated. Argue became temporary House Leader for the CCF in the Commons. Across Canada the Progressive-Conservatives elected two hundred eight members, to only forty-nine for the Liberals and eight for the CCF. It was the last federal election the CCF would fight, and their run for office in Ottawa had ended on a particularly forlorn note.

Yet so popular was the Douglas regime that two years later, mid-term in Diefenbaker's majority rule at Ottawa, Saskatchewan returned the CCF to office provincially with an increased majority. And Allister Grosart lost a one-thousand-dollar election bet with Clarence Fines when the provincial Conservatives failed to capture a single seat.

In the aftermath of the 1958 election, Douglas still saw as inevitable the regrouping of federal political forces, with a coalition on the right and the CCF on the left.

"What real difference is there between the fiscal policies Abbott formulated under Liberal administration and Fleming is following under the Conservatives?" He rejected the idea that the new party then evolving from the CCF, should form a coalition with either Liberals or Conservatives. "Coalitions and gentlemen's agreements are the road to ruin for any political organization," he said.[34] The new party would be forced to go part way up that road in its first tender years of life. But in the long view, for Douglas as for many of his colleagues, the political structure in Canada was destined to shake down into socialist and non-socialist, into left and right.

On the west coast the realignment was rapidly taking place, with the old-line Social Credit party manning the defenses for free enterprise. The British Columbia CCF was still waiting for a breakthrough. In the province Douglas drew huge crowds. In Vernon, in August 1960 1,500 came in pouring rain to hear him, a crowd ten times as large as any previous Vernon gathering in the campaign, and calculated at only one hundred fewer than Premier Bennett's audience in Victoria a day or so earlier, according to Jack Brooks of the Vancouver *Sun*, who added, "The attendance startled even the most optimistic CCF'ers." The New Westminster rally that followed saw another sensational turnout. "I can only recall such meetings during the depression when we were able to fill any hall or arena with the unemployed," a British Columbia M.L.A. wrote to Douglas.[35] But that 1960 fall election was one more occasion when BC voters flocked to support Bennett and rejected the CCF.

Sometimes the rigours of extensive travel were too much for Douglas' health. Late in 1959, travelling in Italy on a very frosty afternoon with an open car window beside him, he contracted a nerve infection which paralyzed the right side of his face. He reached London, where he

was to make a major address to the Chamber of Commerce. He con
sulted a neurologist and was told that he had Bells Palsy.

Douglas said:

> What could I do? My right eye during the day wept, and at nigh
> wouldn't close unless I pushed the lid with my finger. My speech wa
> blurred. I decided I couldn't cancel the engagement.
>
> The next day I raised my countenance and apologized for m
> grotesque appearance. But I said, 'It may not be an unmixed misfor
> tune. This affliction may be the most effective means yet devised fo
> keeping politicians silent. When I return to Canada I intend to bit
> several politicians I know in the hope of infecting them.'
>
> A doctor in the audience recognized it as Bells Palsy and sent m
> a note advising me not to speak for a month and it would clear up;
> had just paid a neurologist seven guineas for that diagnosis. But
> was relieved it wasn't a stroke.

Within weeks he was back in action.

Douglas travelled widely, throughout Canada and abroad, during hi
terms as Premier. Back home in the legislature he called for a response t
world needs. He ended his 1959 address in the Throne Speech debate b
urging the responsibility of the great food-producing plains to a worl
with a shrinking agricultural base. The federal government had becom
alarmed at wheat surpluses and was urging cutbacks in production.

> How can we possibly justify saying to those who produce food whicl
> is essential to life that they ought to curtail their production? Hov
> can we look upon surpluses as being a tragedy in a world where
> according to the Food and Agricultural Organization, half th
> people barely reach or fall below a minimum diet of 2,200 calorie
> per day?
>
> Mr. Speaker, this nation has a responsibility. Canada spent las
> year in assistance to underprivileged and undernourished nations
> three dollars for every one hundred dollars we spent on armament
> for defence. Surely the time has come for a great act of faith.

He was soon to take a further political step, into federal politic
leadership, as his own great act of faith. He believed that what ha
happened in Saskatchewan could happen across the country, and in a
countries. He would not look for instant success, but he believed witl
complete conviction that people everywhere are much alike, and ca
achieve the goals of common cooperative enterprise that he ha
advanced so often in this province.

Douglas left the premiership of Saskatchewan soon after the election of 1960, when provincial affairs appeared well in hand. But before going he had lit the fuse of the incendiary bomb that would tear Saskatchewan apart into its two opposing elements, oust the CCF for an ensuing seven years, and cause his own humiliating defeat in a federal election in Regina.

This was not the way he saw it. For him, it was fulfilling the promise to Saskatchewan that was closest to his heart, the creation of a system whereby anyone could get the medical attention needed, regardless of personal wealth.

The Medicare dispute has been recounted and analyzed at some length.[1] The acrimony of the confrontation was reported widely across Canada, and its repercussions delayed and changed proposals of other governments to implement prepaid health plans.

Saskatchewan had experimented with health schemes for many years, beginning with the Anti-Tuberculosis League in 1929. Several municipalities had tried hiring doctors and keeping them on salary – some schemes went back to 1919. A province-wide government plan could be expected to get support. The doctors themselves had studied the problem and spoken with guarded approval of the insurance principle during depression years when bills went unpaid and doctors' incomes were insecure. In 1932, in fact, and until the war, some Saskatchewan doctors were receiving relief along with the rest of the population – in their case a guaranteed income of fifty to seventy-five dollars a month.

In British Columbia, the provincial government had backed down from implementing a Health Insurance Act because of pressure from the medical profession. A British Columbia Commission recommended a comprehensive government health insurance scheme in 1932, and the bill was introduced in 1935, and passed on April 1, 1936. Although it covered only people earning less than $2400 a year, leaving the doctors free to charge as they liked above that income level, the Medical Association was opposed. When they were invited to consult with an administrative government health insurance commission they balked because they had no real power to change the legislation, " . . . no real progress was made, and none was expected because, while the Commission had wide powers under the Act it would in no way alter the Act itself; the result was that, as far as the Negotiating Committee was concerned, an air of unreality seemed to pervade the whole proceedings."[2]

In other words, the British Columbia medical profession refused to accept legislation passed by the legislature. It was an accurate forerunner of the Saskatchewan experience. The B.C. doctors were successful. They had only to threaten to strike as they did, voting overwhelmingly at meetings in Vancouver and Victoria not to work under the Act. They were unmoved by the results of a B.C. plebiscite, when citizens voted 116,223 for and 80,982 opposed to the Act. In 1937 the B.C. Liberal government postponed the proclamation of the Act *sine die*.

But the B.C. Act had provided only partial coverage. Douglas was convinced that a more generous system, introduced with proper care and consultation, would be accepted by Saskatchewan doctors.

In 1944 he was elected on the promise to set up medical, dental, and hospital services "available to all without counting the ability of the individual to pay."[3]

His government's first move was to make cancer treatment government-supported and free to all, as tuberculosis care had been since 1929. By January 1945 free medical, hospital, and dental care was provided for "blue card" pensioners and indigent people. Mental treatment, and the treatment of polio, became free to all. After a hard struggle to obtain finances, a School of Medicine was opened at Saskatchewan University to increase the supply of doctors. Later, a government Air Ambulance service was set up, making dramatic rescue flights to bring patients to hospital from the remoter northern settlements, and even from isolated farm homes in the south. Geriatric centres were built to provide care for the chronically ill, relieving pressure on acute treatment facilities, and hospital beds were systematically increased to a ratio that made universal access to health a practical possibility.

An experimental health unit was established at Swift Current, where forty doctors served the population of just over 50,000 people. The scheme was financed by a family payment of $48 a year and a land tax, and the doctors received remuneration on a fee-for-service basis. Run on a small scale, it was a testing ground for the provincial program; one of its functions was to keep records and to assess the impact on the health of the people of the region.

Douglas said,

> When I wrote to Dr. Emmett Hall in 1964 to congratulate him on his Report (Hall was commissioned by Diefenbaker in 1961 to study the health needs of Canada and recommend a national health care program) he told me that one of the most useful sources of information to him was the Swift Current Health Region. He said he had begun his work firmly convinced that you need a deterrent fee, a

small charge to be paid by the patient so he won't bother the doctors too much and abuse the system, but the Swift Current experience proved it had no effect at all. The average stay in hospital was less than it was in British Columbia and Alberta where they had hospital schemes with deterrent fees.

The first step toward the province-wide scheme was taken almost as soon as Douglas was in office. As Minister of Health, he appointed a committee to survey health needs and services under Dr. Henry E. Sigerist of Johns Hopkins University.

"Dr. Sigerist was teaching at Sir Johns Hopkins," Douglas said. "He was probably the greatest authority in the world on social medicine. He had a great personality, he got along well with everyone, and he was intrigued by the situation in Saskatchewan and its long record in public health programs – the first anti-tuberculosis program in Canada, started by Saskatchewan farm women – so he came for two years, and actually stayed for five. And we got other outstanding people, Dr. Len Rosenfeldt, Dr. Cecil and Dr. Mendel Sheps – Cecil was in the Army but we got him out. And the great prize was Dr. Fred Mott!

When Sigerist made his first report I said, 'Great. Now where can we get the people to put it into effect? Who is the best man in North America?' Sigersit said, 'Fred Mott. But you can't get him.' I said, 'Why not?' He said, 'He happens to be the Assistant Surgeon-General of the United States Army.'"

But Douglas went after Mott, appealing to the US Surgeon-General to release him for a limited period. Mott, like Sigerist, was interested, and agreed. He quickly assembled a topnotch team who were given the task of producing a complete hospital insurance program – to go into effect on January 1, 1947.

And not a day later.

Hospital construction grants were given to increase bed capacity. The complex task of working out an operating scheme to apply to the budget of every hospital in the province was undertaken. But in November 1946 a delegation from Dr. Mott's working group regretfully told Douglas that the scheme had to be postponed. There was not enough time to complete their preparations. Douglas would not hear of it. January 1 was the target date. He was determined to keep the total health scheme on schedule. And it was a political decision. An election – the first election test for his government – would be held in June 1948 (another promise to the electorate). He was well aware that there would be initial grumbling, he wanted time for the scheme to prove itself.

The Hospital Insurance Plan began as promised on New Year's Day 1947, with Douglas and Dr. Fred Mott on hand at Regina General Hospital to see the first patient admitted under the scheme at a little after midnight, "fortunately a joyful occasion; she was having a child."

Dr. Mott moved on to other things, but in 1971 as Professor of Medical Care at University of Toronto's School of Hygiene, he wrote to Douglas: "My years in Saskatchewan, working at first directly with you, have proved to be the most memorable in a series of exciting assignments, and I shall always be grateful for this privilege you afforded me."[4]

The hospital insurance premium initially was five dollars a person, ten dollars a family. Douglas' mail contained bitter protests from people who objected to the premium and had "never spent a day in hospital in their lives". By 1948 the proportion of those people with first-hand experience in receiving hospital care without getting a bill was sufficient to ensure the Plan's popularity and the re-election of the CCF.

There had been scattered opposition from hospital officials, worried about "government interference". Douglas had reassured them, "We have enough to look after without worrying about whether or not the bedpans in Tisdale are clean." On the whole, the plan was well received by the hospitals. With an assured revenue, they were able to stay out of the red as never before. A sales tax on a limited range of retail goods, a "hospital tax", was the chief source of revenue to subsidize the scheme.

But the hospital insurance, the "blue cards", the free mental and cancer care, were only a prelude to the total, comprehensive medicare scheme Douglas had promised. This would bring the showdown with the doctors.

The first survey committee under Sigerist had included a representative of the Saskatchewan medical profession, Dr. J. Lloyd Brown. Their recommendation for "a system of socialized medical service on a provincial scale, that will guarantee the people the basic services they need," brought no immediate reaction from the doctors' College. Enabling legislation was passed at the fall 1944 session, and plans were moving to divide the province into health regions by the following spring. The first doctors' opposition began to develop in 1945, with requests for professional advisory committees to guide the health commission, and "whose advice should be sought and normally followed". In correspondence with Dr. Brown, Douglas agreed to a permanent independent Commission to administer Medicare, fully representing medical, dental, nursing, and pharmaceutical professions, and promising, "The professional committees shall have unrestricted jurisdiction over all scientific, technical and professional matters pertaining to their own professions, and the Commission shall be guided by their advice."[5] The matter seemed close to agreement. In his reply Dr. Brown spoke of the "splendid degree of cooperation" shown by the Premier.

That was 1945. The CCF government was waiting for the word from Ottawa that a federal health insurance scheme was on its way. It had been a Liberal *promise* since 1919, and federal-provincial consultations and special election promises had made it seem close to actuality in 1945. The federal-provincial conference of 1945 failed to get general agreement, however, and despite Saskatchewan's pleas that Ottawa go into insurance schemes with the provinces that were willing, the whole project went on the federal shelf.

Forced to go it alone, Saskatchewan had to slow down the pace of its Medicare plans. E. A. Tollefson writes: "It would appear that if the province had gone ahead at that time with a health insurance scheme such as that set out in the Premier's letter (to Dr. Brown) there would have been little difficulty in working out the details with the medical profession."[6]

What happened after 1945 was that "times" improved, and the doctors saw less and less advantage in a government administration setting and collecting their fees for them. Several voluntary private insurance schemes came into being, some sponsored by the profession itself. Their coverage was not very wide. They took care of a proportion of more affluent patients, for a limited number of ailments, and their premiums were high. But the doctors believed that with these schemes available to the middle class, and welfare to pay for the needs of the very poor, a comprehensive system could be forgotten.

In 1954 in the Legislature, the Liberal Opposition began to twit Douglas about the delay. Douglas said,

We don't need the Opposition to remind us. I made a pledge with myself long before I ever sat in this house, in the years when I knew something about what it meant to get health services when you didn't have the money to pay for them. I made a pledge that if I ever had anything to do with it, people would be able to get health services just as they are able to get educational services, as an inalienable right of being a citizen of a Christian country.[7]

The prospects for Medicare brightened after 1957, when Diefenbaker at Ottawa brought in a federal-provincial hospital insurance program. After ten years of going it alone, Saskatchewan was able to share part of the cost of its hospital scheme with the federal government.

In April 1959 Douglas announced the introduction of Medicare. It would be based on five principles: prepayment; universal coverage; high quality of service; administration by a public body responsible to the legislature; and "in a form acceptable both to those providing the service and those receiving it."

This time the medical profession made no gesture of acceptance. The doctors' association, the College of Physicians and Surgeons, said firmly in October 1959 that their members "oppose the introduction of a compulsory Government-controlled province-wide medical care plan and declare our support of and extension of health and sickness benefits through indemnity and service plans." Bill Davies, later Health Minister, had been a representative of organized labour on the first survey committee. He said, "About 1950 the doctors' representative signed the document favouring a health care plan under a provincial commission, paid for through taxes. But now it was ten prosperous years later."

Protracted negotiations between Premier Douglas, Health Minister Erb, and G. W. Peacock, Registrar, and other officials of the College continued through the winter of 1959-1960. The College objected to the terms of reference of the committee that would be charged with bringing in a specific plan. It proposed broader terms, it proposed a new sweeping survey of all medical, dental, nursing, hospital, and various other needs, before consideration of the Medicare plan. It wanted no time limit on the committee's deliberations. It changed its mind about representation on the committee.

Even while this correspondence continued to limp between Douglas in Regina and Peacock in Saskatoon, the Saskatchewan College of Physicians and Surgeons was gearing for action. In a circular from its president, A. J. M. Davies, to all Saskatchewan doctors it announced the appointment of

> a three-man committee with office headquarters at 2127 Albert Street, Regina. They will be your listening-post at government level. They will gather, co-ordinate and disseminate important data on medical economics to both the profession and the public . . . They have obtained the loan of a professional public relations officer . . . It is strongly suggested that for purposes of unity and clarity of thought every doctor contact the Special Committee office in writing or by telephone, prior to making statements on policy or medical economic matters. If possible, doctors are urged to send copies of what they said to this office . . . Considerable expense will be incurred but the load will not be heavy upon any one individual doctor. Council, at its next meeting in Saskatoon, will consider the advisability of assessing every member of the College an amount necessary to defray the cost of the Special Committee projects.[8]

Ironically, even as Davies released his circular letter to the doctors, Douglas in the Throne Speech debate at the beginning of the legislative session was mildly rebuking the Liberals: "I notice there is a tendency in some quarters to suggest that the doctors are opposed to this plan but that is not quite fair to them."[9] He expressed confidence that problems relating to the Medicare program would be worked out by the committee which represented the government, the public and the doctors, in a way "satisfactory to all concerned."

"Neither the doctors nor the public have anything to fear from a prepaid medical plan," Douglas told the Legislature. "Instead, there is much to be gained. It means that we can take from thousands of our people the fear which is inherent in illness and the reluctance to go to a doctor at the first sign of evil symptoms."

But the doctors did not see it that way.

The amount assessed by the College was one hundred dollars per doctor. In March Davies followed up with another circular, making it clear that this "is not a voluntary assessment". This circular informed the doctors that they would be receiving information kits and statements of policy. "There is no opportunity for compromise on these principles of policy." Included in the kit were sample speeches for women's groups. It was suggested that doctors tell their women audiences:

> Many times we have sat down in our office with a woman and discussed emotional situations which crop up during pregnancy or other critical periods in a woman's life. We know that under Government administration we would be prevented from rendering these vital services . . . It could very easily be that this type of condition (tension during menopause) must be referred to a psychiatric clinic or a mental hospital, a situation which we, as your personal physician, would deplore.[10]

The Saskatchewan professional association was bolstered by the position of the Canadian Medical Association (CMA), and even more by the American Medical Association which was waging a no-holds-barred campaign against President Kennedy's efforts to introduce a prepaid scheme for the elderly. The Saskatchewan association raised over $60,000 through its assessment of its members, and received a $35,000 gift from the CMA as well as public relations and research staff. They entered vigorously into the 1960 election, on radio, in newspaper advertisements, and in public meetings, urging Douglas' defeat.

The Liberal Opposition expressed sympathy for the doctors but was not prepared to reject Medicare outright. They called for a plebiscite, with no commitment beyond the testing of public approval. The CCF under Douglas declared that they would regard success in the election as a mandate to carry out their program of Medicare. Douglas had no doubt that he carried the province with him. The response to his meetings was wildly enthusiastic. When he informed a vast audience in his final meeting of the campaign, in the Regina Exhibition arena, that if the medical association continued its attack on the government plan he would be prepared to take away their authority to license doctors in the province, there were loud cheers.

Otto Lang, at that time Dean of the College of Law at the University of Saskatchewan and vice-president of the Saskatchewan Liberal Association, talked about the government's "arbitrary power", and "dictatorship".

Coming in on Douglas' side, M. J. Coldwell in a speech during the election campaign said flatly, "The doctors are more concerned here with maintaining high fees than serving the people of Saskatchewan."[11]

Douglas believed that the doctors' hostility came directly from their wallets, and as usual he hoped that altruism would overcome pecuniary interest. He said in a newspaper interview some years later that he saw only two real objections emerging in his long discussions with the doctors, and both had to do with payment. Doctors did not want to accept medicare fees as payment in full; they wanted the schedule to be a minimum, with freedom to charge more if the patient could afford it.

> The second thing – and this of course they would never admit – was that when bills were paid by the Medical Care Commission the T4 slips went to the Department of National Revenue. Every dollar they got was on the books, and they were paying income tax on it. In the next few years after Medicare the per capita income of Saskatchewan doctors was $3000 higher than anywhere else in Canada. I don't think they were earning $3000 more but they were reporting $3000 more.[12]

Douglas felt that more than the Medicare issue decided the outcome of the 1960 election. He thought Ross Thatcher's performance, in his first bid for the Premiership, was clumsy. He recalled a debate in Saskatoon sponsored by the Farmers Union when Thatcher was unable to field questions on agriculture, lost his temper, and was howled down.

But Thatcher, the ex-CCF M.P., the hardware merchant from Moose Jaw, was the leader who would galvanize the forces of Saskatchewan's right-wing Liberals. He successfully divorced his party from Ottawa domination. He was the most adamant of free-enterprisers. He was a businessman, had majored in economics at Queen's University, and had been drawn by the rising fortunes of the CCF into contesting an election, in 1945, as a CCF candidate. Elected with him at that time was another forceful personality, Hazen Argue. Both were successful as CCF candidates in two succeeding federal elections, in 1949 and 1953.

But over the ten-year period at Ottawa, Thatcher found himself increasingly at odds with the CCF. He found more congenial associates on Parliament Hill among Liberals and Conservatives. In 1952 he spoke and voted against the leader of his party, M. J. Coldwell, on the question of old age pensions. Thatcher had arrived at the conclusion that the pensions ought to be based on need instead of being paid universally, as under the existing system.

After that particular vote a CCF federal council meeting considered expelling Thatcher, and it was Douglas who spoke against expulsion, softening the council's wrath. Later he told a friend, "When that meeting was over Thatcher came up to me and offered to take me out to dinner, host me to a big night on the town. I realized then I'd made a mistake."

However, Thatcher's reputation was growing. His home-town paper, the Moose Jaw *Times Herald*, wrote: "Just how much of an individualist Thatcher really is, parliament discovered when he spoke the other day in the budget debate. With an engaging candour and the ringing of real conviction in his voice, he argued against universal old age pensions, universal family allowances, and took a belt, for good measure, at the generosity of the federal superannuation fund."

In 1955 he formally parted company with the CCF, sitting as an Independent for the balance of the term. In May that year he professed his purity as a reformed capitalist in a motion so far right that nobody in the House voted for it, Thatcher and his seconder having chosen to absent themselves when the vote was taken.[13] That motion would have wiped out the government's low-cost annuity scheme, which Thatcher denounced as a drain on the taxpayers' money and as unfair competition to private insurance schemes. Paul Martin for the Liberals, and Donald Fleming for the Conservatives refused to support the motion. On the CCF's behalf, Bert Herridge said: "Fortunately, the philosophy that prompts this amendment is not the philosophy of progressive capitalists. I think we must give them credit for believing in periodic inoculations of relative economic and social justice."

Thatcher ran twice, unsuccessfully, as a federal Liberal, in 1957 and 1958. In 1959 he gained the leadership of the provincial Liberal party; he was reportedly backed by a group of wealthy men who deplored the general "leftist" tendencies of politicians. Blair Fraser wrote of these mysterious backers:

"The charge that they were not 'real Liberals' was borne out by the fact that they put up campaign funds (reportedly $50,000 in donations and pledges) on the express stipulation that Mr. Thatcher must lead the campaign. If he had lost they would have got their money back."[14]

His defection had produced a disgruntled reaction in the CCF, and in Douglas' view he was a back-slider, but his departure provoked nothing like the trauma of the later turnabout by Hazen Argue. The circumstances surrounding Argue's move were highly charged emotionally. Thatcher merely set himself up as the incarnate anti-socialist, the perfect mark, the boldest exponent of no state interference in Canada.

Thatcher attacked by describing Saskatchewan as bound by the shackles of an ideology which would not permit economic growth, and by hotly disputing the achievements of the various crown corporations which the CCF looked on as so many stars in its crown – the bus company, the telephone company, the power company, the insurance company, and the publicly assisted industries of potash, steel, and uranium. In a radio debate broadcast from Mossbank in 1957, Douglas and Thatcher stoutly defended two different sets of figures. To Douglas' chagrin the "debate" did not permit exchange, merely two parallel speeches. Douglas spoke extemporaneously, Thatcher ignored his argument and delivered his own hard-hitting written speech – the result, in the opinion of many listeners, was a draw. A Calgary *Herald* reporter said, "Ross Thatcher emerged from the now famous Mossbank debate as a new power in Saskatchewan politics, not because he won but because he didn't lose."

In 1960 Thatcher seized on the rumours of the formation of a new party which would absorb the CCF. He told a Liberal convention in Saskatoon that the new party would be a labour party dominated by eastern labour leaders, "a party which makes its appeal to class prejudice. . . .

"I concede that our socialist premier is a very astute politician, but even he cannot sell a straight labour-dominated party to agricultural Saskatchewan," he said. "The formation of the new party will ultimately mean the death-knell of socialism in our province."[15]

But in 1960, Douglas' last election as Saskatchewan's premier, he was still unbeatable.

He was winning such fulsome praise as in a column written by Jack Scott of the Vancouver *Sun*:

> This man Douglas is – well, how'll I put it? He's a good deed in a naughty world. He's a breath of clean prairie air in a stifling climate of payola and chicanery and double-talk and pretence, global and local.
>
> Forget the politics. Here's a man who wanted to do something for the improvement of the human race. He chose the method that seemed best to him, quarrel with it if you will. He was motivated by an ideal.
>
> To call him a politician, as you'd call Bennett or Diefenbaker politicians, is to insult him. He was and is a dreamer and a humanitarian, incorruptible, genuine and intellectually honest.

In the 1960 election the CCF increased their majority and Douglas in his Weybourn riding further increased the margin he had won in 1956.

He wrote to the CCF secretary in British Columbia, Harold Thayer: "I think this was probably the hardest election campaign we have fought. As you know, the doctors intruded themselves into the campaign so that we were actually confronted by four opposition groups rather than three. We weathered the storm pretty well, all things considered."

But his success in the 1960 campaign convinced him, prematurely, that Medicare was assured. He did not believe the doctors would continue to resist to the point of withdrawing their services, as they did in 1962. Bill Davies said, "Tommy thought the doctors when they came down to the wire would go along as they had on hospital insurance. But this was completely different. Hospital insurance meant guaranteeing their fees – but Medicare changed their whole way of doing business."

Immediately after the June election the general secretary of the Canadian Medical Association, Dr. A. D. Kelly, issued a conciliatory statement, accepting the democratic decision of the Saskatchewan electorate. But the Saskatchewan association repudiated his words, declaring they were still "unalterably opposed."[16]

240

The government established a committee shortly after the election, under Dr. W. P. Thompson, a former president of Saskatchewan University. Its hearings and studies went on for eight months. In June 1961, Health Minister Erb pressed it for a report on which to base legislation in the fall session, but the best he could get was *two* reports, one recommending a fee-for-service plan under a commission with physician representation, and a minority report signed by the medical representatives and a representative of the Chamber of Commerce, rejecting the total plan and stating, "the quality of medical services rendered under state monopolies tend to achieve a mediocrity which in the long run would not be in the best interest of the health of our people."

Despite the blunt and uncompromising position of the College of Physicians and Surgeons, the government introduced its bill on October 13, 1961, and passed it a month later. It was bitterly opposed by the Liberal Opposition, who now sensed the adamant stand of the doctors.

Having brought the Act into being, having brought Medicare this far, Douglas left the provincial scene to take up his new role as leader of the New Democratic Party. He thought the doctors would bargain hard over the regulations still to be set up under the Act, but he did not expect that when the Act was proclaimed they would refuse to obey it.

He continued to believe, as so many of his admirers did, that Medicare was the greatest achievement of his government's long period of office. In 1967 the federal government passed enabling legislation to set up cost-sharing medical care schemes in the provinces, and one by one, provincial governments entered into these arrangements. Prepaid government medical insurance, with varying premium arrangements, now covers everyone in Canada.

In April 1971 Emmett M. Hall, then a Supreme Court Judge, wrote warmly to Douglas as he left the NDP leadership:

> I just can't let the occasion pass without writing to say that Canada is a very much better country in which to live by reason of your contributions in the political and social action fields.
>
> I can never forget the help and cooperation you gave me in connection with the new St. Paul's Hospital project. It stands today as a monument to your determination that a way would be found to provide for the continuance of this historic institution as a private hospital, and I remember too, vividly as if it were yesterday, that night you came to the Grey Nuns Hospital in Regina to resolve the long dispute over donated services in respect of sisters' salaries which Dr. Mott and his associates were insisting upon and your instantaneous solution when the matter at issue was explained – 'Forget it, boys, you're all wrong.'
>
> I think your greatest and enduring accomplishment was the introduction and putting into effect of Medicare in Saskatchewan. Without your program as a successful one in being, I couldn't have

produced the unanimous report for the Canada-wide universal health recommendations in 1964. If the scheme had not been successful in Saskatchewan, it wouldn't have become nation-wide. Generations to come will be your debtors.[17]

Medicare, once introduced, was soon so well accepted that no political party had the temerity to suggest its abolition. Though the Liberal party took office in 1964 and retained it in 1967, their only change in the plan was to introduce deterrent fees, which the NDP government abolished after 1971.

*　　*　　*

Douglas left Saskatchewan in 1961, the province and the party having expressed their gratitude in a round of testimonials and presentations.

He had a high regard for Woodrow Lloyd, his successor. He believed the Medicare program was safely launched with the passing of the Act, and would crown a sixteen-year record of important achievements. He had done what he could to leave affairs in good shape. But no sooner had he left than catastrophe descended.

The fight by the doctors against the government medical scheme intensified after his departure and led to a strike the following July when the Act was proclaimed in force. The crisis in Saskatchewan that summer of 1962 marked every resident of the province. The fears inspired by the doctors and fanned by the Liberal party convinced many people at least briefly that the CCF *was* a dictatorial, power-mad, ruthless group of politicians who would rather see people die for lack of medical care than back down. The anger crackled in the air. Every business interest, every insurance agent, every local Chamber of Commerce which had privately detested Douglas' brotherhood philosophy, now aided and abetted the doctors' cause with every resource at their disposal. Stores were closed to swell "Keep Our Doctors" rallies and parades and marches on the legislature. Newspapers and radios bristled with accusations. There was, as many testified, a sense of civil war.

The strike petered out after a month or so, largely because the government kept medical services going with British doctors flown in to help in the emergency. Premier Woodrow Lloyd had taken over from Douglas in November. One of his first acts was to remove Health Minister Walter Erb, who was not, he felt, acting firmly enough. He appointed first Bill Davies and later Allan Blakeney to the super-sensitive post. Blakeney agreed with the decision to remove Erb and implement the plan promptly, to give it a chance to work. But Lloyd himself took the full brunt of the doctors' attack. They may have considered him an easier mark than Douglas. But he was, if anything, more resolute in putting the Act into operation. Lloyd was an extremely serious, unsmiling, mild-mannered, dignified person, who took great pains to urge restraint on CCF partisans and to say nothing himself to inflame the situation.

Questioned about the way Lloyd handled the strike, and whether Douglas might have been more successful, participants on the scene defended Lloyd. Some thought he was "steadier" and less likely to arouse further hatred; there was a common feeling that a tougher line in any degree might have made an explosive situation worse. Whether the doctors would have pressed to such lengths against a still-popular Premier remains uncertain.

Lloyd established an administrative commission under the Act, with Donald D. Tansley as chairman. Tansley tried repeatedly to get the Physicians' College to meet with him. The College president at that time, H. D. Dalgleish, rebuffed him by saying, "We regard this Act as a form of civil conscription of the profession of medicine and an attempt to put us under the control of government by political and economic pressure."

In May 1962 Premier Lloyd was hissed at a meeting of the doctors' association which he had requested the privilege of addressing. Erb chose this occasion to announce that he was quitting the CCF to join the Liberals. Erb had been humiliated by his removal from the health portfolio to public works: instead of dealing with doctors, he said, he now talked to charwomen. He was an easy mark for Liberals and militant doctors who assured him he had been treated badly by Lloyd.

As the doctors preyed on the fears of their patients with the announcement that their doors would soon be locked, an elderly priest, Father Athol Murray, was saying to a "Keep Our Doctors" rally in Wilcox: "This thing may break out into violence and bloodshed any day now, and God help us if it doesn't."

There were other inflammatory speeches. Lloyd, by radio, deplored the incitement to violence, and when Opposition Leader Ross Thatcher staged a display at the door of the Legislature, demanding a special session and kicking at the locked door, Lloyd commented coldly that he "saw no point in making a farce of the legislative chamber."

It was a difficult time to be Premier. Frank Scott recalled being in Regina and attending a cabinet meeting. He entered a room full of "doleful" ministers waiting about the big oval table. Lloyd's chair with the high back was still empty and Scott asked, "Where shall I sit? Here?" They said, "Go ahead. No one else wants to sit in it."

A federal election was held in July 1962 and Douglas, running in Regina, was defeated.

The strike lasted about a month. Eastern newspapers deplored the doctors' action. Blakeney had contingency plans ready for emergency services and Graham Spry was recruiting British doctors who were arriving by the plane load. Spry also recommended the perfect arbiter, Lord Taylor, who came in to mediate and eventually produced the Saskatoon Agreement. Blakeney recalls:

The doctors by this time saw they might lose the fight and they couldn't think what to do. Stephen Taylor's job was to get them down off this emotional pitch. He went back and forth between the two groups, spending about four times as much time with them as with us, getting them to focus on their requirements and get down off their emotional high. He was a great showman. He went through his routine about how tired he was, how he had to leave, he had to go fishing. He made a big hit with the press. And he would always park his car ostentatiously in a no-parking zone, with a piece of House of Lords stationery tucked under the windshield wiper.

From Ottawa, absorbed in the need to find a new parliamentary seat after his defeat in Regina, Douglas could only watch the drama play itself out.

By the time the next Saskatchewan election was called, in 1964, the province had other issues besides Medicare to influence the vote. Lloyd was clearly not the leader to win followers passionately to his side, and he was less politically astute. Forgetting the Douglas rule to introduce reforms early in the term of office, to give them time to gain acceptance before the next vote, Lloyd brought in new education measures, which included increased grants to separate schools, close to the 1964 election date, and this contributed to the CCF defeat.

There were other reasons. Brockelbank said:

Sure. The wounds of Medicare went very deep. All kinds of our supporters went completely off the beam. And besides, it's never yet been proven in a democratic country that a party can go on forever. Just the passage of time is a reason for defeat. Twenty years! The people at the 1964 election, the 18-35 year-olds, had no basis of comparison because they knew no other government but ours. It became easy to say things could be better. Things could always be better.

Maybe we became over cautious, not as willing to take a chance.

And the separate schools. The way it was there were some grants to Grade Twelve and some only to Grade Eight. I don't believe in Separate· Schools at all, if you'd never had'em we wouldn't have started 'em. But once you've got 'em that's different. You've got to treat them all alike.

"The CCF in 1964 produced no fresh issues but campaigned on its record, and did that in an impressively undramatic manner."[18]

Thatcher slipped in with a fair margin, electing thirty-three Liberals to the CCF's twenty-five, though the popular vote actually gave the CCF an extra percentage point.

Curiously, some papers gave more space to Douglas who was not a participant in the election than to either Ross Thatcher or Woodrow Lloyd. The Winnipeg *Tribune* carried a story at the top of page one by Don McGillivray of Southam News Service:

. . . this is a requiem for a government which in its best days stirred the blood and the idealism of the people of Saskatchewan . . . Twenty years ago, an earnest, wise-cracking little Baptist parson persuaded the people of Saskatchewan that they could build the new Jerusalem on their dusty, stubborn plains . . . Among the new things was Canada's first bill of rights, hospital insurance plan, pioneering work in mental health, brave attempts to solve the problems of the aged, and government automobile insurance . . . The last great work was medicare and in the crowds of angry protest marchers in that hot Regina summer two years ago, one could sense a shift in the mood of Saskatchewan, an impatience with a government which was wearing out its welcome . . . The Baptist parson is now leading the New Democratic Party, a party which tried to substitute the big battalions for a sense of mission and lost both.

The government he founded in Saskatchewan went down fighting under the old banner of the CCF. There will be recounts and post-mortems . . . But it's the end of an era, for Saskatchewan and for Canada.[19]

The Toronto *Star* the day after the election proclaimed, "For 20 years the CCF government in Regina was the flagship of social change for the whole country . . . remarkably efficient and relatively free from corruption."

But the Saskatoon *Star-Phoenix* would have no part of such sentiments. "After twenty years," it said, "the Saskatchewan voters made a tremendous decision to cast out socialism. The have become very weary of the diaper service provided for them by the Welfare State. After twenty years, Saskatchewan breathes freely once more."

Douglas, in a message to the *Saskatchewan Commonwealth*, said, "Many who were too young to remember what it is like to live under a Liberal regime may now have a chance to savour that experience."

Thatcher, reputed to be the most right-wing defender of free enterprise in Canada, took the province to the polls again in 1967 and was returned with thirty-five seats, to twenty-four for the CCF. Saskatchewan, as usual, swung toward the opposite extreme, and the non-socialists had their inning. In 1971 it was all over. The CCF, revived as the NDP, took office under Premier Allan Blakeney, whose campaign slogan was "NDP – Homecoming 1971". (It proved more successful than the similar slogan adopted in 1972 by George McGovern: "Come Home America!")

Blakeney was interviewed in 1973, in the legislative building – that black-domed elegant structure of pale Tyndal stone beside its formal little artificial lake, precise gardens and planted groves, an oasis in an immeasurable distance of flat plains. In its earlier days of government Regina had tried to compensate for its peculiarly bad physical characteristics as a city – a critic said when it was chosen as the capital of the North

West Territories: "I have never seen in all my travels so wretched a site for a town" – by building the finest legislative building it could manage.

The Executive Council suite in that building is an impressive one. The ceilings are very high, the rooms finely proportioned, the furnishings distinguished. After viewing the Council chamber it is a shock to step into the Premier's office. Here Premier Thatcher left his mark. Against the high carved mouldings, the pale brocade wall coverings, the furniture is cube-shaped metal-framed shiny modern, under a dropped ceiling with fluorescent lights.

But Blakeney has not taken time to think about office furniture. He says, "There are still a vast number of people who look back to those years, 1944 to 1964, who are convinced democratic socialists and believe it is right for Saskatchewan. As though we are now back on the track. We are regarded as the lineal descendant of the Douglas-Lloyd government. We've got back to our roots. The government is only an extension of yourself – that's the ethos of Saskatchewan. It's very widely accepted. But among the young people? I'm not sure."

Saskatchewan in 1974 has a rapidly expanding economy, almost no unemployment, and a land bank policy which, in leasing farms to young farmers, comes significantly close to the use-lease plank in the 1935 platform of the United Farmers of Canada (Saskatchewan Section). The government is promoting the "Saskatchewan Option", a euphemism for a return to the soil as a better way of life.

But the young people? In 1974 four young people at the Regina campus were asked about politics. Two had voted; both had voted NDP though their parents were Liberal. Their reasons had to do with current judgements, for all four showed an astonishing lack of knowledge about their province's immediate past.

They had all received their schooling since 1961, when Douglas left the province. And their schooling had taught them nothing about Douglas, about the doctors' strike (they had never heard of it), about the cooperative movement which makes their province unique. Saskatchewan's history stops, in the classrooms, with the hanging of Riel, and even that is treated delicately as a matter of some controversy. The course in Canadian history offered at matriculation level uses as its text a book written by a University of Toronto professor, J. M. S. Careless, which mentions Douglas by name twice.

Eventually, of course, formal education will include Tommy Douglas, when a safe barrier of time has intervened, just as the wild radical of the Independent Labour Party, Jimmy Maxton, found his way at last into the Glasgow museum. But the present generation of Saskatchewan school children is the loser.

Chapter Sixteen
Founding of a New Party

The old CCF party was created and sustained in the west, and it was ended by a westerner, John Diefenbaker. The lawyer from Prince Albert who became leader, after many tries, of the national Progressive Conservative party, roused the hope of many prairie people that at last one of the *big* parties with a real chance of electoral power at Ottawa, could overcome its eastern industrial bias and speak for "all Canadians" (especially western Canadians). In the 1957 election, the year of Diefenbaker's first incredible rise to federal power, Saskatchewan voters continued to support the CCF: they sent ten CCF M.P.s to Ottawa and only three Conservatives, Diefenbaker, Alvin Hamilton and A. F. Jones of Saskatoon. But in 1958 it was a different story. The famous Diefenbaker sweep that carried two hundred eight Conservatives to victory, included sixteen Conservatives from Saskatchewan and left only one CCF'er, Hazen Argue.

It was a final blow. CCF membership and popular support across the country had been slipping or remaining static; at Ottawa their elected members varied from about ten to twenty. Saskatchewan had always sent the largest contingent. In 1958 the CCF caucus was reduced to eight. M. J. Coldwell, the leader, was defeated in Rosetown-Biggar. In Winnipeg North Centre, the old J. S. Woodsworth seat, Stanley Knowles was defeated too.

There was no longer much argument. The old CCF was getting nowhere in provinces outside Saskatchewan, struggling to win only tiny pockets of support. It had always seen itself as a federal party. What was the use of continuing?

Of course there was still a place for a "left wing" party. If the CCF in its old form could not take hold in other parts of the country, perhaps something else would.

In Canada it had always been assumed that "left wing" meant "farmer-labour". If farmer support could not sustain a national party, the obvious course was to shift the base to labour. This had always been the goal of the eastern party leaders. How else were the great provinces of central Canada to be won? How else had democratic socialist parties come to power in other countries? The trade union base was the international tradition.

The flaw in the argument was that next door to Canada was the biggest industrial nation of the world, where trade unions did *not* support a democratic socialist party, but allied themselves with "free enterprise" parties similar in their economic outlook to Canada's Liberals and Conservatives. Canada's trade unions were largely affiliated with those American unions. There was a thread of political action sentiment running through Canadian trade union history, and a group of top union leaders were active members of the CCF and cherished the notion of a union-supported party. But other union leaders, and vast throngs of union members, did not.

Still, what alternative was there?

There was an additional feeling, particularly in Ontario, of growing distaste for the CCF "style". In Saskatchewan, where people were involved in party processes, the old concepts of political brotherhood were alive. In Ontario they were sour, irrelevant, and empty, a poor joke. The eastern wing had pressed for a changed "image", and had substituted the flat and cautious 1956 Winnipeg Declaration for the prophetic prose of the 1933 Regina Manifesto, only to find, as Desmond Morton wrote: "It was not simply the Regina Manifesto that tied the CCF to the Thirties; it was the name, the faces, the utterances, the ever-present righteousness."[1] Ontario people were tired of all that. The Ontario atmosphere of the 1950s was secular, accelerating, affluent, urban, American. Only a party tuned to this key could hope to get the vote of pragmatic, beer-drinking, car-proud, sports-minded, TV-watching, thousand-strong, "ordinary" voters.

The Mineworkers of Cape Breton had been among the first few unionists who declared themselves to be supporters of the CCF. Assiduously cultivated by David Lewis and other national CCF figures, and ably promoted from within labour's ranks by such men as Charles Millard, Eamon Park, Fred Dowling, and Larry Sefton, union support increased gradually. The merging of the two old labour congresses, the T.L.C. and the C.C.L., into one body, the Canadian Labour Congress (CLC) in 1956, was regarded as a major step toward active union involvement in the CCF. When it was not forthcoming in significant strength, the feeling spread that the CCF itself was out of step with modern times, that a new structure would transform the political left into something the workers could happily endorse and work for.

The initiative came from the leaders of the Canadian Labour Congress, with David Lewis and Stanley Knowles working hard behind the scenes. At the 1958 CLC Winnipeg convention they presented and succeeded in having passed a resolution calling for "a fundamental realignment of political forces in Canada, in a broadly-based people's political movement which embraces the CCF, the labour movement, farmer organizations, professional people and other liberally-minded persons interested in basic social reform and reconstruction through our parliamentary system of government." The word "socialist" was dropped as inapplicable and unnecessary, though it would be re-instated in a 1963 declaration of "Principles and Objectives" of the new party.

Three months later the CCF was slated to hold its national convention. Before that date the election wiped out CCF hopes in its worst post-war defeat. The CCF in convention accepted the invitation of the CLC, and a National Committee for a New Party was formed.

Farm organizatons were asked to name representatives to the Committee, but they declined. The CLC appointed ten, the CCF another ten. A triumvirate of sponsors was desired, so the party could afford a wider, *newer* look, and the solution agreed on was to organize New Party Clubs of non-CCF'ers, presumably to take in the "professional and other liberally-minded" citizens. Ten representatives from these clubs became members of the committee: four of them were farmers and the other six were "middle class professionals."[2] Douglas was on the committee as one of the CCF appointees.

In fact, there was precious little distinction between the New Party Club group and the CCF. With a little careful recruiting, most of the individuals would likely have joined the CCF. The new factor was the CLC. And the CLC played a strange role.

Privately, a score or so of trade union leaders liked to claim a parental role in the New Party; however, their public stance was to disclaim responsibility. They were so convinced that a "labour party" as such would be unacceptable to the voters that they were almost neurotic in attempting to downplay their presence, and in setting up a constitutional form that would put control of the party in the hands of constituency members – exactly as the CCF had always been organized – with only a supportive, affiliate role reserved for the unions. Voting procedures were fixed so that party members at conventions could always outvote affiliate members. In fact, the constitutional structures of the new party and the CCF varied hardly at all.

A casual observer thirteen years later might be excused for asking why the exercise ever took place. The CLC worked very hard, and contributed funds, to launch the New Party with a spectacular mammoth founding convention at which the rafters rang and the people sang. Afterwards, they tactfully and modestly withdrew. The people, the staff, who carried on were in the main the old CCF, with some new faces.

It was an exhaustive and exhausting effort to change and update the "image" of Canada's party of the left, and bring it east.

There was one further reason for the change. The CCF had never gained any ground worth mentioning in the great province of Quebec. Somehow it was hoped the new party would. To begin with, CCF as a name had been untranslatable into French. The new name would come out, handily, as Nouveau Parti (Democratique). David Lewis said, "Our failure to take root in Quebec has been my major disappointment over thirty-eight years. It was the major reason that motivated me – though there were others – to make the change from CCF to NDP."

If these were the reasons for launching a new party in place of the CCF, why was Douglas the man they chose as leader? He was surely, among prominent CCF'ers, the one most identified with moralistic socialism. His association with trade unions had been subject to some strain during the years of his Premiership, though differences had been smoothed out. He had no perceptible rapport with Quebec.

Yet he was the first and only choice of the trade union architects of the new party. Quite simply, he was a success, where others had a record of failure. He had an impressive record in politics over almost twenty-five years. Trade unions had always sought him out eagerly as a favourite guest speaker at mass gatherings. He was in their eyes a popular leader of undoubted appeal. And, there was no real challenger. M. J. Coldwell, defeated at the polls in 1958, had made clear his intention not to continue as leader past the next CCF party convention in 1960, and still less to consider new party leadership.

David Lewis favoured Douglas as leader. Perhaps there was some regret in his decision. It would have meant much to Lewis to move into the leadership role. But he had been curiously reluctant to press for a parliamentary seat. There had been – he said there still was – his family obligation to consider. He had worked for a pittance over many years as CCF national secretary, and felt he must make it up to his family as his children approached university age. The second reason he gave was the fact that he was a Jew, and he doubted whether the Canadian people would accept him. Lewis said:

> I never considered it seriously because I believed he (Douglas) was best for the job. And secondly I wasn't sure at that time, though I may have been wrong, that a Jew at the head of the new party would be best for the movement. I wasn't prepared to load the party with that uncertainty.
>
> Most people who mentioned me for leader were in Saskatchewan, – the caucus, the party, who wanted Tommy to stay, – and Tommy was at first very strongly of this mind. He would point to the fact that I was bilingual and he was not.

There were some in Ontario who would have preferred Lewis. Margaret Stewart, Ontario secretary, saw Douglas as "old fashioned", while Lewis, she said, was adaptable, moved with the times, was more interested in electoral success, and had a broader federal knowledge. Douglas, she thought, was not "tough" enough. Lewis "would sail into an Ontario provincial convention and hypnotize them into turning down some resolution the Council had been working on for months and get it thrown out." Douglas, on the other hand, permitted "all kinds of kooks" to continue as loyal party members in Saskatchewan. Still, when Lewis made it quite clear he would not contest the leadership, Margaret Stewart supported Douglas.

There was one visible alternative.

The one Saskatchewan M.P. elected in 1958 was Hazen Argue, and he had been chosen as House Leader by the small eight-man caucus. Argue had been elected in Wood Mountain (later Assiniboia) as early as 1945, at that time twenty-four years old, the youngest M.P. at Ottawa. He had held his seat against the Conservative tide. He was regarded as a valuable spokesman for western agriculture. But few seriously regarded him as the successor to Woodsworth and Coldwell. Someone, however, suggested the possibility to Argue, and it was taken up by the other Ottawa M.P.s, who had begun to feel slighted by the veteran leaders of the party, especially Lewis. Douglas Fisher was one of that group, first elected in Fort William in 1957 and re-elected in 1958. He said: "We felt we were being treated as lightweights and nitwits by Lewis and Knowles. Actually our 1958-59 performance had been good. My support for Hazen was not based on any antagonism toward Douglas; I didn't know him until the 1960 convention."

Lewis was shocked at Argue's decision to seek the CCF leadership which would become vacant at the 1960 convention. It would be a wind-up convention for the old party: the founding convention for the new party was scheduled for 1961. It was an awkward gap, with Coldwell settled in his determination to step down. Lewis wanted the convention to leave the position vacant.

Others, including Douglas, felt it was a mistake. The party did not want to be headless, Douglas argued. But Lewis went to Argue and persuaded him not to let his name come before the convention.

But at the convention Argue, pressured by an angry Doug Fisher and other caucus members, changed his mind. They threatened that if he gave in to Lewis they would choose someone else in Ottawa to be House Leader. They leaned on him so hard that he let his name go before the convention, and he was duly elected CCF National Leader for its final year. Obviously he had his eye on the leadership of the new party the following year.

Douglas let the events of 1960 take their course, still refusing to accept the invitation to leadership of the new party. He led a successful provincial election in June, and saw the Saskatchewan wing of the party safely through a provincial convention in July, before the federal CCF's last convention in Regina in August. Its purpose would be "to chart the next great political advance", and the relative ease with which the prairie section of the CCF prepared to join the new party was very much due to Douglas' diplomatic skill. Certainly there had been strong debate in Saskatchewan. The president, Carlyle King, for example, had circulated questions for discussion at CCF constituency conventions prior to the provincial gathering:

1. The CLC-CCF Joint National Committee booklet says that the CCF 'has lacked the resources and the manpower to build effective organization in every part of the country.' Will the proposed new political party remedy the situation? How?
2. Is there danger that organized labour might dominate the proposed new political party? If so, wherein lies the danger?
3. Can you combine the memberships of affiliated organizations with memberships of individuals in a democratic political party? How?
4. Is there any significant difference of policy between the CCF and the CLC? If so, what?

The Saskatchewan convention had debated these problems strongly, a process Douglas felt to be worthwhile. He had entered the debate at the end, mildly. He said, "The farmer, who now represents only 14 per cent of Canada's population as against 31 per cent only two decades ago, needs allies. And where can he find them? Only among the men and women who sell the products of their labour just as you sell the products of your labour."

Hazen Argue also took part in the debate to reassure delegates regarding the danger of domination by the unions, pointing out that the party would get one delegate per hundred members, affiliated organizations one delegate per thousand members, under the proposed new party constitution. His soothing words were oddly at variance with the position he was to take just eighteen months later.

The Saskatchewan section voted 521 to 5 for the change.

At the August convention Douglas welcomed the federal delegates to Regina: "It was here twenty-seven years ago that the founders of our movement launched the crusade for a more just and humane society. If we are to match their vision we must forge a political instrument designed to cope successfully with the domestic and international problems of the Atomic Age."

There was no doubt that Douglas sincerely backed the move for a new party. But he was also resolved, during the years the new party was being formed, not to be that new party leader.

In the fall and winter of 1958 Douglas began an extensive tape recording session at the request of the Saskatchewan Archives. Two-hour sessions on Sunday afternoons were given over to a relaxed discussion, in the handsome Executive Council chamber, of his long political career. Chris Higginbotham, a journalist and broadcaster, asked questions, assisted by Allan Turner, Archival Assistant, John Archer, Provincial Librarian and Archivist, and Tim Lee, Douglas' executive assistant. Higginbotham described Douglas as looking much younger than fifty-four, trim and fit, a much admired Premier at the height of his career. Higginbotham began by reminding Douglas of his church background and asking if he regretted the change to politics.

Douglas answered: "There were scores of men ready to take on important church work, but there weren't any prepared to enter the dust and din of the political arena. And I felt somebody had to do it. I'm still convinced somebody had to do it."

His approach to leadership of the new party was again that "somebody had to do it". But in 1958 he still hoped he would not be that "somebody". He told his interviewer he had no federal ambitions.

No, I really haven't. If I'd stayed on in the House of Commons I might have had, and I'm free to say this, that if it became absolutely necessary with the CCF in danger of collapsing across Canada if someone didn't take hold of it, then I might do it. But I would do it reluctantly.

But there is a pull to Saskatchewan. It has an unfortunate history. The climate, the drought. It was late in industrial growth. A stepchild of Confederation. I feel Saskatchewan deserves everything we can give it for the next twenty years.

Douglas' mood throughout the 1958 recordings was buoyant, high-spirited. He tossed off yarns, relishing the memory of early encounters with political opponents.

On June 18, 1961, he made a final recording. The tone was grave. He had at last made up his mind.

"It's not something I'm seeking. I'm not going to go barnstorming. People know my record, the good points and the bad points. If they want me they'll ask me."

There was no question about being asked. He had been besieged by CCF and CLC leaders for over two years.

It was Coldwell who influenced him most.

"Ever since 1941 he has said he hoped I would succeed him some day. And he felt very strongly that all the work he and Woodsworth had done would come to naught unless someone could bring the various factions together in the new party and weld them into a fighting force.

"It's not going to be easy."

Douglas said he had finally, in February, taken the problem to his legislative caucus. They were as concerned as he about the federal scene – the high unemployment, low farm income, and slow economic growth of 1960-61. And that the CCF in Saskatchewan was only a "beachhead".

On February 3, the night before the Legislature opened, there had been the traditional dinner given by the M.L.A.s for the caucus and provincial caucus. Douglas had asked for their decision. He had told them, "Thinking with my heart, I'd rather be here." By April two-thirds of the party council had agreed to accept his move to the federal field. Next he had talked to his Weyburn constituency association, and by vote they with great reluctance also accepted the move.

Douglas recorded his view of political trends.

One of the things that I think influenced me as much as anything to reconsider my position is that I've been appalled in the last twelve months, especially the last six months, at the almost total decline of left-of-centre parties in North America. The whole political spectrum has moved right. The Democrats and Republicans are in a contest to show which is the more reactionary – they're against aid to the farmers, against old age pensions, old age medical care – against almost everything Roosevelt sold to the American people twenty-five years ago. In the United States there is no left-of-centre party. A state like Minnesota that when I was a young man had a Farmer-Labour governor, a farmer-labour legislature and a program almost identical with the CCF, today has a Republican governor and legislature. In Canada, the Liberal party is moving right. The only reason Diefenbaker got elected in 1957 was because he sounded a little left of the Liberals, and it wasn't hard to be left of the Liberals under St. Laurent.

Unless the new party can become a dynamic force in Canada's political life, we'll soon have only a choice between two right-wing parties, and the things most of us have believed in and worked for for twenty-five years will have vanished.

There are fascist trends in Canada – like Smallwood's labour legislation which by the stroke of a pen wiped out a certified union. And the B.C. legislation denying the basic right of civil servants to organize, and legislating that corporations but not unions can contribute to political parties. There are campaigns going in Ontario and Alberta and Quebec for restrictive labour legislation. And under this government there's a gradual sabotage of crown corporations like TCA, the CBC and the Bank of Canada, giving more to their private rivals. Some party must make clear the neglect of the 'public sector' as Galbraith does in writing about the 'affluent society'.

We are allowing our whole society to fall into the hands of corporations and hucksters.

On the international scene, Douglas protested the "echoing of United States policy" and the money "squandered" on the Bomarc missile. He was against nuclear arms for Canada, against the expansion of the "nuclear club" in the world. And he protested the mounting foreign control of Canada's economy.

We should set up a national investment board with real power. Companies setting up in Canada should get their equity capital here, and float their loan capital in the United States. They get their capital and interest back, but you own the industry. We've followed the reverse course for the past thirty years. The United States came in with about 25 per cent of the equity, borrowing in the main the other 75 per cent from Canadian sources, and they staved off Canadian investors with a nice safe investment at a guaranteed interest rate, but when it's all over they own the industry. So they own a good part of the industry in Canada today.

In view of all these trends, Douglas was deeply concerned to see a left-wing party reassert itself. But he was not bubbling with optimism.

"I haven't any illusions that the new party will sweep to power at the present time," he told Higginbotham. "We could get a very effective group in the House, and look for younger people of ability and bring them along, so the new party will eventually form a government. Our first job will be to get the party in shape. I would hope for twenty to thirty good M.P.s in the next election."

There were other considerations in Douglas' mind. He had some suspicion that Hazen Argue was already too close to the Liberals, that he might even have had preliminary talks toward an "understanding" with them, and that he would have led the new party into an alliance. There was always the possibility that Lewis would change his mind, if Douglas continued to refuse. (There was never the remotest possibility of a contest between Lewis and Douglas.) Douglas, however, had begun to have serious doubts that Lewis could win against Argue. Argue had the advantage of being in parliament, of being Leader. Lewis had antagonized too many people in the party. And later, in 1971, Lewis was to show a surprising inability to swing a leadership vote his way even against such a newcomer as James Laxer.

Eleanor McKinnon, Douglas' secretary, had her usual lighter comment on the decision. It had been a hard one, she said, with M. J. and David Lewis putting on a lot of pressure, and the eventual consultation with the caucus and party council. But she was still taken by surprise when Douglas interrupted dictation one day to ask, "If I should decide to let my name stand, and get it, would you go with me to Ottawa?"

"I said yes promptly, without even thinking about leaving my mother and friends in Regina. Though it did occur to me that I'd have to leave my dentist, Benny Booklater, who was a very good dentist."

In July 1961, with the founding convention only a month away, Douglas met his old colleague, Clarence Fines, at the King Edward Hotel in Toronto. Douglas had asked to see him. He wanted to ask Fines' opinion of the move.

"I know he was still undecided," Fines said. "I told him I disagreed very much with the CCF going into the new party, and of him going in as leader. The job wasn't finished by any means in Saskatchewan. And I felt Tommy shouldn't take on anything new, because of his health. I wanted to see him live to enjoy some leisure, just as I had felt in my own case that it was foolish to stay on. But he made the decision the other way, and Saskatchewan lost its CCF government."

For the optimists, there were good signs for the budding new party. Early in 1961 a personable young teacher, Walter Pitman, ran as a New Party candidate in a by-election in traditionally Conservative Peterborough and won. There was unprecedented support for the new party in Quebec through the Quebec Federation of Labour.

The newspapers were taking a lively interest in Douglas. In the Toronto *Telegram* Judith Robinson told of a crowd of one thousand who came to hear and applaud, where only one hundred fifty had turned up for Lester Pearson. In a feature article in *Maclean's*, April 8, 1961, Ralph Allen wrote: "What the New Party Wants that Tommy Douglas Has". He spoke of: "The new party's indispensable man . . . On his lifetime record he is one of the surest vote-getters in the country's history . . . .

"Woodsworth was a good speaker, but Douglas is a far better one, in his own homey and utterly infectious way one of the most effective campaign orators since Laurier."

Two serious issues were uppermost in these late years of the Diefenbaker regime. The country – along with the United States – was experiencing a recession. Canada had half a million unemployed. Foreign investment had suddenly dropped – the heady flow of Yankee dollars – and there was a reverse flow of American earnings out of Canada. Donald Fleming's budget had exacerbated the process by dropping exemptions from the 15 per cent withholding tax on foreign earnings. Construction projects were slowing down; a dollar crisis was building; the GNP growth rate had fallen to one per cent a year.

The second burning issue was whether or not, under the North American Air Defence Command (NORAD), Canada should accept nuclear arms (supplied by the United States) for continental defence.

Douglas' opinions were sought by reporters.

And he was blunt: "We can serve the cause of peace and of the United States too at the United Nations . . . But (our chance to work for peace) will never come so long as we are looked upon as a military satellite of the United States and an appendage of the Pentagon." He denounced both "Mr. Khrushchov intervening in Hungary and Mr. Kennedy intervening in Cuba."

Despite his refusal to campaign on his own behalf, he was getting wide publicity as the likeliest prospect for new party leadership. Hazen Argue, on the other hand, was working feverishly, assisted by his wife Jean, appearing at meetings wherever he could to appeal for support. Lewis had asked him not to enter his name as a candidate. Argue had refused to comply.

Repentant, in 1974, Lewis said,

I as president of the CCF was very much in the wrong in trying to get a unanimous vote for Tommy. It arose out of the tradition we had had – no one had opposed Woodsworth, no one had opposed Coldwell. They were the Chosen.

I met with Hazen and tried to dissuade him from being a candidate. It was wrong. This attitude produced a bitterness around the Hazen-Douglas contest – though it wasn't really a contest; Douglas didn't contest – he was above it.

Hazen told me he was younger than Tommy, he was just as able to put our case across to the Canadian people and he intended to be a candidate.

In August 1961, during five sweltering hot days in Ottawa's vast coliseum, the new party was founded at a huge convention that rocked the rafters and provided tons of lively copy for news media. Clifford Scotton said, "It was the first Canadian political convention that smacked of Show Biz. The banners, flags, hats, buttons, music – ! What a contrast to the usual conventions of CCF people poring over books of resolutions and warding off temptations to enjoy themselves. But the excitement seemed natural."

The convention was also the largest that had ever been held in Canada. There were 2,083 registrations. In addition to adopting a constitution they passed a weighty group of resolutions, prominent among them the guarantee of a job for every Canadian. The conspicuously new development was a large delegation from Quebec, a group by no means passive. They persuaded the party to adopt a statement proclaiming that Canada was a country formed by two founding nations, English and French, and could only survive by recognizing both through a policy of biculturalism and bilingualism throughout Canada. The statement called for "cooperative federalism" in relations between Ottawa and the provinces.

And the name became the New Democratic party (Nouveau Parti Democratique).

Douglas was elected in a wildly cheering, singing, banner-waving mêlée of joy. There was a song for the occasion: "A Douglas for me." In a ringing speech he accepted Diefenbaker's challenge to an election on the issue of "Free Enterprise versus Socialism". Over television he invited more people to join the new party. "We haven't plumbed the depths and found all the answers. We want new ideas. We want eventually to establish a people's government." For a start, he outlined to the convention a program of guided national investment, jobs for the unemployed, parity prices for farmers and fishermen, a comprehensive system of health insurance, and adequate retirement allowances over and above the old age pension.

The vote for leader had gone 1391 for Douglas, to 380 for Argue. After it was announced Argue told the convention he would support the new leader, and he assured the new party "No matter what my role in the years ahead, I shall speak for you, I shall work for you, I shall never let you down."

Six months later the words were recalled in bitter anger by party leaders. The story of Argue's defection from the NDP in 1962 has lost none of its traumatic impact. Coldwell spoke of "treachery", Lewis of "despicable behaviour", Douglas of "betrayal".

Argue had continued as House Leader, with Douglas' blessing, while Douglas wound up affairs in Saskatchewan and began the monumental job of building the new party, waiting for a first opportunity for election to Ottawa.

The initial responses to the party, once the razzle-dazzle of the convention died, were not encouraging. There were five by-elections in Ontario – the NDP lost badly in all of them and found that the desired labour votes and support were not in evidence. A Gallup Poll showed the NDP with only 12 per cent voter support across the country.

In fact, as Desmond Morton points out,[3] the labour movement was fiercely divided, with some strong groups like the Teamsters and Seafarers International Union openly supporting the Liberals, the vast construction industry mainly indifferent, and hot clashes between the NDP and communists in still other unions. There was little chance for the union founders of the NDP to give much force to their Political Action Committees or to rouse a strong grassroots support for the NDP.

Argue obviously saw no future in remaining for the long, hard fight. Neither he nor his wife Jean could face the demotion that would come when Douglas assumed his place as leader. Jean, particularly, had revelled in the cocktail circuit to which Argue's status entitled them.

But it was the manner of his going that shocked not only NDP'ers but journalists and members of other parties as well.

Some rumours were heard that he was having conversations with Ross Thatcher, now Liberal leader in Saskatchewan. When Thatcher had been a CCF member he and Argue had shared an office. When the rumours reached his caucus, Douglas Fisher confronted Argue with them. Argue, an arm around Fisher's shoulder, assured him the rumours were lies.

On February 24, 1962, Argue and his wife arrived in Regina to attend a Saskatchewan Provincial Council meeting. There were genial exchanges with old friends; the Argues stayed throughout the day's business and Argue, at an evening banquet, was applauded as he took his place at the head table alongside Douglas and Premier Woodrow Lloyd. The next morning, a Saturday, he returned to the Council meeting for the concluding session. In the afternoon he turned up at Douglas' home to discuss plans for barnstorming – they would divide the job in coming weeks, while Argue would be in Ottawa and Douglas in Newfoundland. They parted cordially: Douglas drove Argue to his hotel.

A few hours later Argue and his wife drove to Moose Jaw, to Ross Thatcher's home, where they stayed overnight. The next day, Sunday, they all returned to Regina and called a press conference. Argue announced his resignation from the NDP, condemning it passionately as a undemocratic party under the heel of the unions, constituting "a dark and sinister threat to democratic government in Canada."

In Ottawa the federal executive was meeting at the Metcalfe Street party headquarters. Lewis was called from the meeting that Sunday morning to talk to a Canadian Press reporter who said Argue was going to defect from the party.

I disregarded it. I remember turning to Michael Oliver and saying, 'It's nuts. It can't be right.' But after awhile I got another call from another journalist friend, Mark Gayn of the Toronto *Star*. He not only told me this was going to happen but that Argue had arranged for a press conference at 4:00 o'clock. So I telephoned Tommy. He said, 'Aw, come on! I just had Hazen at my house – we discussed an itinerary for me and one for him on the friendliest basis. Hatchets were buried, and he was *just here!*' I said, 'Well you may be right but if I were you I'd be prepared with a statement.' It was a total surprise to me and to Tommy. I've never forgiven Hazen. He had a right to change his mind. I regretted it when other people like Eugene Forsey changed their views, but they had a right. But to lie about it until the very last minute is something that I find very despicable.

Douglas, immediately tackled by reporters, issued a statement saying Argue had apparently already found his spiritual home among the Liberals. "We wish the party well of him."

As a Liberal Argue survived the Diefenbaker forces to win Assiniboia again in June 1962. But in 1963 and again in 1965 he was defeated and, in 1966, again to the tune of many outraged cries, he was appointed to the Senate. One Liberal M.L.A. in Saskatchewan described him as "the orphan of the storm we found on our doorstep four years ago."

Douglas, now without any barnstorming assistance from Argue, was caught up in his first campaign for the federal election expected in the spring of 1962. Irma was seeking an Ottawa apartment. There would be only two of them to share it. Shirley, now 29, was in England. She had won an award in the 1951 Dominion Drama Festival which took her to London and the Royal Academy of Dramatic Art. There were parts for her in plays, movies, and television, and meantime she had married a Canadian medical student, Tim Sick, scion of the Lethbridge and Seattle beer dynasty. There was a first grandchild, Thomas, known as Tad. Joan, now 21, was in her fourth year nursing at the University of Saskatchewan.

Douglas, warmly acclaimed by newspaper editorialists as an important arrival on the federal political scene, was discovering the threadbare condition of the party that had held such a tumultuous convention. They were hardly prepared for the grueling series of elections in the 1960s, as the nation teetered between minority governments under Pearson and Diefenbaker.

Chapter Seventeen
A Difficult Decade

In my opinion the day of mass meetings is almost over. One or two meetings during a campaign serve a useful purpose but they are usually attended by our own supporters. The real work has to be done by person-to-person contacts and by having a small committee in almost every city block and every rural community. These committees, if they are active, can arrange little coffee parties so that the candidates can meet the neighbours, and thus get to know a lot of people who will not go to public meetings.[1]

Douglas was trying, with his new party, to adjust to political facts of life. The champion mesmerizer of mass audiences was acknowledging the ineffectiveness, in the 1960s, of mass audience reaction. His own campaign would depend very heavily on such meetings, more huge and more colourful than ever attempted before, but this was a strategem to win him, as leader, some media attention in a decade of press preoccupation with the uncertain shift of power between Pearson and Diefenbaker.

The zeal that had gone into organizing the NDP founding convention was notably absent in the follow-up. There was confusion, sorting-out, at the constituency level. No crowds thronged to join the New Democratic Party, and there were no inspired bands of organizers out to win and persuade them

"We lost some impetus after the convention. We didn't *take off* in 1962, so it was hard going thereafter," David Lewis said. "It would have been a difficult decade for anyone (as leader). It turned out not to be the decade for the fundamental change and the sweep that we had hoped for."

Diefenbaker, supported by an External Affairs Minister, Howard Green, who believed in peace and goodwill and who said of diplomacy "the most important thing is to be friendly", struck attitudes against the United States and for Great Britain and deflected a large part of the voting public which might have considered the NDP as alternative if both old parties had been in a reactionary phase. Those who were not enthralled by Diefenbaker plumped for Pearson, the essence of good-natured managerial practicality.

The new party could not possibly finance a strong offensive in the unprecedented series of general elections in 1962, 1963, 1965, and 1968

For Douglas there were two by-elections of importance as well – his own. By a highly concentrated opposition attack in 1962, and by constituency mismanagement in 1968, he twice in that decade failed to win personal re-election and had to seek out other seats to get back into the House of Commons.

The beginning, in 1962, was especially calamitous. This was the NDP's first election. They had rounded up a creditable number of candidates, including forty in Quebec, and they had $116,000 to spend. This still meant that while other party leaders criss-crossed the country in their own aircraft Douglas took commercial flights, usually accompanied by Clifford Scotton and one assistant, Thomas Shoyama, with one bulging briefcase. At one stop, when it seemed the briefcase had been lost, Scotton and Shoyama looked at each other and said, "Well there goes the campaign."

An important change in the transition from CCF to NDP had been decentralization of the party. Now all responsibility for elections, federal as well as provincial, rested in provincial hands. It reflected a fairly strong contention that the party ought to concentrate on achieving power in provincial capitals before making a decisive pitch for federal success. But particularly in the first federal campaign this meant a fragmented and weakened approach from the federal viewpoint, and a further obstacle to the new leader. The federal party office confined its efforts during each campaign to channelling aid to Quebec and the Maritimes, and organizing Douglas' own campaign.

In 1962 Diefenbaker was fighting back furiously against a Liberal assault on the ineptness of his government, particularly in the financial field. Canada's foreign reserves were dwindling and after lengthy procrastination the Conservatives pegged the dollar at 92½ cents American. Coldwell described the Diefenbaker regime scornfully as "the poorest parliament in the history of Canada". There had never been, he said, "anything as feeble as the government that sits behind Mr. Diefenbaker ... never a parliament so devoid of courtesy to one another ... never a parliament so lacking in any significant achievement."[2]

The Liberals bragged, as usual, that only they could restore the economy to health – though Pearson's first term after 1963 would be as "inept" as any opposition could desire. Diefenbaker's response to Liberal attack was to champion underdogs, finding a group well suited to this purpose in the various ethnic communities in Canada who were bitterly anti-Russian. He promised to take the cause of self-determination for their conquered homelands to the United Nations, an empty pledge which Douglas called "cruel". Diefenbaker was also helped in the west by large wheat sales concluded by Agriculture Minister Alvin Hamilton.

Reporters were busily assessing the chances of the two big parties, and the impact of such novelties as the Liberal "truth squad" which turned up at Diefenbaker rallies to challenge his grandest assertions.

Douglas was generally praised as a "bantom battler", but there were first indications of press boredom: "The first half hour of his campaign talks he spends on the jokes that used to roll them in the aisles on the vaudeville circuit. Sophisticated audiences might not think his jokes are so funny," wrote the Toronto *Star's* Roy Shields in a despatch from Wakaw, Saskatchewan. Still, he acknowledged that the Wakaw audience was "howling" after the story about the origin of the bagpipes. "The Irish claim they invented the pipes and gave them to the Scots as a joke. But the Scots – not having a sense of humor – kept them, thinking they were a musical instrument. Well, that's not true. The Scots kept the bagpipes because they got them for nothing."

The main message had come across loud and clear. According to Shield's report Douglas had dealt with five main points: one, the "power clique" that owns and controls most of Canada's wealth; two, the nation's stagnant economy ("needs planning"); three, chronic unemployment ("needs retraining programs and more planning"); four, the plight of the farmers ("need parity prices based on cost"); and five, the need for a "peace offensive", rejecting nuclear arms for Canada. Evidence that Canada's economy was in the hands of a "power clique" was produced in Canadian Bureau of Statistics figures: 90 per cent of Canadians own no industrial or commercial stocks; 7 per cent own less than $5000 worth apiece, the remaining 2 per cent of the population own all the remainder.

In Vancouver, Jack Scott saw political courage in the Douglas style:

It's been good to see and hear Tommy Douglas in such fine form. Not the least of his admirable qualities, in my opinion, is that he wages every campaign as if he's utterly convinced of ultimate victory. . . .

Many others of Tommy's political persuasion have gone sour over the years, being so convinced of the rightness of their policies and so dimayed at their inability to set the public afire, but Douglas' optimism seems indestructible.

Since he looks, in early photographs, as if he could not beat up your younger sister, a mutual friend once asked him how he could ever have become the lightweight champion of Manitoba. The answer perhaps helps to explain why he is so durable in the political ring as well.

'I was not an outstanding boxer and was too short in the arm ever to be the best,' Douglas answered, 'but I was fast on my feet, I could hit fairly hard and I always believed I could lick the other boy.'[3]

The final week of the campaign, before voting day on June 18, had been given over to big rallies, a supreme effort on the NDP's part to win a place on the front pages and on TV screen news for their leader. Instead of exhausting Douglas, the mass crowds, surpassing the party's expectations, exhilarated and galvanized him. An overflow audience at Hamilton was followed on the same evening by a vast throng at Toronto's O'Keefe Centre. It was an impressive feat, and according to Ontario NDP Secretary Margaret Stewart it was not planned that way.

An earlier meeting in Hamilton that spring had been poorly organized; Douglas was angry, and informed Mrs. Stewart that Hamilton was to be left off the campaign itinerary as "a waste of time". She had passed on the word to the Hamilton branch of the party. But they set up a meeting for June 12, informing her belatedly of their intentions. Now there was a conflict of dates, for the O'Keefe Centre was booked for June 12 and an all-out pitch to bring in the crowds was well advanced.

Douglas agreed to attend both meetings. It was only a short hop from Hamilton to Toronto; he would do it by helicopter. "I lost about ten pounds hoping the weather would be favourable and there'd be no hitch. There wasn't," Margaret Stewart said. "The Hamilton meeting was a big success. Then he came in by helicopter near the ferry landing where we were all lined up and there was a big motorcade to the O'Keefe."

There had been 1500 in Hamilton; in Toronto, according to the *Star,* there were 6,000 inside and 2,500 listening to loudspeakers outside. Wrote Richard Snell: "The five-foot-six former premier, who seemed to grow three inches when he saw his huge audiences . . . said, 'Pious declarations will neither defeat communism nor give freedom to the Soviet satellite nations, and Mr. Diefenbaker knows it. The only way to triumph over communism is to eradicate the conditions that nourish it . . . hunger, misery, unemployment and poverty."[4] Stretching to his full height Douglas thundered, "Give us seventy seats and we'll turn parliament upside down. Give us a hundred and seventy, and we'll turn the Canadian economy right side up."

Irma Douglas was with her husband in that final week, in the new campaign style of the 1960s. She put in an appropriate word on cue: the *Star* reported that among the official welcoming party at Malton airport when Douglas arrived from the West was Eric Nesterenko of the Chicago Black Hawks. "Mrs. Douglas, the hockey expert in the family, said she was 'thrilled to meet Mr. Nesterenko. He had a wonderful season last year.' "

The rallies were a dazzling success. The looming disaster in the Douglas campaign was back home on his personal battle ground, in Regina.

Douglas had been nominated in Regina on April 26. The guest speaker at his nomination meeting, a huge affair in the Trianon Ballroom, was M. J. Coldwell. And Coldwell drove straight to the heart of the all-pervading issue, Medicare. He said it was not a political or a financial issue, but a moral one. As a prominent Anglican layman he challenged the churches of Regina: "Where are the churches in this fight for a great humanitarian cause? They can stand up and object to bingo . . . but when it comes to a basic moral issue where are they? I challenge the churches to stand up and be counted."

Everyone else in Saskatchewan was standing up and being counted. They were ranged in tight ranks, face-to-face. Medicare split Saskatchewan apart.

Five days before the Douglas meeting, the Regina *Leader-Post* carried front page stories reporting doctors' meetings in Regina, Moose Jaw, and Prince Albert where doctors declared themselves unalterably opposed to the Medical Care Act and stated their refusal to work under it. It was the showdown period – the Act had originally been scheduled to come into effect on April 1 but was postponed until July 1 in the futile hope of winning the doctors' cooperation. Instead, the final three months saw tension build to frightening limits, and during those three months the federal election campaign was held and Douglas sought personal election in Regina.

Two hundred petitions were being circulated in Regina by the "Keep Our Doctors" committee, heavily financed by the Liberal party, during the week of Douglas' nomination. Douglas devoted part of his address to a careful resume of the medicare plan, emphasizing the doctors' right to professional decision-making under it, and asking them to give it "a fair trial". When Mrs. Shirley Toth of Regina, circulating a counter-petition on which she collected 3000 signatures, echoed Douglas' words and asked the doctors to try the plan to see how it would work, a "prominent Regina surgeon" commented, "That would be like putting your head in a noose to see how it feels."[5]

Mrs. Elaine Warne of Regina was one of the active promoters of the doctors' petition. She told reporters, "We're not concerned about facts. The doctors could be dead wrong. What we do know is that they are threatening to leave, and if they do, where will we be?"[6]

Dr. H. D. Dalgleish, president of the College of Physicians and Surgeons, described the act as the "worst piece of legislation in the commonwealth", in fact, "the most serious violation of civil rights since the time of Charles the Second."

The doctors across the province were hanging up signs to inform their patients, "Unless agreement is reached between the present government and the medical profession, this office will close as of July 1."

Douglas back in Regina at a fund-raising banquet on May 18, declared hotly that he knew the government would not back down. He talked of "professional political doctors" in both the US and Saskatchewan who opposed government plans to equalize health costs: "they are not only a disgrace to the medical profession, they are a disgrace to the human race," he charged. And before a meeting of NDP workers the following day he called on Saskatchewan doctors "to stop frightening pregnant women and sick children . . . to confine their attacks to those

264

who can fight back rather than attempting to intimidate the sick and infirm."

Entering the fight with gusto, Douglas may have given no comfort to his successor, Premier Lloyd, who was treading delicately to seek to avert any overt clash in the province.

Douglas had set up his campaign headquarters in the Riverview Shopping Centre. Eleanor McKinnon, working there through those bitter days, recalled the "hate and hostility".

At night when the door was closed teenagers would come up and hiss at us through the glass. In the parades they had they would shout awful things and throw things. We were very much hated. My sister and I found people who wouldn't speak to us. It was so unlike Saskatchewan.

I drove home one day with a taxi-driver. He was a man who could really have benefited from medicare. He had no teeth: he had had them all extracted. He said he had five children and a sick wife. And he blasted me about medicare and about Tommy. There was no arguing with him.

Irma Douglas was receiving threatening phone calls.

People on welfare were phoning up and just raving! The doctors had scared the devil out of them. They would tell their patients, especially a pregnant woman, 'I'm afraid this is the last time I'll be able to see you.' And she would have a fit.

Ted Tulchinsky (who later married our daughter Joan) was one of the young doctors who was on his way overseas when he heard about the strike and phoned Woodrow to see if he could help. He came back and worked throughout the strike. Later he helped organize a community clinic in Saskatoon and his group was really hated by the other doctors. If they were on an elevator in the hospital the other group wouldn't get on with them – they'd wait for the next one. It was hairy.

Morris Shumiatcher, who had been hired by Douglas as his executive assistant in 1945, took sides against him.

The break with "Shumy" was a sad one for Douglas. The young lawyer had resigned from the government in 1949 to enter a more lucrative private practice, and from then on relations had become increasingly strained.

In the early 1950s in the legislature, Liberal members were naming Shumiatcher among those accused of smooth deals in oil exploration and development. Douglas was wholeheartedly ready to defend him.

Dear Shumy: I am enclosing a copy of a speech made by Mr. Danielson on January 11. I am gathering material pointing out the falsehoods in this speech by Mr. Danielson. I see one which concerns yourself and which I know to be quite misleading, namely that you got $25,000 whereas I understand that the payment to be made by Northern Uranium has never been forthcoming and that the 10,000 shares at $1 par value are in all probability worthless. Certainly they are not worth $10,000 at the present rate or in the foreseeable future. Could you and Havard give me a sworn statement regarding this transaction?

The time is coming fairly soon when I am going to call Mr. Tucker and Mr. Danielson on some of these wild and irresponsible innuendoes which they are making. Yours sincerely, Tommy.[7]

On February 9 Shumiatcher sent back a statement "of the facts relative to the permits secured by Havard and myself and assigned to National Petroleums Ltd., and relative to the uranium concession secured by The Search Corporation Ltd. and assigned to Northern Uraniums Ltd." He said: "I am afraid I cannot get Havard to verify the facts, but you may be sure that they are accurate."

Later there was a court case against Shumiatcher launched by Douglas' Attorney-General, Robert Walker, in regard to alleged fraudulent practices in securing oil leases. (Shumiatcher had also built up a file purporting to show that W. W. Cameron, Chairman of the Securities Commission was mentally unbalanced, a tactic which unfuriated Walker.) Shumiatcher was convicted and sentenced, but appealed his case and after protracted hearings the case was dropped by the government – which by this time was under the Premiership of Ross Thatcher.

During the trial Douglas received anguished pleas from members of Shumiatcher's family to stop the proceedings. One letter referred to the "agony suffered over the past five months on account of the bad treatment accorded by certain elements in your government."

Douglas replied at length, pointing out

the Attorney-General had no alternative but to leave it to the court to decide whether or not these witnesses were telling the truth ... When a man is accused of wrongdoing and is convinced of his innocence I think he would prefer to have his good name cleared by the due process of law rather than to have his friends in authority interfere in order to prevent him from having to face his accusers before the Courts.[8]

To which another highly emotional letter came in reply denouncing the "persecution" which the writer believed was tainted by "anti-semitic prejudices".

Attorney-General Walker, by all accounts a scrupulous man, was shocked by a similar appeal by a Regina rabbi, and advised his cabinet colleagues to be on guard against such importunities. "Wachsman says he acts in the role of peacemaker, as if this was 'a matter for a *sincere effort* to be made on both sides' . . . a wildly mistaken concept of the role of the courts and the administration of justice."[9]

Douglas had enjoyed "Shumy's" company; there were good memories of those first years in office. Now in 1962 when the opposition was massing to defeat Douglas, Shumiatcher aligned himself publicly against him. In June he was preparing a series of articles condemning Medicare, to be published in the Regina *Leader-Post* where he would be heralded as a "nationally recognized authority on civil rights".

The Medicare dispute had become a national issue. In Kitchener, Ontario, Douglas described national health insurance as one of the main planks in his platform, one of the first aims of an NDP federal government.

The Liberal party, having adopted national health insurance as part of *their* election platform, was hard put to suggest ways in which their plan would be different and superior to the nefarious Saskatchewan Act. Senator David Croll, speaking in support of the Liberal candidate in York South, added to the confusion when he said that the NDP was "talking nonsense" in suggesting they were the only party that wanted a national insurance plan. Croll proclaimed proudly that the Liberals had advocated it "for a long time", and "I've been a supporter of it as long as I can remember, and I've been thirty-two years in public life."[10] Since the Liberals had been in power, and admirably situated to introduce national health insurance during most of those thirty-two years, the Senator's boast furnished Douglas with some private chuckles and some platform jokes.

Only a few newspaper editors were condemning the medical fraternity of Saskatchewan for its refusal to obey the law. Christopher Young, in the Ottawa *Citizen*, described the Saskatchewan College of Physicians and Surgeons as "behaving like a rabble of anarchists."[11]

In Regina in the federal election of June 18, (as in some other Saskatchewan constituencies) the Liberal strategy was to let Diefenbaker's Tories sweep the field, to defeat the NDP. Professor Norman Ward of the University of Saskatchewan wrote in 1968 that

> many prominent Liberals in the province were active on the anti-Government group that became known as the K.O.D. (Keep Our Doctors Committee), and several Liberal candidates were convinced that Liberal supporters were working to secure the election of Progressive Conservatives in order to ensure the defeat of CCF-NDP candidates . . . . In Regina the local (Liberal) association was so anxious to ensure the defeat of Mr. Douglas that it was reluctant to nominate a candidate and had to be persuaded to do so . . . . The Regina *Leader-Post*, in editorials on June 13 and 16, 1962, seemed to suggest that Liberals vote Conservative. It referred to the election as

a 'matter for electors to decide in terms of their desire to elect or defeat Mr. Douglas.'[12]

Irma Douglas, for whom the campaign was a particularly brutal memory, said, "A lady I took sewing to asked me innocently why it was that the Liberal women were phoning each other to vote Conservative. They pulled the rug out from under Fred Johnson. Ken More, a nice young man but a green politician, was getting the vote. I don't think Tommy could believe that people could be so short-sighted in their own interests. He wasn't prepared for the hysteria."

Cliff Scotton recalls:

I had a prescience about the 1962 campaign in Regina. I left the day before on the excuse of coming back to Ottawa to vote. I had worked for him in the campaign, in a shopping centre near the airport, along with Eleanor McKinnon and Tommy Shoyama. I had a strong premonition that Tommy was going to get clobbered and I hadn't the intestinal fortitude to stay and witness it. He strongly suspected it, but he would never in a campaign let anyone know that disaster was on the horizon.

It was a calculated affair, by the medical profession and business in general, encouraged by the Liberals and Conservatives, who didn't want to see the new party get started. The amounts of money available to the Liberal candidate were astonishing – for a sham battle between the Liberals and Conservatives. It was a considered campaign at the national level to stop the new party in its tracks by knocking off its leader . . . and Saskatchewan campaigns can be very dirty.

Passions in the province were inflamed on the whole issue of Medicare. Families and neighbours were split. One either thought Medicare was the work of God – or the work of the devil. There was really nothing in between.

The official count in Regina Lakeview was: Ken More (P.C.) 22,164; T. C. Douglas (NDP) 12,674; Fred Johnson (Liberal) 7,591; and Arthur Bochme (Social Credit) 1,583. Douglas had indeed been "clobbered".

Blair Fraser of *Maclean's*, writing in 1965, said that Douglas seemed to have ended a distinguished political career in complete disaster and failure. "He was beaten by almost ten thousand votes and came perilously close to losing his deposit . . . a bitter pill . . . for a man who had led his provincial socialists to five consecutive victories and had then retired unbeaten."

"Utterly disgraceful," said Graham Spry. "People who you thought were gentle human beings passed on the most incredible gossip; the most mean approach."

"I felt personally hurt when Tommy was defeated," one of his former

268

cabinet ministers, Bill Davies, said. "There was that feeling of desertion. I remember Tommy that night on TV, as collected and measured as ever. Tommy always recognized the need to look like what the people expect in a leader. I've never seen him when he couldn't smile. He's remarkable."

A young worker, Hans Brown, recalled, "In 1962 when Tommy lost in Regina there was crying in Calgary."

Eleanor McKinnon recalled the mail that poured in. She said that on the morning of election day the NDP provincial secretary, Les Benjamin, admitted to her that Douglas was going to be defeated. On election night there were many friends with him in the Hotel Saskatchewan, and "it was one of the saddest moments of our lives." But Douglas, this small man who with one aide had spent the previous eighteen months criss-crossing Canada in a prodigous attempt to win acceptance for a new party with nothing in its coffers but worn hopes, who had spent the previous week pouring out his message with all the fervour of a crusader in vast auditoria in every large city in Canada, stood up to his personal defeat and awed television viewers who watched him. He quoted the lines from an old Border ballad:

"Fight on, my men, said Sir Andrew Barton,
I am hurt, but I am not slain.
I will lay me down and bleed awhile,
And then I'll rise and fight again."

A TV columnist in Victoria wrote: "For myself, I can only pray that there were many young people up to hear defeated NDP leader T. C. Douglas make his speech. Measured in the tenets of democracy and all those things for which we are supposed to stand – sportsmanship, compassion, humility and understanding – his words were something that surely made all Canadians proud. It was, in brief, a masterpiece."

At the opposite end of Canada, the Charlottetown *Evening Patriot* ran a June 19 editorial:

There are senses in which every party – yes, and Canada as a country – tasted defeat in yesterday's election. It follows that there was nothing exclusive about the defeats suffered by Tommy Douglas, as national leader of the New Democrats, even though they were particularly direct.

But the thing that was exclusive to Mr. Douglas in the election outcome was the spirit of greatness he displayed in accepting his party's defeat, along with his own in Regina. In this he outshone all other party leaders.

He spoke with dignity and graciousness, in quiet words that carried the ring of integrity and sincerity. He wasted not a phrase on self-pity, regrets or recriminations.

The concern he showed was for the cause he represents, and not whatever ups or down may come to him and his party.

There can be no defeat for such a spirit, no matter what happens to the man who is its instrument, so Tommy Douglas continues to shine forth today as a great Canadian – a gallant gentleman, if the country has ever known one.

The hundreds of letters from friends all said in various ways what Marielle Demorest wrote from Richmond, B.C.:

"Harvey and I beg you not to leave the leadership of our party. You are to us the N.D.P. Your great talents are the heart and soul of the success of the N.D.P."

It was Irma who reacted most bitterly to the defeat. She was sure that if Tommy had run in Weyburn it could not have happened. She had thoughts about "getting out of it." She said, "I did think at the time, why bang your head against a stone wall, to help people, if that's all they care?

"We moved to Ottawa almost immediately. It didn't bother me a bit to move. I shouldn't look at it that way, but – ! It didn't get him down as much as me."

Daughter Joan was in London, Ontario, regretting her absence from her parents as she watched TV newscasts. She said, "My mother has a real thing about it. It hit Dad very hard, but with him it's a real fear of being defeated again. He works terribly hard; in his constituency now he has one of the best organizations in Canada."

But in Grace MacInnis' words, "He had the wind knocked out of him for a while."

The Douglases moved to Ottawa where Irma found an apartment at 404 Laurier East, their home for several years following. Eleanor was ensconced at the federal party headquarters on Metcalfe Street and Douglas worked from there until a by-election in November brought him into the House, belatedly.

Lewis said of the somewhat subdued Douglas of this period, "My impression was that it left a permanent scar. He never quite recovered from that slap in the face. Though he was far too strong a person to let it affect the way he functioned."

Nationally, the 1962 election results were: Conservatives one hundred sixteen; Liberals ninety-eight, Social Credit thirty; New Democratic Party nineteen.

The NDP had increased their seats to nineteen from the eight held by the last CCF caucus. The labour vote, instead of coming to "their" new party had, according to a post-election Gallup Poll, gone predominantly to the Liberals, who got 38 per cent of the votes from trade union homes, while Conservatives got 25 per cent and the NDP only 23 per cent. They had elected some important new members, including and especially David Lewis in York South, who promptly became Deputy Leader. But it rankled to be eclipsed in their first election by a resurgent Social Credit group with members from the west as well as Quebec. Social Credit would hold the balance of power in the new parliament, and would swing its support to the Liberals. And the tension in the House guaranteed that a new election would soon follow, as it did ten months later.

On election night, on June 18, 1962, a loyal NDP candidate, Erhart Regier, the winner in the B.C. riding of Burnaby-Coquitlam, offered to resign and invited Douglas to run in his seat. There were several other offers, but Douglas refused them all. Regier resigned on his own initiative. Douglas was presented with a *fait accompli*.

"We were inundated with volunteers in that by-election," Scotton said. Douglas was elected and returned to the House of Commons in November, 1962.

The press was delighted to have him back. Re-introduced to the Speaker by his old associate Stanley Knowles, Douglas had barely reached the seat he had vacated eighteen years earlier, and was standing to acknowledge the greetings of other leaders, when a Conservative backbencher, pretending the diminutive figure could not be seen, shouted, "Stand up!"

Douglas called back, "Fortunately, there are houses of debate where the measurement is from the shoulders up rather than from the shoulders down."

Diefenbaker said Douglas' long career "gave those of us of other political parties some idea of the meaning of eternity," and Pearson for the Liberals and Robert Thompson for Social Credit expressed a warm welcome. Douglas thanked them all. "I would think," he added reflectively, "that any person who started as a private and wound up as a private could at least say he is holding his own."

Douglas was back in Ottawa for the nuclear arms debacle which led directly to the next election. It was an issue in which he was able to state a clear and unequivocal position on behalf of his party, but his earnest pleas to renounce nuclear arms on Canadian soil were drowned in the clatter of the government's downfall. The Conservatives had introduced the Bomarc missiles as part of their NORAD commitment with the United States: they now refused to put nuclear warheads in them. Or at least Howard Green did, and he was backed by Diefenbaker. Other Conservatives disagreed. As for the Liberals, they had at first rejected nuclear arms but had also switched position – on the single decision of Mike Pearson who returned from friendly talks with American military leaders to insist that the weapons should, after all, have their nuclear warhead. For a time Douglas raised a flutter of support in Quebec, where Pierre Elliott Trudeau denounced the Liberals and supported the (unsuccessful) campaign of the NDP candidate Charles Taylor in 1963.

Howard Green recalled that time:

I was much opposed to Canada taking nuclear weapons, thinking it would destroy our initiative in the UN and in the field of disarmament. The NDP supported us, and the Liberals under Pearson were even stronger for it than I was. I thought all my troubles were in my own party.

Then overnight Pearson changed policy completely and endorsed nuclear arms, and then we had trouble in our cabinet, with Diefenbaker coming down on my side. Eventually we were defeated in the House. Only two of the NDP voted with us, Bert Herridge and Colin Cameron. Herridge had been in the same company as I was in the first World War and he stuck by me, and so did Colin Cameron.

The crisis had come in January 1963. The "trouble in our cabinet" referred to by Mr. Green took place when Defence Minister Harkness asserted that the government was "honouring its commitment" to accept nuclear warheads. Diefenbaker equivocated and appeared to deny it, Harkness resigned, there was a note from Washington publicly contradicting Diefenbaker, and two more Tory ministers resigned.

On a vote of confidence in the House, Douglas and most of his party voted for the overthrow of the crumbling government, but could not prevent the old socialists Cameron and Herridge from siding with the anti-nuclear stance of Diefenbaker and Green. Douglas' position was quite simply that Diefenbaker had lost the capability to govern, and a new election was needed. In the election campaign he made quite clear his unchanging opposition to the proliferation of nuclear arms in countries not then possessing them, including Canada.

Back for his second try in Burnaby-Coquitlam, Douglas found that the Liberals had sent in their Number One Bright Boy, Tom Kent, a policy-maker of some stature in the Pearson party, considered to be a man of today, and a top brain. He was expected to give Douglas a hard fight and to keep him so busy in his own riding that his campaign tours would have to be cut short. He disappointed his party on both counts. Whatever his intellectual stature, Kent was no campaigner. He even set up a TV debate to which he invited the press, only to have Douglas "wipe the floor with him" as one gleeful television technician reported. Kent emerged from the studio with his head in his hands.

Irma Douglas spent more time in the home campaign than Douglas did. Again he was off on a gruelling cross-country series of major rallies, climaxed this time in Toronto at Maple Leaf Gardens with a stupefying mass crowd of over 15,000 people. The NDP could at least manage conventions and mass meetings very well.

Severely short of funds, relegated by the press to a minor position, the NDP considered itself fortunate to come through with a loss of only two seats. One was Lewis' York South seat, the other was the Cape Breton beachhead regained the previous year.

"The NDP, despite the valiant campaign of Tommy Douglas, remained static at 14 per cent of the vote," wrote Peter Newman.[13]

While the NDP came back with seventeen instead of eighteen seats, and Social Credit dropped six, the Liberals and Conservatives reversed positions and Pearson took over a Liberal minority government.

It was a time of flux and uncertainty. How soon would Pearson call yet another election, appealing this time for a majority? What should Social Credit and the NDP do in the teetering House of Commons?

Immediately after the election Douglas received a tortured letter from Premier Lloyd of Saskatchewan. Once again all the NDP federal candidates had gone down like ninepins in what had become the Diefenbaker province. Lloyd was anxious about the provincial election which must be held the following year. The position taken by the federal caucus would have great repercussions, and since there was so much anti-Liberal sentiment in Saskatchewan it would be disastrous not to side with Diefenbaker. Surely the outcome of the provincial election was important to the party as a whole?

Douglas replied at length. He said he thought the party in general should be urged

to break the dichotomy of having to choose between Pearson and Diefenbaker. It is like having to choose between being hanged or shot. . . .

I recognize the extent to which the actions of our group in Parliament will affect the political situation in Saskatchewan and to a lesser extent in British Columbia. These are the two provinces in which we can hope for government, with Ontario holding out the prospect of some gains in the provincial field.

If we allow ourselves to be jockeyed into the position of either supporting Pearson or Diefenbaker we are going to tear our movement apart. From some of our people I received passionate letters appealing to us to join with Diefenbaker and the Social Crediters to keep the Liberals out of office. From many others I have been receiving advice which ranges all the way from supporting Pearson to an outright coalition with the Liberals, as advocated by Fred Zaplitney (an NDP M.P. from Manitoba).

It seems to me that we have to break this tug-of-war by taking the position that we are not supporting either of the old-line parties. If there is to be any coalition or working agreement, then it ought to take place between two of the free enterprise parties who have much more in common with each other than they have with us.

I don't think we are going to have too great a problem because I think the Social Credit group will probably support the Liberals mainly because they don't want an election and because they are losing ground in Quebec, the only province where they have had a measure of strength.

At the same time our people have to recognize some of the facts of life. The first fact they must recognize is that most Canadians would like a period of time in which we will be free from the uncertainty of federal elections. The Liberal appeal was mainly based on 'majority government' and the yearning which most Canadians have for political stability. Any political party which acts in an irresponsible manner and gives the impression of wanting to precipitate an election for purely partisan reasons will, in my opinion, be virtually wiped out in the next election.

The second fact we have to recognize is that we need time and we need it badly. We haven't had a real opportunity since the Founding Convention to do basic organization work or to build up the financial resources necessary to put on an effective federal campaign. We are not a major political party at this time and we have to recognize this fact. We polled 1,000,000 votes and slightly over 14 per cent of the popular vote which is a fairly good showing but this doesn't entitle us to call the shots nor to make all the political decisions for the people of Canada. Our job is to play for sufficient time so that when an election comes in two or three years we can be an effective political force in Canada.

My feeling is that we should take a positive and constructive position in the new Parliament. We should state that we want this to be a productive Parliament which will grapple effectively with some of our social and economic problems. We should make it clear that while we do not think either of the old-line parties are likely to go far enough to achieve the results which are desired, nevertheless we will support every measure that moves in the right direction.

It would be irresponsible for us to support 'no confidence' motions against Pearson when there is no alternative government in sight and when a federal election would in all probability only give the Liberals more seats, likely at our expense.

The only issue on which I can see us having a head-on clash with the Liberals would be on nuclear arms. If Pearson is wise he will evade this issue but if he forces it we will have no choice but to oppose him on this question although he can probably count on some of the Social Crediters and Conservatives supporting him in acquiring nuclear warheads.

Those of our supporters who opposed Pearson from the outset have probably lost sight of the fact that this may be precisely what the Liberals would like us to do. If Pearson can bring down some fairly progressive legislation, and if the economic position improves in the next six months he may not be averse to finding a legitimate excuse for going to the country and asking for a clear majority to complete his program. It's my opinion that in this eventuality we could be virtually wiped out, as would most of the Social Crediters in Quebec.

Our strategy should be to give Pearson no excuse for dissolving

Parliament. Diefenbaker will probably carry on a program of constant obstruction and if Pearson decides to use this as an alibi for calling an election there is little we can do about it but the one thing we must not do is provide him with that excuse ourselves and have to go to the country faced with the task of defending ourselves against charges of irresponsibility and doctrinaire obstruction.

Personally I think we're in a good position politically if we play our cards right. We supported the Conservatives as long as they brought down reasonably good legislation and only voted against them when their own Cabinet began to disintegrate. If we support Pearson's legislation whenever it is moving in the right direction we will be in a much stronger position to oppose him if he introduces measures with which we violently oppose or which are unpopular.

In the meantime I think all of our M.L.A.s and others who are addressing public meetings should do everything they can to break this dichotomy of having to choose between Pearson and Diefenbaker. It is like having to choose between being hanged or shot and we must get our people back to the basic principle that we are not concerned with the survival of either of the capitalist parties: we are concerned about building a democratic socialist society.

I hope you have had a good rest and that you are all set to lay the foundations of the next election campaign. I know it will be a tough one but I feel confident that you will come through with flying colours.[14]

Premier Lloyd would have liked, for Saskatchewan's purposes, a tentative alignment with Diefenbaker. Meanwhile in eastern Canada the new party was being tugged in the opposite direction, with invitations from cabinet ministers for informal chats in the interests of "cooperation", all of which the NDP caucus viewed warily, and Douglas most warily of all. A hands-across-party-lines get-together was arranged by the first organizer of the New Party Clubs, Robert Sparham, to include "sensible" NDP'ers and left-wing Liberals and even, perhaps, a Conservative or two. They set up an Exchange for Political Ideas in Canada, vague in its objectives and short-lived. Douglas condemned these diversionary tactics. The party was not yet two years old, already it seemed ready to split off in both directions. Douglas must guide it to more solid ground.

Fortunately, as his letter to Lloyd foresaw, he would not be obliged to occupy the perilous balance-of-power position which betrayed David Lewis in a similar parliamentary set-up between 1972 and 1974. The Social Credit party was prepared to sustain Pearson's Liberals in power, which meant the Liberals could survive any vote in the House. Douglas was in the old familiar position of a powerless small party, able to define its own policy without fear or favour – but seldom listened to when major decisions were being made.

There were parallels and differences between Douglas in 1963 and Lewis in 1972. Both proclaimed an intention to support Liberal legislation they could call "reasonably good", reserving the right to oppose an issue they would consider diametrically contrary to party policy. (With Douglas it was nuclear arms; with Lewis it was income tax exemptions for industry, a measure he had campaigned against. Neither issue, as it happened, became a testing ground.) Both were prepared to support the government for a limited period on votes of confidence, on the grounds that the country at large did not want an "irresponsible" election too soon after the preceding one. Douglas worked with a shorter fuse; on the other hand he knew the NDP vote would not be decisive as long as the Socreds backed Pearson.

Douglas differed from Lewis in emphasizing more strongly the essential importance of staying socialist. He was determined that spokesmen for the party must reiterate this stand. And Douglas was not beguiled into over estimating the size of the NDP on the political stage. He would act like the leader of a small party with a long way to go. Even though personally, as he neared his sixtieth birthday, he might have wished to bask in some kind of borrowed aura of success and power, he looked frankly at the country's 14 per cent support for the NDP and stayed realistically within its limitations. Nor did he ever suggest in anyone's hearing that his present role as a minor party leader was chafing to a former Premier. He had made his choice.

There were initial difficulties of adjustment within his caucus. In Regina he had been supreme. He had been scrupulous in maintaining democratic procedures in his cabinet, but he had unquestionably been at its head. In Ottawa he had to deal with a stubborn group, the remnants of the caucus of eight which had been led first by Argue and then by Bert Herridge, including individualists like Doug Fisher and Arnold Peters who wanted to fly solo, or to argue flat-out for other points of view. Fisher was not in awe of Douglas, whom he regarded as part of an oligarchy which had become "old-fashioned, static". He said "Douglas couldn't be talked to. Sometimes he isolated himself from caucus discussion; he had enormous pride; we couldn't get him to argue out a coherent strategy. Reid Scott and I had a hard time in that caucus from 1962 to 1965; that's why we left politics."

Fisher had learned to admire Lewis, who as deputy leader for several months in 1962 had exhibited freshness and decisiveness. Lewis' performance glowed with the satisfactions of his first season in parliament, where his debating brilliance was acclaimed by the press. Douglas, arriving late in 1962 after his second try, still sobered by his Regina defeat, had to assume leadership of a caucus which generally felt it was doing just fine under Lewis.

Grace MacInnis came into the caucus after 1965, by which time she said the caucus was "pretty harmonious, though we still had some

276

survivors of the previous – well it was a *cactus* instead of a caucus, with a group of prima donnas that has now vanished, but Tommy had to cope with them."

The comparisons and the contest between Lewis and Douglas inevitably existed beneath the surface. Grace MacInnis said, "Ontario presently made up its mind it wanted David. And what Ontario wants Ontario frequently gets."

How was Douglas to go about winning Canada to the NDP? He could press tirelessly for organization, and he did, though his reach from Ottawa into two hundred sixty-four constituencies across the country, tied constitutionally to ten provincial party offices, was necessarily limited. Still he exhorted, encouraged, and taught at every level, smoothing over differences, persuading executives to act like a team facing an opponent instead of a group of strong-willed individuals of varying views. He wanted to spend a great deal of time in the country. In Lewis' opinion he spent too much of that time talking to old socialists, not enough in establishing new political contacts. The other important new factor, taking the place of hundreds of scattered meetings, was television. And here, except on rare occasions, Douglas did not shine. As early as 1962 there were adverse comments about his performance. "Mr. Douglas is getting fairly good crowds at his meetings but he isn't at ease on television where he lacks touch with his listeners. Off stage, Mr. Douglas is a rather nondescript looking man with a slightly antique message. On stage, his face lit by a boyish grin and his expertly-paced oratory catching the mood of the crowd, he is hard to resist," said Don McGillivray."[15]

"He's not photogenic," Grace MacInnis said. "TV isn't kind to him. Even though he's tops with live audiences, better than anyone I know. Well, Trudeau is good on TV and ghastly in the House."

Douglas' worry was showing with his staff. Eleanor McKinnon said, "There was quite a change after 1962. He was more tense. He would be checking back on his staff, something he never used to do. Less *joie de vivre*."

Lewis was returned to the party backroom by the electors in 1963, though he continued to exercise a powerful influence, and he set about ensuring a tight organization in York South for the next election.

Between 1963 and 1965 was a period of slow but positive growth for the NDP. They suffered the calamitous loss of Saskatchewan in 1964 under Premier Lloyd, but that November they won a federal by-election in Waterloo, Ontario, electing Max Saltsman to bring Douglas' party to eighteen in the House of Commons. They were inching upward in the Gallup Poll, while Liberals, wracked by public scandals, and Conservatives, torn by dissent over Diefenbaker's leadership, were losing points in the public's estimation.

Douglas sometimes seemed to accept the new party style ruefully. There was, for example, a fund-raising NDP dinner in Toronto in

December 1964, where in the practice of the "old parties", admission was $50 a plate. Douglas opened his after-dinner speech with: "It's always a pleasure to speak to a group of the underprivileged proletariat."

Douglas led a group of interested observers to Sweden in August 1963. The group included economist Jack Weldon, several CLC officials, and welfare administrators – the objective was to study democratic socialism in its application. Douglas had been much impressed by Israel's economic system on a trip there in 1961, "one of the great highlights of my life." He was equally enthusiastic about Sweden's harmonious labour relationships and advanced social welfare – the minimum time lost in strikes, the efforts to involve workers in the success of their industry, the workers' holidays on the sunny coast of Italy.

Eleanor McKinnon kept account of the trip's lighter moments. Douglas had a particularly hard time with the Swedish diet, and suffered anguish at one private home where the meal appeared to consist of successive courses of herring. "Irma and I struggled through it all, helped by a lot of schnapps," Eleanor said, "but when this *rotten* herring was served – we could smell it in the kitchen before it was served – Tommy copped out, he said it looked delicious but he had to think of his ulcer. The coward! And one morning there was a tremendous smorgasbord for breakfast, all kinds of things but nothing that Tommy was used to eating. George Holmes and Russ Irvine and I were at a different table when we heard a strange spluttering noise. We turned around and there was Tommy – he had taken cornflakes and put what he thought was brown sugar on them, but it turned out to be ground ginger! So he gave in and asked for porridge. There was an enormous Swede named Thorburn Carson looking after us, and he agreed to go and get some oatmeal porridge if Tommy really wanted it. 'I haven't eaten porridge since I was old enough to defend myself!' he announced."

Of Sweden Douglas said,

> I went there of course with all that *Reader's Digest* propaganda about how dull and grim life was – but the people were happy, enjoying life – we went to their boating festivals and beer gardens. I was interested in their labour courts to settle disputes, and the planning of their economy to portion out a percentage of the rising GNP to re-investment, to increased wages, and to social security. I talked to the employers in the Volvo plant and they said, 'Sure, taxes are high and you can't possibly have more than about $50,000 a year in income. Very few have too much and none have too little.'
>
> Sure it's a dull society if what you want is to buy a great piece of land and make yourself a million. You can't do that. A foreigner can't buy Swedish property, or own any part of Sweden.
>
> But you have a feeling of peace and order. And in your apartment block there may be a doctor and his wife, and a truckdriver, and a retired old couple. Their rent is geared to income. The feeling

is so different from Britain – there is no class distinction. There are no slums. Even the old parts of the cities are clean and nice.

From Sweden they travelled to West Germany, where Willy Brandt, who made a strong impression, was embarking on his policy to win the two sides of Germany to tolerate their division, and to achieve a European *detente*. Attending the centennial celebration of the Social Democratic Party in Hamburg, they heard the long roll of comrades killed by the Nazis, and Douglas thought of the irony of senseless accusations in Canada, linking democratic socialism with Hitler, when in fact these men had been among the first of his victims.

If Douglas had entertained any hope of finding in Sweden the key to labour support for his party, he was disappointed. He said,

> I realized that you can't transfer to Canada some of the benefits Sweden has, unless you're able to transfer the cooperation, the educational systems, the understanding. What I learned was that a trade union movement that is just interested in getting more wages for doing less work isn't going to provide the answer to anything.
>
> It was discouraging. But we had a look at the promised land! And of course they have had a long history within a homogeneous community.
>
> I believe purely Canadian unions are coming – solely controlled and operated by Canadians. Our unions can have fraternal relations, but they shouldn't be subservient to the unions of another country. It is time to be master in our own house.

Douglas was for a number of years a member of the executive of the Socialist International, an organization linking the British and Commonwealth Labour Parties with the democratic socialist parties of Europe. Its conferences were solely directed to discussion, occasionally producing resolutions on world issues wherever a common view was found. There were sharp cleavages. Later in the 1960s Douglas tangled with Harold Wilson over support for United States intervention in Vietnam. He was convinced that US help was not as essential to Britain as Wilson thought it was, and that Wilson was following a mistaken policy. He was joined in his attack on the US by Brandt and the Swedes, and got the British policy statement watered down. While he was speaking, Wilson's secretary passed her boss a note, which Wilson later showed Douglas. It said: "I wish you'd said that."

Douglas was concerned with stories of the arrest and detention of social democrats in Malaysia, when five young Malaysians appeared at a Socialist International conference in Helsinki to gain support for their imprisoned comrades. He went on with Irma to a Commonwealth Parliamentary Conference in Kuala Lumpur, where he chose to take part in a panel dealing with civil rights.

On the first day I said, 'When certain socialists who are opposed to violence are imprisoned without charge and held without trial, this country brings into serious question its right to belong to a parliamentary association.' There was no formal reply, but after about three days the socialists turned up at the conference! They had been let out of jail. There was no recrimination shown – but the mere fact that they were there! Some of my Canadian colleagues, particularly George McIlraith, thought this had been very discourteous of me – very inopportune and inappropriate. But I didn't get that reaction from Malaysian officials.

Back in Canada one of the worst of the NDP's problems, an entry to Quebec, seemed to be edging toward solution as Douglas approached the next target date, the 1965 election. Douglas had had long and serious talks with Claude Ryan, editor of *Le Droit*, who had strongly influenced the fledgling NDP's precipitous plunge into two-nationhood in 1961. Douglas said,

> In 1961 there was a strong delegation from Quebec, both francophones and anglophones, at our founding convention, who were convinced that most French-Canadians wanted special status for Quebec, recognition of French Canadian identity and the preservation of their language and culture. So in 1961 we committed ourselves to that policy. I'm not sure that we weren't a bit ahead of ourselves. But the fact is that this is what we are going to be forced eventually to do, though we may not call it 'special status'. Trudeau has given them special status in some respects; the constitution gives them special status.
>
> I spent hours with Claude Ryan on several occasions. He was very sympathetic on some things – on special status, on the federal system he was in complete agreement and wrote very favourable editorials on our position.
>
> Yes, I've also talked to Rene Levesque. And he's just the reverse of Ryan. On economic policy we see eye to eye. On domestic program, reorganizing the economy, and on the importance of Canadian national independence our views are almost identical. What we couldn't agree on was his obsession for pulling Quebec out of Confederation. I got the feeling that he became the captive of his own rhetoric.

A new figure had come forward in Quebec, the first French Canadian of great potential importance for the party after Therese Casgrain. He was Robert Cliche, a lawyer from Beauce, who began appearing with Douglas at press conferences. Moderate, of considerable reputation, he accepted the Beauce nomination for the Nouveau Parti Democratique. "Robert Cliche concealed a brilliant mind, cultural sophistication and a profound sense of his own heritage behind a bear-like exterior. A brilliant platform orator in French and English, he could not hide a warm humanity and a political acumen which had always been a rare combination in the Quebec left. His was one of the finest and most frustrated talents made available to Canadian public life in the sixties."[16]

It was not necessary for the NDP or for Social Credit to conspire to bring down Pearson's minority government. Pearson dissolved parliament in September 1965, to seek a stronger mandate. There were some hopeful signs for the NDP. It had managed to pull ahead financially since the previous election and planned to spend a good round sum – one million dollars – on the campaign. Considerable federal support was going to Quebec, particularly to two Montreal ridings of Mont Royal, where Charles Taylor was running, and Notre Dame de Grace, where the candidate was C. G. Gifford. These two, with Cliche, carried the party's hopes for a Quebec breakthrough. Professor Taylor, half French and half English, was the choice of many to succeed Douglas, in due course, as federal leader. But midway in the campaign an event of considerable national importance occurred, the decision of Pierre Elliott Trudeau to seek a seat in parliament with the Liberals, the party he had so boldly attacked two years earlier. Trudeau ran, and was elected, in Mont Royal, defeating Taylor with ease. A whole new era was opening for the Liberal party, and in the process the NDP's new hopes for Quebec floundered.

The NDP tried to make the most of the good-to-fair media coverage Douglas was getting, reprinting in glossy, four-colour reproduction a Blair Fraser article from *Maclean's* (July 24, 1965) which opined that the party had made a recovery since 1963. "Tommy Douglas, who only three years ago seemed to have ended a distinguished political career in complete disaster and failure . . . (leads a party that) poses a stronger threat than ever before . . . Tommy Douglas himself, after a rather slow and hesitant start, has regained some of the fire and zest that made him in his heyday one of the most formidable campaigners in Canada."

The NDP, with some mathematical dexterity, was talking to the voters about the *bare chance* that they might win a majority in parliament. The main campaign pamphlet, "The Way Ahead for Canada", talked about "guidelines for a New Democratic government" and concluded with a testament of faith by Douglas:

I believe in Canada.
I have faith in its future and am dedicated to its destiny.
I believe that this country has the potential for greatness, not only in material terms, but also in the things of the mind and spirit. . .
With faith in ourselves and a sense of national purpose, we can invite all Canadians – labour and industry, farmer and city dweller, Catholic and Protestant, Gentile and Jew, French-speaking and En-

glish – in a great crusade to make Canada a land where the good things of life will be enjoyed by all.

Out in Burnaby-Coquitlam Douglas was facing a third election with no great qualms. The transfer to British Columbia had been without trauma. Irma Douglas, with her unconquerable good spirit, declared that British Columbia was "great". "You never run out of new things in our kind of life!" The mysteries of a logging and fishing economy had been quickly assimilated. "Saskatchewan has always been more home to me than anywhere else. But I can live anywhere." And Douglas' local popularity was high.

He was tossing off jokes again, refusing to be overawed by his own or anyone else's political destiny. Dave Weston, who in 1964 was executive assistant in his Ottawa office, said he is always aware that he may sound less than credible in describing Douglas as he knew him, because "there were no feet of clay. He was honest and hard-working, with complete integrity. And he'd say things like – at a federal council meeting there was discussion about having the next convention in Toronto, and how to dramatize it. One of the M.P.s said, 'Well, we could have a nude woman riding down Yonge Street on a horse.' And Douglas said, 'What a great idea! It must be a long time since the people of Toronto have seen a horse.' "

His staff was amused by Douglas' occasional encounters with alcohol. Joyce Nash on a plane with him one morning, pretended to be shocked that Douglas ordered a sherry before noon. Douglas said, "It's perfectly alright. I've just checked and it's 1:30 where I'm going."

Cliff Scotton was now his election assistant, and marvelled at Douglas' energy-producing diet of fruit juice, porridge, tea, an occasional poached egg on toast, or rare roast beef sandwich and, at bedtime, brown buttered toast and honey with hot chocolate. Douglas avoided richer refreshments. But once a tight itinerary brought them in a small float plane for a meeting and to spend the night at a lodge at Sproat Lake, out of Port Alberni. Douglas counselled an early bed for the whole party, since their plane would pick them up again at 5:00 a.m. When the lodge manager proposed a bedtime snack, however, Douglas accepted. A lavish buffet had been set out, and a waiter promptly approached with a tray of Manhattans. Douglas downed one, and asked Cliff, "What was that?" Scotton described the composition of a Manhattan. "I knew it wasn't hot chocolate," Douglas said.

He proceeded to delight the group with stories about Lieutenant Governor McNab of Saskatchewan, the king of England, and Mayor Houde of Montreal. Eventually it was 2:00 a.m., and Scotton brought up the matter of the 5:00 a.m. flight. "You're right. I don't know why we didn't get to bed earlier," Douglas said.

Douglas again spoke at mammoth rallies. He was successful, too, in a new election device, the radio "hot line" show. The election results showed a satisfactory advance for the NDP, with twenty-one elected instead of the seventeen in 1963, while the first solid results of union support showed in new Ontario seats gained. And although the party hit a high-water mark in percentage of votes in Quebec, they failed to break through with the election of a single member from that province. Diefenbaker's Conservatives were still sweeping Saskatchewan. Ottawa settled in with another barely larger Liberal government.

The NDP, to journalist Walter Stewart, now looked like "an urban, middle-class party confined mainly to major centres of Ontario, Manitoba and B.C."[17] Walter Young and other federal council members were convinced that the turnaround had begun, that the farmers had been left behind, and labour support was the new fact of life. But it was significant that all the twenty-one elected M.P.s grew up in the CCF.

Douglas' efforts in parliament, as the 1960s moved toward their close, were directed most passionately against the Vietnam war, and Canada's tacit support and active material aid.

From the outset of American intervention, Douglas denounced the United States as "an intruder". He said at a press conference on February 11, 1965, that Canada, as a member of the International Control Commission (ICC) should either take the matter to the UN or ask that the ICC be reconvened. In May he made a major speech in the House, calling US intervention "a new form of colonialism by which Great Powers support puppet governments pliable to their will and prepared to accept economic domination." He described the Diem regime as oppressive and unpopular. Pearson had made known to Washington his approval: "Throughout the long crisis the government has adopted a deferential posture of supine subervience."[18]

Douglas urged on the government a four-point program: first, there should be an immediate end to the bombing of North Vietnam; second, peace negotiations should begin with the Viet Cong admitted as a negotiating member; third, a peace-keeping force should be sent in pending free elections under UN or Geneva Accord auspices; and fourth, Canada should join with other nations to help the people of Vietnam recuperate from the effects of war.

By January 1966 he was denouncing the US policy as "legally indefensible and morally inexcusable."

As the war continued and American voices such as Senator William J. Fulbright and Walter Lippmann were raised in protest, the Canadian government became increasingly uncomfortable with its position. By February 1967, Douglas was rapping External Affairs Minister Paul Martin sharply across the knuckles for refusing to condemn the United States, for "delivering an apologia for doing nothing", and worse, for supplying arms to the US without any guarantee that they would not be used in Vietnam:

My information is that the Canadian government has already appealed to the United States government and asked for assurance that none of the $300 million worth of armaments we sell them each year will go to Vietnam. My information is that that plea has been rejected . . . While a loss of $300 million in our trading position would be serious, I am not prepared to get $300 million of trade at the cost of seeing villages annihilated and defenceless people killed . . . The use of anti-personnel bombs and the use of napalm has made the war in Vietnam a bloody and barbaric incident that has no equal in our time. . .

Most of the war and bloodshed that we have seen in our lifetime has come because of the cowardly silence of governments in days gone by. I was a member of the House when the Liberal government withdrew Dr. Riddell from the League of Nations because he dared to suggest oil sanctions against Mussolini – he was rocking the boat. I stood in my place in this House and protested against the sale of copper, scrap iron and nickel to Japan when Japan invaded Manchuria. We were told we must not rock the boat, and this silence, this apathy and inaction have brought us again and again into the maelstrom of war.

The Official Opposition under Diefenbaker had stopped government business to debate foreign affairs, but their motion had merely deplored the inadequacy of time for such debate, and the lack of a clear statement by the government on Asia and Middle East policy. The NDP amended the motion to specifically condemn the United States for continued bombing of North Vietnam, and managed to get twenty Conservatives, including Diefenbaker, to vote with them. The rest of the Tory party split with their leader to support the Liberals.

Another supreme issue, related also to Liberal "subservience", was the encroachment of American ownership of Canadian resources and industry. Douglas had protested the trend since the end of World War Two. Eric Kierans, now a member of Pearsons' Cabinet, "violated protocol" according to some critics in 1966 to protest the action of American parent companies for milking their subsidiaries in Canada to help their balance of payments problem, at the expense of Canada's position. Douglas staunchly supported Kierans' bluntness, earning words of gratitude from Kierans. His gratitude would not be enough, however, to prevent him dealing the NDP a hard blow in the next election.

Douglas twitted Walter Gordon, the deposed Minister of Finance, who "three years ago started out with high hopes of buying back the Canadian economy. Now he is sitting with some other former ministers in the penalty box."

Douglas warned,

Foreign investors now control major segments of our economy in the fields of manufacturing, mining and smelting, oil production and refining, rubber industry, farm machinery and auto and aircraft manufacturing. Foreign investors are now moving into insurance and financing fields. Our objection to this is not based on any sentimental grounds. It does not make much difference to a Canadian whether he is exploited by a Canadian capitalist or a U.S. capitalist . . . Our objection is that increasingly the important decisions affecting the well-being of Canadians are being made outside of Canada by people who have loyalty to other countries than ours. We had a very good example of that this summer when three milling companies in Canada, subsidiaries of U.S. corporations, refused to mill flour for the Canadian government because that flour was being sold to Russia, which in turn intended to send it to Cuba. These corporations are doing business in Canada under the protection of Canadian laws with Canadian resources and Canadian workers, yet they feel that their loyalty is not to the country in which they are located but to the country in which their parent company is located. Surely this is untenable. . . .

Absorption always begins with economic control followed by cultural assimilation by control of press, radio, television and periodicals. We should not forget that history teaches us that political power inevitably follows economic power, and that once a nation has tremendous sums of money invested in another country it must begin to exercise an influence on the political activity of that nation.

Someone has suggested that we have passed the point of no return, but I personally do not believe that. Rather I think we should ask ourselves whether we are prepared to pay the price which will be necessary to regain control of the Canadian economy.[19]

But Douglas was getting no kudos outside his own party for such forthright statements. The press in Canada was enjoying a season of king-making, a sense of power in the personality play between Diefenbaker and Pearson, which they saw as a clash of earth-shaking consequence dependent on one man's lisp and the other man's trembling jowls. They would turn their skills to a dazzling build-up of Pierre Trudeau based on even slighter evidence in 1968. And in 1966 many had made up their minds that Douglas was *passé*.

A particularly significant article appeared in the *Star Weekly* on January 8, 1966. It was written by Walter Stewart, who later was to lead the press reaction against the Trudeau myth in a best-selling book called *Shrug*. In 1966 Stewart wrote "The Tough, Lonely Man in the Middle", which showed Douglas as hard-driving but corny, quoted extensively from Walter Young and others who accused Douglas of lack of leadership, and most significantly dwelt at length on the contrast with his deputy leader, David Lewis. "Douglas exhibits a curious weakness in the councils of his own party. Many people who know the internal workings of the NDP claim that David Lewis, one of the five national vice-presidents and M.P. for a Toronto riding, holds greater sway than Douglas in internal matters." A close associate is quoted as saying, "He's not at all a warm man, not like David Lewis, for instance." Another anonymous "aide" is quoted as saying, "Here you had this man back in parliament for the first time in nearly twenty years, still suffering from the brutal transition from leader of a government to the defeated head of a minor party. Beside him was this brilliant guy Lewis, so smart, so sure, and his obvious successor. If Douglas developed a bit of inferiority feeling, it's hardly to be wondered at."

As far as Douglas was concerned, Lewis was by no means "his obvious successor". Though it was an unnerving experience, as he entered the 1968 election campaign in his west coast riding, to have David's son Stephen arrive by plane for the express purpose of asking him to step down from the leadership in Lewis' favour. Stephen Lewis was influenced by a group of younger Ontario party men. David Lewis did not sanction the mission: he realized that it would be "misrepresented" as a brash or cruel act on Stephen's part. "But at least he had the guts to say it to his face," Lewis said.

Douglas' reply was that he had no intention of holding on to the leadership beyond the time when he could be of service to the party. However it was hardly the time to abandon leadership, on the brink of an election. He realized that the sixties had developed a youth cult – and he was considerably "over thirty", the extreme bounds of reliability in the terms of the decade. He was, in fact, almost sixty-four. He was much concerned to see younger people bid for the party's top job. But that did not indicate a switch to a man four years younger than himself.

The media was so enraptured by the Trudeau sunburst in 1968 that Douglas might have considered himself lucky to be granted any front page or television space. In fact, he stayed in the picture not by luck but by pursuing a rigorously hard campaign which, in mid-June, actually raised hopes that the party would fare moderately well, and in the end produced twenty-two seats and a gain in the popular vote.

The Conservatives had deposed Diefenbaker for their new man, Robert Stanfield, and the titillating contrast between the staid, drawling Nova Scotian and Trudeau, the "swinger" from Mont Royal, was enough for yards of copy. Yet Douglas managed to score, near the close of the campaign in a three-way national television debate in which both Trudeau and Stanfield appeared oddly stiff and dull, while Douglas sparkled and scored points with ease. Television with real live opponents next him in the studio was a different matter from speaking alone into the shadowed lens of a hovering camera.

Douglas' success in the debate excited his followers. Hans Brown, working in the campaign and later Douglas' executive assistant, offered the comment: "He had his ups and downs on TV, but at that big debate in '68 he was magnificent! He had his hair done, all puffed out and shiny, looked like a million bucks. The way he bounced up out of his chair, zapped those questions off really sharp! Of those three people – he beat the shit out of them on every question. Everybody had low expectations, but we (his staff) just floated out of the place. His forte is debate, face to face."

And Douglas recaptured a large share of Saskatchewan seats. This was perhaps the real triumph of the 1968 campaign. He appeared in Regina at a big rally in the Armouries, where 7000 people gave him a tremendously warm reception. The fever of the Medicare dispute had passed, Diefenbaker as a national leader had come and gone, and they were with Tommy again. There were repeated ovations, and at the end Douglas' assistants, Doug Rowland and Bruce Lawson, were waiting backstage to extricate him quickly from well-wishers and whisk him off to his hotel to rest. They had seen the dense crowd, blocking the aisles and every row of seats, so they proposed the back door. Douglas would have none of it. He leaped down from the very high stage; he made his way into the crowd. They caught his hands and called out to him, and he to them. He reached the back of the hall at last, he stood to shake hands with hundreds more, and the tears and the shining eyes were not to be forgotten.

Regina in 1968 elected two NDP members, and elsewhere in the province the party elected five others. The seven more than compensated for losses in Ontario and British Columbia. It also meant that those who had been so certain that the party's base was moving eastward had to revise their calculations once again.

But Douglas' hard campaign in Saskatchewan and other provinces meant too little time spent in his own riding, and he was punished by a second personal defeat. Burnaby-Coquitlam had disappeared in redistribution and the new Burnaby-Seymour riding included a section of North Vancouver where prospects were unknown – Douglas had been reassured by a confident campaign committee that all was well; only Irma appeared worried as election day approached. The Liberal, Ray Perrault who had been provincial leader, beat him by little more than a hundred votes.

Trudeau and his Liberals swept the country. The NDP hopes for a break-through in Quebec were wiped out. Douglas appeared to feel as badly about Cliche's defeat as his own. Cliche had run this time in Duvernay, he had been given a good chance of winning until the Liberals sent in Eric Kierans. It was Cliche's final attempt. Douglas said, "Until two weeks before the election he had the seat won. When I was there, many were conceding him the election. Then Kierans came in and made a great impact – he had been a popular minister in the Lesage government – and the Liberals were sweeping everything. He defeated Robert.

It was a great tragedy for our party. Robert was the kind of person who could have broken the log jam in Quebec."

Once again Douglas was out of the House as it met in a post-election session. And this time he was prepared to remain out. He refused to consider the resignation of another member to open up a seat for him. He insisted that each of them had fought hard for election and should serve his or her term. At a federal council meeting Douglas announced – and made known to the press – that he would step down at the next party convention in 1969.

Suddenly, in July, the NDP's veteran west coast socialist, Colin Cameron, died. The riding, where Cameron had a large very loyal following, in due course invited Douglas to run. Douglas accepted. He knew that many in Cameron's riding considered him "right wing"; he spent time meeting and talking with key members of the party.

Trudeau was in no great hurry to accommodate the NDP by calling a by-election in Nanaimo-Cowichan-and-the-Islands. In the interval Douglas and his new constituency committee organized an invincible campaign. They were opposed by a Liberal who bore another revered name among B.C. socialists, Eric Winch, a local magistrate. The sprawling constituency was canvassed five times. No tiny island was too remote for a visit from Douglas. Early in 1969 Douglas pummelled his opponents in a by-election victory.

He was back in Ottawa for the final term of his leadership. Now he listened to those who pressed him not to resign in 1969. Where were the potential young leadership aspirants? Ed Broadbent had been elected in June 1968 but was still untried. Douglas agreed merely to give notice at the 1969 convention, and, if re-elected by that sovereign group, to continue as leader for another two years. The party would be given time to find a successor.

Chapter Eighteen
The Waffle, the Black Panthers and the FL Q

Douglas' leadership was not contested at the 1969 federal convention; the party accepted his decision to carry on for a final two years, while new, young aspirants would test out their positions and look to new waves of redefined democratic socialism to sweep them to the forefront. It did not happen quite that way.

Several thought they perceived such a current and made haste to seize it: Stephen Lewis in Ontario saw his chance as a young, articulate spokesman of the sixties who would brighten and accelerate the party in his province. His ideological position, however, was not radical at all, and far from uniting a new generation of socialists behind him he was quickly confronted by the Canadian manifestation of the American New Left, the Waffle Movement. Stephen Lewis found himself relying on the support of the most pragmatic and cautious elements of the party and the trade union movement. Ontario entered into yet another depressing period of conflict, between the conspiratorial Wafflers and the hardened resistance of elected officers. It ended, as usual, in a ritual cleansing and the weary party pressed on, attempting to come to terms with current Ontario society and without a strong sense of direction, a reform party dealing with issues one by one as they arose. But it was now an established party; it counted in Ontario politics; there was that much gained.

More spectacular advances took place in the western provinces where the NDP formed governments under Schreyer in Manitoba in 1969, under Blakeney in Saskatchewan in 1971, and under Barrett in British Columbia in 1972. In Manitoba success came with the breakthrough in rural areas and among non-Anglo-Saxon groups; in Saskatchewan it was a strong re-emergence of a particularly sturdy political philosophy; in British Columbia it was a new radical alignment with diverse elements in the community and a perceived distance between the party and the trade unions.

There was a decline of initiative and influence from the federal headquarters of the party which still worked with a diminished staff out of an antique, cramped red brick building in downtown Ottawa. Much that happened at the federal office reflected provincial conflicts in the party. This followed from changed party structure. The control of elections was almost entirely in the hands of provincial executives, which set up committees to handle federal election campaigns. Although policy study exercises took place at the federal level, and a growing research branch supported the parliamentary activities of the caucus members, the placing of election control in the hands of the provinces led to a decentralized party.

The Waffle episode, for example, was played out in Ontario, Saskatchewan, British Columbia, and Manitoba, but did not produce clearly defined antagonists in the federal caucus. A confrontation might easily have developed there, however, under David Lewis' leadership, for Lewis was chafing during this period over the activities of Waffle adherents and the disrepute they brought to the party. Douglas took a different line.

Inevitably denounced as weakness, his instinctive response was to accept the main thrust of Waffle declarations – which seemed to make eminent good sense – their concern for the conservation of Canada's energy resources and for the runaway takeover of the Canadian economy by American corporate enterprise. He not only tolerated but liked James Laxer, the grave, gentle-mannered professorial leader of the Waffle group, who was highly suspect among other party officers because his background included a father nurtured in the Communist Party of Canada.

Douglas said,

The Waffle was a recent development, late in my term as leader. It was the sort of thing we've always had in the CCF and the NDP, as in all democratic socialist and labour parties – a left wing.

I've never quarrelled with their right to be a bit ahead of the party. My dread has never been that the party will be too radical. My dread has been that the party will settle into a rut and become complacent. People who act a gadflies are useful in keeping you from becoming so over-cautious in order to get the support of the middle class that you dilute the party, tone it down until it becomes indistinguishable from, say, a Liberal Party.

My quarrel with some of these left wing groups however is twofold – but I have never openly quarrelled with them; though I have argued with them I have never denied their right to be, never taken any move to discriminate against them, – first, they tend to become idealistic and unrealistic. In Saskatchewan, for example, they said why not nationalize the potash industry? Without thinking of cost or priorities – should you do without rural electrification or natural gas or northern air services? You can, instead, set up a Potash Board to which the developers must sell their products, and you have made the company simply a contractor to go out and produce the stuff and sell it to you. But these doctrinaire people insist on nationalization.

290

And, two, they tend to become people who feel that being doctrinaire and extreme makes them very special people. They are always proving their purity. In the process they cut off everyone to the right and left of themselves. They become a small group – to use Nye Bevan's term – engaging in political masturbation.

You have to carry other people with you, in politics. My father used to say, 'Go as far and fast as you can, but never get too far ahead of your own troops.' I remember Bill Irvine at the CCF founding convention saying about the controversial issue of compensation to private companies, 'We are now setting up a political party. If people aren't prepared to follow us, why start it?'

I am very sorry about Mel Watkins and Jim Laxer. They have developed an overweening pride. They have become completely unrealistic.

I felt that Saskatchewan worked its way out of the Waffle situation more easily than Ontario did. I remember the long sessions in Saskatchewan at conventions and councils when they wanted to expel somebody. I've always opposed expelling anybody, unless it is apparent that he's a member of another party. But short of that, I'm opposed to expelling anybody.

Some members in some areas suffer from expulsionitis. And sometimes you expel somebody who, if you'd had a little more patience, would have stayed and come to his senses as he got older. And you also make martyrs of them, which is a dangerous thing to do.

I remember people back in the forties and fifties who were about to be expelled, but weren't, and they stopped reading books and got to know what's going on in the world, and are now good members.

My answer to these so-called left-wingers, and some of them are not as radical as I am – I suggest one night a week out canvassing to find out what the average person is thinking. We are supposed to deal with the problems people have, not the problems we think they have.

The Waffle movement espoused a Quebec element which stopped just short of separatism, promoting "self determination". Since this was interpreted to mean a unilateral right to decide constitutional matters, without reference to other authorities within the Canadian structure, it was not a policy Douglas could accept. At the very end of his term as leader, in February 1971, the new little band of quasi-separatists took over the Quebec NDP. Douglas listened to its leader, Raymond Laliberte, who explained that his real concern was for economic reform, but he felt the separatist idea was something Quebec had to get out of its system, and he believed that a stand for "self determination" would pacify them without actually producing a separate state. Obviously it could lead to a much more independent Quebec within Confederation, considerably beyond the "special status" concept which Douglas had accepted (though he considered it premature) in 1961.

"Special status" for Quebec was now a fact as Lesage pointed out in his announcement to his legislature: "I used all the means that Providence has given me so that Quebec, in the end would be recognized as a province with a special status in Confederation. And I have succeeded." Douglas hoped that a pattern of amicable accommodation had been found, within Confederation.

But Douglas did not challenge the Laliberte group. In part he was no doubt deterred because of his short remaining tenure of office, and hesitated to embark on an exercise of authority which would mean expelling the Quebec section of the party, small, ineffective, and rebellious as it was. In part he was inhibited by his own sense of not fully understanding Quebec. For many years he had held firmly to the view that Quebeckers were exactly like all other Canadians, their main problem being the atrociously bad economic and social conditions they endured, and he reamed off figures to show their rates of unemployment and low levels of income. Their cultural and language obsessions were to some degree a smokescreen, he had felt, and could all be settled sensibly once the basic economic situation was made right. In Ottawa, and after many talks with Claude Ryan (who supported "self determination") and Charles Taylor, he had become convinced that the complex cultural issue was indeed a major concern – but one which he felt personally reluctant to judge.

In this aspect of the Waffle struggle he temporized and refrained from forcing the issue, though he was not in sympathy with the "self determination" stand which was hailed by the Wafflers with great excitement as a prodigious victory against the NDP "establishment".

His attitude on the other Waffle concerns – conservation of energy and foreign ownership – was very sympathetic, though he consistently argued against the idea of wholesale nationalization. He could see a promising road, too, in the "industrial democracy" they talked of – the worker involvement in his own plant operation – as a way out of the classic confrontation between employer and employee.

The Waffle Manifesto (for an Independent Socialist Canada) had been pushed forward at the 1969 convention where the battles between its numerous supporters and the counter group, led by David Lewis, who successfully put forward an alternative manifesto, completely eclipsed other party business or any interest in the leadership problem, which was merely put in abeyance until 1971.

Following the 1969 convention Waffle and anti-Waffle forces hardened. Most members of recognized stature in the party withdrew their support from Laxer and Watkins.

The struggle was resolved in the provinces. At Ontario's 1970 convention Douglas ("unintentionally" according to his executive assistant Hans Brown, who sympathized with the Waffle group) gave a mighty assist to the Waffle cause by liberally endorsing their position on energy. Brown said:

> Laxer and another Waffler were running for the provincial seats on federal council, against Desmond Morton and Bob Mackenzie. Laxer cracked the slate, beating out Mackenzie, so that the two elected were Morton and Laxer. What had happened was that Douglas spoke on energy resources and Canadian sovereignty and independence, all the great issues and had the crowd in the palm of his hand, getting one ovation after another. Just before he ended he mentioned two good books everybody should read, *Silent Surrender* by Kari Levitt, and *The Continental Energy Poker Game* by Laxer. Everybody whipped out their pencils, looked for a clean corner of a page to write down the books Tommy thought they should read. A moment or two later here's Jim Laxer's name on a ballot!
>
> Tommy also pissed off the Toronto crowd in that speech because he talked about some nationalization of energy – not the whole thing, but transmission lines, yes, they ought to be under public control. It just so happened that just before he spoke there had been a violent debate at the mikes over a Waffle motion on this issue. It had been held over for his speech. So next day when the motion came on again, Stephen and some others went to the mikes and said they had changed their minds, they accepted most of the resolution. There wasn't much else they could do.
>
> Douglas always carried terrific moral authority within the party. It was quite amazing. He would in caucus deliberately hold back, because whenever he intervened in debate he turned the tide.

Douglas persisted in believing that the Waffle leaders should and could be absorbed into the party. Immediately after the 1971 leadership convention at which Laxer had made a strong showing, the federal council rejected Waffle nominees to the executive of the party. Douglas wrote to a Nova Scotian party member: "Like yourself, I was very disappointed that Jim Laxer and Mel Watkins were not elected to the Federal Executive."[1]

Later Douglas told Hans Brown that he hoped Laxer would pick a good riding in the 1972 federal election and win a seat in parliament – instead Laxer withdrew his candidature and his party membership.

When the Waffle struggle began in Saskatchewan Premier Lloyd was accused of being "too soft". Douglas was upset by the charges, and kept in close touch with Lloyd, who resigned as leader partly because of this division, partly because of ill health. Some years earlier Douglas had written to Lloyd: "I'm delighted to hear about the Youth Convention. This is the best news I've heard in a long time. I've never had any doubt about the faithful supporters of our generation but as you know I've always been concerned about our failure to really set the young people on fire. I think this is happening now and it bodes well for the future."[2]

A moderate group kept control of the Saskatchewan party under Allan Blakeney, without much vituperation. When the Waffle wing was frustrated by its failure to score heavily in convention voting it withdrew, and the party expressed regret. One young Waffle member, John Richards, was elected as an M.L.A., and served as the solitary, ornamental, independent radical.

Blakeney said, "Douglas' reaction was shaped by his Saskatchewan experience. The Waffle ideas don't scare many people in Saskatchewan. They've heard most of this before. Secondly, Douglas knows that every democratic socialist party, when it gets into office has a tendency to move to the centre. He knew the party must not snuff out any of these new ideas, no matter how wild they may appear, if the party is to renew itself. They are the raw materials of some pretty good stuff".

But quite aside from tactics, Douglas' attitude toward the Waffle was determined by his own inherent radicalism. He was never merely a reformer. He was convinced of the need for very deep and fundamental change. In April 1968 he had said to the British Columbia convention: "Our movement is fundamentally concerned with the basic structure of society itself." In too many ways, he said, Canada was "a society of shabby values." He would never give up hoping to see those values replaced by better ones.

*   *   *

Douglas never brought his family into the public limelight, but in the autumn of 1969, his older daughter Shirley made headlines in the United States and Canada on her own account. She was arrested in Los Angeles for activities in an organization called the Friends of the Black Panthers.

Shirley, after her divorce from Tim Sick, had married Don Sutherland, the popular star of M*A*S*H, and was living in Beverly Hills with her small family, Thom and three-year-old twins, Rachel and Keifer. She had involved herself in the overseas program of the Unitarian Service Committee; now, in California, she took up the cause of raising funds and assisting with a Black Panther program to provide breakfasts for underprivileged children. Don Sutherland was hospitalized with spinal meningitis when the police episode took place.

"Shirley," said Hans Brown, "got into radical causes in L.A., she was all gung ho about them, and Tommy was very supportive. He may have felt she got herself into some needless scrapes, but for idealistic motives – a chip off the old block; he kind of liked that."

Some Canadian journalists found that Douglas' ready defence of his daughter made him "seem more like flesh and blood." Immediately after news of her arrest in Los Angeles, on a charge of conspiring to obtain ten hand grenades for the Black Panthers – a charge that proved to be a police frame-up – Douglas called a press conference in Ottawa. He spoke, said the Toronto *Star's* Frank Jones, "in touchingly personal terms, and said, 'I am proud of the fact that my daughter believes, as I do, that hungry children should be fed whether they are Black Panthers or white Republicans'."[3]

Brown said, "Tommy had arrangements made so fast! He was down there in a flash. The press down there mobbed him at the airport. They were in so tight he couldn't move. They had been told he was the 'leader of the Communist Party in Canada'! He told me after he got back that to get through he gave one of them a kick in the shins. I said I didn't see that on TV."

Canadian TV coverage showed the familiar, small, cocky figure, smiling politely and answering the questions with disarming sincerity, though reporters had got the impression from Los Angeles police that he was a sinister figure from the communist underworld.

Shirley Sutherland recalled,

There is no way of understanding the poverty in Los Angeles until you've seen it. I went downtown and I was appalled by the standard of living. There were so many children going to school without breakfast – and those same children were ending up in juvenile court – so I was more than happy to work on it, to raise money. We had two or three really fine breakfast programs going at that time.

There was a police frame-up, about four o'clock one morning when I was asleep, only the three children and a maid there with me, the men came in, only one of them in uniform, and held us all against the wall, my oldest son and I with guns pointing at us. I didn't know why they were there or what they expected to find. (It was at the apartment of an associate in the Friends of the Black Panthers, Donald Freed, that a package containing hand grenades was picked up in the police search. The package had been planted there by an undercover policeman, according to the evidence produced in court. Freed and Shirley Sutherland were released and the charges against them dismissed.)

I was held for about four days. Luckily Benjamin Spock was in town and began immediately arranging bail. I began to understand the many cases I had read about in the papers, many of them were frame-ups like mine. I started to realize why people are afraid of the police in the United States. The paranoia of the police system itself is really frightening.

I called Tommy the next day. He is always marvellous – he just said, 'Are you alright? Anything we can do for you? Mind if I come down?' Never said he was worrying! He flew down within twenty-four hours. He helped get me the best lawyer we could find. And with

295

the police – I overheard one of them say to another, 'I hope this guy realizes what's going on. He acts very calm.' But Tommy understood the situation very well, better than I did.

In the 1974 interview from her California home, Shirley Sutherland said,

> I thought the McCarthy period was over when I came to the States, but it's a long way from it. Maybe because I was so much younger in Saskatchewan, politics seemed so much simpler there!
>
> For Tommy, there never really was anything but work. He *never* plays. He has never understood how you can play. When I grew older I discovered that men *play* – that families have people in for dinner and play bridge!
>
> I had always known he was well loved in Saskatchewan – that was why the 1962 defeat was the most terrible thing that ever happened – but I discovered he is also well known in other countries, in London and Rome. I'm always meeting people who met him many years ago, and ask for him. Eleanor Roosevelt said to me, 'Take care of him. He's a marvellous person.'
>
> Tommy is a very different kind of politician. He has never done anything to make 'politics' a dirty word. Yes, I would enjoy politics very much myself. I am at a point now where I want to think of some of these options.

*　　*　　*

The TV commentators who were dismissing Douglas as corny and old-fashioned in those years, saw in Pierre Trudeau fantastic qualities of appeal to Canadians. They were assessing Trudeau in terms of his television image, the erotic vision in a little box, the relationship to the viewer which McLuhan sees as essentially "cold". That is, removed. Trudeau was a god to be adored – at least in the minds of his most enthusiastic admirers. But was this empathy?

In Douglas' terms, as he told Southam news reporter Ben Tierney,

> Trudeau is completely bereft of human compassion in personal terms. He thinks in theoretical terms that, you know, we should do something for the poor and the needy. But, in terms of understanding a young person out of work, or a student who can't get money to go back to university, or the problems of an unemployed man with five kids. . . . Well, he doesn't understand because he's never come up against it.
>
> I don't know whether he's ever worked with, or lived with, or talked with, day in and day out, people who are really up against the crunch. And he reacts like this when he's crossed in the House of

Commons. You get all the marks of arrogance of the spoiled little rich boy who always had what he wants, and who bites the carpet and kicks his feet when he's thwarted. . . .

Trudeau is a very complex character . . . There isn't any doubt that he is an intellectually competent person.[4]

In October 1970 this charismatic, arrogant, and complex Prime Minister committed one of the most audacious acts in Canadian history. He invoked the sweeping powers of the War Measures Act to deal with a small, fragmented terrorist group which he saw allied with the growing separatist cause in Quebec. By first sending in military troops to conspicuously guard public figures in Ottawa and Quebec, and by extraordinarily inflammatory statements by members of his Cabinet, he helped produce in Canada a state of panic against the activities of a handful of terrorists – whom James Cross, one of their victims, described afterwards as "six kids trying to start a revolution".[5] There was little doubt, in the statements Trudeau made in the House of Commons and outside, that the real adversary in his mind was separatism, manifested in the provincial Parti Québecois which was challenging the Liberal government of Quebec, and within more immediate range a citizens' organization, Front de Rassemblement et d'Action Populaire (FRAP), which was for the first time challenging the almost dictatorial powers in Montreal of Mayor Drapeau and his city manager, Lucien Saulnier, good Liberals both.

Against this massive government retaliation, Tommy Douglas and the group he led in the House of Commons were the only ones to stand absolutely opposed. The War Measures Act confers on the government the absolute powers of a police state. Douglas declared that it was impossible to see anything in the situation to warrant the proclamation of an Act designed to protect a nation in the throes of total war. He pushed for concrete evidence of the "apprehended insurrection", given as cause for invoking the Act. No concrete evidence was ever forthcoming. Four years later, many members of the public at large are still convinced that Trudeau saved them from a bloody revolution. Few, if any, serious analysts now believe that the October Crisis was more than a political act dealing in inflated fear. Perhaps it is too soon to use the word "hoax", but history may do so.

Douglas saw it as Canada's Reichstag fire. He said,

The government was hoodwinked into believing it was a much more dangerous situation than actually existed, largely because the city of Montreal was going to hold an election and FRAP was putting up candidates and Drapeau, who had every seat on the Council, was desperately afraid not that he would be beaten but that there would be enough members in there to investigate some of the things that were going on in Montreal. I think Drapeau and Saulnier worked on

297

Bourassa, who was completely inexperienced, and on Marchand and convinced them, as Marchand's speech in the House showed, that they were on the brink of a revolution. Marchand's speech sounded like a man from Mars: there were thousands of rifles, thousands of machine guns. And all the firearms collected by the police could be found anytime in the little city of Nanaimo!

Trudeau was possibly really hoodwinked into believing it was the beginning of a Quebec revolution by the separatists, the FLQ, and certain elements in the Confederation of National Trade Unions (CNTU). I think he's very intelligent, it's hard to believe he could have bought this.

The other explanation which may prove to be the right one is that he saw this as a chance to do two things – first, to crush the separatist movement. Almost all the PQ organizers were picked up. One of them in Hull came to me and claimed they put a telephone book on each side of his head and battered him with police sticks trying to get him to give them information about other PQ supporters in the Hull area. And, second, to convince English Canada that here was a strong man who could keep Quebec in its place.

Trudeau had a taste for the heroic. The clincher in his 1968 sweep to success was a televised scene at a Montreal auditorium the night before the election, when he calmly stood his ground against separatist demonstrators and rioters (it was St.-Jean Baptiste Day) while lesser men around him ducked and fled. In 1971, his pale taut image on the TV screen following the murder of one of the FLQ's kidnapped victims, Pierre Laporte (a crime committed *after* the War Measures Act was invoked), when he said "I am speaking to you at a moment of grave crisis." made a wonderfully dramatic impact. It is, in fact, impossible to substitute the figure of any preceding Canadian Prime Minister in the role of Pierre Trudeau during the October Crisis.

Against such bravura, which had caught thousands of Canadians ashamed of their own dullness and timidity, only Douglas, sixty-six year-old leader of the democratic socialist party, was not prepared to give way. He did not believe the loose band of terrorists who had used the name *Front de Liberation du Québec* to cover sporadic bombings over a period of seven years, was in fact a revolutionary force. He knew – as Trudeau knew – that most separatists in Quebec were peaceful advocates of independence, in a duly recognized political party which entered elections under the leadership of Rene Levesque, who repeatedly denounced the FLQ as madmen. He, like Trudeau, opposed the political views of that party. He was not prepared – as Trudeau apparently was – to introduce extreme wartime measures against the FLQ with the wider intent of halting the separatist trend.

Neither did he suppose for a moment that he would win any

gratitude from Quebec in opposing Trudeau's stand. It was not the preservation of their civil rights that worried Quebeckers that October. On the contrary, there was a mounting fear and horror because of the bombing incidents and the kidnapping of the British diplomat, James Cross; Trudeau won more applause in Quebec than anywhere else in the country for the imposition of the Act that resulted in rounding up over four hundred people who were later released because they were guilty of nothing at all. Meanwhile the kidnappers were caught by ordinary police methods. Yet eventually, Douglas' single-handed opposition to the War Measures Act will be seen as the strongest single act of his career. Not to give in to a panic of that dimension takes a great deal of what is commonly described as guts.

The "October Crisis" is a gaudy bit of Canadian history. A small band of FLQ terrorists, later exiled to Cuba, kidnapped James Cross but did not harm him. There were publicly conducted negotiations for his release in exchange for twenty-three FLQ terrorists held in connection with earlier crimes. An unrelated group of three men decided to take additional action, called themselves another FLQ "cell", and kidnapped the Quebec Labour Minister, Pierre Laporte. It was at this point that Premier Bourassa became panic-stricken and Trudeau became determined that no concessions would be made to either set of kidnappers.

Douglas said: "Once when I said to him, 'Isn't Bourassa over-reacting and frightening you?' he said, 'No, I have to be on the phone to him every hour to try to put some backbone in him. He wants to give in to them.' "

It was Trudeau who ordered military guards to protect all public figures in Ottawa and various public buildings in Quebec, and Trudeau who moved to introduce the War Measures Act.

Douglas was one of those who scoffed at the soldiers on guard in every official back garden in Ottawa, and was embarrassed by the clanking corporal in his own wake. "I told him I didn't need him," Douglas said, "but they had their orders. I had a short fellow from Cape Breton for a while; I used to kid him that I was looking after him. I felt we were all making ourselves a bit ridiculous."

At 10:30 in the evening of October 15, Prime Minister Trudeau invited Douglas with the other Opposition leaders to his office, and informed them that he planned to introduce the War Measures Act. Douglas expressed his astonishment; he asked that instead legislation to strengthen police power, if necessary, be introduced for consideration in the House of Commons.

At 4:00 a.m. the Act was proclaimed and police without warrants swooped down on hundreds of people, chiefly in the Montreal area and took them into custody without specific charges being laid and with minimal latitude in informing relatives and friends. Rounded up were students, artists, a doctor, journalists, and bystanders.

The news broke in the eight o'clock broadcast of the CBC.
Hans Brown said,

One of the really exciting things about working with Tommy was
that he had a real sense of political honesty, tremendous political
reactions. I went to the office that morning, I was talking to Eleanor
about how terrible it was, and in walked Tommy. He still didn't know
what regulations under the Act would be used but he responded
with all his civil libertarian instincts to the fore!

And the other amazing thing was how quick he was. His intellectual grasp of the thing in his speech that morning in contrast to
Stanfield's which was bloody awful. Tommy had come in about 9:30.
We tried to get a copy of the regulations. We called a snap caucus for
about a quarter to ten because the House was to meet at eleven. At
about a quarter after ten the messenger brought the regulations and
I took them in. Brewin and Tommy looked them over. Tommy stood
up and said, 'we're going to fight this.' Everybody pulled behind him.
He took it back to his office to go over it and he walked into the
House and gave a fantastic speech.

That caucus decided not to attempt any amendments – to totally
reject the government's bill. Brewin talked of "over-reaction", discussed
the unprecedented use of an open writ for search. One member wondered if the NDP could possibly hope to educate the public in this
fashion during a time of crisis. But the caucus appeared solid. When the
vote in the house came, four would vote the other way.

At eleven o'clock the Prime Minister spoke to a tense House, regretting the serious action he had felt he must take. Stanfield followed,
obviously still mystified by the lack of adequate information from the
government. He called the measures too sweeping but indicated a wil-
lingness to support the government in stamping out terrorism. He said,
"I apologize for not making my remarks more succint." In a television
address that evening he would declare his party's support, with misgivings, for the Act.

Several years later, Stanfield admitted he was wrong in giving that
support. He had yielded to tremendous pressure within his party but on
sober second thought he believes the government was not justified in
taking such power into its hands.

Douglas roundly protested the government move. He spoke of "using a sledgehammer to crack a peanut", a phrase that shocked the anxious listeners, brought a rebuke from the Ottawa *Citizen's* Christopher
Young as a "mistimed wisecrack" and jeers from the Liberal benches.

Douglas in his speech reminded the Liberals that they had once
moved to drop Section 98 from the Criminal Code (a law which made
communism illegal) because of the "very real liberal philosophy that you
should not condemn a person for his beliefs but only for his acts."

There were adequate laws to deal with such crimes as sedition, but instead of using them, the government had "put on a dramatic performance to cover its own ineptitude."

Douglas' speech was deliberate and explicit. He began by agreeing with the course the government had pursued to this point. He agreed with Trudeau that acceding completely to the demands of the kidnappers for the release of twenty-three people convicted of violent crimes would have been wrong. He agreed, moreover, that the cautious moves toward negotiation which the government had made thus far were right; with the lives of two men at stake they could do no less.

But now had come a point when he could not support the government. The government, apparently, "has information that civil disturbances are likely to break out on a large scale and that sabotage is anticipated in menacing proportions". Since he must assume the government's fears were based on information not yet available to others, they might be justified. In that case the government had two valid options, they could "utilize all the powers under the treason sections of the Criminal Code and the sections dealing with seditious intentions. . . There is also the offensive weapons provision and . . . the government could have acted under that authority."

If the government believed these powers were not enough then they had a second option, to come before parliament and ask for additional special powers. Instead, they had "over-reacted" by invoking the War Measures Act, the first time this had ever been done in peacetime. "There have been civil disturbances in Canada before . . . . Governments have been able to secure from Parliament the necessary power and authority to deal with these situations."

He said, "We are prepared to support the government in taking whatever measures are necessary to safeguard life and to maintain law and order in this country. But, Mr. Speaker, we are not prepared to use the preservation of law and order as a smokescreen to destroy the liberties and the freedom of the people of Canada."

The Liberals and some Conservatives shouted and jeered. There were cries of "shame!" When Douglas said, "I wonder if the honourable gentlemen opposite who are making so much noise have stopped to consider that today the Prime Minister holds more power in his hands than any Prime Minister in the peacetime history of Canada?" there were cries of "Thank God!"

So Douglas went on: "Right now there is no constitution in this country, no Bill of Rights, no provincial constitutions. This government now has the power by Order in Council to do anything it wants – to intern any citizen, to deport any citizen, to arrest any person and to declare any organization subversive or illegal. These are tremendous powers to put into the hands of the men who sit on the treasury benches.

"If my friends will look at the regulations they will find that if the

301

police in their judgement decide that some person is a member of a subversive organization – not just of the FLQ but of any organization that the police decide is subversive – or if he contributes to such a party or that he communicates any of the ideas or doctrines of such a party that person may be arrested and detained for ninety days. At the end of ninety days he has the power to appeal to a superior court judge to set a date for his trial and that may be postponed for some time. He may be denied bail."

While the House kept up its uproar, he pressed on: "A person in Canada may be held for ninety days or more without any opportunity to prove his innocence, to prove that he does not belong to a subversive organization or to prove that the organization to which he belongs is not subversive in spite of what may be in the minds of those who ordered the arrest. The regulations give the power to seize property and hold it for ninety days. It is a resurrection of the Padlock Law. These are very serious powers. If the government requires those kinds of powers, surely in a democracy they should have asked the democratically elected representatives of the people to give them those powers."

But those duly elected representatives were rushing to hand in their power to the Prime Minister.

The most revealing statement from Trudeau was provoked by Douglas' speech. As Hansard records it:

> Mr. Douglas: I would point out to the Prime Minister that the best way to stop people turning to violence is to remove the root causes which make them frustrated with the democratic process.
> Mr. Trudeau: *And let Quebec separate?* That is what they want.[6]

"Within half an hour of Tommy's speech," said Hans Brown, "we received about thirty telegrams, all opposing our stand. The next week there were about 6,000 letters, 95 per cent opposed."

Following Douglas in the Commons on October 16, cabinet ministers Marchand and Turner added to the hysteria of the hour. George Bain, writing in the *Globe and Mail* and one of the few journalists to question the Trudeau move strongly from the outset, protested on October 19:

> Canadians have been asked to accept that the government is contending with some concerted menace – and most of them appear to have done so – but they have been entrusted with precious little information on which to make judgements. . . .
> The most alarming speech was that of Jean Marchand, the Minister of Regional Economic Expansion, who . . . said that these people, the FLQ, have infiltrated every strategic place in the province of Quebec, and . . . that 'the state of Quebec and the federal state are truly in danger in Canada.'
> These are disturbing things Mr. Marchand is talking about . . .

Pierre Trudeau himself would have scoffed at any one of them had they been suggested to him a month ago. If that is the case, a very great deal of extremely important information has come into the government's hands recently, not much of which has been passed on to the country."[7]

But not many questioned the government's hidden evidence. Most were simply scared, and accepted Trudeau's brave stand against unknown threats to the state in a spirit of blind trust. They upbraided Douglas and the NDP for not making the act of faith unanimous.

One day after the proclamation of the War Measures Act, a tragic consequence, the trigger-happy trio of terrorists holding Pierre Laporte for ransom murdered their victim. Only Rene Levesque, in a statement that was harshly condemned, suggested that the murder might not have happened except for the government's massive show of force in invoking the War Measures Act. But Douglas could have recalled that in his first statement that Friday, October 16, he had warned: "The government has done exactly what the FLQ wanted." He said that such desperate people always aim for an open confrontation between the government and themselves. "The government has fallen right into the trap."

The horror that followed Laporte's murder, the mounting fears stirred by the government's allusions to massed revolutionary forces, had their effect on some of the NDP members. Reacting to the vituperative mail from their constituents, Barry Mather, Max Saltsman, Frank Howard, and Mark Rose broke with their party when the vote came. The remaining fifteen voted with Douglas.

Even as they moved into the Chamber for the vote, David Lewis turned to ask Douglas if he really felt that what they were doing was wise. Douglas answered, "I am going to vote against this if I am the only person who does."

In the press gallery as the sixteen NDP Members stood to vote in opposition, a reporter murmured "Hari kari".

A Gallup Poll in December showed unprecedented support for the Liberals at 59 per cent, while NDP support had plummetted to 13 per cent.

The NDP reaffirmed their position by voting against the bill brought in by the government to replace the War Measures Act, the "Public Order Act" which contained almost all the same provisions. This time they were joined by a solitary Conservative, David Macdonald.

A few lonely letters of approval turned up in Douglas' overflowing mailbag. One was from Dave Barrett, who had just been chosen by the British Columbia NDP as their leader.

Dear Tommy: There are times when I am really puzzled as a politician, why it should always fall to our lot to have to take the right moral position on every issue. My political instincts, while being tugged emotionally in one direction, were calmed by the correct and courageous position you took on the use of the War Measures Act. Time will of course prove you right again.

I do not think that the average Canadian citizen appreciates the depth of freedom that has been curtailed by the use of the War Measures Act. Someone had to take the right position, the moral position, the principled position. I am glad that that someone was you.

I am sure you will receive much abusive material, but if it is any comfort to you, my reaction is that J. S. Woodsworth, if he were alive, would be very proud of your position as the honourable successor to the new ground he broke politically in this country. Yours very truly, Dave."[8]

By May 1971 the Gallup Poll stood at Liberals 42 per cent, NDP 23 per cent. In the middle of August the Canadian Press reported:

Various charges laid under last October's War Measures Act have been dropped by the Crown against more than thirty persons, including labour leader Michel Chartrand, lawyer Robert Lemieux and teacher Charles Gagnon.

The Crown has sent registered letters to 32 persons. . . .

The Act was invoked Oct. 16 to fight terrorism after the Oct. 5 kidnapping of British diplomat James Cross and Pierre Laporte, former Quebec labour minister, abducted Oct. 10.

Mr. Laporte was found dead Oct. 18 and Mr. Cross was released Dec. 4.

Nearly five hundred persons were arrested under the act which gave the police powers to arrest without warrant and detain without bail. Only about sixty persons were eventually charged.[9]

The report noted that Paul Rose and Francis Simard had been convicted of murdering Mr. Laporte; Jacques Rose and Bernard Lortie were awaiting trial; and six other persons had been convicted of helping in the kidnapping or assisting the murderers to hide from police. All these were convicted of criminal acts under the criminal law of Canada. The kidnappers of Cross had been put on a plane to Cuba.

Three people had, in fact, been convicted of association with the FLQ and advocating its aims.

Douglas had not improved his position in Quebec by his action, though it could hardly be said that it had worsened. He had always been handicapped in that province by his seeming inability to master the French language. Frank Scott recalled with delight Douglas' startling self-introduction to a Montreal group, "Je ne sais que trois mots français: bon soir, mademoiselle, combien?" After which he elucidated NDP doctrine in English. Cliff Scotton said,

304

It astonished me in a person who is such a fantastic mimic in Ukrainian, Irish or Scottish accents. In French he sounded worse than Diefenbaker! I remember one flight from Vancouver to Quebec City and I was running him through 'la plume de ma tante' but it came out absolutely *appalling*. We just looked at each other and shrugged. He could speak in English in Montreal and get an ecstatic response, but he regretted that he couldn't speak to them in French with the quality of speech and the depth of emotion he wanted to use.

Douglas supported the Official Languages Act because he believed it was fair that French-speaking Canadians should be able to conduct their affairs with the federal government in their own language. He said, "I suppose we could have won ten or twelve more seats in western Canada by attacking the Official Languages Act. Every time I go on an open line radio show in the west people say, 'Why don't we all speak English?' You have to go back and explain to them the rights originally guaranteed to the French who were here first. . ."

It was, as Dave Barrett had said, depressing.

But Douglas believes the position the NDP took on the War Measures Act will be vindicated. He noted that separatism, far from being smashed, had increased to 30 per cent of the provincial vote. "It's not going to go away. The strong arm methods aren't going to work. They never have. I don't want to see Quebec leave Confederation, but I wouldn't have one drop of blood shed to keep them in Confederation. It's possible we will have to work out methods to separate and then work out agreements, though I hope it won't come to that. It would be better than a civil war. The Americans are still suffering from the civil war they fought a hundred years ago."

Chapter Nineteen
The Leadership Change

There was little evidence in 1970 that Douglas was losing much if any of his vigour. In that year he travelled 87,000 miles, in and out of Ottawa to every section of Canada. During the week he bounced into his office each morning, brisk and ready for action.

"Stamina!" Cliff Scotton, national secretary, moaned, "I would come back from a trip with him worn out, dragged down and he'd be still dancing about. He's as resilient as a wire spring."

Hans Brown, a lanky political science graduate of Toronto University signed on as Douglas' executive assistant in 1969, over the protests of David Lewis: Brown had worked for Lewis in York South riding in 1968, an abrasive relationship that crackled with shouting matches. The presence of Brown in the leader's office was a continued irritant to Lewis, who described the place as "a nest of Wafflers." Douglas, more than once, came to Brown's defence in acrimonious encounters with Lewis. When he discussed the "Waffle problem", Douglas spoke of his assistant:

> Hans was a very good example. Hans enjoyed sessions of talk, he was an admirer of Horowitz and Marcuse. There were some who wanted him fired. I asked them for any instance where he betrayed a trust, passed on any confidential information from our office to cause us harm. He worked hard, he's competent, he's one of the best executive assistants I ever had, and he's enthusiastic. And now he himself, as provincial secretary in B.C. (during Barrett's successful campaign), has tossed the Waffle thing out the window.

Brown described Douglas at work.

> People warned me he'd be hard to work for. Demanding. A stickler. I always found him not that way. Really pleasant. He wanted everything very precise. He was always working like the devil. He had two Christmases in Jamaica, other than that maybe two weekends off in the whole two years.
>
> He worked at a ferocious pace and he liked to be sure that everybody else was working ferociously too. When I started, he went down to the U.N. for two weeks. My idea was to sign all his mail and get it all done so there'd be nothing when he came back. He was not

pleased! So the next time he was away for a week we piled up all his mail, done and ready for his signature, on his desk, a tremendous stack. He sat down, obviously pleased, pulled over the stack and started going through it. It was tangible proof that we'd been working hard while he was gone. Then he bounced in with all the signed letters. He read almost everything that went out of the office.

I looked after the office and he didn't interfere with me. That's why I quit when David became leader because I knew David, Sophie and the whole darn clan would be there... Tommy is much more sensitive to people than David. David's in many ways remarkably insensitive to people's feelings. Tommy's more diplomatic and tactful, he always has the ability to greet you as though he's really interested in seeing you, whereas David shakes your hand but he's looking over your shoulder to see if there's anyone more important around.

During the leadership contest (to replace him), Douglas was very interested in how the race was going, but impeccably neutral. I filled him in on what was coming from the rumour mill.

Douglas is fantastic as a riding man. There can't be many ridings that get that kind of service. It's hard to get there, but he's out there almost every second weekend. He sends 'M.P.s at Work' to 1200 people in his riding every week. He'd come back from his riding with a pocketful of little pieces of paper, little notes he'd scribbled down, and he wanted us to get on them right away. There were regular radio speeches, once or twice a month, for the stations on the Island, and press releases to the Island papers.

He got 71 per cent of the vote last time (in 1972).

He has fantastic health. He was only sick once in those two years. I never saw anything like him. It made me tired just watching him running upstairs. And his darned diet – prunes, bran muffins – it kept him regular, it was great for that, every morning he'd be down to the can at the same time.

He read the papers regularly every day and marked them for clipping. He took the paper himself before we saw it. All done in three-quarters of an hour. It took the staff longer to do the clipping out.

He's interested in getting things done. Translating philosophy into action. Practical programs for people and the whole process of persuading people to raise their sights, to go after things that may be a little tough but can be got if you really put your mind to it.

If the experts couldn't figure out how to do it, get another bunch of experts. He said that to me often – find the experts who can.

I enjoyed working with him. There was only one occasion, he was in a bad mood, I don't know why, grumpy for about a week. I took in the mail and he just grunted and I walked back and mentioned to Irene, you know, 'What a rotten mood!' She was grimacing at me, and I turned around and there was Tommy right behind me with a stack of mail. He never said anything, just put down the mail and out he went. The next morning, I'm telling you, bright and shining! He'd snapped right out of it. That was the only time.

Scotton considered that Douglas had an unusual rapport not only with young men like Hans Brown but all those others of the new generation. Certainly he had a strong sense of being *entrusted* to pass on to them a very valuable commodity. He wrote, in 1971: "It is important that we have change. The absence of a democratic socialist party in the United States is one of the reasons why the young people there have taken to the streets."[1]

But the Ottawa media had, by and large, decided to write Douglas off, as out-of-touch with modern ways. Some were enthralled with their self perceived roles as king-makers, especially after the dizzy ascent and decline of Diefenbaker and the vertical take-off of Trudeau, in all of which they could believe they had played a part. Now, many of these political scribes saw, in David Lewis, whose parliamentary jousts with Trudeau had delighted them, a possibly important asset, for they were currently bent on deflating and "exposing" the Mighty Pierre. They built up Lewis and played down Douglas. Lewis was modern, urban, and masterful, Douglas was antique, rural, and much too gentle.

Occasionally they spoke of him in a kindly manner: "There is still a hint of 1930's dustbowl socialism about him, an evangelical drive that seems out of place among the smooth academics and articulate activists of the party today . . . Douglas seems to be the kind of man who neatly puts his slippers in the same place under the bed every night."[2]

Everyone conceded his sincerity; many found it easy to speak affectionately. Howard Green, well removed from current politics, ruminated in his Vancouver study, "He might be considered too straightforward by some people. Some people think that to be a successful leader you have to be a bit tricky. I don't think so . . . He and I have always been good friends. Sometimes it's easier to be friends with people of other parties than some of your own."

And among NDP'ers the comparisons were continual and inevitable.

Grant MacNeil, nonagenarian, said, "David's quite a chap. He's an able parliamentarian, he annoys Trudeau and makes a fool of Stanfield. But Douglas – I wouldn't say he was ever behind the times. He's always ahead of the times. But they are two different types."

Frank Scott said, "To some degree perhaps Tommy is too much the popular preacher. He needs a style that is more serious. It must have been galling for David – that slightly offhand manner of Tommy's was a little galling to sit under. We should have had David earlier."

And Margaret Stewart, former Ontario secretary, said, "I always felt it was a mistake that David didn't take the leadership at the beginning (in 1961). David has tremendous intellectual stature. A magnificent voice. I think he's superb. The press was hard on Tommy, but some of it was justified. He was an old-fashioned Saskatchewan socialist."

Scotton mused, "It is an ironic thing to me that of all the people I know, Tommy's essential philosophic and ideological ideas remain as fresh as ever. He *did* have an old-fashioned approach. Yet he is extremely adaptable to the times."

The centre of these diverse assessments kept his thoughts to himself. Walter Stewart had tried hard to probe his personality and had been forced to conclude:

> Douglas is a curious combination of the austere and the amiable. He's cool, resilient, shrewd; he has no friends outside politics and few within. He has erected such a barrier between himself and the world that no one I talked to – and I have talked to dozens of the people who know him best – has been able to penetrate it. . . .
>
> Perhaps the most curious aspect of his personality is his inner reserve . . . . Despite his public reputation, he is not a firebrand, this careful, ascetic man. When he shows emotion – and he often does, as his speeches rise to crescendo on the wings of poetry or the Bible – it is emotion superbly controlled and used. Even his humour is a tool, rather than a quality of the man.[3]

In a profound sense, Douglas' public speeches *were* the man. He revealed himself in them as he never did in private conversation. On November 27, 1970, he spoke to an NDP audience in Prince Albert:

> Sometimes people say to me, 'Do you feel your life has been wasted? The New Democratic Party has not come to power in Ottawa.' And I look back and think that a boy from a poor home on the wrong side of the tracks in Winnipeg was given the privilege of being part of a movement that has changed Canada. In my lifetime I have seen it change Canada.
>
> When you people sent me to the House of Commons in 1935, we had no universal old age pension. We have one now. It's not enough, but we have one. We had no unemployment insurance. We had no central Bank of Canada, publicly owned. We didn't have a wheat board, didn't have any crop insurance, didn't have a Canada Pension plan, didn't have any family allowances.
>
> Saskatchewan was told that it would never get hospital insurance. Yet Saskatchewan people were the first in Canada to establish this kind of insurance, and were followed by the rest of Canada. We didn't have Medicare in those days. They said you couldn't have Medicare – it would interfere with the 'doctor-patient relationship'. But you people in this province demonstrated to Canada that it was

possible to have Medicare. Now every province in Canada either has it or is in the process of setting it up.

And you people went on to demonstrate other things with your community health clinics. You paved the road, blazing a trail for another form of health service, to give people better care at lower cost. You did these things. You have demonstrated what people can do if they work together. There is almost no limit to what people can do if they work together, rather than work against; if you build a cooperative society rather than a jungle society.

Thirty-five years is a long time to have been in public service. I now sort of feel like an antiquarian. I say to the young people here: I can look back to the time when you went into the kitchen and said, 'What's cooking?' And now you can go in and say, 'What's thawing?' I can remember when grandma wore a night cap – now she drinks one. I can remember when I was a small boy, I would get a nickel for taking out the ashes – and now my grandson gets a quarter for turning up the thermostat.

Sure things have changed. Hair has gone down and skirts have gone up. But don't let this fool you. Behind the beards and the miniskirts, the long hair, this generation of young people, take it from me, is one of the finest generations of young people that have ever grown up in this country. Sure they're in rebellion against a lot of our standards and values and well they might be. They have got sick and tired of a manipulated society. They understand that a nation's greatness lies not in the quantities of its goods but in the quality of its life. This is a generation of young people who are in revolt against the materialism of our society. They may go to extremes at times but this is a generation with more social concern, with a better understanding of the need for love and involvement and cooperation than certainly any generation I have seen in my lifetime.

Now the government says we will try to get the economy going again. But if we get it going again, inflation will start again. Do you see what that means? To those of you who have been through it before, it's not new, but I say to the younger people here, what they are telling you is that you can't have prosperity without inflation, and if you get rid of inflation, you have unemployment and recession. In other words, they are saying we can't have a society in which we'll have prosperity and affluence and a stabilized economy. That's a terrible admission. They are saying we have got to have either booms or busts, with the booms getting shorter and the busts getting longer.

Here are some of the things we have been suggesting. The first thing we say is instead of contracting the Canadian economy, we should expand the Canadian economy. Do you realize what it means to have contracted the Canadian economy? The Economic Council of Canada said that as a result of our lack of economic growth, the fact that our factories are not working at full capacity, we have half a million unemployed, which means that we are losing every year in potential wealth production six thousand million dollars. That's $300 for every man, woman and child, of wealth that we don't create and can't enjoy. People say, where will the government get the money to do what the New Democratic Party recommends? Of that $6 billion, two billion of it, one-third would find its way in taxes into the coffers of the government. More money that would come in if we were operating at full capacity.

We ought to expand our economy. There ought not to be one idle able-bodied person in Canada. We need a million new homes in Canada. We need schools. We need recreation centres. We need nursing homes, housing projects, particularly for old people and for people on low incomes. We've got pollution in this country that needs to be cleaned up before we strangle ourselves in our own filth. We need a reforestation program. Many things need to be done. We could put every able-bodied person in this country to work, not just making holes and filling them up but doing useful work. That's the first thing we ought to do.

The second thing we ought to do is to recognize that we haven't had inflation in Canada. What we have had is maladministration of income. What do I mean by that? Well, what is inflation? According to the economic text books, inflation is too much money chasing too few goods. Do you think there is too much money chasing too few goods? Where has this too much money been? Any around here? Do you think the old age pensioners get too much money? Or the unemployed? Or the farmers? Or the fishermen? The Economic Council of Canada says that there are five million Canadians who live below the poverty line. Do you think they've got too much money? That's a quarter of our population, living in poverty.

What about this too few goods? How many supermarkets have you seen close at two o'clock in the afternoon because they haven't got any more goods to sell? We're not short of goods. What we have is inequitable and unfair distribution of income. Raising the old age pension would put money into the pockets of people who spend it. Unemployment insurance of $100 a week would be spent and the economy would begin to move again.

The other thing we could do to redistribute income is to bring in tax reforms. The Carter Commission said that too large a share of the taxes falls on people with incomes of under $10,000 a year. The commission said that if we made the banks, the insurance companies, the mining companies, the gas companies, and those who live off capital gains pay taxes the same as the rest of us do, we would lower the income tax by 15 per cent for everybody with incomes under $10,000 a year and the government would still have $600 million a year more coming in than is coming in at the present time.

The principal thing we have to do if we are going to redistribute income is that we have to deal with the sections of our economy that have the least protection from the vagaries of the market system. I'm talking about farmers, fishermen, and primary producers. Regarding farmers: have you read the report of the Agricultural Task Force? It says that the top third of the farmers are big farmers and they can stay in business, probably with the help of the feed companies and the meat packing companies. The next third of the farmers can probably last another ten or twenty years. The bottom third, the small farmers, must be got rid of immediately. But they don't say where they're to go.

They don't say where a man who is fifty or sixty years of age, on a quarter section of land, is going to go when they take him off the farm. I'll tell you where he's going to go. He's going to go into the city and go on welfare. This is a program that is going to denude and depopulate this country.

They talk about only having 150 to 200 grain centres in the west. The towns will be seventy-five miles apart and nothing in between them, just wasteland. Little towns of 1,500 and under will fade away; branch lines being closed and rails pulled up. Is this how they're going to build this nation? Is this what the pioneers opened up this great country for? The farmers should speak out against this program before it is too late.

Whether people want change or not, change is coming. The rising generation is going to insist on change, and they're going to bring about change. What we have to decide is whether that change will be brought about violently and bloodily, which would be a tragedy, because when you bring about change by violence and when you get to office by force, you have to stay in office by force, and you get a dictatorship. We have the means in Canada to bring about social change by the process of evolution, by the parliamentary system, by the democratic process. That's why it must grow. It is a means by which the young people can make change, can make it peacefully, can make it democratically. For that reason the New Democratic Party must continue to live. I charge you to give your lives and your money and your best effort to see that it lives and it grows and it succeeds.

This was his conviction, his personal statement, his only revelation. No one was allowed to probe for a different or more private Tommy Douglas.

There were some eleventh-hour appeals to Douglas to continue as leader beyond 1971. He rejected them. Certainly the two-year interval he had given the party to produce a successor had not been easy for him. The leadership was not easy. He would be well out of it.

During the hotly contested five-man race at the April 1971 convention, Douglas kept his own counsel. This time there would be no laying on of hands. Lewis had to fight hard for his title. He was ahead on every ballot, but only on the fourth count did he emerge as the clear winner over James Laxer.

The convention paid tribute to Douglas in an evening of celebration, and the House of Commons suspended its usual sitting to allow NDP M.P.s to attend, and M.P.s of other parties, as House Leader MacEachen suggested, to watch it all on their television sets: "We want him to know as he is basking in the glow of congratulatory comments tonight that we also acknowledge the contribution he has made."

And now his mailbag swelled with letters of warmth and gratitude.

"You have left an indelible mark . . . May you go on enjoying the reassurance that your life has been dedicated to truth. . .

"For several years I have intended to write you and thank you for the work you did. . .

"At the time your CCF government took office in Saskatchewan, I was a disgrunted Liberal and with many others, we voted for you, more to get the Liberal party out of office and clean house and then turn you out and have a new and honest Liberal party back in office. You brought in legislation no honest man could disagree with. . .

"To me you will always be the leader. . .

"Theoretically I am in favour of an early retirement age but I would like to see you continue. . .

"We shall be forever grateful. . .

"Your leadership has been of great importance to me. . .

"I am happy to know that you intend to contest the next election and as you said, 'if God gives you strength and the electors give you votes' you will be back in the House of Commons. . .

"You were a fair and personally friendly adversary. . .

"You certainly looked wonderful on the TV Monday night. . .

"On the whole I disagree with you, but I believe that you in particular, Mr. Douglas, are sincere, and I hope that the new leader of the NDP will be as compassionate as you are. . .

"You have always been a favourite of mine because of your sincerity and love of battle. . .

Walter Pitman, Ontario M.P.P., wrote: "As an old politician I am not easily moved by speeches but as I sat alone in my office listening to the tributes to your service and your own response, I was overwhelmed by the memories of the past decade. There have been victories and defeats, but never in those years have I had to excuse the actions of my leader. I have been proud to know you – and to have had your guidance over this critical period."

To all of which Douglas replied, ". . . with all the speeches that have been made and the editorials that have been written about me in recent days, I would be less than human if I were not flattered and less than honest if I believed them all."[4]

He was particularly delighted when the Ottawa West NDP Association rather ineptly arranged a "memorial" dinner in his honour. "I've always wondered what it would be like to attend my own funeral. I said, 'Here's my chance.' "

That November he was to receive another tribute in Helsinki, Finland, when the Conference of the Socialist International presented him with an embossed silver tray honouring his leadership in Canada and on the Socialist International executive. Only one person, Kier Hardie, had received such recognition in the years before 1971. The General Secretary Hans Janitschek, wrote to him, "Please accept the thanks of the Socialist International for having made the sun of socialism rise in North America."

Now he was able to breathe a little more freely. He could enjoy the quiet of the cottage at Wakefield, north of Ottawa, where Irma Douglas said his chief diversion was to chop wood and pile it in the cellar, and to take an occasional brisk swim. Douglas' grandchildren, Joan Tulchinsky's children, Danny and Joel, were persuaded that he excelled in this sport: they had once seen him swim clear across Sharbot Lake, and they once passed the hours travelling by car from Winnipeg assessing their grandfather's chances of getting across the various lakes en route. The only one they were quite sure he couldn't make, was Lake Superior.

The December holidays in Jamaica could stretch out a little longer. In 1972 Ottawa papers carried a front page story. Douglas and his wife had encountered a mugger one night in Kingston, Jamaica, and Douglas had belted him. The next day a modified version of the affair appeared at Douglas' request. It hadn't been quite that bad, Douglas said, and he didn't want to reflect any discredit on Jamaica.

In parliament, Douglas took up the role of private member. "For a while," said Grace MacInnis, "he was noticeably quiet. Then he perked up. He threw himself into the energy issue. And he has done everything possible to make things easy for David."

The Conservatives also include in their ranks an ex-leader. Diefenbaker took every occasion to grab the spotlight from Stanfield, to embarrass, contradict, disagree with, and attempt to undermine him. To the left, in the NDP rows, Douglas quietly deferred to Lewis.

No one acknowledged this more readily than Lewis himself.

I have always had respect, affection and admiration for him over the years, but it is nothing to the respect, affection and admiration I've had for him since I became leader. You have to be a really big person to act as he has done. Without discussing it, he has deliberately shunted things in my direction if they came to him first, because people still thought of him as leader. It's commitment to the party and it's a personal decency.

And he's become the most effective energy critic in the country. A hell of a lot more knowledgeable than Donald Macdonald, the energy minister. It's really remarkable, he studies, he works, he learns.

Only once in the party's recollection, had Lewis and Douglas personally crossed swords. At a 1969 meeting of the federal executive, Lewis said bluntly that he thought it was a mistake for Douglas to change his mind and stay on after having announced his intention to step down at the 1969 convention. By this time there were open expressions of support for Lewis as leader. Douglas had made up his mind to continue for a final two years, obviously in the hope of finding someone else, preferably younger than Lewis, to succeed him. Though he never at any time hinted at a lack of confidence in Lewis, his decision to stay on was in itself evidence of such misgiving. Or was it entirely a desire to keep the way open for a younger man?

Few contradictions in human personality have matched, in Canadian public life, this contrast between Tommy Douglas and David Lewis, each in his way so close to the heart and nerve centre of his party. The freely recorded comments of party followers show the sharp cleavage, for to consider Douglas unique in leadership was to see great fault in Lewis, and the opposite stance was equally true. Both men were aware of the schism. They were not friends. They knew that a contest between them for leadership would have ended the democratic socialist party in Canada. They never permitted that contest to take place. But for two years Douglas held the leadership against the open intention of Lewis to succeed him and during those two years Douglas actively encouraged the "far left" elements of the party, against the bitter resistance of Lewis. Far from "laying on hands", he demonstrated an obvious determination to guide the party in a direction that would not permit Lewis to be acclaimed leader after him.

It was not done for the crass purpose of arranging Lewis' defeat or humiliation at the hands of Jim Laxer. It was done with an extraordinarily stubborn intention of keeping the party open to the left, expanding, radical, but responsible (as he believed the majority to be), his kind of party, as long as he remained its leader. When he must step down, then let the next leader, *whoever that might be*, guide the party in *his* way. Douglas would set his own stamp on the party to the end of his term. Lewis, so it appeared would take over. Then let the next responsibility be his.

So that if for two years Lewis was showing overt signs of dissatisfaction with Douglas' leadership, Douglas was just as clearly showing his lack of enthusiasm for Lewis as successor.

The biographers of David Lewis will not have much trouble getting at the psyche. Lewis is an egoist. He is brilliant and intuitive. He can despise people as Douglas cannot. He can be inflamed with the almost sensual rewards of a majestic cause in which he is involved. Douglas is likely to duck that final sensuality, to take escape in flippancy.

Both fight hard, with tremendous resources of skill and determination. But Douglas would knock an opponent out, then pick him up, dust him off, shake his hand and smile.

For Lewis, the battles are personal and bruising. In a favourite phrase, he is "passionately opposed" to whatever he opposes. His own blood is mixed with the dust of war. And he is apt to be somewhat sickened at the thought of forgiveness.

Lewis has remained committed throughout a lifetime to the democratic socialist cause because he continues to hate and oppose the privileged top managers of society, and because he is intellectually convinced of the superiority of the socialist argument.

Douglas has remained committed to the same cause because he sees people as capable of relieving the world's distress, and he wants to help them toward it.

Both men are politically acute, but their tactics broadly differ.

Biographers of Lewis will find their work rewarding. Biographers of Douglas will always feel fenced off. Is he the more complex, layered with teaching and self-discipline, removing from sight the elemental responses we expect to discover in most men?

In earlier years he liked instructing young boys because he enjoyed their uncomplicated nature, generous, joyful, scrappy, frolicksome. He could have been a Mr. Chips.

But his supreme moments were with "mankind" in the mass, the great audiences that extend beyond the doors of the hall, out through the city, and out over the earth. He is essentially a leader of men.

Chapter Twenty
Postlude

In December 1973 an organization called the Douglas-Coldwell Foundation convened a weekend seminar in Regina. It was the first discussion
conference attempted by the Foundation. The chairman was T. C. Douglas, and its roster of distinguished participants included Gunnar and
Alva Myrdal of Sweden, Michael Harrington of the United States, Premier Schreyer of Manitoba, and such noteworthy Canadian professionals as Charles Taylor, Jack Weldon, Meyer Brownstone, and Randolph
Harding. One of its panels talked about "Energy Resources and Use",
and it was this topic that created most interest, for the world had recently
been informed that the Arab oil producers would boycott the United
States and several other countries for political reasons; they had then
proceeded to raise the price of oil to unprecedented levels. The price
increase would create havoc in the economies and financial systems of all
countries buying oil. The immediate reaction was to look to domestic
sources, and estimate their extent. Canada was forced to acknowledge
the finite nature of this nation's oil, a situation that spectral voices had
announced to the government without visible impact for years.

Douglas had taken a keen interest in "the energy problem" for five or
six years past. He had fought against the continental policy fondly pursued by Americans, which meant they could use up all their own oil and
gas and then have Canada's. Under strong NDP pressure, in the minority government situation that existed in Ottawa, the government had put
export controls on gas and oil, and instituted a temporary price freeze on
oil sold within Canada, to shield Canadians from the skyrocketing world
price.

Then, in early December, the NDP had carried out one of its most
successful coups in the balance-of-power situation which they controlled.
Resources Minister Macdonald had introduced in the Commons on December 3 a bill to establish an Allocation Board, but no further measures
to meet the emergency shortages. The price freeze was to be lifted on
January 1, 1974. Speaking in the Commons on Wednesday, December 5,
Douglas, the party's energy spokesman, had threatened the government
with withdrawal of support unless three important measures in oil policy
were announced "within the next day or two". He had asked for an
extension of the price freeze until the end of winter, a commitment to

build the long-postponed pipeline from Toronto east to Montreal, so that all eastern Canada could use Canadian oil instead of depending on uncertain imports, and he had asked for the establishment of a National Petroleum Corporation to enter into the exploration and development of new fields of oil and to acquire at least one existing private oil company.

On Thursday Prime Minister Trudeau announced a new oil policy. One by one, he ticked off the new measures: the price freeze would be extended, the pipeline would be built, the government would set up a National Petroleum Corporation. The NDP benches were rocking with joy as the third item was announced. Douglas' face was wreathed in smiles.

It was a cocky, ebullient Douglas who chaired the Regina seminar. His obvious mastery of the dimensions of the energy question added sparkle and depth to those sessions. Finally, on Sunday the ninth, he drew the seminar to a close, thanking the important visitors, talking of future plans. But not just for the continuance of the Foundation and its work. For the continuance of socialist ideals in western society.

He was, as Cliff Scotton remarked, "vintage" Douglas. He joked about the esoteric folly of some socialists, which reminded him of the old Quaker's remark to his wife, "Everyone seems a bit queer but thee and me, and sometimes I have my doubts about thee". He set forth his remarks on energy in three points, he always said three points, it came from being a minister and harking back to the Trinity, the truth was he could only remember three points at a time.

And finally there was the call to go on with the socialist struggle. "For I believe that within every man there lies a more compassionate human being, a more cooperative member of society . . . We can give man hope and . . . Man lives by hope."

On the platform with him, Cliff Scotton, who had travelled with him on many campaign trails, could hardly contain his glee. It was so delightfully crazy and unexpected, the old Douglas again in this quiet academic group, leading on to the New Jerusalem and beating swords into plough-shares – while everyone out there in the audience sat on the edge of their dam' chairs and the radiant faces hung on every word. He thought, "Tommy, you're supposed to be winding up a conference on a very abstract subject and here you are leading us to the barricades."

Douglas sat down. Scotton leaned over. "Tommy, what in the devil are you running for?" Douglas said, "Why – . The presidency of the Douglas-Coldwell Foundation."

The audience streamed out, bemused.

"I can't bear the thought of Tommy ever *losing* those powers he has," one man said, on the point of tears.

*　　*　　*

One day the following April, during the Easter recess, we are to make up a small party to visit several points in Douglas' riding. Douglas' agenda

318

was drawn up weeks ahead. This day, Thursday, April 18, 1974, fits into the middle of a six-day trip which includes, on Tuesday, a consultation between the Nanaimo Indian Band and the Water Board, with an evening address to the Nanaimo Jaycees; on Wednesday, an address to the Mock Parliament at Lake Cowichan Senior Secondary School, and in the evening a meeting of Gabriola Island Ratepayers; on Thursday our trip to Sooke and Port Renfrew; on Friday an Open Line Show at CHUB, Nanaimo, and a coffee party; on Saturday a day-long Federal Constituency meeting at Ladysmith; on Sunday the annual meeting of the Cowichan Malahat NDP, and in the evening attendance at the Nanaimo Curling Bonspiel. On Monday he is to fly back to Ottawa.

On this Thursday morning Jim Gorst, M.L.A. for Esquimalt, an attractive dark-haired young man in his thirties, is to meet Douglas at 10:00 o'clock at the cafe in the Colwood Shopping Centre just outside Victoria. Gorst is late; he has a headache, his new constituents have been giving him trouble over some of Barrett's legislation. It is twenty after ten when we reach the shopping centre.

Douglas has been there since ten. He has had an interview with a couple of reporters; Gorst is annoyed to find the photographers have taken their pictures and left. Douglas, who will be seventy in a few months, looks trim in a light brown suit, a printed silk brown and white tie. He is talking with half a dozen people about shortages of construction materials; some of the people, inevitably, have retired from Saskatchewan and they remind him of the Depression and old campaign meetings on the prairies.

Douglas has already driven seventy-five miles from Nanaimo, where he and Mrs. Douglas keep a small apartment. We are joined by Gorst's young assistant, Gordon Neville. We will take two cars as far as Sooke, where we will be back for an evening meeting. Driving to Sooke, Douglas talks about the riding and the variety of transport required to get around it, sometimes he charters a seaplane from Vancouver to reach some of the islands. The road today will be up over the mountains to Port Renfrew, pretty rough in places. There is another road across the Island from Nanaimo but you can only use it in the evenings when the MacMillan-Bloedel trucks are off it. He talks about the meeting Tuesday with the Nanaimo Indian Band. They have had their water cut off. He is going to see Chretien as soon as he gets back to Ottawa.

At Sooke we rejoin Gorst. Our first stop is a brown-shingled home in a beautiful location on the Sooke River. Jim and Irene Barron have a sizable group of neighbours in for coffee, with hot biscuits and cheese, hot sausage rolls, and cake. The conversation is amiable and low key, but, surprisingly, most concerned with international and national monetary problems, and how these lead to inflation. One young woman raises the question of pension rights for housewives. Douglas discusses ways to extend the Canada Pension Plan to include women who work at home.

Outside, he walks with Jim Barron to look at a boat on the river and to see his garden: Jim grows tiny, delicate, orchids.

We leave for Port Renfrew. Douglas notes that we will be half an hour late. It is a curving, gravel road above the Strait of Juan de Fuca. We talk about the potential disaster of oil spills on this coast if American tankers turn it into a permanent route. Douglas has visited Washington in 1973 with members of other parties to try to talk the Americans into abandoning Cherry Point as a major refining and distributing centre. If the distributing centre was nearer San Francisco the Americans could take a route farther out to sea. The Canadians offered to supply Cherry Point and the area around it, but there was no deal.

Douglas wonders why he left his raincoat in his own car at Sooke. It never fails to rain at Port Renfrew. But this day we are lucky; cloudy but no rain.

B.C. Forest Products owns the town, at the mouth of the Juan de Fuca River. There were about a hundred registered voters in the last election and almost all voted NDP, but now there is trouble. The residents are buying their homes from the company after renting them for many years, and there are questions of assessment. Many are angry with the government.

Phyllis Smith, the school librarian, has arranged a coffee party. She has laid out twenty cups but she doesn't know how many will turn up. She has told people this is their chance to air their complaints, and did they ever get this opportunity with a Social Credit M.L.A.? Before the coffee party, Douglas and Gorst visit with a Citizen's Activity group at the school. They talk about possible grants to underwrite their craft projects and Gorst thinks it went fine.

The people drift in to the coffee party. A young lad wants a provincial grant to rent a boat, to set him up in business for rescue operations during the summer. He was able to salvage small boats and bring in people who got in trouble last summer, and people want the service, but he needs an adequate boat. He has written Barrett but had no reply. Douglas listens carefully and gets Neville to write it all down, to be checked.

Some of the people have brought their beefs. One Social Credit supporter complains about the government car insurance. Douglas discusses rates with her. A brawny, sandy-haired Scot, demands, "don't you believe in freedom of choice?" apparently about everything. He has come to Canada because he thought it was a free country. Douglas discovers that he and his young wife moved first to the United States, but when his wife became pregnant they moved on to Canada because of the public health insurance. He says to the Scot, "Let's take one question at a time." But the young man has worked up his courage to come to the house to assail the socialist member of parliament and he is not going to be put off by reasonable discussion. At one point he objects to an intervention by Gordon Neville. "What right has he to say something? He's your chauffeur isn't he?" Douglas raps back, "Hasn't he as much right to speak as anyone here?" On the return trip he will say, in disgust, "I find I have less and less patience with these fellows."

Douglas obtains particulars about an underpaid and overworked nurse at Port Renfrew, who is considered to be part-time. He finds she has been attending the children from the adjoining Indian reserve and he thinks she may be entitled to federal money: he makes a note and puts it in his pocket.

By this time it is late and we are due to eat supper at the food kitchen next the single men's quarters, courtesy of the International Woodworkers of America (IWA). Douglas goes on into the bunkhouse to shake hands with the men who had finished supper before we arrived; we wait in the car. Douglas comes out and says he made it brief because most of them are listening to the Rangers and the Canadiens at Madison Square Gardens.

It is now late; we will have to drive hard to get back to Sooke for the meeting. The scenery is rugged and fascinating. We drive through the reserve and see an elderly Indian burning out the interior of a dugout canoe.

Jim wonders if he has flu. There was a pile-up of bills when the Legislature adjourned for the Easter recess. There are still estimates to pass for twelve departments and the Tories are filibustering. Douglas says, "Let them talk. They'll get tired of it when the warm weather comes. Don't let them goad you into clamping down so they can say you muzzled them." It would be better to send the estimates to committees. With several going at once the press doesn't cover them all and the Opposition lets up.

The game is on. The Rangers win before we get back to Sooke.

The Legion Hall, decorated with two small "Douglas" signs on the platform, is rapidly filling up. A few people, surprisingly, speak to each other in French. There are several Indian faces. Many of the younger men have come in their rough denim clothes and heavy boots – these are work clothes, not hippie apparel.

A chairwoman introduces Douglas with a talk about accountability.

Douglas talks about the balance-of-power situation in Ottawa. The NDP takes credit for legislation they have persuaded the government to pass: pensions now will rise with the cost of living; there is a much bigger family allowance and a reduction in income tax; and the government has kept the freeze on oil prices. But now "there are questions on which it doesn't seem possible to get the government to move." There may be an election soon.

People are standing at the back of the hall. Douglas invites them to find seats at the front. "It's bad enough to listen to me without getting sore feet."

Mostly he talks about inflation, about the need for selective price controls and a more powerful Prices Review Board. He talks about the unfair tax structure and the $4,700,000,000 owed to the government by corporations in deferred taxes. "*You* try deferring your taxes until it's more convenient to pay them!"

Most of the questions, which go on for an hour, are complex, and are concerned with the practicality of lower mortgage rates for home building and aspects of inflation. Douglas spends a long time on them, carefully. He outlines the growth of inflation from the heavy spending of the United States in the Vietnam war.

There is a question about the World Football League. Douglas sides with the government on that one. He says if we don't back the Canadian Football League we might as well play for a Nixon Cup instead of a Grey Cup.

He answers questions about population growth and economic growth. The "no growth" people must realize we can not freeze our economy at present levels. Not all Canadians have a decent standard of living. While there is imbalance across the world we cannot impose restrictions that affect the well-being of poorer nations.

Serious questions merit serious answers. But he is concise, he is global, sometimes he throws in a joke to keep people on their toes.

The dour chairwoman brings the question period to a close. She tells Douglas it has been the best political-economics lecture she has ever heard. The meeting breaks up.

Douglas is more exhilarated than he has been all day. He is in no hurry to leave. He talks quietly, warmly, with knots of people, moving out slowly into the dark. The air has become very cool.

All of us except Douglas are returning to Victoria in Gorst's car; we slump against the seats, tired from the long day.

Douglas comes up to say goodby. He leans in, advises quietly, "Jim be sure to see a doctor if that headache doesn't clear up."

He walks briskly back to his own car. People are still calling out to him. He has seventy-five miles to drive back to Nanaimo, tomorrow morning there will be the Open Line show and the coffee party, and the following days other meetings with the people he represents in parliament. Back in Ottawa he will catch up on world developments in the energy crisis, and he will be ready at Question Period on Monday.

It is hard to say goodnight to this man. The Honourable Member for Nanaimo-Cowichan-The Islands. Jerusalem's forerunner.

Footnotes

Chapter 1

1. H. V. Morton, *In Search of Scotland*, (London: Methuen and Company, 1929).
2. Robert Keith Middlemas, *The Clydesiders*, (Hutchison of London, 1965).
3. *Ibid.*
4. *Ibid.*
5. *Ibid.*

Chapter 2

1. See D. C. Masters, *The Winnipeg General Strike*, (Toronto: University of Toronto Press, 1950).
2. See Earle Beattie, "The Strike That Terrified All Canada", *Maclean's Magazine*, June 1, 1952.
3. K. McNaught, "J. S. Woodsworth and a Political Party for Labour, 1896 to 1921", *Canadian Historical Review*, 1949.
4. Chas. Gilbert to TCD, Premier Douglas Papers, Saskatchewan Archives.

Chapter 3

1. Ralph Allen, "The Land of Eternal Change", *Maclean's Magazine*, June 25, 1955.
2. Davin was elected three times as a Conservative to the federal House of Commons. He sold the paper in 1895 to a Liberal, Walter Scott, on condition that the paper would continue to support him editorially. The support was withdrawn in the 1896 election and in 1900 Scott ran against Davin and defeated him, later becoming Saskatchewan's first Premier. Davin committed suicide.
3. Hugh MacLennan, "The Saskatchewan", *Rivers of Canada*, (Toronto: Macmillan of Canada, 1974).
4. W. L. Morton, "The Bias of Prairie Politics", *Transactions of the Royal Society of Canada*, Vol. XLIX, Series III, Sec. 2, June 1955.
5. Edgar McInnis, *Canada, A Political and Social History*, (New York: Rinehart & Company, 1947).
6. *Ibid.*
7. Duff Spafford, "The Left Wing 1921-1931", in *Politics in Saskatchewan*, eds. Norman Ward and Duff Spafford, (Don Mills: Longmans Canada Limited, 1968), pp. 54-55.
8. The best account is W. L. Morton, *The Progressive Party in Canada*, (Toronto: University of Toronto Press, 1950).
9. See W. Calderwood, *The Rise and Fall of the Ku Klux Klan in Saskatchewan*, (University of Saskatchewan, unpublished thesis, 1968).
10. Saskatoon *Star-Phoenix*, June (?), 1928.
11. See Also Patrick Kyba, "Ballots and Burning Crosses – the Election of 1929", in *Politics in Saskatchewan, op. cit.*
12. Escott M. Reid, "The Saskatchewan Liberal Machine before 1929", *The Canadian Journal of Economics and Political Science*, Vol. II, No. 1, 1936.
13. James H. Gray, *Red Lights on the Prairies*, (Toronto: Macmillan of Canada, 1973).

Chapter 4

1. TCD to Max C. Stuart, Regina, November 15, 1949. Premier Douglas Papers, Saskatchewan Archives.
2. See Stanley Duane Hanson, *The Estevan Strike and Riot, 1931,* (University of Saskatchewan, unpublished M.A. thesis, 1971).
3. The grievances leading to the dispute were produced as evidence before the Wylie Commission, appointed in September, 1931. A full account appears in *The Estevan Strike and Riot, 1931, ibid.*
4. Estevan *Mercury*, December 3, 1931.
5. Kenneth McNaught, "J. S. Woodsworth and a Political Party for Labour, 1896 to 1921", *op. cit.*
6. *Ibid.*
7. British Columbia *Federationist*, January 2, 1919.
8. Richard Allen, *The Social Passion*, (Toronto: University of Toronto Press, 1971).

Chapter 5

1. From *Socialism* by Michael Harrington. Copyright © 1972 by Michael Harrington. Reprinted by permission of the publishers, Saturday Review Press/ E. P. Dutton & Co., Inc.
2. See Harrington, *ibid.*
3. See for example Andrew Milnor, "The New Politics and Ethnic Revolt, 1929- 1938", in *Politics in Saskatchewan, op. cit.*

Chapter 6

1. Walter D. Young, *The Anatomy of a Party: the National CCF 1933-1961*, (Toronto: University of Toronto Press, 1969).
2. *Ibid.*, p. 32.
3. *Ibid.*, p. 81.
4. *Ibid.*, p. 87.
5. *Ibid.*, p. 177.
6. As quoted in *The First Ten Years*, CCF anniversary publication, 1942.
7. See Gerald L. Caplan, *The Dilemma of Canadian Socialism – The CCF in Ontario*, (Toronto: McClelland and Stewart Limited, 1973).
8. Interview with W. C. Good, April 1957, when Good was eighty-one years old.
9. Caplan, *op. cit.*, p. 39.
10. D. Lewis to F. Scott, July 12, 1937. CCF Papers, Public Archives of Canada.
11. Caplan, *op. cit.*, p. 68.
12. In the *25th Anniversary*, CCF souvenir publication, 1957.
13. Allen, *The Social Passion, op. cit.*
14. Young, *The Anatomy of a Party, op. cit.*, p. 159, and quoting Daniel Bell, "Notes on Authoritarian and Democratic Leadership", in A. Gouldner, ed., *Studies in Leadership*, (New York: 1950), p. 405.
15. Frank Scott. Notes for an address to a Quebec convention. August, 1955.
16. TCD to M. J. Coldwell, December 6, 1936. CCF Papers, Public Archives of Canada.
17. W. L. Morton, "The Bias of Prairie Politics", *op. cit.*

Chapter 7

1. Professor Gordon O. Rothney to TCD, April 17, 1971. Premier Douglas Papers, Saskatchewan Archives.
2. TCD, "The More Things Change. . . ", Ottawa *Journal*, December 18, 1973.

324

3. Blair Fraser, "The Prairies' Political Preachers", *Maclean's Magazine*, June 25, 1955.
4. House of Commons *Debates*, February 24, 1936.
5. Ottawa *Journal*, January 29, 1974.
6. House of Commons *Debates*, June 16, 1936.

Chapter 8

1. House of Commons *Debates*, February 11, 1936.
2. *Ibid.*, January 25, 1937.
3. See Young, *The Anatomy of a Party, op. cit.*, p. 91.
4. Ralph Allen, *Maclean's Magazine*, April 1961.

Chapter 9

1. Stanley Knowles to David Lewis, November 20, 1943. CCF Papers, Public Archives of Canada.
2. See Caplan, *The Dilemma of Canadian Socialism, op. cit.*, pp. 88 to 107.
3. Saskatchewn *Commonwealth*, Special Issue, August 10, 1960.
4. Saskatoon *Star-Phoenix*, May 23, 1944.
5. David Lewis to T. C. McLeod, October 26, 1944. CCF Papers, Public Archives of Canada.

Chapter 10

1. S. M. Lipset, *Agrarian Socialism, the Cooperative Commonwealth Federation in Saskatchewan*, (University of California Press, 1950).
2. Dean E. McHenry, *The Third Force in Canada. The Cooperative Commonwealth Federation 1932-1948*, (University of California Press, 1950).
3. Evelyn Eager, "The Conservatism of the Saskatchewan Electorate", in *Politics in Saskatchewan, op. cit.*, p. 15.
4. H. D. to TCD, February 15, 1946. Premier Douglas Papers, Saskatchewan Archives.
5. TCD to H. D., May 15, 1946. Premier Douglas Papers, Saskatchewan Archives.
6. Harrington, *op. cit.*
7. *Ibid.*
8. Blair Fraser, "The Prairies' Political Preachers", *Maclean's, op cit.*
9. TCD to L. W., November 14, 1946. Premier Douglas Papers, Saskatchewan Archives.
10. J. G. M. to TCD, June 14, 1948. Premier Douglas Papers, Saskatchewan Archives.
11. TCD to J. G. M., June 23, 1948. Premier Douglas Papers, Saskatchewan Archives.
12. G. S. to TCD, December 9, 1946. Premier Douglas Papers, Saskatchewan Archives.
13. S. D. to TCD, December 6, 1946. Premier Douglas Papers, Saskatchewan Archives.
14. Young, *The Anatomy of a Party, op. cit.*, p. 151. Reference: F. C. Engelmann, "The Cooperative Commonwealth Federation of Canada: A Study of Membership Participation in Policy Making". Unpublished Ph.D thesis. (Yale, 1954), p. 79.
15. Desmond Morton, *NDP: the Dream of Power*, (Toronto: Hakkert, 1974), p. 15.
16. Evelyn Eager, "The Paradox of Power in the Saskatchewan CCF, 1944-1961", in *The Political Process in Canada*, Ed., J. H. Aitchison, (Toronto: University of Toronto Press, 1963).
17. *Ibid.*

18. TCD to Mackenzie King, October 12, 1942. Premier Douglas Papers, Saskatchewan Archives.
19. J. H. Sturdy to TCD, May 17, 1945. Premier Douglas Papers, Saskatchewan Archives.
20. N. G. G. to TCD, July 24, 1949. Premier Douglas Papers, Saskatchewan Archives.
21. C. E. S. Franks, "The Legislature and Responsible Government", *Politics in Saskatchewan, op. cit.*, pp. 32, 35, 37.
22. Beatrice Trew to author, February 8, 1974.

Chapter 11

1. J. R. to TCD, March 13, 1951. Premier Douglas Papers, Saskatchewan Archives.
2. Wilfred Eggleston, *Saturday Night*, August 24, 1946.
3. Saskatoon *Star-Phoenix*, August 7, 1946.
4. Regina *Leader-Post*, December 30, 1946.
5. *Ibid.*, July 14, 1947.
6. C. Higginbotham. Taped interview with TCD, 1958.
7. Unsigned: circa 1945. Premier Douglas Papers, Saskatchewan Archives.
8. TCD to Beland Honderich, July 19, 1956. Premier Douglas Papers, Saskatchewan Archives.
9. Toronto *Star*, July 23, 1956.

Chapter 12

1. TCD to David Lewis, August 18, 1944. Premier Douglas Papers, Saskatchewan Archives.
2. M. H. to TCD, May 28, 1952. Premier Douglas Papers, Saskatchewan Archives.
3. TCD to C. R., February 2, 1955. Premier Douglas Papers, Saskatchewan Archives.
4. J. Corman to C. Fines, March 12, 1953. Premier Douglas Papers, Saskatchewan Archives.
5. C. Higginbothom, *Off the Record: The CCF in Saskatchewan*, (Toronto: McClelland and Stewart Limited, 1948).
6. William Kilbourn, *Pipeline*, (Toronto: Clarke, Irwin, 1970).
7. TCD to Rt. Hon. L. St. Laurent, November 29, 1955. Premier Douglas Papers, Saskatchewan Archives.
8. Rt. Hon. L. St. Laurent to TCD, December 9, 1955. Premier Douglas Papers, Saskatchewan Archives.
9. TCD to M. J. Coldwell, December 15, 1955. Premier Douglas Papers, Saskatchewan Archives.
10. Kilbourn, *Pipeline, op. cit.*, p. 92.
11. Higginbotham, *Off the Record, op. cit.*

Chapter 13

1. Grace MacInnis to TCD, March 19, 1945. Premier Douglas Papers, Saskatchewan Archives.
2. TCD to G. MacInnis, April 3, 1945. Premier Douglas Papers, Saskatchewan Archives.
3. J. R. Tucker to TCD, April 30, 1945. Premier Douglas Papers, Saskatchewan Archives.
4. BUP dispatch from Regina, April 25, 1947. Special to the Vancouver *Sun*.

5. F. De Laronde to TCD, March 2, 1946. Premier Douglas Papers, Saskatchewan Archives.
6. TCD to V. F. Valentine, September 3, 1953. Premier Douglas Papers, Saskatchewan Archives.
7. TCD to A. J. E. Liesemer, June 19, 1952. Premier Douglas Papers, Saskatchewan Archives.
8. D. Kennedy to M. Shumiatcher, September 25, 1945. Premier Douglas Papers, Saskatchewan Archives.
9. TCD to A. J. E. Liesemer, June 19, 1953. Premier Douglas Papers, Saskatchewan Archives.
10. TCD to Rev. T. A. Hamilton, February 2, 1956. Premier Douglas Papers, Saskatchewan Archives.
11. A. M. to TCD, April 9, 1956. Premier Douglas Papers, Saskatchewan Archives.
12. TCD to Therese Casgrain, March 28, 1961. Premier Douglas Papers, Saskatchewan Archives.
13. Sid Boyling to TCD, September 14, 1955. Premier Douglas Papers, Saskatchewan Archives.
14. *25th Anniversary Booklet, op. cit.*

Chapter 14

1. E. to TCD, August 1, 1944. Premier Douglas Papers, Saskatchewan Archives.
2. TCD to David Lewis, August 15, 1944. Premier Douglas Papers, Saskatchewan Archives.
3. *Maclean's Magazine*, April, 1961.
4. TCD to E. B. Jolliffe, January 25, 1945. Premier Douglas Papers, Saskatchewan Archives.
5. TCD to P. R., July, 1948. Premier Douglas Papers, Saskatchewan Archives.
6. TCD to E. Roper, July 7, 1952. Premier Douglas Papers, Saskatchewan Archives.
7. Calgary *Herald*, August 2, 1952.
8. TCD to MJC, December 9, 1952. Premier Douglas Papers, Saskatchewan Archives.
9. MJC to TCD, December 18, 1952. Premier Douglas Papers, Saskatchewan Archives.
10. TCD to MJC, December 22, 1952. Premier Douglas Papers, Saskatchewan Archives.
11. TCD to all Cabinet Ministers, April 28, 1953, Premier Douglas Papers, Saskatchewan Archives.
12. TCD to Russ Brown, May 19, 1953. Premier Douglas Papers, Saskatchewan Archives.
13. Judith Robinson, Toronto *Telegram*, July 30, 1953.
14. Ottawa *Citizen*, August 11, 1953.
15. David Lewis to TCD, May 30, 1950. Premier Douglas Papers, Saskatchewan Archives.
16. *Ibid*.
17. TCD to David Lewis, June 6, 1950. Premier Douglas Papers, Saskatchewan Archives.
18. T. Casgrain to TCD, February 7, 1955. Premier Douglas Papers, Saskatchewan Archives.
19. TCD to T. Casgrain, February 7, 1955. Premier Douglas Papers, Saskatchewan Archives.
20. T. Casgrain to TCD, April 16, 1955. Premier Douglas Papers, Saskatchewan Archives.

21. *Canadian Forum*, April 1952.
22. David Lewis to TCD, June 21, 1939. CCF Papers, Public Archives of Canada.
23. David Lewis to TCD, October 16, 1944. CCF Papers, Public Archives of Canada.
24. David Lewis to TCD, July 19, 1944. CCF Papers, Public Archives of Canada.
25. David Lewis to TCD, August 16, 1945. Premier Douglas Papers, Saskatchewan Archives.
26. W. O. Clunk to Lorne Ingle, October 25, 1950. CCF Papers, Public Archives of Canada.
27. TCD to W. O. Clunk, November 21, 1950. CCF Papers, Public Archives of Canada.
28. TCD to David Lewis, April, 1956. Premier Douglas Papers, Saskatchewan Archives.
29. Lorne Ingle to TCD, April 8, 1957. Premier Douglas Papers, Saskatchewan Archives.
30. TCD to Lorne Ingle, April 17, 1957. Premier Douglas Papers, Saskatchewan Archives.
31. Eugene Forsey to TCD, July 5, 1957. Premier Douglas Papers, Saskatchewan Archives.
32. John Wellbelove to TCD, June 1957. Premier Douglas Papers, Saskatchewan Archives.
33. TCD to John Wellbelove, June 17, 1957. Premier Douglas Papers, Saskatchewan Archives.
34. *Maclean's Magazine*, April 8, 1961.
35. Arthur J. Turner to TCD, September 5, 1960. Premier Douglas Papers, Saskatchewan Archives.

Chapter 15

1. See Robin F. Badgley and Samuel Wolfe, *Doctors' Strike: Medical Care and Conflict in Saskatchewan*, (Toronto: Macmillan Company of Canada, 1967); and E. A. Tollefson, *Bitter Medicine*, (Saskatoon: Modern Press, 1963).
2. Wallace A. Wilson, M.D., "Health Insurance – A Flashback", *The British Columbia Medical Journal*, Vol. 2, No. 12, December 1960.
3. TCD, speech at Biggar, Saskatchewan, May 18, 1944.
4. F. D. M. to TCD, May 17, 1971. Douglas Papers, Ottawa.
5. TCD to J. L. Brown, September 19, 1945. Premier Douglas Papers, Saskatchewan Archives.
6. Tollefson, *Bitter Medicine, op. cit.*
7. TCD. Saskatchewan Legislature *Debates*, April 1, 1954.
8. A. J. M. Davies, to all Doctors in Saskatchewan, February 17, 1960. Premier Douglas Papers, Saskatchewan Archives.
9. TCD. Saskatchewan Legislature *Debates*, February 17, 1960.
10. Quoted in Badgley and Wolfe, *Doctors' Strike, op. cit.*
11. Saskatoon *Star-Phoenix*, May 30, 1960.
12. TCD interview with Ben Tierney, Ottawa *Citizen*, March 26, 1971.
13. House of Commons *Debates*, July 25, 1955.
14. Blair Fraser, *Maclean's Magazine*, October 24, 1959.
15. Regina *Leader-Post*, November 22, 1960.
16. Regina *Leader-Post*, June 10, 1960.
17. E. M. Hall to TCD. April 26, 1971. Douglas Papers, Ottawa.
18. N. Ward, "The Contemporary Scene", in *Politics in Saskatchewan, op. cit.*, p. 297.
19. The Winnipeg *Tribune*, April 23, 1964.

Chapter 16

1. Morton, *NDP: The Dream of Power, op. cit.*
2. *Ibid.*
3. *Ibid.*

Chapter 17

1. TCD to F. C., June 7, 1961. Premier Douglas Papers, Saskatchewan Archives.
2. Regina *Leader-Post*, April 26, 1962.
3. Jack Scott, Vancouver *Sun*, June 15, 1962.
4. Richard Snell, Toronto *Star*, June 13, 1962.
5. Regina *Leader-Post*, May 4, 1962.
6. *Ibid.*
7. TCD to M. S., January 26, 1952. Premier Douglas Papers, Saskatchewan Archives.
8. TCD to M. W. March 2, 1961. Premier Douglas Papers, Saskatchewan Archives.
9. R. W. to Cabinet, April 11, 1961. Premier Douglas Papers, Saskatchewan Archives.
10. Toronto *Star*, May 10, 1962.
11. Ottawa *Citizen*, May 19, 1962.
12. N. Ward, "The Contemporary Scene", in *Politics in Saskatchewan, op. cit.* pp. 290, 291, 302 ff.
13. Peter Newman, *Renegade in Power*, (Toronto: McClelland and Stewart Limited, 1963).
14. TCD to Woodrow Lloyd, May 1, 1963. Douglas Papers, Ottawa.
15. Ottawa *Citizen*, June 1, 1962.
16. Morton, *NDP: The Dream Of Power, op. cit.*
17. Walter Stewart, "The Tough, Lonely Man in the Middle", *Star Weekly*, January 8, 1966. Reprinted with permission Toronto *Star/Star Weekly*.
18. House of Commons *Debates*, May 28, 1965.
19. *Ibid.*, January 20, 1966.

Chapter 18

1. TCD to G. S., April 27, 1971. Douglas Papers, Ottawa.
2. TCD to Woodrow Lloyd, October 22, 1964. Douglas Papers, Ottawa.
3. Toronto *Star*, October 18, 1969.
4. Ottawa *Citizen*, March 27, 1971.
5. Toronto *Star*, December 7, 1970.
6. House of Commons *Debates*, October 16, 1970, p. 200.
7. George Bain, Toronto *Globe and Mail*, October 19, 1970. Reprinted with permission, *The Globe and Mail*, Toronto.
8. David Barrett, M.L.A., to TCD, October 20, 1970. Douglas Papers, Ottawa.
9. Ottawa *Citizen*, August 16, 1971.

Chapter 19

1. TCD to G. H., May 7, 1971. Douglas Papers, Ottawa.
2. Frank Jones, Toronto *Star*, October 18, 1969.
3. Walter Stewart, "The Tough, Lonely Man in the Middle" in *Star Weekly*, January 8, 1966.
4. TCD to Emmett M. Hall, May 13, 1971. Douglas Papers, Ottawa.

Index